Lecture Notes in Computer Science   11950

Founding Editors

Gerhard Goos
Juris Hartmanis

The series Lecture Notes in Computer Science (LNCS), including its subseries Lecture Notes in Artificial Intelligence (LNAI) and Lecture Notes in Bioinformatics (LNBI), has established itself as a medium for the publication of new developments in computer science and information technology research, teaching, and education.

LNCS enjoys close cooperation with the computer science R & D community, the series counts many renowned academics among its volume editors and paper authors, and collaborates with prestigious societies. Its mission is to serve this international community by providing an invaluable service, mainly focused on the publication of conference and workshop proceedings and postproceedings. LNCS commenced publication in 1973.

Zoltán Porkoláb · Viktória Zsók
Editors

Composability, Comprehensibility and Correctness of Working Software

8th Summer School, CEFP 2019
Budapest, Hungary, June 17–21, 2019
Revised Selected Papers

 Springer

Editors
Zoltán Porkoláb ⓘ
Eötvös Loránd University
Budapest, Hungary

Viktória Zsók ⓘ
Eötvös Loránd University
Budapest, Hungary

ISSN 0302-9743   ISSN 1611-3349 (electronic)
Lecture Notes in Computer Science
ISBN 978-3-031-42832-6   ISBN 978-3-031-42833-3 (eBook)
https://doi.org/10.1007/978-3-031-42833-3

Cover illustration: 3COWS, Designed and drawn by Balázs Dénes Róbert. Used with his kind permission.

This Springer imprint is published by the registered company Springer Nature Switzerland AG
The registered company address is: Gewerbestrasse 11, 6330 Cham, Switzerland

Paper in this product is recyclable.

Preface

This volume presents the revised lecture notes of selected talks given at the eighth Central European Functional Programming School, CEFP 2019, held during 17–21 June in Budapest, Hungary at Eötvös Loránd University, Faculty of Informatics.

The summer school was organized in the spirit of intensive programmes. CEFP involves a large number of students, researchers, and teachers from across Europe.

The intensive programme offered a creative, inspiring environment for presentations and exchange of ideas on new specific programming topics. The lectures covered a wide range of programming subjects.

We are very grateful to the lecturers and researchers for the time and effort they devoted to their talks and lecture notes.

The lecture notes were each carefully checked by reviewers selected from experts. Each paper had two reviews involving external reviewers as well. The review process was a single-blind one. Out of the thirteen papers submitted, eleven were accepted for publication.

Seven tutorials of the partner universities and four student papers were selected from the students' workshop presentations organized for the participants of the summer school. Based on the reviews, the papers were revised and checked by the lecturers and student authors.

We would like to express our gratitude for the work of all the members of the Programme Committee and the Organizing Committee.

The web page of the event is https://people.inf.elte.hu/cefp/.

June 2023

Zoltán Porkoláb
Viktória Zsók

Organization

The 8th CEFP 2019 Summer School was organized by Eötvös Loránd University, Faculty of Informatics, Budapest, Hungary.

The school was supported by Erasmus+ projects. This volume is part of the dissemination of the results of the Erasmus+ Key Action 2 (Strategic Partnership for Higher Education) project No. 2017-1-SK01-KA203-035402: "Focusing Education on Composability, Comprehensibility and Correctness of Working Software".

Program Committee Chairs

Viktória Zsók   Eötvös Loránd University, Budapest, Hungary
Zoltán Porkoláb   Eötvös Loránd University, Budapest, Hungary

Contents

Main Lectures

Writing Internet of Things Applications with Task Oriented Programming

Mart Lubbers$^{(\boxtimes)}$ ⓘ, Pieter Koopman ⓘ, and Rinus Plasmeijer

Radboud University, Nijmegen, Netherlands
{mart,pieter,rinus}@cs.ru.nl

Abstract. The Internet of Things (IoT) is growing fast. In 2018, there was approximately one connected device per person on earth and the number has been growing ever since. The devices interact with the environment via different modalities at the same time using sensors and actuators making the programs parallel. Yet, writing this type of programs is difficult because the devices have little computation power and memory, the platforms are heterogeneous and the languages are low level. Task Oriented Programming (TOP) is a declarative programming language paradigm that is used to express coordination of work, collaboration of users and systems, the distribution of shared data and the human-computer interaction. The mTask language is a specialized, yet full-fledged, multi-backend TOP language for IoT devices. With the bytecode interpretation backend and the integration with iTask, tasks can be executed on the device dynamically. This means that—according to the current state of affairs—tasks can be tailor-made at run time, compiled to device-agnostic bytecode and shipped to the device for interpretation. Tasks sent to the device are fully integrated in iTask to allow every form of interaction with the tasks such as observation of the task value and interaction with Shared Data Sources (SDSs). The entire IoT application—both server and devices—are programmed in a single language, albeit using two embedded Domain Specific Languages (EDSLs).

Keywords: Task Oriented Programming · Interpretation · Functional Programming · Internet of Things

1 Introduction

1.1 Internet of Things

The IoT is growing rapidly and it is changing the way people and machines interact with the world. The term IoT was coined around 1999 to describe the communication of Radio-frequency Identification (RFID) devices. RFID became more and more popular the years after but the term IoT was not associated with it anymore. Years later, during the rise of novel network technologies, the term IoT resurged with a slightly different meaning. Today, the IoT is the term for a system of devices that sense the environment, act upon it and communicate with

Z. Porkoláb and V. Zsók (Eds.): CEFP 2019, LNCS 11950, pp. 3–52, 2023.
https://doi.org/10.1007/978-3-031-42833-3_1

each other and the world. At the time of writing, there is about one connected device per person in the world of which many are part of an IoT system. Gartner estimates that of these connected devices, there are about 5.8 billion IoT devices or endpoints connected[1]. They are already in everyone's household in the form of smart electricity meters, smart fridges, smartphones, smart watches, home automation and in the form of much more. While the number of devices seems to be growing exponentially fast, programming IoT applications is difficult. The devices are a large heterogeneous collection of different platforms, protocols and languages resulting in impedance problems.

The devices in IoT systems are equipped with various sensors and actuators. These range from external ones such as positioning, temperature and humidity to more internal ones like heartbeat and respiration [12]. When describing IoT systems, a layered architecture is often used to compartmentalize the technology. For the intents and purposes of this paper the four layer architecture defined by ITU-T (International Telecommunications Union - Telecommunication Standardization Sector) will be used as visualized in Fig. 1.

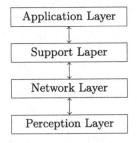

Fig. 1. The four layered IoT architecture as described by the ITU-T.

The first layer is called the perception layer and contains the actual endpoints with their peripherals. For example in home automation, the sensors reading the room and the actuators opening the curtains are in the perception layer. As a special type of device, it may also contain a Sensor Network (SN). A SN is a collection of sensors connected by a mesh network or central hub. The network layer is the second layer and it consists of the hardware and software to connect the perception layer to the world. In home automation, this layer may consist of a specialized IoT technology such as Bluetooth Low Energy (BLE) or ZigBee but it may also use existing technologies such as WiFi or wired connections. The third layer is named support layer and is responsible for the servicing and business rules surrounding the application. One of its goals is to provide the API, interfaces and data storage. In home automation this provides the server storing the data. The fourth and final layer in this architecture is the application layer. The application layer provides the interaction between the user and the

[1] Gartner (August 2019).

IoT system. In home automation, this layer contains the apps for to read the measurements and control the devices.

The perception layer often is a heterogeneous collections of microcontrollers, each having their own peculiarities, language of choice and hardware interfaces. The hardware needs to be cheap, small-scale and energy efficient. As a result, the Microcontroller Units (MCUs) used to power these devices do not have a lot of computational power, a soupçon of memory, and little communication bandwidth. Typically the devices do not run a full fledged OS but a compiled firmware. This firmware is often written in an imperative language that needs to be flashed to the program memory. It is possible to dynamically send the program to the program memory using Over the Air (OTA) programming [6,7]. Program memory typically is flash based and only lasts a couple of thousand writes before it wears out[2]. While devices are getting a bit faster, smaller, and cheaper, they keep these properties to an extent. The properties of the device greatly reduce the flexibility for dynamic systems where tasks are created on the fly, executed on demand and require parallel execution. These problems can be mitigated by dynamically sending code to be interpreted to the MCU. With interpretation, a specialized interpreter is flashed in the program memory once that receives the program code to execute at runtime.

1.2   Task Oriented Programming

TOP is a declarative programming paradigm designed to model interactive systems [39]. A task is an abstract representation of a piece of work that needs to be done. It provides an intuitive abstraction over work in the real world. Just as with real-life tasks and workflow, tasks can be combined in various ways such as in parallel or in sequence. Furthermore, tasks are observable which means it is possible to observe a—partial—result during execution and act upon it by for example starting new tasks. Examples of tasks are filling in a form, sending an email, reading a sensor or even doing a physical task. The task itself abstracts away from implementation details such as the interface, the communication and the sharing of data.

In many implementations the value observable in a task is a three state value that adheres to the transition diagram seen in Fig. 2. If a task emits no value, it means that the task has not made sufficient progress to produce a complete value. It might be the case that some work has been done but just not quite enough (e.g. an open serial port with a partial message). An unstable value means that a complete value is present but it may change in the future (i.e. a side effect). A web editor for filling in a form is an example of a task that always emits an unstable value since the contents may change over time. Stable values

---

[2] Atmel, the producer of AVR microprocessors, specifies the flash memory of the MCU in the Arduino UNO to about 10,000 cycles. This specification is a minimal specification and most likely the memory will be able to sustain many more writes. However, even if the memory can sustain ten times the amount, it is still a short time. .

never change. When the continue button has been pressed, the contents of the web editor is relayed, the values can never change, hence it is stable.

$$NoValue \longleftrightarrow Unstable \longrightarrow Stable$$

Fig. 2. State diagram for the legal transitions of task values

Tasks can communicate using task values but this imposes a problem in many collaboration patterns where tasks that are not necessarily related need to share data. Tasks can also share data using SDSs. SDSs are an abstraction over any data. An SDS can represent typed data stored in a file, a chunk of memory, a database etc. SDSs can also represent external impure data such as the time, random numbers or sensory data. Similar to tasks, transformation and combination of SDSs is possible. In this architecture, tasks function as lightweight communicating threads.

1.3   iTask

The iTask system originated as a system for developing distributed collaborative interactive web applications and the TOP paradigm grew from it [37]. It is suitable to model collaboration in almost any domain (see Subsect. 5.2).

The iTask system is implemented as an EDSL hosted in Clean [9]. Compiling the embedded TOP specification results in a multi-user distributed webserver offering an interface to users for actually doing the work. By default, implementation details such as the graphical user interface, serialization and communication are automatically generated. Section B gives a non-comprehensive overview that is sufficient for the exercises and examples in this paper.

In iTask a task is implemented as an event-driven stateful rewrite function. This means that, when there is an event, the function is executed with the current state of the system and the event as arguments. As a result, it produces a new state and either a value or an exception. If a value is produced, it consists of a task value, an update to the user interface and a rewritten function. The current state of a task can be represented by the structure of the tasks and their combinators and is dubbed the task tree [29].

SDSs in iTask are based on Uniform Data Sources (UDSs). UDSs are a type safe, uniform and composable abstraction over arbitrary data through a read-/write interface [34]. This interface is extended with parametric lenses to also allow fine-grained control over accessing subsets of the data and filtering notifications [13]. Any type in the host language Clean is an SDS when it implements the RWShared class collection that contains the read, write and notification functions. The iTask library contains SDSs for storing data in files, databases, memory but also to provide access to system information such as date, time and random streams. Furthermore it contains combinators to apply all types of transformations to SDSs. Multiple SDSs can be combined to form new SDS,

SDSs modelling collections can be filtered, information of an SDS can determine the lens on another one and the data modelled by an SDS can be transformed.

Examples. Example 1 shows a simple example of an iTask application, more examples are available in Sect. B. In the application, the user can enter a family tree and when they are finished, view the result. The screenshots in Figs. 3 and 4 show this workflow. Lines 1 to 7 define the data types, `Family` and `Person` are record types with named fields and `Gender` is an algebraic data type. For any first order type, the necessary machinery housed in the iTask generic function collection can be derived automatically [3]. The collection contains functions for deserialization, serialization, editors, pretty printing and equality. Line 9 shows the derivation of the generic functions for the types in this example. The actual task is of type `Task Family` and shown at Line 11. The workflow consists of two tasks, the first task is for entering (Line 13) and the second one for viewings (Line 14). They are combined using a sequential task combinator (`>>=`) that results in a continue button being shown to the user. At the start of the workflow, the form is empty, and thus the continue button is disabled. When the user enters some information, the continue button enables when there is a complete value. However, the value may still change, as can be seen in the third figure when the partner tickbox is ticked and a recursive editor appears.

```
1    :: Family = { person     :: Person,  partner      :: Maybe Person
2                 , children   :: [Family]
3                 }
4    :: Person = { firstName :: String,  surName      :: String
5                 , gender    :: Gender,  dateOfBirth :: Date
6                 }
7    :: Gender = Male | Female | Other String
8
9    derive class iTask Family, Person, Gender
10
11   enterFamily :: Task Family
12   enterFamily
13   =          Hint "Enter a family tree:" @>> enterInformation []
14   >>= λres→Hint "You Entered:"            @>> viewInformation  [] res
```

Example 1. Source code for some example iTask tasks.

1.4 TOP for the IoT

IoT devices are often doing loosely related things in parallel. For example, they are reading sensors, doing some processing on the data, operating actuators and communicating with the world. The TOP paradigm is an intuitive description language for theses tasks. Furthermore, due to the execution semantics of tasks, seemingly parallel operation due to interleaving comes for free. Unfortunately, running iTask tasks on the device is not an option due to the high memory requirements of the software. Therefore, mTask has been created, a

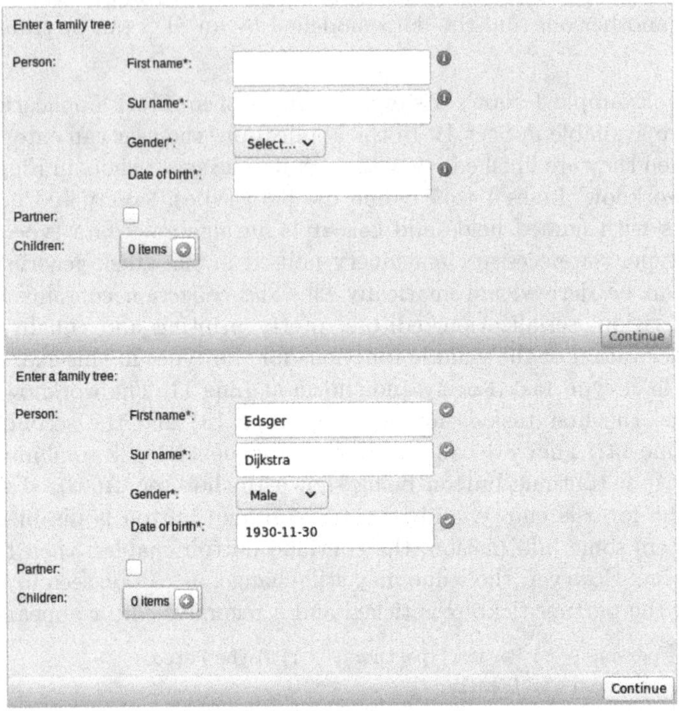

Fig. 3. The initial user interface and the enabling of the continue button for the example application.

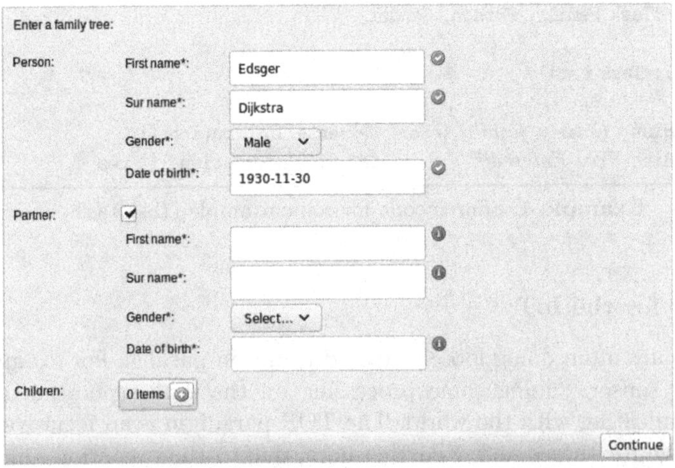

Fig. 4. The user interface after the user ticks the Partner box.

TOP language for small memory environments like IoT devices that also contains constructions to interact with the peripherals as well. It compiles the tasks to bytecode and sends them to the IoT device at run time. This allows the creation of dynamic applications, i.e. applications where tasks for the IoT devices are tailor-made at runtime and scheduled when needed.

1.5 Structure of the Paper

This section contains the introduction to IoT, TOP and iTask. The mTask ecosystem is explained in Sect. 2 followed by a language overview in Sect. 3. Section 4 contains gradually introduces more mTask concepts and provides a step by step tutorial for creating more interesting IoT applications. Section 5 contains the related work and Sect. 6 concludes with discussions. Background material on EDSL techniques is available in Sect. A. An iTask reference manual containing all the tasks and functions required for the exercises can be found in Sect. B and Sect. C contains detailed instructions on setting up an mTask development distribution.

Inline code snippets are typeset using a `teletype` font.

|| Program definitons are typeset in listings with a double left vertical border

Definition 1. This is an example definition.

| Program examples are typeset in listings with a single left and bottom border

Example 2. This is an example example.

Exercise 0 (The title of the example exercise). Exercises are numbered and typeset like this. The filename of the skeleton—located in the distribution, see Sect. C—is typeset in teletype and placed between brackets (`fileName`).

2 mTask system architecture

2.1 Blink

Traditionally, the first program that one writes when trying a new language is the so called *Hello World!* program. This program has the single task of printing the text *Hello World!* to the screen and exiting again. On microcontrollers, there often is no screen for displaying text. Nevertheless, almost always there is a rudimentary single pixel screen, namely an—often builtin—LED. The *Hello World* equivalent on microcontrollers blinks this LED.

Example 3 shows how the logic of a blink program might look when using the Arduino C++ dialect. The main event loop of the Arduino language continuously calls the user defined `loop` function. Blink's `loop` function alternates the state of the pin representing the LED between `HIGH` and `LOW`, turning the LED off and on respectively. In between it waits for 500 ms so that the blinking is actually visible for the human eye. Compiling this results in a binary firmware that needs to be flashed onto the program memory.

Translating the traditional blink program to mTask can almost be done by simply substituting some syntax as seen in Example 4. E.g. `digitalWrite` becomes `writeD`, literals are prefixed with `lit` and the pin to blink is changed to represent the actual pin for the builtin LED of the device used in the exercises. In contrast to the imperative Arduino C++ dialect, mTask is a TOP language and therefore there is no such thing as a loop, only task combinators to combine tasks. To simulate this, the `rpeat` task can be used, this task executes the argument task and, when stable, reinstates it. The body of the `rpeat` contains similarly named tasks to write to the pins and to wait in between. The tasks are connected using the sequential `>>|.` combinator that for all intents and purposes executes the tasks after each other.

Exercise 1 (Blink the builtin LED). Compile and run the blink program to test your mTask setup (`blinkImp`). Instructions on how to install mTask and how to find the example code can be found in Sect. C.

```
void loop() {
  digitalWrite(BUILTIN_LED, HIGH);
  delay(500);
  digitalWrite(BUILTIN_LED, LOW);
  delay(500);
}
```

Example (3) Blink in Arduino.

```
blink :: Main (MTask v ()) | mtask v
blink = {main = rpeat (
          writeD d2 (lit True)
    >>|. delay (lit 500)
    >>|. writeD d2 (lit False)
    >>|. delay (lit 500)
  )}
```

Example (4) Blink in mTask

2.2 Language

The mTask language is a TOP EDSL hosted in the pure lazy functional programming language Clean [9]. An EDSL is a language embedded in a host language created for a specific domain [23]. The two main techniques for embedding are deep embedding—representing the language as data—and shallow embedding—representing the languages as function. Depending on the embedding technique, EDSLs support one or multiple backends or views. Commonly used views are pretty printing, compiling, simulating, verifying and proving properties of the program. Deep and shallow embedding have their own advantages and disadvantages in terms of extendability, type safety and view support that are described in more detail in Sect. A.

2.3 Class Based Shallow Embedding

There are also some hybrid approaches that try to mitigate the downsides of the standard embedding techniques. The mTask language is using class-based—or tagless—shallow embedding that has both the advantages of shallow and deep embedding while keeping the disadvantages to a minimum [10]. This embedding technique is chosen because it allows adding backends and functionality orthogonally, i.e. without touching old code. E.g. adding functionality orthogonally is useful to add constructions for interact with new peripherals without requiring other backends to implement them. At the time of writing there is bytecode generation, symbolic simulation and pretty printing available as a backend.

Definition 2 shows an illustrative example of this embedding technique using a multi backend expression language. In class-based shallow embedding the language constructs are defined as type classes (`intArith` and `boolArith`). In contrast to regular shallow embedding, functions in class based shallow embedding are overloaded in the backend and in the types. Furthermore, the functions can be overloaded and contain class constraints, i.e. type safety is inherited from the host language. Lastly, extensions can be added easily, just as in shallow embedding. When an extension is made in an existing class, all views must be updated accordingly to prevent possible runtime errors. But when an extension is added in a new class, this problem does not arise and views can choose to implement only parts of the collection of classes.

```
class intArith v where
  lit :: t → v t                    | toString t
  add :: (v t) (v t) → (v t)  | + t
  sub :: (v t) (v t) → (v t)  | - t

class boolArith v where
  and :: (v Bool) (v Bool) → (v Bool)
  eq  :: (v t)    (v t)    → (v Bool) | == t
```

Definition 2. A minimal class based shallow EDSL.

A backend in a class based shallowly EDSL is just a type implementing some of the classes which makes adding backends relatively easy. It is even possible to create partial backends that do not support all classes from the language. The type of the backend are often—e.g. in the `PrettyPrinter` type—phantom types, only there to the resulting expression type safe. Example 5 shows an example of two backends implementing the expression Domain Specific Language (DSL).

```
:: PrettyPrinter a = PP String
runPrinter :: (PrettyPrinter t) → String
runPrinter (PrettyPrinter s) = s

instance intArith PrettyPrinter where
  lit x = PP (toString x)
  add (PP x) (PP y) = PP (x +++ "+" +++ y)
  ...
instance boolArith PrettyPrinter where ...
```

```
:: Evaluator a = Eval a
runEval :: (Evaluator a) → a
runEval (Eval a) = a

instance intArith Evaluator where ...
instance boolArith Evaluator where ...
```

Example 5. A minimal class based shallow EDSL.

A downside of using classes instead of functions is that the more flexible implementation technique makes the type errors more complicated. Also, as a consequence of using classes instead of data, a program wanting to use the same expression twice has to play some tricks (see Example 2). If the language supports rank-2 polymorphism, it can use the same expression for multiple backends. Another solution is to create a combinator backend that combines the two argument backends in a single structure.

```
printAndEval :: (∀v: v t | intArith, boolArith v) → (String, t)
printAndEval c = (runPrinter c, runEval c)

:: Two l r a = Two (l a) (r a)
printAndEval' :: (Two PrettyPrinter Evaluator t) → (String, t)
printAndEval' (Two (PP t) (Eval a)) = (t, a)

instance intArith (Two l r) | intArith l & intArith r where
  lit x = Two (lit x) (lit x)
  add (Two lx rx) (Two ly ry) = Two (add lx ly) (add rx ry)
instance boolArith (Two l r) | boolArith l & boolArith r where
  eq (Two lx rx) (Two ly ry) = Two (eq lx ly) (eq rx ry)
```

Example 6. Using multiple backends simultaneously in a shallow EDSL.

2.4 DSL design

To leverage the type checker of the host language, types in the mTask language are expressed as types in the host language, to make the language type safe. However, not all types in the host language are suitable for microcontrollers that may only have 2KiB of RAM so class constraints are therefore added to the EDSL functions (see Definition 3). The most used class constraint is the `type` class collection containing functions for serialization, printing, iTask constraints etc. Many of these functions can be derived using generic programming. An even stronger restriction on types is defined for types that have a stack representation. This `basicType` class has instances for many Clean basic types such as `Int`, `Real` and `Bool` but also for tuples. The class constraints for values in mTask are omnipresent in all functions and therefore often omitted throughout this paper for brevity and clarity.

Furthermore, expressions overloaded in backend add all mTask classes as constraints. To shorten this, a class collection is defined that contains all standard mTask classes to relieve this strain. However, classes for peripherals—or other non standard classes that not all backends have—need to be added still.

```
class type t | iTask, ... ,fromByteCode, toByteCode t
class basicType t | type t where ...

class mtask v | arith, ..., cond v

someExpr :: v Int | mtask v
readTempClass :: v Bool | mtask, dht v
```

Definition 3. Classes and class collections for the mTask EDSL.

The mTask language is a TOP language and therefore supports tasks. For seamless integration, the `TaskValue` type from iTask is used for task values in mTask as well (see Definition 4). The leafs are basic tasks (i.e. editors) and the forks are task combinators. Every evaluation step, the task tree is traversed from the root up and nodes are rewritten while at the mean time keeping track of the task value of the tree as a whole. This means that there is a difference in execution between expressions and tasks. Expressions are always evaluated completely and therefore block the execution. Tasks on the other hand have small evaluation steps to allow seemingly parallel execution when interleaved.

```
:: TaskValue t = NoValue | Value a Bool //from iTasks
:: MTask v t :== v (TaskValue t)
```

Definition 4. The mTask task types.

2.5 Backends

The classes are just a description of the language. It is the backend that actually gives meaning to the language. There are many backends possible for a TOP programming language for tiny computers. At the time of writing, there is a pretty printing, symbolic simulation and bytecode generation backend. These lecture notes only regard the bytecode generation backend but the other backends will be briefly discussed for completeness sake.

Pretty Printer. The pretty printing backend produces a pretty printer for the given program. The only function exposed is the `showMain` (Definition 5) function which runs the pretty printer and returns a list of strings containing the pretty printed result as shown in Example 7. The pretty printing function does the best it can but obviously cannot reproduce the layout, curried functions and variable names.

```
:: Show a // from the mTask Show library
showMain :: (Main (Show a)) → [String] | type a
```

Definition 5. The entrypoint for the pretty printing backend.

```
blink :: Main (MTask v Bool) | mtask v
blink =
  fun λblink = (λstate→
        writeD d13 state
    >>|. delay (lit 500)
    >>=. blink o Not)
  In {main = blink true}

Start :: [String]
Start = showMain blink

// output:
// let f0 a1 = writeD(D13, a1) >>=λa2.(delay 1000) >>| (f0 (Not a1)) in (f0 True)
```

Example 7. Pretty printing backend example.

Simulator. The simulation backend produces a symbolic simulator embedded in iTask for the given program. When task resulting from the `simulate` function presents the user with an interactive simulation environment (see Definition 6, Example 8 and Fig. 5). From within the environment, tasks can be rewritten, peripheral states changed and SDSs interacted with.

```
:: TraceTask a // from the mTask Show library
simulate :: (Main (TraceTask a)) → [String] | type a
```

Definition 6. The entrypoint for the simulation backend.

```
Start :: *World → *World
Start w = doTasks (simulate blink) w
```

Example 8. Simulation backend example.

2.6   Bytecode

Programs written in mTask are compiled to bytecode to be integrated in iTask. The microcontroller stores the tasks in their RAM, leaving the program memory untouched. In TOP, it is not uncommon to create tasks every minute. Writing the program memory of an MCU every minute would wear a typical MCU out within a week (see footnote 2).

A complete specification of an mTask program—including the SDSs and peripherals—of type t has the following type in the host language: :: `Main (` `MTask BCInterpret t)`. Under the hood, `BCInterpret` is a monad stack that generates the bytecode when executed. Interplay between mTask and iTask happens via three different constructions that are visualized in Fig. 6.

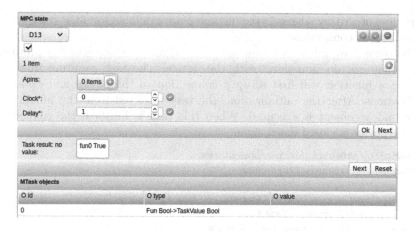

Fig. 5. Simulator interface for the blink program.

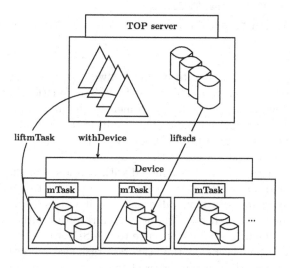

Fig. 6. The world of TOP applications that supports devices.

Connecting Devices. For a device to be suitable for mTask, it needs to be able to run the Run-time System (RTS). At the time of writing, the RTS is ported to Arduino compatible xtensa boards such as the LOLIN D1 Mini and NodeMCU, Arduino compatible AVR boards such as the Arduino UNO, and for platforms running OSs such as Linux, Windows or MacOS regardless of the architecture.

The `withDevice` function offers access to a specific device given the communication specification (see Definition 7). The first argument of the function contains the information about the connection that is used to communicate with the device. Any reliable sequential character based connection is suitable as a means of communication between the device and the server. In the mTask system at the time of writing, `channelSync` instances are available for TCP connections and serial port connections.

The second argument is a function that—given a device handle—produces a task that can do something with the device. The task resulting from the `withDevice` function will first setup a connection to the device and exchange specifications. After the initialization, the task retrieved from the function in the second argument is executed. When this task is finished, the connection with the device is closed down again.

```
:: MTDevice  // Abstract device representation
:: Channels  // Communication channels

class channelSync a :: a (Shared Channels) → Task ()
withDevice :: a (MTDevice → Task b)
  → Task b | iTask b & channelSync, iTask a

instance channelSync TCPSettings, TTYSettings
```

Definition 7. Connecting mTask devices to an iTask server

Lifting Tasks. Sending a task to a device always occurs from within iTask and is called *lifting* a task from mTask to iTask. The function for this is called `liftmTask` (see Definition 8). The first argument is the mTask program and the second argument is the device handle. The resulting task is an iTask proxy task representing the exact state of the mTask task on the device.

Under the hood it first generates the bytecode of the mTask task by evaluating the monad. This bytecode is bundled with metadata of the (lifted) SDSs and peripherals and sent to the device. The device executes the task and notifies the server on any changes in task value or when it writes a lifted SDS. These changes are immediately reflected in the server resulting either in a changed observable task value or a server side write to the SDS to which the lifted SDS was connected. On the server side, the `liftmTask` task also subscribes to all lifted SDS so that when the SDS on the server changes, the device can be notified as well. The result is that this lifted task reflects the exact state of the mTask task.

```
liftmTask :: (Main (MTask BCInterpret u)) MTDevice → Task u | iTask, type u
```

Definition 8. Lifting an mTask to an iTask task.

2.7   Skeleton

Subsect. 2.1 showed an example mTask task that blinks the builtin LED. This is not yet a complete Clean/iTask program that can be executed. A skeleton follows that can be used as a basis for the exercises that is explained line by line. Future snippets will again only give the mTask code for brevity.

```
1  module blink
2
3  import StdEnv, iTasks                    //iTasks imports
4  import Interpret, Interpret.Device.TCP //mTask imports
5
6  Start :: *World → *World
7  Start w = doTasks main w
8
9  main :: Task Bool
10 main = enterDevice >>= λspec→withDevice spec
11   λdev→liftmTask blink dev -|| viewDevice dev
12 where
13   blink :: Main (MTask v Bool) | mtask v
14   blink = ... //e.g. blink from Listing 4
```

Example 9. An mTask skeleton program.

Line 1 declares the name of the module, this has to match the name of the file-name. Line 3 import StdEnv and iTasks libraries, these imports are required when using iTasks. Line 4 imports the Interpret—the mTask bytecode backend—and Interpret.Device.TCP—the TCP device connectivity modules. Both imports are always required for these exercises. Line 6 and 7 gives the Start function, the entry point for a Clean program. This start function always calls the iTask specific entry point called doTasks that starts up the iTask machinery and launches the task main.

The main task first starts with an editor on Line 10. This editor presents an interface to the user connecting to the server for it to select a device as seen in Fig. 7. The enterDevice task allows selecting devices from presets and allows changing the parameters to select a custom device. After entering the IP address the device shows, the task continues with connecting the device withDevice that takes a function requiring a device and resulting in a task. This function (Line 11) executes the blink task and shows some information about the device at the same time. Line 13 and 14 contain the actual task, for example the task shown in Example 9.

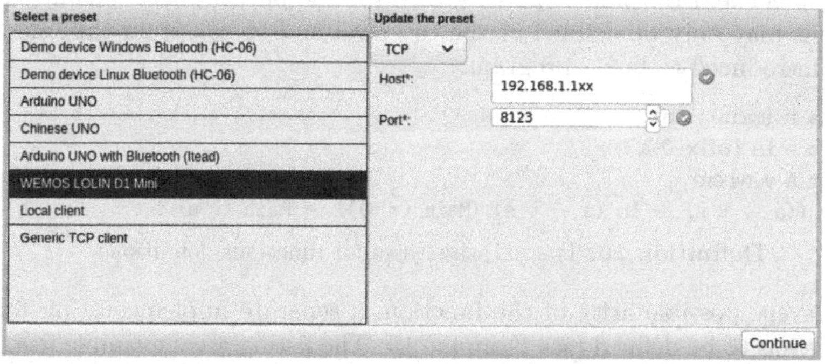

Fig. 7. The interface for the enterDevice task.

3   mTask language

3.1   Expressions

The classes for expressions—i.e. arithmetic functions, conditional expressions and tuples—are listed in Definition 9. Some of the class members are oddly named (e.g. +.) to make sure there is no name conflict with Clean's builtin overloaded functions that are of a different kind (* instead of *→*). There is no need for loop control due to support for tail call optimized recursive functions and tasks. The types speak for themselves but there are a few functions to explain. The lit function lifts a value from the host language to the mTask domain. For tuples there is a useful macro (topen) to convert a function with an mTask tuple as an argument to a function with a tuple of mTask values as an argument.

```
class arith v where
  lit :: t → v t | type t
  (+.) infixl 6 :: (v t) (v t) → v t    | basicType, +, zero, t
  ...
  (==.) infix 4 :: (v a) (v a) → v Bool | basicType, == a
  ...
class cond v where
  If :: (v Bool) (v t) (v t) → v t | type t
class tupl v where
  first  :: (v (a, b))  → v a    | type a & type b
  second :: (v (a, b))  → v b    | type a & type b
  tupl   :: (v a) (v b) → v (a, b) | type a & type b
```

Definition 9. The mTask classes for arithmetic, conditional and tuple expressions.

3.2   Functions

Functions are supported in the EDSL, albeit with some limitations. All user defined mTask functions are typed by Clean functions so that they are type-safe and are first class citizens in the DSL. They are defined using the multi-parameter typeclass **fun**. The first parameter (a) of the typeclass is the shape of the argument and the second parameter (v) is the backend (see Definition 10). Functions may only be defined at the top level and to constrain this, the **main** type is introduced to box a program.

```
:: Main a = {main :: a}
:: In a b = In infix 0 a b
class fun a v where
  fun :: ((a → v s) → In (a → v s) (Main (v u))) → Main (v u) | ...
```

Definition 10. The mTask classes for functions definitions.

For every possible arity of the function, a separate implementation for the **fun** class has to be defined (see Example 10) The listing gives example instances for arities zero to two for backend **T**. Defining the different arities as tuples of arguments instead of a more general definition forbids the use of curried functions. All functions are therefore known at compile time and when a function is called, all arguments are always known which is beneficial for keeping the memory requirements low.

```
:: T a // a backend
instance fun () T
instance fun (T a) T | type a
instance fun (T a, T b) T | type a & type b
```

Example 10. Different class instances for different arities in mTask functions.

To demonstrate the use, Example 11 shows examples for two functions. The `type` constraint on the function arguments forbid the use of higher order functions because functions do not have instances for all classes of the collection. The functions (`sum`, `factorial`) constructs the program that calculates the result of the arguments. In the bytecode backend, there is full tailcall optimization and therefore, writing `factorial` as `factorial`' pays off in memory usage.

```
sum :: Int Int → Main (v Int)
sum x y =
  fun λsum = (λ(l, r)→1 +. r) In
  {main = sum (lit x, lit y)}

factorial :: Int → Main (v Int) | mtask v
factorial x =
  fun λfac = (λi→
    If (i ==. lit 0) (lit 1) (i *. fac (i -. lit 1)))
  In {main = fac (lit i)}

factorial' :: Int → Main (v Int) | mtask v
factorial' x =
  fun λfacacc = (λ(n,a)→
    If (n ==. lit 0) a (facacc (n -. lit 0, n *. a)))
  In fun λfac = (λi→
    facacc (i, lit 1))
  In {main = fac (lit i)}
```

Example 11. Example mTask functions.

Functional Blinking. The mTask blink implementation does not show the advantage of function or TOP. With functions, the blink behaviour can be lifted to a function to make the program more functional and composable (see Example 12). The function takes a single argument, the state and recursively calls itself. It creates an infinite task that first waits 500 ms. Then it will write the current state to the pin followed by a recursive call to with the inverse of the state.

```
blinkTask :: Main (MTask v Bool) | mtask v
blinkTask
  = fun λblink = (λx→
        delay (lit 500)
    >>|. writeD d2 x
    >>=. blink o Not)
  In {main = blink (lit True)}
```

Example 12. A functional mTask translatation of Hello World! (`blink`)

Exercise 2 (Blink the builtin LED with a different interval). Change the blinking interval of the functional blink program (`blink`).

3.3 Basic Tasks

Definition 11 shows the classes for the basic tasks in mTask. Interaction with peripherals also occurs through basic tasks and they are shown later. To lift a value in the expression domain to the task domain, the basic task `rtrn` is used. The resulting task will forever yield the given value as a stable task value. The `rpeat` task continuously executes the argument task, restarting it when it yields a stable value. The resulting compound task itself never yields a value. The `delay` task emits no value while waiting for the elapsed number of milliseconds. When enough time elapsed, it returns the number of milliseconds that it overshot the target time as a stable value.

```
class rtrn v where
  rtrn :: (v t) → MTask v t | type t
class rpeat v where
  rpeat :: (MTask v a) → MTask v () | type a
class delay v
  delay :: (v Int) → MTask v Int | type n
```

Definition 11. The mTask classes for basic tasks.

3.4 Parallel Task Combinators

Task combinators can be divided into two categories, namely parallel and sequential combinators. In parallel combination, the evaluation of the two tasks are interleaved, resulting in seemingly parallel execution. In contrast to iTask, there are only two parallel combinators available in mTask. Definition 12 shows the class definitions. Both combinators execute the two argument tasks in an interleaved fashion resulting in parallel execution.

```
class .&&. v where
  (.&&.) infixr 4 v :: (MTask v a) (MTask v b) → MTask v (a, b) | ...
class .||. v where
  (.||.) infixr 3 v :: (MTask v a) (MTask v a) → MTask v a | ...
```

Definition 12. The mTask classes for parallel task combinators and the rules for combining the value.

The resulting task value for the conjunction combinator .&&. is a pair of the task values of the children. The resulting task value for the disjunction combinator .||. is a single task value, giving preference to the most stable one. The exact task value production is explained as a Clean function in the listing below.

```
(.&&.) :: (TaskValue a) (TaskValue b) → TaskValue (a, b)
(.&&.) (Value l s1) (Value r s2) = Value (l, r) (s1 && s2)
(.&&.) _              _          = NoValue

(.||.) :: (TaskValue a) (TaskValue a) → TaskValue a
(.||.) (Value _ True) _          = Value l True
(.||.) (Value _ _)    (Value r True) = Value r True
(.||.) NoValue        r          = r
(.||.) l              _          = l
```

Definition 13. The rules for the task value of the parallel combinators.

When using the parallel combinator .&&. the result is something of type v (a, b). This means that it is a tuple in the mTask language and not in the host language and therefore pattern matching the tuple directly is not possible. For that, the topen macro is defined as can be seen in the listing together with an example of the usage.

```
topen :: (v (a, b) → c) (v a, v b) → c | tupl v
topen f x :== f (first x, second x)

firstPinToYield :: MTask v Int
firstPinToYield = readA A0 .||. readA A1 >>~. rtrn

sumpins :: MTask v Int
sumpins = readA A0 .&&. readA A1 >>~. topen λ(x, y)→rtrn (x +. y)
```

Example 13. An example of the usage of the parallel combinators.

3.5   Threaded Blinking

Now say that we want to blink multiple blinking patterns on different LEDs concurrently. Intuitively we want to lift the blinking behaviour to a function and call this function three times with different parameters as done in Example 14.

```
void blink (int pin, int wait) {
  digitalWrite(pin, HIGH);
  delay(wait);
  digitalWrite(pin, LOW);
  delay(wait);
}

void loop() {
  blink (1, 500);
```

```
  blink (2, 300);
  blink (3, 800);
}
```

Example 14. Naive approach to multiple blinking patterns in Arduino C++.

Unfortunately, this does not work because the `delay` function blocks all further execution. The resulting program will blink the LEDs after each other instead of at the same time. To overcome this, it is necessary to slice up the blinking behaviour in very small fragments so it can be manually interleaved [17]. Example 15 shows how to implement three different blinking patterns in Arduino using the slicing method. If we want the blink function to be a separate parametrizable function we need to explicitly provide all references to the required state. Furthermore, the `delay` function can not be used and polling `millis` is required. The `millis` function returns the number of milliseconds that have passed since the boot of the MCU. Some devices use very little energy when in `delay` or sleep state. Resulting in `millis` potentially affects power consumption since the processor is basically busy looping all the time. In the simple case of blinking three LEDs on fixed intervals, it might be possible to calculate the delays in advance using static analysis and generate the appropriate `delay` code. Unfortunately, this is very difficult in general when the thread timings are determined at run time. Manual interleaving is very error prone, requires a lot of pointer juggling and generally results in spaghetti code. Furthermore, it is very difficult to represent dependencies between threads, often state machines have to be explicitly programmed by hand to achieve this.

```
long led1 = 0, led2 = 0, led3 = 0;
bool st1 = false, st2 = false, st3 = false;

void blink(int pin, int delay, long *lastrun, bool *st) {
  if (millis() - *lastrun > delay) {
    digitalWrite(pin, *st = !*st);
    *lastrun += delay;
  }
}

void loop() {
  blink(1, 500, &led1, &st1);
  blink(2, 300, &led2, &st1);
  blink(3, 800, &led3, &st1);
}
```

Example 15. Threading three blinking patterns in Arduino.

Blinking multiple patterns in mTask is as simple as combining several calls to an adapted version of the `blink` function from Example 9 with a parallel combinator as shown in Example 16. The resulting task tree of a single blink function call can then be visualized as in Fig. 8.

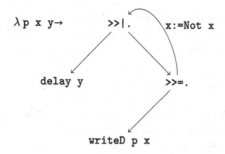

Fig. 8. The task tree for the blink task.

```
1  blink :: Main (MTask v Bool) | mtask v
2  blink
3    = fun λblink = (λ(p, x, y)→
4          delay y
5       >>|. writeD p x
6       >>=. λx→blink (p, Not x, y))
7    In {main = blink (d1, true, lit 500)
8        .||. blink (d2, true, lit 300)
9        .||. blink (d3, true, lit 800)}
```

Example 16. An mTask program for blinking multple patterns. (`blinkThread`)

Exercise 3 (Blink the builtin LED with two patterns). Adapt the program in Example 16 so that it blinks the builtin LED with two different patterns concurrently. The times for the patterns are queried from the user.

The function signature for `blink` becomes (`blinkThread`)

```
blink :: Int Int →  Main (MTask v Bool) | mtask v
```

You should `enterInformation` to get the information from the user (see Sect. B.2).

3.6   Sequential Task Combinators

The second way of combining tasks is sequential combination in which tasks are executed after each other. Similar to iTask, there is one Swiss army knife sequential combinator (`>>*.`) which is listed in Definition 14. The task value yielded by the left-hand side is matched against all task continuations (`Step v t u`) on the right-hand side, i.e. the right-hand side tasks observes the task value. When one of the continuations yields a new task, the combined task continues with it, pruning the left-hand side. All other sequential combinators are derived from the step combinator as default class member instances. Their implementation can therefore be overridden to provide a more efficient implementation. For example, the `>>=.` combinator is very similar to the monadic bind, it continues if and only if a stable value is yielded with the task resulting from the function. The `>>~.`

combinator continues when any value, stable or unstable, is yielded. The >>|.
and >>.. combinators are variants that do not take the value into account of the
aforementioned combinators.

```
class step v where
  (>>*.) infixl 1 :: (MTask v t) [Step v t u] → MTask v u | ...

  (>>=.) infixl 0 :: (MTask v t) ((v t) → MTask v u) → MTask v u | ...
  (>>=.) m f = m >>*. [IfStable (λ_→lit True) f]
  (>>~.) infixl 0 :: (MTask v t) ((v t) → MTask v u) → MTask v u | ...
  (>>~.) m f = m >>*. [IfValue (λ_→lit True) f]
  (>>|.) infixl 0 :: (MTask v t) (MTask v u) → MTask v u | ...
  (>>|.) m f = m >>=. λ_→f
  (>>..) infixl 0 :: (MTask v t) (MTask v u) → MTask v u | ...
  (>>..) m f = m >>~. λ_→f

:: Step v t u
  = IfValue    ((v t) → v Bool) ((v t) → MTask v u)
  | IfStable   ((v t) → v Bool) ((v t) → MTask v u)
  | IfUnstable ((v t) → v Bool) ((v t) → MTask v u)
  | IfNoValue                   (MTask v u)
  | Always                      (MTask v u)
```

Definition 14. The mTask classes for sequential task combinators.

The following listing shows an example of a step in action. The readPinBin
function will produce an mTask task that will classify the value of an analog
pin into four bins. It also shows how the nature of embedding allows the host
language to be used as a macro language.

```
readPinBin :: Main (MTask v Int) | mtask v
readPinBin = {main = readA A2 >>*.
  [ IfValue (λx→x <. lim) λ_→rtrn (lit bin)
  \\ lim←[64, 128, 192, 256]
  & bin←[0..]]}
```

Example 17. An example task using sequential combinators.

3.7 Shared Data Source

In mTask it is also possible to share data between tasks type safely using SDSs.
Similar to functions, SDSs can only be defined at the top level.

The sds class contains the function for defining and accessing SDSs. With the
sds construction function, local SDSs can be defined that are typed by functions
in the host language to assure type safety. The other functions in the class are
for creating get and set tasks. The getSds returns a task that constantly emits
the value of the SDS as an unstable task value. setSds writes the given value to
the task and re-emits it as a stable task value when it is done.

Definition 18 and Example 15 present the definitions and an example. The artificial example shows a task that mirrors a pin value to another pin using an SDS.

```
:: Sds a
class sds v where
    sds     :: ((v (Sds t)) → In t (Main (MTask v u)))
        → Main (MTask v u) | type t & type u
    getSds :: (v (Sds t))          → MTask v t | type t
    setSds :: (v (Sds t)) (v t) → MTask v t | type t
```

Definition 15. The mTask class for SDS tasks.

```
localvar :: Main (MTask v ()) | mtask v
localvar = sds λx=42 In {main =  rpeat (readA D13 >>~. setSds x)
                                .||. rpeat (getSds x  >>~. writeD D1)}
```

Example 18. An example mTask task using SDSs.

3.8   Lifted Shared Data Sources

The `liftsds` class is defined to allow iTask SDSs to be accessed from within mTask tasks. The function has a similar type as `sds` and creates an mTask SDS from an iTask SDS so that it can be accessed using the class functions from the `sds` class. Definition 16 and Example 19 show an example of this where an iTask SDS is used to control an LED on a device. When used, the server automatically notifies the device if the SDS is written to and vice versa. The `liftsds` class only makes sense in the context of actually executing backends. Therefore this class is excluded from the `mtask` class collection.

```
:: Shared a // an iTasks SDS
class liftsds v | sds v where
    liftsds :: ((v (Sds t)) → In (Shared t) (Main (MTask v u)))
        → Main (MTask v u) | type t & type u
```

Definition 16. The mTask class for iTask SDSs.

```
lightSwitch :: (Shared Bool) → Main (MTask v ()) | mtask v & liftsds v
lightSwitch s = liftsds λx=s In {main = rpeat (getSds x >>~. writeD D13)}
```

Example 19. An example mTask task using iTask SDSs.

3.9   Interactive Blinking

Example 17 showed that Clean can be used as a macro language for mTask, customizing the tasks using runtime values when needed. SDSs can also be used to interact with the mTask tasks during execution. This can for example be used to let the user control the blinking frequency. Example 20 shows how the blinking frequency can be controlled by the user using SDSs.

```
1   main :: Task Bool
2   main = enterDevice >>= λspec→withDevice spec
3     λdev→withShared 500 λdelayShare→
4        liftmTask (blink delayShare) dev
5      -|| updateSharedInformation [] delayShare <<@ Title "Interval"
6   where
7     blink :: (Shared s Int) → Main (MTask v Bool) | mtask, liftsds v & RWShared s
8     blink delayShare =
9       liftsds λdelaysh=delayShare
10      In fun λblink = (λx→
11              writeD d2 x
12        >>|. getSds delaysh
13        >>~. delay
14        >>|. blink (Not x))
15      In {main = blink (lit True)}
```

Example 20. An mTask program for interactively changing the blinking frequency. (`blinkInteractive`)

Line 3 shows the creation of the controlling iTask SDS using `withShared` (see Sect. B.4).

Line 4 and 5 compromise the device function for `withDevice`. It lifts the `blink` task to iTask and provides the user with an `updateSharedInformation` for the delay SDS. The `blink` task itself is hardly modified. Line 9 lifts the SDS to an mTask SDS using `liftsds` (see Subsect. 3.8). Note that the `>>~.` combinator is used since the `getSds` task always yields an unstable value. The lifted SDS can be accessed as usual using the `getSds` task (Line 12). The value this yields is immediately fed to `delay`. The mTask machinery takes care of synchronising the SDSs, when the user changes the delay, it is automatically reported to the device as well.

Exercise 4 (Blink the builtin LED on demand). Adapt the program in Example 20 so that the user can control whether the LED blinks or not.

The `blink` function will then have the following type signature (`blinkInteractive`):

```
blink :: (Shared s Bool) → Main (MTask v Bool) | mtask, liftsds v & RWShared s
```

3.10   Peripherals

Interaction with the General Purpose Input/Output (GPIO) pins, and other peripherals for that matter, is also captured in basic tasks. Some peripherals need initialization parameters and they are defined on the top level using host language functions similar to SDSs and functions. Typically from tasks reading peripherals such as sensors an unstable value can be observed.

General Purpose Input/Output. For each type of pin, there is a function that creates a task that—given the pin—either reads or writes the pin. The class for GPIO pin access is shown in Definition 17. The readA/readD task constantly yields the value of the analog pin as an unstable task value. The writeA/writeD writes the given value to the given pin once and returns the written value as a stable task value. Note that the digital GPIO class is overloaded in the type of pin because analog pins can be used as digital ones as well.

```
class aio v where
  readA  :: (v APin) → MTask v Int
  writeA :: (v APin) (v Int) → MTask v Int

class dio p v | pin p where
  readD  :: (v p) → MTask v Bool
  writeD :: (v p) (v Bool) → MTask v Bool

:: Pin = AnalogPin APin | DigitalPin DPin
class pin p :: p → Pin | type p
instance pin APin, DPin
```

Definition 17. The mTask classes for GPIO tasks.

Peripherals. All sensors have the same general structure in their classes and to illustrate this, the Digital Humidity and Temperature sensor (DHT) and LED matrix are shown. Using the DHT function, the device can be initialized with the correct parameters and used safely within the task. The temperature and humidity task respectively query the temperature and the relative humidity from the sensor and yield it as an unstable task value. This interface matches the C++ interface very closely but the semantics have been transformed to be suitable as a task. Note that this class is not part of the mtask class collection and needs to be added as a separate constraint. At the time of writing, mTask supports in a similar fashion DHTs, LED matrices, ambient light sensors, passive infrared sensors, sound level sensors and air quality sensors.

```
:: DHT
:: DHTtype = DHT11 | DHT21 | DHT22

class dht v where
  DHT         :: p DHTtype ((v DHT) → Main (v b)) → Main (v b) | pin p & ...
  temperature :: (v DHT) → MTask v Real
  humidity    :: (v DHT) → MTask v Real
```

Definition 18. The mTask classes for the DHT.

```
:: LEDMatrix

class LEDMatrix v where
  ledmatrix :: DPin DPin ((v LEDMatrix) → Main (v b)) → Main (v b) | type b
  LMDot     :: (v LEDMatrix) (v Int) (v Int) (v Bool) → MTask v ()
```

```
LMIntensity :: (v LEDMatrix) (v Int) → MTask v ()
LMClear     :: (v LEDMatrix) → MTask v ()
LMDisplay   :: (v LEDMatrix) → MTask v ()
```

Definition 19. The mTask classes for the LED matrix.

4 IoT applications with TOP

The following subsections are a hands-on introduction to writing more complex applications in mTask and iTask. Both mTask and iTask are hosted in Clean which has a similar syntax to Haskell. Peter et al. provide a concise overview of the syntactical differences [1]. The skeletons for the exercises are listed between brackets and can be found in the `mTask/cefp19` directory of the distribution[3]. Section C contains detailed setup instructions. Solutions for all exercises are available in Sect. D.

4.1 Hardware and Client

For the examples we use the WEMOS LOLIN D1 mini[4] (Fig. 9). The D1 mini is an ESP8266 based prototyping board containing 1 analog and 11 digital GPIO pins and a micro USB connection for programming and debugging. It can be programmed using MicroPython, Arduino or LUA.

It is assumed that they are preinstalled with the mTask RTS and that it has the correct shields attached. Details on how to compile and run the mTask RTS on the device can be found in Sect. C.4.

The devices are installed on a three-way splitter and setup with an OLED, SHT and Matrix LED shield. The OLED shield is used for displaying runtime during operation. When booting up, it shows the WiFi status and when connected it shows the IP address that one should enter in the device selection screen of the server application. Furthermore, the OLED screen contains two buttons that can be accessed from within mTask to get some kind of feedback from the user. The SHT shield houses a DHT sensor that can be accessed from mTask as well. The LED matrix can be accessed through mTask and can be used to display information.

4.2 Temperature

Reading the ambient temperature off the device is achieved using the DHT sensor connected as a shield to the main board. The DHT shield contains an SHT30 sensor. When queried via I^2C, the chip measures the temperature with a $\pm 0.4\,°C$ accuracy and the relative humidity with a $\pm 2\%$ accuracy.

It is accessed using the mTask `dht` class (see Subsect. 3.10). For example, the following program will show the current temperature and humidity to the

---

[3] https://ftp.cs.ru.nl/Clean/CEFP19/.
[4] https://wiki.wemos.cc/products:d1:d1_mini.

Fig. 9. The mainboard of the WEMOS LOLIN D1 mini.

user. The yielded values from the `temperature` and `humidity` tasks are in tenths of degrees and percents respectively instead of a floating point value. Therefore, a lens is applied on the editor to transform them into floating point values.

```
1  main = enterDevice >>= λspec→withDevice spec
2      λdev→liftmTask temp dev >&> viewSharedInformation () [ViewAs templens]
3  where
4      templens = maybe (0.0, 0.0) λ(t, h)→(toReal t / 10.0, toReal h / 10.0)
5
6      temp :: Main (MTask v (Int, Int)) | mtask, dht v
7      temp = DHT D4 DHT22 λdht→{main=temperature dht .&&. humidity dht}
```

Example 21. An mTask program for measuring the temperature and humidity. (`tempSimple`)

Exercise 5 (Show the temperature via an SDS). Modify the application so that it writes the temperature in an SDS. Writing the temperature constantly in the SDS creates a lot of network traffic. Therefore it is advised to create a function that will memorize the old temperature and only write the new temperature when it is different from the old one. Use the following template (`tempSds`):

```
main = enterDevice >>= λspec→withDevice spec
    λdev→withShared 0 λsh→
          liftmTask (temp sh) dev
       -|| viewSharedInformation "Temperature" [ViewAs templens] sh
where
    templens t = toReal t / 10.0

    temp :: (Shared s Int) → Main (MTask v ()) | mtask, dht, liftsds v & RWShared s
```

With the `writeD` functions from mTask (see Subsect. 3.10) the digital GPIO pins can be controlled. Imagine a heater attached to a GPIO pin that turns on when the temperature is below a given limit.

Exercise 6 (Simple thermostat). Modify the previous exercise so that a thermostat is mimicked. The user enters a temperature target and the LED will turn on when the temperature is below the target. To quickly change the temperature measure, blow some air in the sensor. Use the following template (`thermostat`):

```
main = enterDevice >>= λspec→withDevice spec
  λdev→withShared 0 λtempShare→
        withShared 250 λtargetShare→
        liftmTask (temp targetShare tempShare) dev
   -|| viewSharedInformation "Temperature" [ViewAs tempfro] tempShare
   -|| updateSharedInformation "Target" [UpdateAs tempfro λ_→tempto] targetShare
where
  tempfro t = toReal t / 10.0
  tempto  t = toInt t * 10

  temp :: (Shared s1 Int) (Shared s2 Int)
     → Main (MTask v ()) | mtask, dht, liftsds v & RWShared s1 & RWShared s2
  ...
```

4.3   LED matrix

Fig. 10. *The Answer* printed on the LED matrix.

The LED matrix shield can be used to display information during the execution of the program. Every LED of the 8×8 matrix can be controlled individually using the functions from Subsect. 3.10. The program in Example 22 shows an iTask program for controlling the LED matrix. It allows toggling the state of a given LED and clear the display.

To present the user with a nice interface (Fig. 11), a type is created that houses the status of an LED in the matrix. The main program is very similar to previous programs, only differing in the device part. The >ˆ* combinator is a special kind of **parallel** combinator that—instead of stepping to a continuation—forks off a continuation. This allows the user to schedule many tasks in parallel. Continuations can be triggered by values or by actions. In this example, only actions are used that are always enabled. One action is added for every operation and when the user presses the button, the according task is sent to the device.

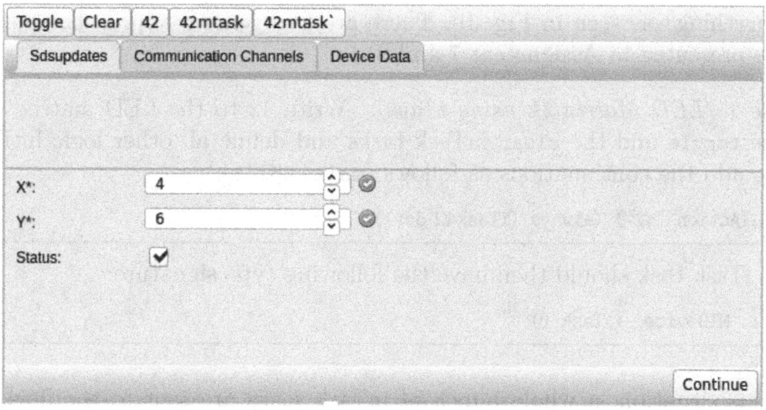

Fig. 11. The user interface for the LED matrix application

The `toggle` and `clear` tasks are self-explanatory and only use LED matrix mTask functions (see Definition 19).

```
1  :: Ledstatus = {x :: Int, y :: Int, status :: Bool}
2  derive class iTask Ledstatus
3
4  main = enterDevice >>= λspec→withDevice spec
5    λdev→ viewDevice dev >^*
6      [OnAction (Action "Toggle") (always (
7          enterInformation () [] >>= λs→liftmTask (toggle s) dev
8        >>~ viewInformation "done" []))
9      ,OnAction (Action "Clear") (always (
10         liftmTask clear dev
11       >>~ viewInformation "done" []))
12     ] @! ()
13 where
14   dot lm s = LMDot lm (lit s.x) (lit s.y) (lit s.status)
15
16   toggle :: Ledstatus → Main (MTask v ()) | mtask, LEDMatrix v
17   toggle s = ledmatrix D5 D7 λlm→{main=dot lm s >>|. LMDisplay lm}
18
19   clear :: Main (MTask v ()) | mtask, LEDMatrix v
20   clear = ledmatrix D5 D7 λlm→{main=LMClear lm >>|. LMDisplay lm}
```

Example 22. An interactive mTask program for interacting with the LED matrix. (matrixBlink)

Toggling the LEDs in the matrix using the given tasks is very user intensive because for every action, a task needs to be launched. Extend the program so that there is a new button for printing the answer to the question of life, universe

and everything[5] as seen in Fig. 10. There are two general approaches possible
that are presented in Assignment 7 and 8.

Exercise 7 (LED Matrix 42 using iTask). Write 42 to the LED matrix using
only the `toggle` and the `clear` mTask tasks and define all other logic in iTask
You can add the continuations as follows (`matrixBlink`):

```
OnAction (Action "42") (always (iTask42 dev))
```

The iTask task should then have the following type signature:

```
iTask42 :: MTDevice → Task ()
```

In this situation, a whole bunch of mTask tasks are sent to the device at
once. This strains the communication channels greatly and is a risk for running
out of memory. It is also possible to define printing 42 in solely in mTask. This
creates one bigger task that is sent at once.

Exercise 8 (LED Matrix 42 using mTask). Write 42 to the LED matrix as a
single mTask task. This results in the following continuation (`matrixBlink`):

```
OnAction (Action "42mtask") (always (liftmTask mTask42 dev))
```

The mTask task should then have the following type signature:

```
mTask42 :: Main (MTask v ()) | mtask, LEDMatrix v
```

4.4 Temperature Plotter

This final exercise is about creating temperature plotter with an alarm mode.
This application uses all components of the device and communicates with the
server extensively. I.e. the LED matrix to show the plot, the OLED shield buttons
to toggle the alarm, the builtin LED to show the alarm status and the DHT shield
to measure the temperature. Figure 12a shows an implementation in action.
Figure 12b shows the user interface for it.

Exercise 9 (Temperature plotter). There are several tasks that the plotter needs
to do at the same time

Plot The main task of the program is to plot the temperature over time on the
LED matrix. The range of the graph is specified in the `limitsShare` and may
be changed by the user.

Report The temperature has to be reported to the server every interval. This is
achieved by writing the current temperature in the lifted `tempShare` SDS. The
server is automatically notified and the user interface will update accordingly
Preferably it only writes to the SDS when the temperature has changed.

---

[5] The exact question is left as an exercise to the reader but the answer is 42 [2].

(a) The temperature plotter in action.   (b) The temperature plotter UI.

Fig. 12. The reference implementation of the plotter in action

Set alarm When the temperature is higher than a certain limit, the builtin LED should turn on. The current limit is always available in the lifted `alarmShare`.

Unset alarm When the alarm went off, the user should be able to disable it by pressing the A button that resides on the OLED shield.

The exercise is quite elaborate so please keep in mind the following tips:

– Start with the preamble and a skeleton for the tasks.
  The preamble should at least lift the SDSs and define the peripherals (LED matrix and DHT).
– Use functions for state as much as possible.
  Especially for measuring the temperature, you do not want to write to the temperature SDS every time you measure. Therefore, keep track of the old temperature using a function or alternatively a local SDS.
– Write functions for routines that you do multiple times.
  For example, clearing a row on the LED matrix is a tedious job and has to be done every cycle. Simplify it by either writing it as a Clean function that generates all the code or an mTask function that is called.

Create the plotter using the following template (`plotter`):

```
BUILTIN_LED := d3
ABUTTON := d4

main = enterDevice >>= λspec→withDevice spec
  λdev→withShared (220, 250) λlimitsShare→
        withShared 1000 λwaitShare→
        withShared 0 λtempShare→
        withShared 250 λalarmShare→
        liftmTask (temp limitsShare waitShare tempShare alarmShare) dev
    -|| updateSharedInformation "Graph Min/Max (C, C)" [] limitsShare
    -|| updateSharedInformation "Granularity (ms)" [updater] waitShare
    -|| viewSharedInformation "Temperature (C)" [ViewAs tempfro] tempShare
    -|| updateSharedInformation "Alarm (C)" [UpdateAs tempfro λ_→tempto] alarmShare
where
```

```
  tempfro t = toReal t / 10.0
  tempto  t = toInt t * 10

  updater :: UpdateOption Int Int
  updater = UpdateUsing (\x→(x, x)) (const fst)
    (panel2
      (slider <<@ minAttr 5 <<@ maxAttr 10000)
      (integerField <<@ enabledAttr False))

temp :: (Shared s1 (Int, Int)) (Shared s2 Int) (Shared s3 Int) (Shared s4 Int)
  → Main (MTask v ())
  | mtask, dht, liftsds, LEDMatrix v
  & RWShared s1 & RWShared s2 & RWShared s3 & RWShared s4
temp limitsShare delayShare tempShare alarmShare =
  ...
```

5   Related Work

The novelties of the mTask system can be compared to existing systems in several categories. It is an interpreted (Subsect. 5.1) TOP (Subsect. 5.2) language that may seem similar at first glance to Functional Reactive Programming (FRP) (Subsect. 5.3), it is implemented in a functional language (Subsect. 5.4) and due to the execution semantics, multithreading is automatically supported (Subsect. 5.5).

5.1   Interpretation

There are a myriad of interpreted programming languages available for some of the bigger devices. For example, for the popular ESP8266 chip there are ports of MicroPython, LUA, Basic, JavaScript and Lisp. All of these languages except the Lisp dialect uLisp (see Subsect. 5.4) are imperative and do not support multithreading out of the box. They lay pretty hefty constraints on the memory and as a result do not work on smaller MCUs. A interpretation solution for the tiniest devices is Firmata, a protocol for remotely controlling the MCU and using a server as the interpreter host [44]. Grebe et al. wrapped this in a remote monad for integration with Haskell that allowed imperative code to be interpreted on the MCUs [18]. Later this system was extended to support multithreading as well, stepping away from Firmata as the basis and using their own RTS [19]. It differs from our approach because continuation points need to be defined by hand there is no automatic safe data communication.

5.2   Task Oriented Programming

TOP as a paradigm with has been proven to be effective for implementing distributed, multi-user applications in many domains. Examples are conference management [36], coastal protection [27], Command & Control (C2) [8], incident coordination [28], crisis management [24] and telemedicine [48]. In general, TOP results in a higher maintainability, a high separation of concerns and more effective handling of interruptions of workflow. IoT applications contain a distributed and multi-user component, but the software on the device is mostly follows multiple loosely dependent workflows A TOP language μTasks developed by Piers is specialized for embedded systems. It is a non-distributed TOP EDSL hosted in Haskell designed for embedded systems such as payment terminals [35]. They showed that applications tend to be able to cope well with interruptions and be more maintainable. However, the hardware requirements for running the standard Haskell system are high.

5.3 Functional Reactive Programming

The TOP paradigm is often compared to FRP and while they appear to be similar—they both process events—, in fact they are very different. FRP was introduced by Elliot and Hudak [15]. The paradigm strives to make modelling systems safer, more efficient, composable [5]. The core concepts are behaviours and events. A behaviour is a value that varies over time. Events are happenings in the real world and can trigger behaviours. Events and behaviours may be combined using combinators. Stutterheim et al. showed that FRP concepts such as events, behaviours and signal transformers can be expressed in TOP using tasks and SDSs as well [45].

The way FRP, and for that matter TOP, systems are programmed stays close to the design when the domain matches suits the paradigm. The IoT domain seems to suit this style of programming very well in just the device layer[6] but also for entire IoT systems.

For example, Potato is an FRP language for building entire IoT systems using powerful devices such as the Raspberry Pi leveraging the Erlang Virtual Machine (VM) [47]. It requires client devices to be able to run the Erlang VM which makes it unsuitable for low memory environments. The authors state that it should be possible to create lesser demanding node software using other languages such as C or Java but this is future work.

The emfrp language compiles a FRP specification for a microcontroller to C code [41]. The Input/Output (IO) part, the bodies of some functions, still need to be implemented. These IO functions can then be used as signals and combined as in any FRP language. Due to the compilation to C it is possible to run emfrp programs on tiny computers. However, the tasks are not interpreted and there is no communication with a server.

Juniper [21] and arduino-copilot [22] are FRP language for creating Arduino programs by compiling the specification to C++. The languages do not contain built-in interaction with the server nor do they support interpretation.

---

[6] While a bit out of scope, it deserves mention that for SN, FRP and stream based approaches are popular as well [46].

5.4   Functional Programming

Haenisch showed that there are major benefits to using functional languages for IoT applications. They showed that using function languages increased the security and maintainability of the applications [20]. Traditional implementations of general purpose functional languages have high memory requirements rendering them unusable for tiny computers. There have been many efforts to create a general purpose functional language that does fit in small memory environments, albeit with some concessions. For example, there has been a history of creating tiny Scheme implementations for specific microcontrollers. It started with BIT [14] that only required 64KiB of memory, followed by PICBIT [16] and PICOBIT [43] that lowered the memory requirements even more. More recently, Suchocki et al. created Microscheme, a functional language targeting Arduino compatible microcontrollers. The *BIT languages all compile to assembly while Microscheme compiles to C++, heavily supported by C++ lambdas available even on Arduino AVR targets. An interpreted Lisp implementation called uLisp also exists that runs on microcontrollers with as small as the Arduino UNO [25].

5.5   Multitasking

Applications for tiny computers are often parallel in nature. Tasks like reading sensors, watching input devices, operating actuators and maintaining communication are often loosely dependent on each other and are preferably executed in parallel. MCUs often do not benefit from an OS due to memory and processing constraints. Therefore, writing multitasking applications in an imperative language is possible but the tasks have to be interleaved by hand [17]. This results in hard to maintain, error prone and unscalable spaghetti code.

There are many solutions to overcome this problem in imperative languages.

If the host language is a functional language (e.g. the aforementioned Scheme variants) multitasking can be achieved without this burden relatively easy using continuation style multiprocessing [49]. Writing in this style is complicated and converting an existing program in this Continuation Passing Style (CPS) results in relatively large programs. Furthermore, there is no built-in thread-safe communication possible between the tasks. A TOP or FRP based language benefits even more because the programmer is not required to explicitly define continuation points.

Regular preemptive multithreading is too memory intensive for smaller microcontrollers and therefore not suitable. Manual interleaving of imperative code can be automated to certain extents. Solutions often require an Real-Time Operating System (RTOS), have a high memory requirement, do not support local variables, no thread-safe shared memory, no composition or no events as described in Table 1 adapted from Santanna et al. [40, p. 12]. The table compares the solutions in the relevant categories with mTask.

Table 1. An overview of imperative multithreading solutions for tiny computers with their relevant characteristics. The characteristics are: sequential execution, local variable support, parallel composition, deterministic execution, bounded execution and safe shared memory (Adapted from Santanna et al. [40, p. 12]).

Language		Complexity				Safety	
Name	Year	Seq. ex.	Loc. var.	Par. comp.	Det. ex.	Bound. ex.	Safe. mem.
Preemptive	many	✓	✓			rt	
nesC	2003				✓	async	
OSM	2005		✓	✓			
Protothreads	2006	✓			✓		
TinyThreads	2006	✓	✓		✓		
Sol	2007	✓	✓	✓	✓		
FlowTask	2011	✓	✓				
Ocram	2013	✓	✓		✓		
Céu	2013	✓	✓	✓	✓	✓	✓
mTask	2018	✓	✓	✓	✓	✓*[a]	✓[b]

[a] Only for tasks, not for expressions.
[b] Using SDSs.

5.6 mTask history

A first throw at a class-based shallowly EDSL for MCUs was made by Pieter Koopman and Rinus Plasmijer in 2016 [38]. The language was called Arduino Domain Specific Language (ARDSL) and offered a type safe interface to Arduino C++ dialect. A C++ code generation backend was available together with an iTask simulation backend. There was no support for tasks or even functions. Some time later an unpublished extended version was created that allowed the creation of imperative tasks, SDSs and the usage of functions. The name then changed from ARDSL to mTask.

Mart Lubbers extended this in his Master's Thesis by adding integration with iTask and a bytecode compiler to the language [31]. SDS in mTask could be accessed on the iTask server. In this way, entire IoT systems could be programmed from a single source. However, this version used a simplified version of mTask without functions. This was later improved upon by creating a simplified interface where SDSs from iTask could be used in mTask and the other way around [32]. It was shown by Matheus Amazonas Cabral de Andrade that it was possible to build real-life IoT systems with this integration [4].

The mTask language as it is now was introduced in 2018 [26]. This paper updated the language to support functions, tasks and SDSs but still compiled to C++ Arduino code. Later the bytecode compiler and iTask integration was added to the language [33]. Moreover, it was shown that it is very intuitive to write MCU applications in a TOP language [30]. One reason for this is that a lot of design patterns that are difficult using standard means are for free in TOP (e.g. multithreading). Furthermore, Erin van der Veen has been working on a green computer analysis and is working on support for bounded data types.

6   Discussion

These lecture notes give a complete introduction to the design and use of the mTask system. Furthermore it provides a hands-on tutorial for writing IoT applications with it.

The number of IoT devices is increasing evermore but programming them is as difficult and error-prone as it ever was. Most programs written for IoT devices are collections of loosely dependent parallel tasks which makes programming the devices using TOP very natural. The mTask language is a multi-backend device-agnostic TOP language specialized for IoT tasks. It contains a backend that will compile the program to bytecode that is then sent to the device. The backend is fully integrated in iTask which means that tasks that are sent to the device act as regular iTask tasks, i.e. their task value can be observed and they can interact with SDSs on the server. There is no impedance problem in the mTask ecosystem since all code is written in a single language, albeit in two EDSLs. The bytecode generation backend of mTask—and iTask for that matter—make heavy use of generic programming techniques to relieve the programmer of the burden to hand-craft specifics such as the user interface, the communication protocol or serialization. The execution semantics of the tasks makes them similar to lightweight threads—for which there is typically no support on microcomputers due to the lack of an OS. This allows programmers to create multitasking applications just by using parallel combinators. Reasonably complex IoT applications spanning all layers of IoT can be written in a concise and safe way using the mTask system.

Future work may be practical topics such as extending the number of supported platforms or extending the language with more features. For example, adding lenses and combinators to SDSs may improve the expressiveness of the language. Also, type errors in the DSL are presented to the programmer as type errors in the host language. As a result of class based shallow embedding, the type errors are quite complicated. It would be interesting to see whether techniques for mitigating this problem can be applied to mTask as well [42]. The execution model of the mTask system lets the server send arbitrary code to the device to be executed. This may pose a problem if the server, the communication technique is not to be trusted or can be snooped on. At the time of writing a student is working on analysing this problem in his thesis. Finally it would be interesting to allow the user instead of the programmer to write mTask tasks from scratch. This can be achieved by creating a type-safe editor in iTask that constructs tasks.

Acknowledgements. This paper constitutes the adapted lecture notes for the hands-on course presented at the Central European Functional Programming School (CEFP) in Budapest between 17 and 21 June 2019. This research is partly funded by the Royal Netherlands Navy. Furthermore, we would like to thank the reviewers for their valuable comments.

A   Embedded Domain Specific Language Techniques

An EDSL is a language embedded in a host language created for a specific domain [23]. EDSLs can have one or more backends or views. Commonly used views are pretty printing, compiling, simulating, verifying and proving the program. There are several techniques available for creating EDSLs. They all have their own advantages and disadvantages in terms of extendability, type safety and view support. In the following subsections each of the main techniques are briefly explained. An example expression DSL is used as a running example.

A.1   Deep Embedding

A deeply EDSL is a language represented as data in the host language. Views are functions that transform *something* to the datatype or the other way around. Definition 20 shows an example implementation for the expression DSL.

```
:: Expr
   = LitI  Int
   | LitB  Bool
   | Var   String
   | Plus  Expr Expr
   | Eq    Expr Expr
```

Definition 20. A deeply embedded expression DSL.

Deep embedding has the advantage that it is easy to build and views are easy to add. On the downside, the expressions created with this language are not necessarily type-safe. In the given language it is possible to create an expression such as `Plus (LitI 4)(LitB True)` that adds a boolean to an integer. Extending the Algebraic Datatype (ADT) is easy and convenient but extending the views accordingly is tedious since it has to be done individually for all views.

The first downside of this type of EDSL can be overcome by using Generalized ADTs (GADTs) [11]. Example 21 shows the same language, but type-safe with a GADT. GADTs are not supported in the current version of Clean and therefore the syntax is hypothetical. However, it has been shown that GADTs can be simulated using bimaps or projection pairs [11]. Unfortunately the lack of extendability remains a problem. If a language construct is added, no compile time guarantee can be given that all views support it.

```
:: Expr a
   =      Lit  a                          → Expr a
   | ∃e: Var    String                    → Expr e
   |      Plus  (Expr Int)  (Expr Int)    → Expr Int
   | ∃e: Eq     (Expr e)    (Expr e)      → Expr Bool & == e
```

Definition 21. A deeply embedded expression DSL using GADTs.

A.2 Shallow Embedding

In a shallowly EDSL all language constructs are expressed as functions in the host language. An evaluator view for the example language then can be implemented as the code shown in Definition 22. Note that much of the internals of the language can be hidden using monads.

```
:: Env   = ...              // Some environment
:: DSL a :== (Env → a)

Lit :: a → DSL a
Lit x = λe→x

Var :: String → DSL Int
Var i = λe→retrEnv e i

Plus :: (DSL Int) (DSL Int) → DSL Int
Plus x y = λe→x e + y e

Eq :: (DSL a) (DSL a) → DSL Bool | == a
Eq x y = λe→x e == y e
```

Definition 22. A minimal shallow EDSL.

The advantage of shallowly embedding a language in a host language is its extendability. It is very easy to add functionality because the compile time checks of the host language guarantee whether or not the functionality is available when used. Moreover, the language is type safe as it is directly typed in the host language, i.e. `Lit True +. Lit 4` is rejected.

The downside of this method is extending the language with views. It is nearly impossible to add views to a shallowly embedded language. The only way of achieving this is by reimplementing all functions so that they run all backends at the same time. This will mean that every component will have to implement all views rendering it slow for multiple views and complex to implement.

B   iTask reference

This appendix gives a brief overview of iTask. It is by far extensive but should cover all iTask constructions required for the exercises. Some examples from [45] can be found in Sect. B.6.

B.1 Types

The class collection `iTask` is used throughout the library to make sure the types used have all the required machinery for iTask. This class collection contains only generic functions that can automatically be derived for any first order user defined type. Example 23 shows how to derive this class.

```
:: MyName =
  { firstName :: String
  , lastName  :: String
  }
derive class iTask MyName
```

Example 23. Derive the iTask class for a user defined type.

B.2   Editors

The most common basic tasks are editors for entering, viewing or update information. For the three basic editors there are three corresponding functions to create tasks as seen in Definition 23.

```
enterInformation  :: d [EnterOption m]        → Task m | iTask m & toPrompt d
updateInformation :: d [UpdateOption m m] m → Task m | iTask m & toPrompt d
viewInformation   :: d [ViewOption m]      m → Task m | iTask m & toPrompt d
```

Definition 23. The definitions of editors in iTask.

The first argument of the function is something implementing toPrompt. There are toPrompt instances for at least String—for a description, (String, String)—for a title and a description and ()—for no description.

The second argument is a list of options for modifying the editor behaviour. This list is either empty or contains exactly one item. The types for the options are shown in Definition 24. Simple lenses are created using the *As constructor. If an entirely different editor must be used, the *Using constructors can be used.

```
:: ViewOption a
  =∃v: ViewAs      (a → v)              & iTask v
  | ∃v: ViewUsing  (a → v) (Editor v) & iTask v
:: EnterOption a
  =∃v: EnterAs     (v → a)              & iTask v
  | ∃v: EnterUsing (v → a) (Editor v) & iTask v
:: UpdateOption a b
  =∃v: UpdateAs    (a → v) (a v → b)            & iTask v
  | ∃v: UpdateUsing (a → v) (a v → b) (Editor v) & iTask v
```

Definition 24. The definitions of editors in iTask.

Example 24 shows an example of such an editor using a lens. The user enters a temperature in degrees Celsius and the editor automatically converts the result to a temperature in Fahrenheit which is in turn the observed task value.

```
tempFahrenheit :: Task Real
tempFahrenheit = enterInformation "Enter the temperature in degrees Celsius"
  [EnterUsing λc→c*(9.0/5.0) + 32]
```

Example 24. An example of an editor that converts the entered value to a different unit in iTask.

B.3   Task Combinators

There are two flavours of task combinators, namely parallel and sequential that are all specializations of their Swiss-army knife combinator step and parallel respectively.

Parallel Combinators. The two main parallel combinators are the conjunction and disjunction combinators shown in Definition 25.

The -&&- has semantics similar to the mTask .&&. combinator. The -||- has the same semantics as the mTask .||. combinator. The -|| and ||- executes both tasks in parallel but only looks at the value of the left task or the right task respectively.

```
(-&&-) infixr 4 :: (Task a) (Task b) → Task (a,b) | iTask a & iTask b
(-|| ) infixl 3 :: (Task a) (Task b) → Task a     | iTask a & iTask b
( ||-) infixr 3 :: (Task a) (Task b) → Task b     | iTask a & iTask b
(-||-) infixr 3 :: (Task a) (Task a) → Task a     | iTask a
```

Definition 25. The definitions of parallel combinators in iTask.

Example 25 shows an example of a task that, using the disjunction combinator, asks the user for a temperature either in degrees Celsius or Fahrenheit using the task from Example 24. Whichever editor the user edits last, will be the observable task value.

```
askTemp :: Task Real
askTemp =   enterInformation "Temperature in Fahrenheit" []
       -||- tempFahrenheit
```

Example 25. An example of parallel task combinators in iTask.

Sequential Combinators. All sequential combinators are derived from the >>* combinator as shown in Definition 26. With this combinator, the task value of the left-hand side can be observed and execution continues with the right-hand side if one of the continuations yields a Just (Task b). The listing also shows many utility functions for defining task steps.

```
(>>*) infixl 1 :: (Task a) [TaskCont a (Task b)] → Task b | iTask a & ...
:: TaskCont a b
  = OnValue           ((TaskValue a) → Maybe b)
  | OnAction Action ((TaskValue a) → Maybe b)

:: Action = Action String //button

always      :: b                (TaskValue a) → Maybe b
never       :: b                (TaskValue a) → Maybe b
hasValue    :: (a → b)          (TaskValue a) → Maybe b
ifStable    :: (a → b)          (TaskValue a) → Maybe b
ifUnstable  :: (a → b)          (TaskValue a) → Maybe b
```

```
ifValue      :: (a → Bool) (a → b) (TaskValue a) → Maybe b
ifCond       :: Bool b             (TaskValue a) → Maybe b
withoutValue :: (Maybe b)          (TaskValue a) → Maybe b
withValue    :: (a → Maybe b)      (TaskValue a) → Maybe b
withStable   :: (a → Maybe b)      (TaskValue a) → Maybe b
withUnstable :: (a → Maybe b)      (TaskValue a) → Maybe b
```

Definition 26. The definitions of sequential combinators in iTask.

Example 26 shows an example of the step combinator that forces the user to enter a number between 0 and 10. If the user enters a different value, the continue button will remain disabled.

```
numberBetween0and10 :: Task Int
numberBetween0and10 = enterInformation "Enter a number between 0 and 10" []
    >>* [OnAction (Action "Continue") $ ifValue (λi→i <= 10 && i >= 0) $ λi→return i]
```

Example 26. An example of parallel task combinators in iTask.

Derived from the >>* combinator are all other sequential combinators such as the ones listed in Definition 27 with their respective documentation.

```
// Combines two tasks sequentially. The first task is executed first.
// When it has a value the user may continue to the second task, which is
// executed with the result of the first task as parameter.
// If the first task becomes stable, the second task is started automatically.
(>>=) infixl 1 :: (Task a) (a → Task b) → Task b | iTask a & iTask b

// Combines two tasks sequentially but explicitly waits for user input to
// confirm the completion of
(>>!) infixl 1 :: (Task a) (a → Task b) → Task b | iTask a & iTask b

// Combines two tasks sequentially but continues only when the first task has a
// stable value.
(>>-) infixl 1 :: (Task a) (a → Task b) → Task b | iTask a & iTask b

// Combines two tasks sequentially but continues only when the first task has a
// stable value.
(>-|) infixl 1
(>-|) x y :== x >>- λ_ → y

// Combines two tasks sequentially but continues only when the first task has a
// value.
(>>~) infixl 1 :: (Task a) (a → Task b) → Task b | iTask a & iTask b

// Combines two tasks sequentially just as >>= but the result of the second
// task is disregarded.
(>>^) infixl 1 :: (Task a) (Task b) → Task a| iTask a & iTask b

// Execute the list of tasks one after another.
sequence :: [Task a] → Task [a] | iTask a
```

Definition 27. The definitions of derived sequential combinators in iTask.

B.4   Shared Data Sources

Data can be observer via task values but for unrelated tasks to share data, SDSs are used. There is an publish subscribe system powering the SDS system that makes sure tasks are only rewritten when activity has taken place in the SDS. There are many types of SDSs such as lenses, sources and combinators. As long as they implement the `RWShared` class collection, you can use them as an SDS. Definition 28 shows two methods for creating an SDS, they both yield a `SimpleSDSLens` but they can be used by any task using an SDS.

```
sharedStore :: String a → SimpleSDSLens a | iTask a
withShared  :: b ((SimpleSDSLens b) → Task a) → Task a | iTask a & iTask b
```

Definition 28. The definitions for SDSs in iTask.

With the `sharedStore` function, a named SDS can be created that acts as a well-typed global variable. `withShared` is used to create an anonymous local SDS.

There are four major operations that can be done on SDSs that are all atomic (see Definition 29). `get` fetches the value from the SDS and yields it as a stable value. `set` writes the given value to the SDS and yields it as a stable value. `upd` applies an update function to the SDS and returns the written value as a stable value. `watch` continuously emits the value of the SDS as an unstable task value. The implementation uses a publish subscribe system to evaluate the watch task only when the value of the SDS changes.

```
get   ::              (sds () r w) → Task r | iTask r & iTask w & RWShared sds
set   :: w            (sds () r w) → Task w | iTask r & iTask w & RWShared sds
upd   :: (r → w) (sds () r w) → Task w | iTask r & iTask w & RWShared sds
watch ::              (sds () r w) → Task r | iTask r & iTask w & RWShared sds
```

Definition 29. The definitions for SDS access tasks in iTask.

For all editors, there are shared variants available as shown in Definition 27. This allows a user to interact with the SDS.

```
updateSharedInformation :: d [UpdateOption r w] (sds () r w) → Task r | ...
viewSharedInformation   :: d [ViewOption r]     (sds () r w) → Task r | ...
```

Definition 30. The definitions for SDS editor tasks in iTask.

```
sharedUpdate :: Task Int
sharedUpdate = withShared 42 λsharedInt→
      updateSharedInformation "Left" [] sharedInt
 -||- updateSharedInformation "Right" [] sharedInt
```

Example 27. An example of multiple tasks interacting with the same SDS in iTask.

B.5   Extra Task Combinators

Not all workflow patterns can be described using only the derived combinators. Therefore, some other task combinators have been invented that are not truly sequential nor truly parallel. Definition 31 shows some combinators that might be useful in the exercises.

```
//Feed the result of one task as read-only shared to another
(>&>) infixl 1 :: (Task a) ((SDSLens () (Maybe a) ()) → Task b) → Task b | ...
```

```
// Sidestep combinator. This combinator has a similar signature as the >>*
// combinator, but instead of moving forward to a next step, the selected step is
// executed in parallel with the first task. When the chosen task step becomes
// stable, it is removed and the actions are enabled again.
(>^*) infixl 1 :: (Task a) [TaskCont a (Task b)] → Task a | iTask a & iTask b
```

```
// Apply a function on the task value while retaining stability
(@) infixl 1 :: (Task a) (a → b) → Task b
// Map the task value to a constant value while retaining stability
(@) infixl 1 :: (Task a) b → Task b
```

```
// Repeats a task indefinitely
forever :: (Task a) → Task a | iTasks a
```

Definition 31. The definitions for hybrid combinators in iTask.

B.6 Examples

Some workflow task patterns can easily be created using the builtin combinator as shown in Examples 28.

```
maybeCancel :: String (Task a) → Task (Maybe a) | iTask a
maybeCancel panic t = t >>*
  [ OnValue (ifStable (return o Just))
  , OnAction (Action panic) (always (return Nothing))
  ]

:: Date //type from iTasks.Extensions.DateTime
currentDate :: SDSLens () Date () // Builtin SDS

waitForDate :: Date → Task Date
waitForDate d = viewSharedInformation ("Wait until" +++ toString d) [] currentDate
  >>* [OnValue (ifValue (\now → date < now) return)]

deadlineWith :: Date a (Task a) → Task a | iTask a
deadlineWith d a t = t -||- (waitForDate d >>| return a)

reminder :: Date String → Task ()
reminder d m = waitForDate d >>| viewInformation ("Reminder: please " +++ m) [] ()
```

Example 28. Some workflow task patterns.

C   How to Install

This section will give detailed instructions on how to install mTask on your system. The distribution used also includes the example skeletons.

C.1   Fetch the CEFP distribution

Download the CEFP version of mTask distribution for your operating system as given in Table 2 and decompress the archive. The archives is all you need since it contains a complete clean distribution. The windows version contains an IDE and Clean Project Manager (`cpm`). Mac and Linux only have a project manager called `cpm`.

Table 2. Download links for the CEFP builds of mTask.

OS	Arch	URL
Linux	x64	https://ftp.cs.ru.nl/Clean/CEFP19/mtask-linux-x64.tar.gz
		Requires GCC
Windows	x64	https://ftp.cs.ru.nl/Clean/CEFP19/mtask-windows-x64.zip
MacOS	x64	https://ftp.cs.ru.nl/Clean/CEFP19/mtask-macos-x64.tar.gz
		Requires XCode

C.2   Setup

Linux. Assuming you uncompressed the archive in `~/mTask`, run the following commands in a terminal.

```
# Add the bin directory of the clean distribution to $PATH
echo 'export PATH=~/mTask/clean/bin:$PATH' >> ~/.bashrc
# Correctly set CLEANHOME
echo 'export CLEANHOME=~/mTask/clean' >> ~/.bashrc
# Source it for your current session
source ~/.bashrc
```

Windows. You do not need to setup anything on windows. However, if you want to use `cpm` as well, you need to add the `;C:\Users\frobnicator\mTask\clean` to your `%PATH%`[7].

MacOS. Assuming you uncompressed the archive in `~/mTask`, run the following commands in a terminal.

```
# Add the bin directory of the clean distribution to $PATH
echo 'export PATH=~/mTask/clean/bin:$PATH' >> ~/.bash_profile
# Correctly set CLEANHOME
echo 'export CLEANHOME=~/mTask/clean' >> ~/.bash_profile
# Source it for your current session
source ~/.bashrc
```

---

[7] Instructions from https://hmgaudecker.github.io/econ-python-environment/paths.html.

C.3   Compile the Test Program

Note that the first time compiling everything can take a while and will consume quite some memory.

Windows.   Assuming   you   uncompressed   the   archive   in `C:\Users\frobnicator\mTask`. Connect a device or start the local TCP client by executing `C:\Users\frobnicator\mTask\client.exe`

IDE

- Open the IDE by starting `C:\Users\frobnicator\mTask\clean\CleanIDE.exe`.
- Click on File ⟩ Open or press Ctrl + O ond open `C:\Users\frobnicator\mTask\mTask\cefp19\blink.prj`.
- Click on Project ⟩ Update and Run or press Ctrl + R .

cpm Enter the following commands in a command prompt or PowerShell session:

```
cd C:\Users\frobnicator\mTask\mTask\cefp19
cpm blink.prj
blink.exe
```

Linux & MacOS.   Assuming you uncompressed the archive in ~/mTask. Connect a device or start the local TCP client by executing ~/mTask/client. In a terminal enter the following commands:

```
cd ~/mTask/cefp19
cpm blink.prj
./blink
```

C.4   Setup the Microcontroller Unit

For setting up the RTS for the MCU, the reader is kindly referred to here[8].

D   Solutions

```
main :: Task Bool
main = enterDevice
  >>= λspec→enterInformation "Enter the intervals (ms)"
  >>= λ(i1, i2)→withDevice spec
    λdev→liftmTask (blink i1 i2) dev -|| viewDevice dev
where
```

---

[8] https://gitlab.science.ru.nl/mlubbers/mTask/blob/cefp19/DEVICES.md.

```
blink :: Int Int → Main (MTask v Bool) | mtask v
blink x y
  = fun λblink = (λ(p, x, y)→
          delay y
      >>|. writeD p x
      >>=. λx→blink (p, Not x, y))
  In {main = blink (d4, true, lit x)
        .||. blink (d4, true, lit y)}
```

Solution 3. Blink the builtin LED with two patterns

```
main :: Task Bool
main = enterDevice >>= λspec→withDevice spec
  λdev→withShared True λblinkOk→
        liftmTask (blink blinkOk) dev
    -|| updateSharedInformation "Blink Enabled" [] blinkOk
where
  blink :: (Shared s Bool) → Main (MTask v Bool) | mtask, liftsds v & RWShared s
  blink blinkShare = liftsds λblinkOk=blinkShare
    In fun λblink = (λx→
          writeD d2 x
      >>|. delay (lit 500)
      >>|. getSds blinkOk
      >>*. [IfValue (λx→x) (λ_→blink (Not x))])
    In {main = blink (lit True)}
```

Solution 4. Blink the builtin LED on demand

```
temp :: (Shared s Int) → Main (MTask v ()) | mtask, dht, liftsds v & RWShared s
temp tempShare =
  DHT D4 DHT22 λdht→
  liftsds λsTemp = tempShare
  In fun λmonitor = (λx→temperature dht
    >>*. [IfValue ((!=.)x) (setSds sTemp)]
    >>=. monitor)
  In {main = monitor (lit 0)}
```

Solution 5. Show the temperature via an SDS

```
temp :: (Shared s1 Int) (Shared s2 Int) → Main (MTask v ())
  | mtask, dht, liftsds v & RWShared s1 & RWShared s2
temp targetShare tempShare =
  DHT D4 DHT22 λdht→
      liftsds λsTemp = tempShare
  In liftsds λsTarget = targetShare
  In fun λmonitor = (λx→temperature dht
    >>*. [IfValue ((!=.)x) (setSds sTemp)]
    >>=. monitor)
  In fun λheater = (λst→getSds sTemp .&&. getSds sTarget
    >>*. [IfValue (tupopen λ(temp, target)→temp <. target &. Not st)
```

```
    λ_→writeD d4 (lit True)
     ,IfValue (tupopen λ(temp, target)→temp >. target &. st)
    λ_→writeD d4 (lit False)]
 >>=. heater)
 In {main = monitor (lit 0) .||. heater (lit True)}
```

Solution 6. Simple thermostat

```
iTask42 :: MTDevice → Task ()
iTask42 dev = liftmTask clear dev
 >-| sequence [liftmTask (toggle {x=x,y=y,status=True}) dev\\(x,y)←fourtytwo] @! ()
      //Four
fourtytwo = [(0, 5), (0, 4), (0, 3), (0, 2) ,(1, 2), (2, 2), (2, 3) ,(2, 1), (2, 0)
      //Two
      ,(4, 5), (5, 5), (6, 4), (6, 3), (5, 2), (4, 1), (4, 0), (5, 0), (6, 0)]
```

Solution 7. LED Matrix 42 using iTask

```
mTask42 :: Main (MTask v ()) | mtask, LEDMatrix v
mTask42 = ledmatrix D5 D7 λlm→{main = LMClear lm >>|.
 foldr (>>|.) (LMDisplay lm) [dot lm {x=x, y=y, status=True} \\ (x,y) ← fourtytwo]}
```

Solution 8. LED Matrix 42 using mTask

```
temp :: (Shared s1 (Int, Int)) (Shared s2 Int) (Shared s3 Int) (Shared s4 Int)
 → Main (MTask v ()) | ...
temp limitsShare delayShare tempShare alarmShare =
 DHT D4 DHT22 λdht→
 ledmatrix D5 D7 λlm→
   liftsds λsLimits = limitsShare
 In liftsds λsDelay = delayShare
 In liftsds λsTemp   = tempShare
 In liftsds λsAlarm  = alarmShare
 In fun λprint = (λ(targety, currentx, currenty)→
   If (currenty ==. lit 8)
     (LMDisplay lm)
     (LMDot lm currentx currenty (targety ==. currenty)
       >>|. print (targety, currentx, currenty +. lit 1)))
 In fun λmin = (λ(x, y)→If (x <. y) x y)
 In fun λcalcy = (λ(up, down, val)→
   min (down, (val -. down) /. ((up -. down) /. lit 7)))
 In fun λplot = (λx→
       getSds sLimits
   >>~. tupopen λ(gmin, gmax)→temperature dht
   >>~. λy→print (min (lit 7, calcy (gmin, gmax, y)), x, lit 0)
   >>|. setSds sTemp y
   >>|. getSds sDelay
   >>~. delay
   >>|. plot (If (x ==. lit 7) (lit 0) (x +. lit 1))
 )
```

```
In {main = plot (lit 0)
    .||. rpeat (readD BUILTIN_LED >>*. [IfValue Not (writeD ABUTTON o Not)])
    .||. rpeat (getSds sAlarm .&&. getSds sTemp
    >>*. [IfValue (tupopen λ(a, t)→t >. a) λ_→writeD ABUTTON (lit False)]
)}
```

Solution 9. Temperature plotter

References

1. Achten, P.: Clean for Haskell98 Programmers (2007)
2. Adams, D.: The Hitchhiker's Guide to the Galaxy Omnibus: A Trilogy in Four Parts, vol. 6. Pan Macmillan (2017)
3. Alimarine, A.: Generic Functional Programming. Ph.D., Radboud University, Nijmegen (2005)
4. Amazonas Cabral De Andrade, M.: Developing real life, task oriented applications for the internet of things. Master's thesis, Radboud University, Nijmegen (2018)
5. Amsden, E.: A survey of functional reactive programming. Technical report (2011)
6. Baccelli, E., et al.: Reprogramming low-end IoT devices from the cloud. In: 2018 3rd Cloudification of the Internet of Things (CIoT), pp. 1–6. IEEE (2018)
7. Baccelli, E., Doerr, J., Kikuchi, S., Padilla, F., Schleiser, K., Thomas, I.: Scripting over-the-air: towards containers on low-end devices in the internet of things. In: IEEE PerCom 2018 (2018)
8. Bolderheij, F., Jansen, J.M., Kool, A.A., Stutterheim, J.: A mission-driven C2 framework for enabling heterogeneous collaboration. In: Monsuur, H., Jansen, J.M., Marchal, F.J. (eds.) NL ARMS Netherlands Annual Review of Military Studies 2018. NA, pp. 107–130. T.M.C. Asser Press, The Hague (2018). https://doi.org/10.1007/978-94-6265-246-0_6
9. Brus, T.H., van Eekelen, M.C.J.D., van Leer, M.O., Plasmeijer, M.J.: Clean — a language for functional graph rewriting. In: Kahn, G. (ed.) FPCA 1987. LNCS, vol. 274, pp. 364–384. Springer, Heidelberg (1987). https://doi.org/10.1007/3-540-18317-5_20
10. Carette, J., Kiselyov, O., Shan, C.C.: Finally tagless, partially evaluated: tagless staged interpreters for simpler typed languages. J. Funct. Program. **19**(05), 509 (2009). https://doi.org/10.1017/S0956796809007205
11. Cheney, J., Hinze, R.: First-class phantom types. Technical report, Cornell University (2003)
12. Da Xu, L., He, W., Li, S.: Internet of things in industries: a survey. IEEE Trans. Ind. Inform. **10**(4), 2233–2243 (2014)
13. Domoszlai, L., Lijnse, B., Plasmeijer, R.: Parametric lenses: change notification for bidirectional lenses. In: Proceedings of the 26nd 2014 International Symposium on Implementation and Application of Functional Languages, p. 9. ACM (2014)
14. Dubé, D.: BIT: a very compact Scheme system for embedded applications. In: Proceedings of the Fourth Workshop on Scheme and Functional Programming (2000)
15. Elliott, C., Hudak, P.: Functional reactive animation. In: ACM SIGPLAN Notices, vol. 32, pp. 263–273. ACM (1997)
16. Feeley, M., Dubé, D.: PICBIT: a scheme system for the PIC microcontroller. In: Proceedings of the Fourth Workshop on Scheme and Functional Programming, pp. 7–15. Citeseer (2003)

17. Feijs, L.: Multi-tasking and Arduino: why and how? In: Chen, L.L., et al. (eds.) Design and Semantics of form and Movement. 8th International Conference on Design and Semantics of Form and Movement (DeSForM 2013), Wuxi, China, pp. 119–127 (2013)
18. Grebe, M., Gill, A.: Haskino: a remote monad for programming the arduino. In: Gavanelli, M., Reppy, J. (eds.) PADL 2016. LNCS, vol. 9585, pp. 153–168. Springer, Cham (2016). https://doi.org/10.1007/978-3-319-28228-2_10
19. Grebe, M., Gill, A.: Threading the Arduino with Haskell. In: Van Horn, D., Hughes, J. (eds.) TFP 2016. LNCS, vol. 10447, pp. 135–154. Springer, Cham (2019). https://doi.org/10.1007/978-3-030-14805-8_8
20. Haenisch, T.: A case study on using functional programming for internet of things applications. Athens J. Technol. Eng. **3**(1), 29–38 (2016)
21. Helbling, C., Guyer, S.Z.: Juniper: a functional reactive programming language for the Arduino. In: Proceedings of the 4th International Workshop on Functional Art, Music, Modelling, and Design, pp. 8–16. ACM (2016)
22. Hess, J.: Arduino-copilot: arduino programming in haskell using the Copilot stream DSL (2020). http://hackage.haskell.org/package/arduino-copilot
23. Hickey, P.C., Pike, L., Elliott, T., Bielman, J., Launchbury, J.: Building embedded systems with embedded DSLs. In: ACM SIGPLAN Notices, vol. 49, pp. 3–9. ACM Press (2014). https://doi.org/10.1145/2628136.2628146
24. Jansen, J.M., Lijnse, B., Plasmeijer, R.: Towards dynamic workflows for crisis management (2010)
25. Johnson-Davies, D.: Lisp for microcontrollers (2020). https://ulisp.com
26. Koopman, P., Lubbers, M., Plasmeijer, R.: A task-based DSL for microcomputers. In: Proceedings of the Real World Domain Specific Languages Workshop 2018 on - RWDSL 2018, Vienna, Austria, pp. 1–11. ACM Press (2018). https://doi.org/10.1145/3183895.3183902
27. Lijnse, B., Jansen, J.M., Nanne, R., Plasmeijer, R.: Capturing the netherlands coast guard's sar workflow with itasks (2011)
28. Lijnse, B., Jansen, J.M., Plasmeijer, R., others: Incidone: a task-oriented incident coordination tool. In: Proceedings of the 9th International Conference on Information Systems for Crisis Response and Management, ISCRAM, vol. 12 (2012)
29. Lijnse, B., Plasmeijer, R.: iTasks 2: iTasks for end-users. In: Morazán, M.T., Scholz, S.-B. (eds.) IFL 2009. LNCS, vol. 6041, pp. 36–54. Springer, Heidelberg (2010). https://doi.org/10.1007/978-3-642-16478-1_3
30. Lubbers, M., Koopman, P., Plasmeijer, R.: Multitasking on microcontrollers using task oriented programming. In: 2019 42nd International Convention on Information and Communication Technology, Electronics and Microelectronics (MIPRO), Opatija, Croatia, pp. 1587–1592 (2019). https://doi.org/10.23919/MIPRO.2019.8756711
31. Lubbers, M.: Task oriented programming and the internet of things. Master's thesis, Radboud University, Nijmegen (2017)
32. Lubbers, M., Koopman, P., Plasmeijer, R.: Task oriented programming and the internet of things. In: Proceedings of the 30th Symposium on the Implementation and Application of Functional Programming Languages, Lowell, MA, p. 12. ACM (2018). https://doi.org/10.1145/3310232.3310239
33. Lubbers, M., Koopman, P., Plasmeijer, R.: Interpreting task oriented programs on tiny computers. In: Proceedings of the 31st Symposium on Implementation and Application of Functional Languages, IFL 2019, Singapore, Singapore. Association for Computing Machinery, New York (2019). https://doi.org/10.1145/3412932.3412936

34. Michels, S., Plasmeijer, R.: Uniform data sources in a functional language, p. 16. Unpublished manuscript (2012)

35. Piers, J.: Task-oriented programming for developing non-distributed interruptible embedded systems. Master's thesis, Radboud University, Nijmegen (2016)

36. Plasmeijer, R., Achten, P.: A conference management system based on the iData Toolkit. In: Horváth, Z., Zsók, V., Butterfield, A. (eds.) IFL 2006. LNCS, vol. 4449, pp. 108–125. Springer, Heidelberg (2007). https://doi.org/10.1007/978-3-540-74130-5_7

37. Plasmeijer, R., Achten, P., Koopman, P.: iTasks: executable specifications of interactive work flow systems for the web. ACM SIGPLAN Not. **42**(9), 141–152 (2007)

38. Koopman, P., Plasmeijer, R.: A shallow embedded type safe extendable DSL for the Arduino. In: Serrano, M., Hage, J. (eds.) TFP 2015. LNCS, vol. 9547, pp. 104–123. Springer, Cham (2016). https://doi.org/10.1007/978-3-319-39110-6_6

39. Plasmeijer, R., Lijnse, B., Michels, S., Achten, P., Koopman, P.: Task-oriented programming in a pure functional language. In: Proceedings of the 14th Symposium on Principles and Practice of Declarative Programming, pp. 195–206. ACM (2012)

40. Sant'Anna, F., Rodriguez, N., Ierusalimschy, R., Landsiedel, O., Tsigas, P.: Safe system-level concurrency on resource-constrained nodes. In: Proceedings of the 11th ACM Conference on Embedded Networked Sensor Systems, p. 11. ACM (2013)

41. Sawada, K., Watanabe, T.: Emfrp: a functional reactive programming language for small-scale embedded systems. In: Companion Proceedings of the 15th International Conference on Modularity, pp. 36–44. ACM (2016)

42. Serrano, A.: Type error customization for embedded domain-specific languages. Ph.D. thesis, Utrecht University (2018)

43. St-Amour, V., Feeley, M.: PICOBIT: a compact scheme system for microcontrollers. In: Morazán, M.T., Scholz, S.-B. (eds.) IFL 2009. LNCS, vol. 6041, pp. 1–17. Springer, Heidelberg (2010). https://doi.org/10.1007/978-3-642-16478-1_1

44. Steiner, H.C.: Firmata: towards making microcontrollers act like extensions of the computer. In: NIME, pp. 125–130 (2009)

45. Stutterheim, J., Achten, P., Plasmeijer, R.: Maintaining separation of concerns through task oriented software development. In: Wang, M., Owens, S. (eds.) TFP 2017. LNCS, vol. 10788, pp. 19–38. Springer, Cham (2018). https://doi.org/10.1007/978-3-319-89719-6_2

46. Sugihara, R., Gupta, R.K.: Programming models for sensor networks: a survey. ACM Trans. Sensor Netw. **4**(2), 1–29 (2008). https://doi.org/10.1145/1340771.1340774

47. Troyer, de, C., Nicolay, J., Meuter, de, W.: Building IoT systems using distributed first-class reactive programming. In: 2018 IEEE International Conference on Cloud Computing Technology and Science (CloudCom), pp. 185–192 (2018). https://doi.org/10.1109/CloudCom2018.2018.00045

48. van der Heijden, M., Lijnse, B., Lucas, P.J.F., Heijdra, Y.F., Schermer, T.R.J.: Managing COPD exacerbations with telemedicine. In: Peleg, M., Lavrač, N., Combi, C. (eds.) AIME 2011. LNCS (LNAI), vol. 6747, pp. 169–178. Springer, Heidelberg (2011). https://doi.org/10.1007/978-3-642-22218-4_21

49. Wand, M.: Continuation-based multiprocessing. In: Proceedings of the 1980 ACM Conference on LISP and Functional Programming - LFP 1980, Stanford University, California, United States, pp. 19–28. ACM Press (1980). https://doi.org/10.1145/800087.802786

Paint Your Programs Green: On the Energy Efficiency of Data Structures

Rui Pereira[1,2,3,4], Marco Couto[3,4], Jácome Cunha[3,5], Gilberto Melfe[2], João Saraiva[3,4], and João Paulo Fernandes[5,6(✉)]

[1] C4 — Centro de Competências em Cloud Computing (C4-UBI), Covilhã, Portugal
[2] Universidade da Beira Interior, Covilhã, Portugal
[3] HASLab/INESC Tec, Porto, Portugal
marco.l.couto@inesctec.pt
[4] Universidade do Minho, Braga, Portugal
{ruipereira,saraiva}@di.uminho.pt
[5] Universidade do Porto, Porto, Portugal
{jacome,jpaulo}@fe.up.pt
[6] Laboratório de Inteligência Artificial e Ciência de Computadores (LIACC), Porto, Portugal

Abstract. This tutorial aims to provide knowledge on a different facet of efficiency in data structures: energy efficiency. As many recent studies have shown, the main roadblock in regards to energy efficient software development are the misconceptions and heavy lack of support and knowledge, for energy-aware development, that programmers have. Thus, this tutorial aims at helping provide programmers more knowledge pertaining to the energy efficiency of data structures.

We conducted two in-depth studies to analyze the performance and energy efficiency of various data structures from popular programming languages: Haskell and Java. The results show that within the Haskell programming language, the correlation between performance and energy consumption is statistically almost identical, while there are cases with more variation within the Java language. We have presented which data structures are more efficient for common operations, such as *inserting* and *removing* elements or *iterating* over the data structure.

The results from our studies can help support developers in better understanding such differences within data structures, allowing them to carefully choose the most adequate implementation based on their requirements and goals. We believe that such results will help further close the gap when discussing the lack of knowledge in energy efficient software development.

Keywords: Green Software · Data Structures · Energy Efficient Programming

© The Author(s), under exclusive license to Springer Nature Switzerland AG 2023
Z. Porkoláb and V. Zsók (Eds.): CEFP 2019, LNCS 11950, pp. 53–76, 2023.
https://doi.org/10.1007/978-3-031-42833-3_2

1   Introduction

In his 1976 book [1], Niklaus Wirth coined one the most famous Computer Science equations that today still persists:

$$Algorithms + Data\ Structures = Programs$$

The elegance and sharpness of the equation provides decisive support for the argument that mastering programming can not be achieved without the combined knowledge of both algorithms and data structures. A recurring example is taught early to computer science students: if you know you have a sorted list, you can use that knowledge to more efficiently search for an element in that list. Indeed, you may use binary search instead of performing search sequentially.

While both terms in Wirth's addition are equally relevant, in this tutorial we focus on the *Data Structures* portion. In a message shared through Git's mailing list [2], Linus Torvalds further argues that:

".. the difference between a bad programmer and a good one is whether he considers his code or his data structures more important. Bad programmers worry about the code. Good programmers worry about data structures and their relationships".

Our goal is to provide a detailed comparison of a large set of data structure implementations. We expect the information we provide to be useful both to computer science students who pedagogically seek to extend their knowledge on data structures as well as professional programmers who seek to use the most efficient structures in their products.

Our (methodological) approach is to take as case studies two well-know, publicly available and widely used data structure libraries, in two different programming languages, Haskell and Java. This approach is well aligned with the fact that most, if not all, modern programming languages come with such supporting libraries that programmers are free to explore and use. In fact, providing such libraries is often seen as decisive for the language to succeed [3]. As Kernighan and Pike mention:

"Every program depends on algorithms and data structures, but few programs depend on the invention of brand new ones" [4].

With our work, we aim to provide even more knowledge about data structures, and namely on their efficiency. In fact, we analyze the efficiency of a data structure under two lenses: based on i) its runtime performance, and on ii) its energy efficiency. While the former has historically received the most attention, the fact is that the energy consumption is becoming a significant concern for programmers [5–8], where studies argue that this is due to *the lack of knowledge* and *the lack of tools*. Actually, the energy efficiency of data structures has recently concerned a significant number of researchers [9–16].

A general question whose answer we seek to provide with our research is:

RQ How do different data structure implementations compare, both in terms of runtime and energy efficiency?

To answer this research question we conducted two in-depth studies to analyze the performance and energy efficiency of various data structures from popular programming languages: Haskell and Java.

For Haskell, we considered the well-known Edison library of purely functional data structures, and for Java, we used the Java Collections Framework (JCF) standard data structure library. Both libraries provide many different implementations for the same group of data structures, such as Sets, Lists, and Associative Collections/Maps. For each of these groups, we study the energy consumption of their different implementations for common data strctures operations, such as *inserting, iterating, removing*, etc., elements. Our results show that within the Haskell programming language, the correlation between execution time and energy consumption is statistically almost identical, indicating that program's runtime and energy consumption are related. For the Java language, however, there are cases where more efficient (*i.e.* faster) implementations of data structures also consume more energy, and *vice-versa*.

The remaining sections in this tutorial are organized as follows: Sect. 2 presents a brief overview of the three different types of data structures we have studied, and describes the different implementations that exist in the Haskell and Java programming languages; Sect. 3 describes our experimental setup for both programming languages, detailing what operations we considered and how we measured their energy consumption; Sect. 4 presents the results of our experiment, with a discussion of the observations we have found; Sect. 5 looks at an overview of related research work; Finally, Sect. 6 concludes our tutorial and presents our final thoughts.

2 Data Structures Libraries

Data structures are one of the most important building blocks for computation [17]. While we use algorithms to define a solution to solve a problem, we use data structures to store and organize our data in very specific ways so that it can be searched and managed very efficiently [18,19].

While there are countless amounts of different data structures within all the various existing programming languages, they mostly follow one of the well defined high-level structure abstractions which exist. In this tutorial, and throughout our experiments, we will focus on three types: *Ordered Sequences, Non-repeating unique sets*, and *Key-Value Pairs*. In Haskell, abstractions of these types can be found in *Sequences, Collections*, and *Associative Collections*, and in Java in the *Lists, Sets*, and *Maps* abstractions.

Ordered Sequences represent a countable number of ordered values or objects, where that same value or object can be repeated more than once. *Non-repeating unique sets* store unique values or objects, without any particular order.

Finally, *Key-Value Pairs* stores data in a pair that is known as (key, value), where for each stored unique key there is a value or object associated to it. Each entry contains exactly one unique key and its corresponding value.

In the following sections, we will go into some more detail as to what data structures we analyzed for respectively, and give a simple description of each data structure as to further understand their differences.

2.1   Haskell Data Structures

Our analysis on the Haskell data structures relies on Edison, a mature and well documented library of purely functional data structures [20,21]. Edison provides different functional data structures for implementing three types of abstractions: Sequences, Collections, and Associative Collections.

While these implementations are available in other programming languages, e.g., in ML [21], here we focus on their Haskell version. While this version already incorporates an extensive unit test suite to guarantee functional correctness, it can admittedly benefit from the type of performance analysis we consider here [22].

Presented in Table 1, are the implementations that are available for each of the abstractions considered by Edison. These implementations can also be consulted in the *EdisonCore* [23] and *EdisonAPI* [24] packages. Some of the listed implementations are actually *adaptors*. This is the case, e.g., of `SizedSeq` that adds a size parameter to any implementation of Sequences. Besides `SizedSeq`, also `RevSeq`, for Sequences, and `MinHeap` for Collections are adaptors for other implementations. Finally, we split the Collections abstraction between Sets and Heaps, as to avoid confusion between Haskell Collections and Java Collections.

Table 1. Abstractions and Implementations available in Edison.

Sets & Heaps	Associative Collections	Sequences
		BankersQueue
		SimpleQueue
EnumSet		BinaryRandList
StandardSet		JoinList
UnbalancedSet	AssocList	RandList
LazyPairingHeap	PatriciaLoMap	BraunSeq
LeftistHeap	StandardMap	FingerSeq
MinHeap	TernaryTrie	ListSeq
SkewHeap		RevSeq
SplayHeap		SizedSeq
		MyersStack

Sets and Heaps. The first set implementation, *EnumSet*, is based on bit-wise operations. But in order to use this implementation, there must not contain more distinct elements than the number of bits in the Word type. The *StandardSet* is based on size balanced binary trees, and is an overlay over a set instance provided by the Data.Set module. Finally, the *UnbalancedSet* is based on unbalanced binary search trees.

The *LazyPairingHeap* is a heap implementation with a heap-ordered tree, the shape of which is governed by the odd or even number of children. Another heap-ordered (binary) tree is the *LeftistHeap*, which is maintained conformant with a "leftist property". *MinHeap* is an adaptor for other heap implementations, which keeps the minimum element separately. Somewhat similar to the *LeftishHeap* is the *SkewHeap*, which is a self-adjusting implementation. Finally, *SplayHeap* is based on a Splay Tree (akin to a balanced binary search tree, but not maintaining explicit balance information).

Associative Collections. An *AssocList* is a simple list of associations (key-value pairs). The *PatriciaLoMap* is an associative collection based on little-endian Patricia Trees. Finally, the *StandardMap* is an associative collection based on size balanced trees, while *TernaryTrie* models finite maps as ternary search trees.

Sequences. The *ListSeq* is the standard list implementation available in Haskell's Prelude ([a]). Based on two (front/rear of the sequence) of these standard lists is the *BankersQueue* implementation, which abides by the invariant that: the front shall be at least as long as the rear. Also the sizes of the lists are tracked explicitly. The *BinaryRandList* implementation uses a linear data structure, maybe empty, or with two distinct substructures modeling a list that has an even, or odd, number of elements.

By using a balanced binary tree as an underlying implementation, the *BraunSeq* maintains the invariant that the left subtree's size is equal or at most one element larger than the right subtree's size. The *FingerSeq* implementation is based of a FingerTree, a general-purpose data structure. The *JoinList* is based on a leaf-tree data-structure, while the *MyersStack* uses a binary tree and permits accesses to the nth element.

The *RandList* relies on a data structure that is a list of complete binary trees (maintained in non-decreasing order of the trees sizes). It provides efficient access to random elements contained in it, and primitive list operations that run as fast as the ones defined for the Haskell's standard list data structure. Somewhat similar to the *BankersQueue* is the *SimpleQueue*, which is also based on two standard Haskell lists (front/rear of the sequence). The rear list is maintained in reverse order, so that its first element is the last element of the sequence, and abides by the invariant that: the front shall be empty only if the rear is also empty.

Finally, a *SizedSeq* is an adaptor for other sequence implementations, which keeps track of the sequence's size explicitly, and a *RevSeq* is to keep the sequence in the opposite order (useful if we have a sequence implementation that offers fast/slow access to the front/rear respectively, and we need the opposite behavior).

2.2   Java Data Structures

The Java programing language includes a standard data structure library known as the Java Collections Framework (JCF)[1]. In JCF the different data structures are organized in three groups which implement the interfaces List[2], Set[3], or Map[4], respectively. These are very similar to the three types of Haskell data structure implementations we chose previously. We evaluated the following implementations shown in Table 2.

Table 2. Java data structures available in the JCF library.

Lists	Sets	Maps
		ConcurrentHashMap
ArrayList		ConcurrentSkipListMap
AttributeList		HashMap
CopyOnWriteArrayList	ConcurrentSkipListSet	HashTable
LinkedList	CopyOnWriteArraySet	LinkedHashMap
RoleList	HashSet	Properties
RoleUnresolvedList	LinkedHashSet	SimpleBindings
Stack	TreeSet	TreeMap
Vector		UIDefaults
		WeakHashMap

From the considered data structures, we should point out that, as with the Haskell data structures, Java data structures are also very different from each other, even within the same group. Each particular implementation has distinct properties, and will be further described.

Lists. According to the documentation, for the List abstraction, the *ArrayList* collection is the underlying structure of 4 collections: *CopyOnWriteArrayList*, *AttributeList*, *RoleList*, and *RoleUnresolvedList*. The first, *CopyOnWriteArrayList*, is a fully thread-safe List implementation, while highly costly since every mutable operation results in a fresh copy of the underlying array. As for the other 3, they all represent a collection intended to store a specific type of objects; for

---

[1] Java Collections Framework: https://docs.oracle.com/javase/7/docs/technotes/guides/collections/index.html.

[2] JCF List Interface: https://docs.oracle.com/javase/7/docs/api/java/util/List.html.

[3] JCF Set Interface: https://docs.oracle.com/javase/7/docs/api/java/util/Set.html.

[4] JCF Map Interface: https://docs.oracle.com/javase/7/docs/api/java/util/Map.html.

compatibility reasons, it also supports the storage of other objects, although it makes the collections lose their initial purpose.

The *Vector* collection is roughly equivalent to *ArrayList*, except that it is synchronized. However, a *Vector* has a different reallocation strategy: by default, when the number of inserted elements is the same as the actual capacity, it doubles the underlying array's capacity, whereas the *ArrayList* increases the capacity by 50%. The *Stack* collection extends *Vector*, and in addition to inheriting all its properties, it extends it with the standard stack operations: push, pop, peek, isEmpty, and search.

Finally, the *LinkedList* collection appears as the only List implementation that does not use an internal array to store data, but a sequence of doubly-linked items, each with 3 components: the stored element, and the pointers to the previous and next elements. This makes the standard element insertion operation (which is at the end of the list) rather inefficient, since it involves adding the element, and update 3 pointers. On the other hand, in a scenario where elements are forced to be inserted at the head of the list, it only needs to add the element and update the pointer to the next element, making this collection more efficient than any other List for this specific scenario, as the others would need to shift all elements one position, add the new element, and finally update the indices.

Sets. As with all set implementations, the following implementations contain unique elements only. The *ConcurrentSkipListSet* is a naturally ordered list of non-repeated values, useful for concurrently executing insertion, removal, and access operations by multiple threads. The *CopyOnWriteArraySet* internally uses the *CopyOnWriteArrayList*, thus it is a set where every mutable operation results in a fresh copy of the underlying array.

The *HashSet* is a set implementation which makes use of a hash table (actually a *HashMap* instance) to store elements. The insertion does not generally maintain the same iteration order, and this implementation offers constant time performance for basic operations if the hash function equally disperses the elements. While *HashSet* internally uses a *HashMap*, the *LinkedHashSet* uses a *LinkedHashMap* (which takes advantage of *LinkedList*). The *LinkedHash-Set* maintains the order of elements inserted, contrary to the normal *HashSet*. Finally, *TreeSet* internally uses a *TreeMap*, allows self-defined ordering of elements (or natural ascending order if none is defined) and is known to scale very well as with all *tree* structures, allowing for good performances (guaranteed $O(n \log n)$) of insertion, removal, and retrieval operations.

Maps. The *HashMap* and *HashTable* are roughly the same, as they use the same underlying structure (a hash table with pre-defined buckets upon initialization), and therefore operational methodology. The only difference lies in the fact that the former is unsynchronized and allows null values as both key and value.

LinkedHashMap and *TreeMap* are the remaining Map implementations which offer standard mapping structures and operations. The difference between them and the previous referred implementations is the internal structure used. *Linked-HashMap* is essentially a hash table which handles collisions using the chaining mechanism (i.e., using linked lists instead of buckets). On the other hand, *TreeMap* uses a Red-Black tree to store its elements, making update/list operations more costly but any search/access operation much more efficient. Both of these implementations guarantee a predictable order of its elements.

From the remaining considered Map implementations, the *ConcurrentHashMap* and *ConcurrentSkipListMap* both offer a concurrent-supported version of a hash table. The former uses a *HashMap* as internal structure, while the latter supports mechanisms to maintain the order of its elements. The remaining 5 collections are all special implementations of either *HashMap* or *HashTable*. For instance, the *WeakHashMap* is an *HashMap* which can have its elements discarded by the garbage collector when they are no longer in ordinary use, and *SimpleBindings* only supports String values as keys. As for the last two *HashTable* based implementations, the *Properties* collection is a hash table with built-in support for persistence, while *UIDefaults* typically represents a table of defaults for Java Swing components, but can be instantiated with other objects.

3   Experimental Setup

One of our goals is to compare the energy consumption of different data structure implementations within the same abstract data structures categories (lists, maps, etc.). For this, we designed two independent studies which simulate the different ways to use such structures and their operations within two popular programming languages: *Haskell* and *Java*.

In this section we present the design of our study. Due the nature of *Haskell* and *Java* being very different languages, the designs slightly varied for each language to reflect the possibilities and limitations present. Thus, whenever deviations occur in the design, we detail each language separately.

3.1   Haskell Operations

Our benchmark implementation is inspired by a publicly available micro-benchmark [25] which evaluates the runtime performance of different implementations of Java's JCF API, and has been used in previous studies to obtain energy measurements [9,13,15]. Here we considered the benchmark operations and their corresponding Edison functions presented in Table 3.

Most operations in the underlying benchmark have straightforward correspondences in the implementation functions provided by Edison. This is the case, for example, of the operation add, which can naturally be interpreted by functions insert, for Heaps, Sets and Associative Collections. For Sequences, the underlying ordering notion allows two possible interpretations for adding an element to a sequence: in its beginning or in its end. In this case, we defined add as follows, to alternately use both interpretations:

With the previous definition, add s n m inserts the n aditional {n+m-1, n+m-2, n+m-3, ..., m} to s.

Table 3. Edison functions used to implement the benchmark operations.

Operation	Sequences	Sets	Heaps	Associative Collections
add	lcons, rcons	insert	insert	insert
addAll	append	union	union	union
clear	null, ltail	difference	minView, delete	difference
contains	null, filter	member	member	member
containsAll	foldr, map	subset	null, member, minView	submap
iterator	map	foldr	fold	map
remove	null, ltail	deleteMin	deleteMin	null, deleteMin
removeAll	filter	difference	minView, delete	difference
retainAll	filter	intersection	filter, member	intersectionWith
toArray	toList	foldr	fold	foldrWithKey

```
add ::  Seq Int -> Int -> Int -> Seq Int
add seq 0 _ = seq
add seq n m = add (x 'cons' seq) (n-1) m
 where
  x =  m + n - 1
  cons = if even n then rcons else lcons
```

The operations we consider are listed in Table 4, and they all can be abstracted by the format:

$$iterations * operation(base, aditional)$$

This format reads as: iterate *operation* a given number of times (*iterations*) over a data structure with a *base* number of elements. If *operation* requires an additional data structure, the number of elements in it is given by *aditional*. All the operations are suggested to be executed over a base structure with $100K$ elements. For instance, for the addAll operation, the second entry in the table suggests adding 1000 times all the elements of a container with 1000 elements to the base structure (of size $100K$).

In a few cases, however, we needed to simplify concrete operations for specific abstractions. This simplification was performed whenever a concrete operation failed to terminate within a 3 h bound for a given implementation. In such cases, we repeatedly halved the size of the base data structure, starting at 100000, 50000 and so on. When the data structure size of 3125 was reached without the bound being met, we started halving the number of iterations. With this principle in mind, no change was necessary for Heaps and Sets. For Associative Collections and Sequences, however, this was not the case. Table 5 lists the operations whose inputs or numbers of iterations were adjusted. The elements in boldface of this table are the ones that differ from the original benchmark.

For different reasons, we excluded some implementations from our experimental setting. This was the case of RevSeq and SizedSeq, for Sequences, and MinHeap for Heaps, since they are adaptors of other implementations for the corresponding abstractions. EnumSet, for Sets, was not considered because it can

Table 4. Benchmark Operations.

iterations	operation	base	aditional
1	add	100K	100K
1000	addAll	100K	1000
1	clear	100K	n.a.
1000	contains	100K	1
5000	containsAll	100K	1000
1	iterator	100K	n.a.
10000	remove	100K	1
10	removeAll	100K	1000
10	retainAll	100K	1000
5000	toArray	100K	n.a.

Table 5. Modified Haskell Benchmark Operations.

abstraction	iterations	operation	base	aditional
Associative Collections	1	clear	**50000**	n.a.
	2500	remove	**3125**	1
	10	retainAll	**25000**	1000
	2500	toArray	**3125**	n.a.
Sequences	1	add	**3125**	**50000**
	625	containsAll	**3125**	1000

only hold a limited number of elements, which makes it not compatible with the considered benchmark. As said before, PatriciaLoMap and TernaryTrie are not totally compatible with the Associative Collections API, so they could not be used in our uniform benchmark. Finally, MyersStack, for Sequences was discarded since its underlying data structure has redundant information in such a way that fully evaluating its instances has exponential behavior. Thus, the remainder of the structures shown in Table 1 were considered.

3.2 Java Operations

For our Java operations, we replicated the same 10 operations shown in Table 3 by either directly using the generic JCF API list for each corresponding interface, or using several methods of the API. Shown in Table 6 are the JCF methods used to implement the benchmark operations. Each of these mirror directly the operations performed in the previous section, for example alternatively adding a new element to a list in the beginning and the end.

Table 6. JCF methods used to implement the benchmark operations.

Operation	Lists	Sets	Maps
add	add, add(Index)	add	put
addAll	addAll	addAll	putAll
clear	clear, ltail	clear	clear
contains	contains, filter	contains	containsKey
containsAll	containsAll, map	containsAll	keySet, containsAll
iterator	iterator, hasNext, next	iterator, hasNext, next	iterator, hasNext, next, getKey, getValue
remove	remove	remove	remove
removeAll	removeAll	removeAll	keySet, removeAll
retainAll	retainAll	retainAll	keySet, retainAll
toArray	toArray	toArray	entrySet, toArray

To evaluate the different implementations of each of the described methods, we followed the same approach considered in the previous section, and populated the data structures in each implementation with the same *base* size as presented in Table 4, while also following the same number of iterations (*iterations*) per benchmark operation. Additionally, when a second data structure is required, that is, for operations addAll, containsAll, removeAll and retainAll, we have adopted yet again the same *aditional* size shown in Table 4, but containing half existing values from the original structure and half new values, all shuffled with a seed. We use both existing and new values to balance the effort that is being imposed on the operations. Finally, the modifications which were applied in Table 5 were also applied in our study on Java data structures as to maintain consistency. These modifications are shown in Table 7.

Several data structures were not evaluated as they are quite particular and non-comparable in their usage. In particular, JobStateReasons (Set) only accepts JobStateReason objects, IdentityHashMap (Map) accepts strings but compares

Table 7. Modified Java Benchmark Operations.

abstraction	iterations	operation	base	aditional
Maps	1	clear	**50000**	n.a.
	2500	remove	**3125**	1
	10	retainAll	**25000**	1000
	2500	toArray	**3125**	n.a.
Lists	1	add	**3125**	**50000**
	625	containsAll	**3125**	1000

its elements with the identity function, and not with the equals method. The remainder of the data structures, shown in Table 2 all follow the same expected outputs and allow the insertion of more generic objects and thus were considered.

3.3 Measuring Energy Consumption

To precisely measure the energy consumption of the data structures within our tests, we used Intel's Running Average Power Limit [26] (RAPL). RAPL is an interface provided by modern Intel processors to allow setting custom power limits to the processor packages. Using this interface one can access energy and power readings via a model-specific register (MSR). RAPL uses a software power model to estimate the energy consumption based on various hardware performance counters, temperature, leakage models and I/O models [27].

The precision and reliability of RAPL have been extensively studied [28–30], showing that, although there is in general an offset between RAPL estimations and the corresponding physically measured values, the general behavior over time is consistent between the two observations. And, for server machines, which are the ones we target, this offset is actually insignificant.

RAPL interfaces operate at the granularity of a processor socket (package). There are MSRs to access 4 domains:

– PKG: total energy consumed by an entire socket
– PP0: energy consumed by all cores and caches
– PP1: energy consumed by the on-chip GPU
– DRAM: energy consumed by all DIMMs

The client platforms have access to {PKG, PP0, PP1} while the server platforms have access to {PKG, PP0, DRAM}.

Criterion. For our Haskell data structure study, we have extended Criterion to be able to measure the amount of energy consumed during the execution of a benchmark. Criterion [31] is a micro-benchmarking library that is used to measure the performance of Haskell code. It provides a framework for both the execution of the benchmarks and the analysis of their results, and is robust enough to filter out noise coming, e.g., from the clock resolution, the operating system's scheduling or garbage collection.

In our extended version of Criterion, energy consumption is measured in the same execution of the benchmarks which is used to measure runtime performance. This benchmark environment can be found at the corresponding Github page[5].

jRAPL. For our Java data structure study, we used **jRAPL** [32] which is a framework for profiling Java programs using RAPL. jRAPL allows us to obtain energy measurements on a method level, proving a fine grained measurements. The benchmark environment which was used to measure Java data structures with jRAPL can be found at the corresponding Github page[6].

Execution Environment. In our Haskell study, we ran the experiment on a machine with 2 × 10-core Intel Xeon E5-2660 v2 processors (Ivy Bridge microarchitecture, 2-node NUMA) and 256GB of DDR3 1600MHz memory. This machine runs the Ubuntu Server 14.04.3 LTS (kernel 3.19.0-25) OS. The compiler was GHC 7.10.2, using Edison 1.3, and a modified Criterion library. Also, all experiments were performed with no other load on the OS.

In our Java study, we ran the experiment on a: Linux 3.13.0-74-generic operating system, 8GB of RAM, and Intel(R) Core(TM) i3-3240 CPU @ 3.40 GHz. This system has no other software installed or running other than necessary to run this study, and the operating system daemons. Both the Java compiler and interpreter were versions 1.8.0_66.

Additionally, prior to executing a test, we ran an initial "warm-up" where we instantiated, populated (with the designated *base size*), and performed simple actions on the data structures. This "warm-up" was to avoid unstable measurements during the virtual-machine's Just-In-Time compilation and "warm-up" phase [33]. Each test was executed 25 times [34], and the median values for both the time and energetic consumption were extracted (of the specific test, and not the initial "warm-up" as to only measure the tested methods). This was not necessary for the Haskell study, as Criterion automatically executed initial 'warm-ups' and executed the study as many times as was necessary until it converged into a final value.

4   Comparing Data Structure Energy Consumption

This section presents the results we gathered from the two studies previously defined in Sect. 3. We highly recommend and assume the images containing the results are being viewed in color. The following subsections will present our findings, observations, and discussions for the Haskell and Java programming language, respectively.

---

[5] Haskell Data Structures Benchmark: http://green-haskell.github.io/.
[6] Java   Data   Structures   Benchmark: https://github.com/greensoftwarelab/ Collections-Energy-Benchmark/tree/master/PaintYourPrograms.

4.1   Haskell Data Structures

We split our observations between the 4 data structure types of Sets, Heaps, Associative Collections, and Sequences, respectively. Additionally, we only present the graphical results which are discussed in our observations, but all results for all operations on all abstractions are available at the companion website[7].

Additionally, we have confirmed that our analyses in the remainder of this section are statistically valid, by calculating correlation coefficients given by Spearman's non parametric measure. Indeed, we studied the correlation between execution time and energy consumption within each of the 4 abstractions that we considered. For this, we calculated 4 correlation coefficients, considering in each two data series: i) the execution time and ii) the energy consumption, for all the operations within the respective abstraction. We found that these variables are strongly correlated, which is indicated by the correlation coefficients and respective p-values given in Table 8.

Table 8. Correlation between time and energy consumption for the analyzed abstractions.

Abstraction	Spearman Correlation	p-value
Sets	1	2.2e−16
Heaps	0.9993902	<2.2e−16
Associative Collections	1	<5.976e−06
Sequences	0.9999531	<2.2e−16

Sets. We have observed that for each combination of implementation and benchmark operation, taking longer to execute also implies more energy consumption. The *UnbalancedSet* implementation is less efficient (both in terms of runtime and energy footprint) than *StandardSet* for all benchmark operations except contains.

The results on the comparison between both implementations for the clear operation of the benchmark are presented in Fig. 1. In Figs. 1(a) and (b) we compare the absolute values obtained for the runtime execution and energy consumption, respectively. In Fig. 1(c) we compare the proportions of time and energy consumption: the *StandardSet* implementation consumes 29.4% of the time and 27.9% of the energy spent by *UnbalancedSet*.

For Sets, for all operations of the benchmark, the differences between the proportions of either time or energy consumption are always lower than 1.49%.

Heaps. As we have observed for Sets, our experiments suggest that energy consumption is proportional to execution time. Concrete evidence of this is shown in Figs. 2(a) and 2(b), with the comparison between proportions of runtime and

---

[7] Companion website with the experiment's results: http://green-haskell.github.io/.

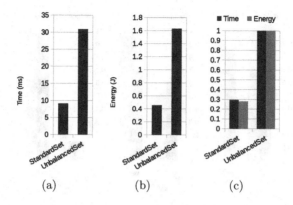

Fig. 1. Results of the clear operation for Haskell Sets

energy consumption for add and toArray, respectively, for each of the considered implementation.

Overall, the *LazyPairingHeap* implementation was observed to be the most efficient in all benchmark operations except for add. *SkewHeap* and *SplayHeap* implementations were the least efficient in 5 operations each. The proportions of runtime and energy consumption differ in at most 2.16% for any operation in any implementation of Heaps.

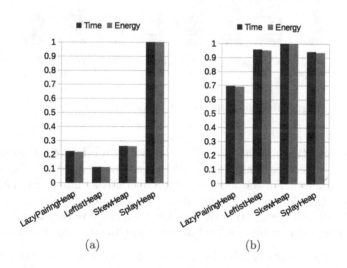

Fig. 2. Results of the add (a) and toArray (b) operations for Heaps

Associative Collections. Energy consumption was again proportional to execution time. The *AssocList* was observed to be less efficient for all but the add

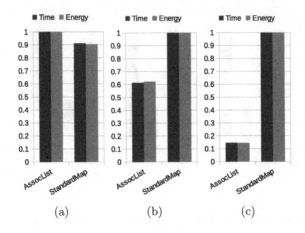

Fig. 3. Results of addAll (a), add (b), and iterator (c) for Associative Collections

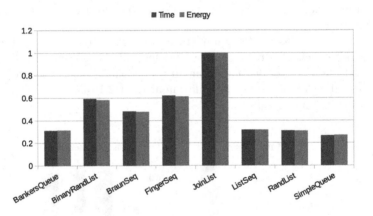

Fig. 4. Results of the remove operation for Sequences

and iterator operations. In the cases where *AssocList* was less efficient than *StandardMap*, the difference ranged from 9%, for addAll (depicted in Fig. 3(a)), to 99.999% for retainAll. For the add and iterator operations, illustrated in Figs. 3(b) and (c), *StandardMap* took approximately 40% and 85% more time and energy than *AssocList*. The proportion of consumed energy was (marginally, by 1%) higher than the proportion of execution time only for the add operation.

Sequences. The results obtained for Sequences also show that execution time strongly influences energy consumption. This is illustrated in Fig. 4 for the remove operation. The observed proportions across all operations and implementations differ at most in 1.9%, for the add operation.

4.2 Java Data Structures

Our observations in this section are split between the 3 data structure types of Sets, Maps, and Lists, respectively. Additionally, we only present the graphical results which are discussed in our observations, but all data results for all operations on all abstractions are available at the GitHub website[8].

As in the previous section, we have confirmed that our analyses in the remainder of this section are statistically valid, by calculating correlation coefficients given by Spearman's non parametric measure.

Indeed, we studied the correlation between execution time and energy consumption within each of the 3 abstractions that we considered. We calculated the 3 correlation coefficients, considering in each two data series: i) the execution time and ii) the energy consumption, for all the operations within the respective abstraction. We found that these variables are strongly correlated, which is indicated by the correlation coefficients and respective p-values given in Table 9, more so for the Maps and Lists, and slightly less so for the Sets.

This result is expected, as execution time is a variable in the energy equation. Although statistically its is shown that the more time the Java benchmarks took, the more it also consumed, the proportions differ much more than in the previous Haskell study. Additionally, there are several cases where a faster operation is not the more energy efficient one, and vice-versa. We will touch on some examples in the following paragraphs.

Table 9. Correlation between time and energy consumption for the analyzed Java abstractions.

Abstraction	Spearman Correlation	p-value
Sets	0.811208	4.1e$-$258
Maps	0.958147	<0.0
Lists	0.956052	<0.0

Sets. Of the three abstractions, the Set implementations were the ones with the lowest Spearman Correlation of 81%. Based on the observations here, the *TreeSet* implementation is clearly the one which tends to consume the least amount of energy in 8 of 10 cases, and is the fastest in 6 of 10 cases.

The results on the comparison between the 4 implementations for the addAll, containsAll, and toArray operations of the benchmark are presented in Fig. 5a), b) and c), respectively. These values are the proportion of energy and time compared to the slowest and most energy consumption one, *ConcurrentSkipListSet*.

While for our Haskell Sets the differences between the proportions of time and energy are always lower than 1.49%, we see a larger variation for the Java

---

[8] Companion website with the experiment's results: https://github.com/greensoftwarelab/Collections-Energy-Benchmark/tree/master/PaintYourPrograms.

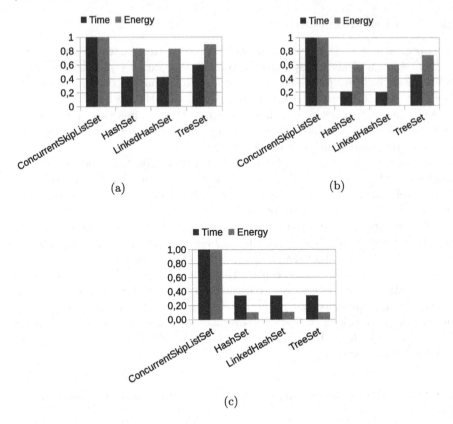

Fig. 5. Results of the addAll, containsAll, and toArray operations operation for Java Sets

Sets. Such an example can be seen in Fig. 5 with the proportions varying between 23%–40%.

Maps. Energy consumption was again proportional to execution time. For the Map implementations, the *TreeMap* and *ConcurrentHashMap* were the most efficient in 3 of 10 cases each. On the other hand, *TreeMap* and *UIDefaults* were the fastest implementations in 3 of 10 cases each.

Figure 6a), b), and c) show the results on the comparison between several of the Map implementations for the add, contains, and remove operations, respectively. Once again, the bars represent the proportion of energy and time compared to the slowest and most energy consuming one. In Fig. 6a), the worst implementation was the *ConcurrentSkipListMap*, in b) it was *SimpleBinding* and *HashMap* for energy and time respectively, and in c) it was *UIDefaults* and *TreeMap* for energy and time respectively.

Again, the results show us that the differences, within a given implementation, between the proportions of time and energy have a much larger varia-

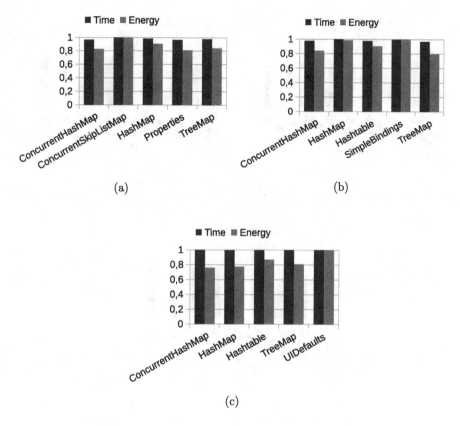

Fig. 6. Results of the add, contains, and remove operations for Maps

tion than which were seen in the Haskell Associative Collections, with differences between 0.1%-38%.

Lists. Yet again, there was a strong correlation between energy consumption and execution time. For the List implementations, almost all were the most energy efficient in at least one operation, with *RoleList* as the most energy efficient in 3 of 10 cases. For execution time, *RoleList* was the fastest in 4 of 10 cases with *LinkedList*, *RoleUnresolvedList*, and *ArrayList* having the fastest times in 2 of 10 cases each.

Figure 7a), b), and c) show the results on the comparison between several of the List implementations for the add, addAll, and remove operations, respectively. In Fig. 7a), the worst implementation was the *CopyOnWriteArrayList*, in b) it was *LinkedList* and *CopyOnWriteArrayList* for energy and time respectively, and in c) it was *CopyOnWriteArrayList*.

The differences between the proportions of time and energy for the Java Lists are, yet again, larger than those seen in Haskell Sequences varying between 0.1%–50%. In Fig. 7b), we even see an example where a data structure is more energy efficient than it is performance efficient, in the case of *LinkedList*.

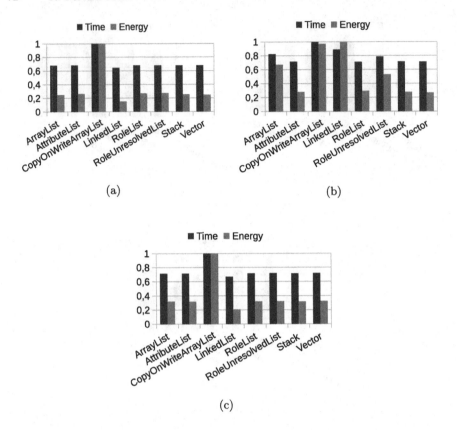

(a)

(b)

(c)

Fig. 7. Results of the add, addAll, and remove operations for Lists

5   Related Work

Data structures are a fundamental, unavoidable part of software development. As we have previously seen, each different data structure implementation has their own benefits, drawbacks, and performance. In recent years however, the analysis of the energy efficiency of such implementations has drawn the attention of many researchers.

Manotas *et al.* [13] developed the *SEEDS* framework, which was the first automated support for optimizing the energy usage of applications by making source code-level changes. They implemented a very specific instance of this framework to improve the energy consumption of projects using Java's Collections API, producing good results. *SEEDS* dynamically follows a trial and error method, testing each possible alternative, until the most energy efficient one is found.

A study by Pinto *et al.* [9] studied the energy efficiency specifically on Java's thread-safe collections, based on traversal, insertion, and removal operations. They were able to improve up to 17% energy savings by switching out collections, showing how such simple changes can reduce the energy consumption considerably. Such similar findings were shown by Hasan *et al.* [12], where they looked at the Java Collections Framework (8 collections), Apache Commons Collections (5 collections), and Trove (4). They measured the energy costs of iterations, insertions (beginning, middle, and end for *Lists*), and random access/query. A study they performed showed how switching out one *List* for a worse one can decrease energy consumption by 300%, or improve the energy consumption by 36%.

Another study, more focused on map data structures within Android, analyzed the CPU time, memory usage, and energy consumption in *HashMap*, *ArrayMap*, and *SpareArray* variants [10]. The latter two implementations were developed to be more performance efficient than *HashMap*. They found that *ArrayMap* was less energy efficient, and *SpareArray* was more energy efficient, when compared to *HashMap*.

Oliveira *et al.* developed a tool called *CT+* [16], based on results and work from a previous study of theirs [35], which applies a static analysis on a program and recommends energy-efficient Java collections, while accounting for the impact of loops and differentiates thread-safe and thread-unsafe collections. This tool is similar to the one presented by Pereira *et al.* [14], called *jStanley*, where it uses results from a previous study [15] to recommend energy efficient collections based on method usage per collection, across varying population sizes. *jStanley* is simpler in nature in regards to the static analysis, where it does not differentiate loops and thread-safe or thread-unsafe collections.

The studies conducted by Lima *et al.* [11,36] analyzed the energy behavior of various Haskell sequential and concurrent data structures. They too were able to show how making changes on which data structures are used can have large impacts, saving up to 60% of energy in one of their settings. The latter study further explored Haskell's thread-management constructs, and showed that the replacement of `forkIO` by `forkOn` lowered the energy consumption.

Finally, the study and results for the Haskell and Java experiments we presented in this tutorial were based off the work from [11,36], and an adaptation of the benchmarking framework used in [15], respectively.

6   Conclusions

As energy efficiency continues to be a big concern for software developers, due to climatic or economic costs, we must properly understand the energy footprint our choices in software development have. With this work, we analyzed a key part in software development: data structures. We looked at common operations on data structures within the Haskell and Java programming language, and measured the energy consumed while performing such tasks in different implementation scenarios.

Through performing our experiment and presenting their results, we have answered our *RQ How do different data structure implementations compare, both in terms of runtime and energy efficiency?* We found that for Haskell programs, execution time is more closely tied with energy consumption. While for Java programs this correlation still existed, it was not as strict. We found data structures which were more energy efficient than performance efficient, and vice-versa. In both cases, we have provided results on what data structure implementation should be used in a given operation scenario. Thus, the programmer can have more information present when choosing the most adequate implementation.

With our work, we aim to provide even more knowledge pertaining to the efficiency of data structures, based on their runtime performance, and on their energy efficiency. While the former has historically received the most attention, the fact is that the energy consumption is becoming a significant concern for programmers [5–8], where studies argue that this is due to *the lack of knowledge* and *the lack of tools*. We believe that with this work, we have contributed to further close the gap when discussing *the lack of knowledge* in energy efficient software development, a concern which has also brought the attention of a significant number of researchers [9–16].

References

1. Wirth, N.: Algorithms + Data Structures = Programs. Prentice Hall PTR (1976)
2. Torvalds, L.: Message to Git mailing list: Re: Licensing and the library version of git (2006)
3. Aho, A.V., Hopcroft, J.E., Ullman, J.: Data Structures and Algorithms, 1st edn. Addison-Wesley Longman Publishing Co., Inc. (1983)
4. Kernighan, B.W., Pike, R.: The Practice of Programming. Addison-Wesley Professional (1999)
5. Manotas, I., et al.: An empirical study of practitioners' perspectives on green software engineering. In: 2016 IEEE/ACM 38th International Conference on Software Engineering (ICSE), pp. 237–248. IEEE (2016)
6. Pang, C., Hindle, A., Adams, B., Hassan, A.E.: What do programmers know about software energy consumption? IEEE Softw. **33**(3), 83–89 (2016)
7. Pinto, G., Castor, F., Liu, Y.D.: Mining questions about software energy consumption. In: Proceedings of the 11th Working Conference on Mining Software Repositories, pp. 22–31. ACM (2014)
8. Pinto, G., Castor, F.: Energy efficiency: a new concern for application software developers. Commun. ACM **60**(12), 68–75 (2017)
9. Pinto, G., Liu, K., Castor, F., Liu, Y.D.: A comprehensive study on the energy efficiency of Java's thread-safe collections. In: 2016 IEEE International Conference on Software Maintenance and Evolution, ICSME 2016, Raleigh, NC, USA, 2–7 October 2016, pp. 20–31 (2016)
10. Saborido, R., Morales, R., Khomh, F., Guéhéneuc, Y.-G., Antoniol, G.: Getting the most from map data structures in Android. Empir. Softw. Eng. **23**(5), 2829–2864 (2018). https://doi.org/10.1007/s10664-018-9607-8
11. Lima, L.G., Melfe, G., Soares-Neto, F., Lieuthier, P., Fernandes, J.P., Castor, F.: Haskell in green land: analyzing the energy behavior of a purely functional language. In: Proceedings of the 23rd IEEE International Conference on Software Analysis, Evolution, and Reengineering (SANER 2016), pp. 517–528. IEEE (2016)
12. Hasan, S., King, Z., Hafiz, M., Sayagh, M., Adams, B., Hindle, A.: Energy profiles of Java collections classes. In: Proceedings of the 38th International Conference on Software Engineering, pp. 225–236. ACM (2016)
13. Manotas, I., Pollock, L., Clause, J.: SEEDS: a software engineer's energy-optimization decision support framework. In: Proceedings of the 36th International Conference on Software Engineering, pp. 503–514. ACM (2014)

14. Pereira, R., Simão, P., Cunha, J., Saraiva, J.: jStanley: placing a green thumb on Java collections. In: Proceedings of the 33rd ACM/IEEE International Conference on Automated Software Engineering, ASE 2018, pp. 856–859. ACM, New York (2018)
15. Pereira, R., Couto, M., Saraiva, J., Cunha, J., Fernandes, J.P.: The influence of the Java collection framework on overall energy consumption. In: Proceedings of the 5th International Workshop on Green and Sustainable Software, GREENS 2016, pp. 15–21. ACM (2016)
16. de Oliveira Júnior, W., dos Santos, R.O., de Lima Filho, F.J.C., de Araújo Neto, B.F., Pinto, G.H.L.: Recommending energy-efficient Java collections. In: 2019 IEEE/ACM 16th International Conference on Mining Software Repositories (MSR), pp. 160–170. IEEE (2019)
17. Aho, A.V., Ullman, J.D.: Foundations of Computer Science. Computer Science Press Inc. (1992)
18. Bell, C.G., Newell, A.: Computer structures: readings and examples. Technical report, Carnegie-Mellon University, Department of Computer Science, Pittsburgh, PA (1971)
19. Shaffer, C.A.: A Practical Introduction to Data Structures and Algorithm Analysis. Prentice-Hall Inc. (1997)
20. Okasaki, C.: An overview of Edison. Electron. Notes Theor. Comput. Sci. $41(1)$, 60–73 (2001)
21. Okasaki, C.: Purely Functional Data Structures. Cambridge University Press, Cambridge (1999)
22. Dockins, R.: Edison, Haskell communities and activities report 2009. https://www.haskell.org/communities/05-2009/html/report.html
23. Dockins, R.: EdisonCore package. http://hackage.haskell.org/package/EdisonCore-1.3
24. Dockins, R.: EdisonAPI package. http://hackage.haskell.org/package/EdisonAPI-1.3
25. Lewis, L.: Java Collection Performance (2011). http://dzone.com/articles/java-collection-performance
26. David, H., Gorbatov, E., Hanebutte, U.R., Khanna, R., Le, C.: RAPL: memory power estimation and capping. In: 2010 ACM/IEEE International Symposium on Low-Power Electronics and Design (ISLPED), pp. 189–194. IEEE (2010)
27. Weaver, V.M., et al.: Measuring energy and power with PAPI. In: 2012 41st International Conference on Parallel Processing Workshops, pp. 262–268. IEEE (2012)
28. Rotem, E., Naveh, A., Ananthakrishnan, A., Weissmann, E., Rajwan, D.: Power-management architecture of the Intel microarchitecture code-named sandy bridge. IEEE Micro $32(2)$, 20–27 (2012)
29. Hähnel, M., Döbel, B., Völp, M., Härtig, H.: Measuring energy consumption for short code paths using RAPL. SIGMETRICS Perform. Eval. Rev. $40(3)$, 13–17 (2012)
30. Desrochers, S., Paradis, C., Weaver, V.M.: A validation of DRAM RAPL power measurements. In: Proceedings of the Second International Symposium on Memory Systems, MEMSYS 2016, pp. 455–470. ACM (2016)
31. O'Sullivan, B.: Criterion: robust, reliable performance measurement and analysis (2009). http://www.serpentine.com/criterion/
32. Liu, K., Pinto, G., Liu, Y.D.: Data-oriented characterization of application-level energy optimization. In: Egyed, A., Schaefer, I. (eds.) FASE 2015. LNCS, vol. 9033, pp. 316–331. Springer, Heidelberg (2015). https://doi.org/10.1007/978-3-662-46675-9_21

33. Barrett, E., Bolz-Tereick, C.F., Killick, R., Mount, S., Tratt, L.: Virtual machine warmup blows hot and cold. Proc. ACM Program. Lang. 1(OOPSLA), 52 (2017)
34. Hogg, R.V., Tanis, E.A.: Probability and Statistical Inference, vol. 993. Macmillan, New York (1977)
35. Fernandes, B., Pinto, G., Castor, F.: Assisting non-specialist developers to build energy-efficient software. In: 2017 IEEE/ACM 39th International Conference on Software Engineering Companion (ICSE-C), pp. 158–160. IEEE (2017)
36. Lima, L.G., Soares-Neto, F., Lieuthier, P., Castor, F., Melfe, G., Fernandes, J.P.: On Haskell and energy efficiency. J. Syst. Softw. **149**, 554–580 (2019)

Energy Efficient Software in an Engineering Course

João Saraiva[(⊠)] and Rui Pereira

Department of Informatics, University of Minho HASLab/INESC TEC,
Braga, Portugal
{saraiva,rui.pereira}@di.uminho.pt

Abstract. Sustainable development has become an increasingly important theme not only in the world politics, but also an increasingly central theme for the engineering professions around the world. Software engineers are no exception as shown in various recent research studies. Despite the intensive research on green software, today's undergraduate computing education often fails to address our environmental responsibility.

In this paper, we present a module on energy efficient software that we introduced as part of an advanced course on software analysis and testing. In this module students study techniques and tools to analyze and optimize energy consumption of software systems. Preliminary results of the first four instances of this course show that students are able to optimize the energy consumption of software systems.

Keywords: Sustainable Software Development · Energy Efficient Software

1 Introduction

The world is increasingly aware of and concerned about sustainability and the green movement. Computers and their software play a pivotal role in our world, thus it has a special responsibility for social development and the welfare of our planet. In this century, the situation is becoming critical since software is everywhere! The widespread use of computer devices, from regular desktop computers, to laptops, to powerful mobile phones, to consumer electronics, and to large data centers is changing the way software engineers develop software. Indeed, in our *internet of things* age there are new concerns which developers have to consider when constructing software systems. While in the previous century both computer manufacturers and software developers were mainly focused in producing very fast computer systems, in this century energy consumption is becoming the main bottleneck when developing such systems [1].

Non wired/mobile devices are our everyday computers and not only do they need energy efficient hardware, but also need energy efficient software. While the computer hardware manufacturers have for several decades already, done a considerable amount of research/work on developing energy efficient computers, only

Z. Porkoláb and V. Zsók (Eds.): CEFP 2019, LNCS 11950, pp. 77–97, 2023.
https://doi.org/10.1007/978-3-031-42833-3_3

recently have the programming language and software engineering communities started conducting research on developing energy efficient software, the so-called green software. Indeed, green software is nowadays a very active research area, as shown by the organization of specific research events on this area (for example, the ICT4S[1] and IGSCC[2] conferences, and the GREENS[3], RE4SuSy[4], and SUSTAIN-SE[5] workshops), the many research papers being published in top conferences on, for example, green data structures [2–5],green software libraries [6,7], green rankings of software languages [8], energy greedy programming practices/-patterns [9–13], and green repositories [14], etc.

While research in green software is rapidly increasing, several recent studies with software engineers show that they still miss techniques and tools to develop greener software [1,15–17]. For example, in [17] a large survey on green software is presented with the following conclusions:

> *"A survey revealed that programmers had limited knowledge of energy efficiency, lacked knowledge of the best practices to reduce software energy consumption, and were unsure about how software consumes energy. These results highlight the need for training on energy consumption."*

In fact, all those recent studies show that academia should not only define new advanced techniques and tools for green software developing, but it should also educate software engineers towards greener software development. Obviously, this education should be provided from the very beginning of a software engineer career. Unfortunately, today's undergraduate computing education often fails to address our social and environmental responsibility [18]. Indeed, energy efficiency and sustainability should be part of an undergraduate curriculum in software engineering.

This document presents a module on green software as part of a discipline on software engineering that is given in the MSc program on "Engenharia Informática" at University of Minho, Portugal. The course introduces green software as a new nonfunctional requirement in software engineering: minimizing software energy consumption is a key concern. Techniques to monitor, instrument and measure energy consumption by software systems are introduced. To understand the impact of how programmers develop software on energy consumption, we focus our energy analysis and optimization on the software's source code. Thus, a catalog of energy greedy programming practices is presented to students- that we call red smells - together with corresponding source code optimizations that reduce such possibly abnormal consumption, named green refactorings. Using this catalog, students have to build in a lab environment a successful experiment for software energy consumption. This paper briefly presents

---

[1] https://conf.researchr.org/series/ict4s.

[2] https://www.igscc.org/.

[3] https://greens.cs.vu.nl/.

[4] http://birgit.penzenstadler.de/re4susy/.

[5] https://sites.google.com/view/sustainablese-workshop/home.

our catalog of smells/refactorings, developed in the context of the Green Software Laboratory (GSL) project[6]. Then, we present the first preliminary results where students used this catalog to optimize the energy consumption of a given software system. The results show that students do understand the impact of software over energy consumption, are able to locate red smells in its source code and to apply appropriate refactorings to optimize the software as to reduce energy consumption.

2 Energy Efficient Software in Higher Education

2.1 Sustainable Development and Its Dimentions

Over the past decade, interest in topics related to sustainability has grown steadily. In fact, sustainability is studied from various angles, for example, economic, political, institutional, cultural or ethical ones, and thus it is difficult to arrive at a common definition that covers nearly all of its aspects. The broader socio-political concept of sustainability, as presented by the World Commission on Environment and Development in their 1987 report [19], addresses the well-known conflicts between environment and development goals by formulating sustainability *"as the ability to make development sustainable to ensure that it meets the needs of the present without compromising the ability of future generations to meet their own needs."*.

In the extensive discussion and use of this concept, it is commonly agreed that the central component of sustainable development is best described by considering the following three dimensions of sustainability [20]:

- *Economic:* An economically sustainable system must be able to produce goods and services, and to avoid extreme sectoral imbalances which damage agricultural or industrial production.
- *Environmental:* An environmentally sustainable system must maintain a stable resource base, avoiding over-exploitation of renewable resources, and depleting non-renewable resources only to the extent that investment is made in adequate substitutes.
- *Social:* A socially sustainable system must achieve distributional equity, adequate provision of social services health and education, gender equity, and political accountability and participation.

2.2 Sustainable Development in Higher Education

There are several works studying how to integrate the concept of sustainable development into higher education in meaningful ways and to address the three main dimensions of sustainability and their different combinations [21–23]. For example, at the university institutional level, [22] presents a procedure at the University of Gävle in Sweden, designed to stimulate integration of the concept

---

[6] http://greenlab.di.uminho.pt/.

of sustainable development into courses and research projects. In that study, faculty members were asked to classify their courses and research funding applications regarding their contributions to sustainable development. The method of classifying courses provides a framework to approach sustainable development from common definitions, but still allows for individual approaches to integrating it in courses and research. The study shows that it is possible to integrate the concept of sustainable development into higher education. However, the system needs further development in order to show instructors and researchers that the integration of sustainability is seen as important to the university administration so that it stimulates faculty members to integrate sustainable development in their courses.

At the national level, the paper [21] describes the process of promoting the disciplinary exploration of sustainable development in the curricula of Dutch Universities and the lessons learned with that process. The Finnish Government included the promotion of sustainable development in its development plan for education and research in 2003. This development plan is a key steering tool for the Finish ministry of education [24]. In 2010, eight public universities in Hong Kong signed the Hong Kong Declaration to recognize the vital role of the higher education sector in the efforts to deal with the challenges caused by climate change and to include the collective voices from Hong Kong public universities in the global sustainability community. In [25] a study reviewed what the eight public universities in Hong Kong have accomplished in promoting sustainability.

Sustainable development is also a concern for worldwide institutions, like for example ACM: the world's largest association of computing professionals. As advocated in [26] information systems can be a driving force for sustainability improvements and, as a consequence, ACM members could and should play a critical role in creating and implementing an information strategy. In fact, ACM promotes sustainability and in 2017, SIGPLAN[7] formed the climate committee to study the climate impact of conferences and possible steps that SIGPLAN might take in response. ACM hosts a number of annual scientific meetings at various locations throughout the world. While such meetings are important for furthering important research, the air travel required for participate in such meetings is a significant source of greenhouse gas emissions, which in turn is a significant contributor to environmental change. In their preliminary report on *Engaging with Climate Change: Possible Steps for SIGPLAN*, the climate committee (among other things) presents a number of alternative models such a physical/virtual hybrids, multi-hub conferences, and regional conferences, with the goal to reducing carbon footprints. To make its members aware of the conference participation impact on climate, ACM also provides a CO_2 footprint calculator for conferences: https://co2calculator.acm.org/.

Sustainability in the ACM Computer Science Curricula. While technical issues are central to the computing curriculum, they do not constitute a complete educational program in the field. Students must also be exposed to the larger

---

[7] The ACM Special Interest Group on Programming Languages.

societal context of computing to develop an understanding of the relevant social, ethical, legal and professional issues.

Sustainability was first introduced in the ACM Computer Science 2008 curricular guidelines, and in that same year [27] presented a policy on computing education for sustainability for adoption by ACM SIGCSE[8]. In the Computer Science Curricula 2013, ACM further recognized the enormous impact that computing has had on society at large emphasizing a sustainable future and placing added responsibilities on computing professionals.

The outcome of this was the definition of core topics on sustainability which include the identification of ways to be a sustainable practitioner by taking into consideration cultural and environmental impacts of implementation decisions (e.g. organizational policies, economic viability, and resource consumption). The exploration of global social and environmental impacts of computer use and disposal (e-waste). And, the assessment the environmental impacts of design choices in specific areas such as algorithms, operating systems, networks, databases, or human-computer interaction.

2.3   Energy Efficient Software in Higher Education

In recent years, sustainable and energy efficient (green) software became a very active software engineering research field. However, there are several studies showing that software engineers still lack knowledge of how to reason and improve energy consumption of their software systems.

In [16] a detailed study on energy-related questions on StackOverflow - a question and answer site for (non) professional software developers[9] - showed that software developers are aware of the energy consumption problems but the many questions they asked rarely got appropriate answers. They also suggested eight strategies to reduce energy consumption through software modification. A large empirical study of how developers think about energy when they write requirements, design, construct, test, and maintain their software is presented in [15]. After surveying 464 developers (from ABB, Google, IBM, and Microsoft) and 18 in-depth interviews with Microsoft employees the study overall conclusions are: *"green software engineering practitioners care and think about energy when they build applications; however, they are not as successful as they could be because they lack the necessary information and support infrastructure."*. In [17] it is shown that programmers know little about energy consumption: *"The programmers in our study lacked knowledge and awareness of software energy- related issues. More than 80 percent of them didn't take energy consumption into account when developing software."*. And, authors suggest that the strategies discussed in [16] *"should be part of programmers' education. In addition, development tools can be created to identify unnecessary energy consumption and suggest how to reduce it. Educators could develop slides, videos, projects, and assignments as part of an undergraduate curriculum for energy efficiency and sustainability."*.

---

[8] The ACM Special Interest Group on Computer Science Education.
[9] http://stackoverflow.com.

A recent article at CACM [1] discusses energy efficiency as a new concern for software developers, showing that: developers currently do not know how to write, maintain and evolve green software. They lack the knowledge on how to measure, profile and optimize energy consumption, and they lack tools to help them in these tasks.

Despite the intensive research on green software and all these recent studies showing the lack of knowledge and language/tool support software engineers are currently facing, there is little undergraduate computing education in green software engineering. Misconception among developers and researchers persist, rooted in a lack of coherent understanding of sustainability, and how it relates to software systems research and practice, also makes it difficult [28]. [28] presents a cross-disciplinary initiative to create a common ground and a point of reference for the global community of research and practice in software and sustainability, to be used for effectively communicating key issues, goals, values and principles of sustainability design for software-intensive systems.

Nevertheless, there is some work advocating the introduction of sustainability in undergraduate education. In [29] a first study of what is the current state of teaching sustainability in the software engineering community is presented. The paper reports the findings from a targeted survey of 33 academics on the presence of green and sustainable software engineering in higher education. The major findings suggest that sustainability is under-represented in the curricula and the main reasons are:

- lack of awareness,
- lack of teaching material,
- high effort required,
- lack of technology and tool support.

A list a group of barriers for sustainability integration into computing education is also discussed in [18]. Two strategies to sustainability integration in computing are presented: the developing of a new course or the development of modules easily plugged into existing courses. This short paper gives a very general view of the organization of such a course. However, it does not include any discussion on the course objectives and whether they were achieved by students or not.

A systematic approach for teaching software engineering for sustainability and its qualitative evaluation is presented in [30]. The proposed course blueprint articulated a candidate set of modules. This is an intensive week-long course, given at a summer school where participants had different backgrounds. In [31] a course on learning and teaching computing sustainability is also briefly described. They are adapting an existing course on professionalism in computing to incorporate more of these sustainability modules, such as: green mobile cloud computing systems; integration of green clouds and the Internet of things; energy saving solutions and trade-offs; sensors and monitoring software tools for evaluating energy use, among other topics. [32] presents an experiment with integrating issues of sustainability with information technology in both introductory and upper-level computer science courses. The course discusses several case studies that illustrate the many creative ways that IT is being used to address sustainability: transportation and logistics, supply chain management, etc. In [23] it is described the design of the course *Software Engineering Sustainability* that introduces the sustainable concept into educational programs for software engineers. The course has been being delivered at the National Aerospace University "Kharkiv Aviation Institute" in Ukraine.

A survey on green software education with 21 well-known researchers and educators in the green software/computing field is presented in [33]. This survey confirms the lack of courses and educational material for teaching green software in current higher education It also highlights three key pedagogical challenges in teaching green software, and provide existing solutions and guidelines to address these challenges.

At the Texas State University in USA, Ziliang Zong offers a full course on Advanced Green Computing[10] which covers hardware and software techniques to improve the energy-efficiency of computing systems. Topics include best practices in building energy-efficient data centers and mobile devices, current trends in reducing the energy consumption of processors and storage components, energy-aware resource management, software optimizations, and hands-on experience on power-measurable systems. The objectives of this course is that students will be able to:

- Analyze research papers and evaluate existing research ideas.
- Compare experimental results from different algorithms.
- Evaluate the strengths and weaknesses of different approaches.
- Design experiments and collect experimental results on power measurable systems

Patricia Lago and Ivano Malavolta coordinate the Master track in Software Engineering and Green IT at the Master's in Computer Science[11] offered at Vrije Universiteit Amsterdam, The Netherlands. The combination of Software Engineering and Green IT in one track provides the students with the instruments necessary to gain a holistic understanding of large-scale and complex software systems, to manage their evolution, assess their quality and environmental impact, quantify their value and sustainability potential, and organize their development in different local and distributed contexts. Students graduating in this track are experts of:

- Architecture design of software-intensive systems
- the role of software for sustainability (including energy efficiency, socio-technical, ecologic and economic impact)
- software engineering techniques for critical analysis and decision-making
- benefits and challenges of developing and maintaining sustainable software
- the pervasive role of software-intensive systems in the digital society
- data-driven measurement and assessment of software quality

---

[10] CS 7333 - Advanced Green Computing, https://cs.txstate.edu/academics/course_det ail/CS/7333/.

[11] https://vuweb.vu.nl/en/education/master/computer-science.

3   Software Analysis and Testing with a Green Flavor

In this section we discuss in detail the module on green software we offer as part of a non mandatory discipline on software engineering, more precisely on software analysis and testing, that is given in the fourth year of our five year MSc program.

As mentioned in several papers advocating the inclusion of sustainability and green software in computing education [28–30,34–37], we present green software as a module of an already existing course. Moreover, we focus this module in making future software engineers aware of the impact of programming practices on software energy consumption.

3.1   Green Software: A Multidisciplinary Module

The green software module requires a multidisciplinary course combining several software engineering techniques and principles, namely:

Source Code Analysis and Transformation: In order to analyze and transform software systems we introduce two powerful source code manipulation techniques: Strategic and Aspect Oriented Programming. Strategic programming is a generic tree traversal techniques that allows for expressing powerful abstract syntax tree analysis and transformations [38,39]. Aspect oriented programming is introduced to allow developers to instrument the base source code without adding the energy monitoring intrusive code, but keeping it in one aspect that is later weaved to the base program [40].

Green Aspect: In order to monitor the energy consumption, students need to traverse and instrument the source code with calls to APIs providing energy measurements at runtime. In our course we consider two types of measurements: energy estimation provided by manufacturers of the CPUs, namely the RAPL framework developed by Intel [41,42], or using hardware with energy sensors, like for example the ODroid hardware board[12].

Source Code Smells and Metrics: Code smells represent symptoms of poor implementation choices when developing software. Code smells are not faults, they make program understanding difficult, and possibly indicate a deeper problem in the software. Software metrics are usually used to detect source code smells, for example, a too long method smell.

Green Aspect: In our module on green software we present a catalog of energy greedy programming practices [13]. This catalog can also be seen as a energy smell catalog, where software metrics can be used to detect such smells in the source code.

---

[12] http://www.odroid.com.

Program Refactoring: refactoring is a controlled source-to-source transformation technique for improving the design of an existing (source code) software system [43, 44]. Its essence is applying a series of small semantic-preserving transformations. Refactorings are usually associated with code smells: for each smell there is a refactoring that eliminates it.

Green Aspect: We associate refactorings to the catalog of energy smells so that students can use a green refactoring to eliminate red smells. Because the main focus of refactoring is to improve comprehensibility, several refactorings may negatively affect energy consumption. Students also analyze how refactorings available from Java IDEs affect energy consumption. The catalog of green refactorings for Java data structures is supported by the jStanley tool [2].

Technical Debt: Technical debt describes the gap between the current state and the ideal state of a software system [45]. The key idea of technical debt is that software systems may include hard to understand/maintain/evolve artefacts, causing higher costs in the future development and maintenance activities. These extra costs can be seen as a type of debt that developers owe the software system.

Green Aspect: In our module we introduce the concept of Energy Debt [46] as the amount of unnecessary energy that a software system uses over time, due to maintaining energy code smells for sustained periods.

Software Testing and Benchmarking Infrastructures: Software testing aims at ensuring that a software system is defect free. We present the usual levels of testing: unit, integration, system, regression and beta testing. Automated test case generation and property based testing is also studied in this course. Code coverage and mutation-based testing is used to assess the quality of the test suite. Moreover, we use testing framework and benchmarks infrastructures, like Google's Caliper[13] in order to execute programs.

Green Aspect: To measure energy consumption, the source code needs to be executed with proper inputs. We use system testing, where the automated test case generation techniques produces *real* inputs of the program under testing.

Fault Localization: When a software systems fails running the defined/generated test suite, programmers need to locate the fault and fix it. Fault localization techniques locate software faults in the program's source code [47]. Spectrum-based Fault Localization (SFL) relies on test cases to run the program and it uses statistical methods to assign probabilities of being faulty to source code components (methods, classes, statements, etc.) [48].

Green Aspect: Abnormal energy consumption can be seen as a software fault. In our course we defined a variant of SFL to locate energy leaks in the source code: Spectrum-based Energy Leak Localization (*SPELL*) [49,50], and students can use it to locate such energy hot-spots in their software.

---

[13] http://code.google.com/p/caliper/.

Automated Program Repair: The goal of automated program repair is to take a faulty program and a test suite, and automatically produce a patch that fixes the program [51]. The test suite provides the correctness criterion in this case, guiding the repair towards a valid patch.

Green Aspect: SPELL adapts fault localization to the green software realm, while green refactorings eliminate red smells aiming at improving energy efficiency of programs. We combine these two techniques in order to automate the energy-aware repair of energy inefficient software systems [52,53].

3.2   Green Software: Module Objectives

The objectives of the green software module are:

- Be able to instrument, monitor and measure the energy consumption of software systems.
- Become aware of the impact of programming practices on energy consumption.
- Become familiar with the research problems in the field of green software engineering.

Course Duration, Organization and Evaluation: The module of green software is part of the software analysis and testing course. It is a one semester long course with 5 ECTS. It is a non mandatory course included in the second semester of the fourth year of the master program on software engineering at Minho University.

The students have 3 h per week in the classroom: one hour in a seminar room, where all theories and techniques are presented. The remaining two weekly hours are laboratory classes where students have the chance to experiment the introduced techniques for software energy consumption. The evaluation consists of two components: an individual written exam, and a group project on analyzing and optimizing the energy consumption of a given software system. The considered software system is the students project developed in the introductory course to object oriented programming the semester before (by second year students). The idea is to provide students in the course with a simple, non fully optimized system.

In order to analyze and optimize the energy consumption of Java based software systems, we present the students a catalog of energy-greedy Java programming practices. The main goal is to make students aware of some features of Java's source code that may indicate an abnormal energy consumption of the software. The students are also presented with a possible solution by performing a refactoring of the source code into a more energy efficient one. Moreover, software tools that locate such features and (semi) automatically optimize the code are also presented. In laboratory sessions the students are able to experiment with smell detection and optimization. Then, outside of class, students have to work in group (three students per group) and apply the catalog/tools in order to optimize the energy consumption of a real software project.

3.3   Green Software: Module Supporting Tools

In the context of the Green Software Laboratory project [54] we have developed several tools that support the laboratory classes, namely:

– *SPELL* [50]- A toolkit to measure the energy consumption of a Java based program and detect potential energy hot spots through an adapted Spectrum-based Fault Localization technique.
– *jStanley* [2] - An Eclipse plugin that automatically refactors Java collections to more energy efficient ones.
– *Chimera* [13]: An energy-greedy Android pattern testing framework for Android.
– *E-Debitum* [55] - A SonarQube extension to manage the Energy Debt of Java/Android-based software systems.
– *GreenSource* and *AnaDroid* [14] - A repository of android source code applications tailored for green software analysis and a tool to static analyze and dynamically monitor the energy consumption of such applications.

4   Energy Efficent Software: Students Assessment

We introduced this module on green software as part of the software analysis and testing course in the scholar year of 2017/2018. In the 2020/2021 scholar year we offered the fourth instance of the course, totaling 141 students enrolled across all four instances.

In the first four instances of this module students were quite positive in their reception of the material and the way it was incorporated in the course. In fact across all editions, 59% of students obtained at least a B for the module project, with the average module grade (written exam and project) being a C.

As shown in Fig. 1, most students received a positive evaluation on the group project where they have to analyze and optimize the energy consumption of a given software system. With the green software background acquired in the course, students were not only able to measure energy consumption of a software system, but also to optimize its energy consumption. Indeed, the catalog of energy smells and corresponding green refactorings, introduced in the theoretical classes, provided insights how energy may be abnormally consumed by software and pointed to the exact locations of where to improve/refactor the source code.

In order to assess the green software learning outcomes of individual students, the written exam includes questions on green software, as well. In the second instance of the course, offered in the 2018–2019 scholar year, we defined a specific question regarding green software. This one question has been repeated in the following two instances so that we have a larger set of answers.

In this exam question on green software, students are asked to identify energy smells in the source code of a given Java class (approx. 100 lines long), and to refactor each of the identified smells by hand. The given Java source code contains six of the smells included in the red smells catalog we present in the theoretical classes. The following subsection presents a brief description of the red smells catalog, and in Sect. 4.2 we analyze the students' answers in detail.

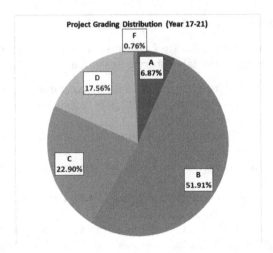

Fig. 1. Project grade distribution across all four editions.

4.1 A Catalog of Energy Smells and Refactorings

In the theoretical classes we present a catalog of Java-based energy smells and associated refactorings reported in the green software literature [5,56,57]. The following lists the subset of smells that occur in the given Java source code for the exam question.

Data Structures: Most languages offer mechanisms to manipulate data structures. Java is no exception with the Java Collections Framework (JCF). There are several research papers analyzing the energy behavior of such Java structures [2,3,5,58] showing very different energy efficiencies.

String Manipulation: Strings are widely used when developing software, with modern languages providing special syntax/operators to manipulate them. Java uses the String class and includes the "+" operator to concatenate them. However, the `StringBuilder` class in the Java library exploits buffering, and is more energy efficient. Thus, every occurrence of the string concatenation "+" in the source code is an energy smell and it should be refactored to a `StringBuilder`.

Lambda Expressions: Java 8 adopted lambda expressions as a mechanism to manipulate its collections. However, the execution of Java streams has several efficiency problems, either by doing more traversals than necessary, or creating intermediate data structures. In fact, Java 8 streams are still an order of magnitude slower than hand-written loops [56,59,60]. Thus, the use of Java streams is an energy smell and the refactoring considers a for-loop instead. IntelliJ IDEA[14] refactoring source code system provides such a detection and refactoring.

---

[14] https://www.jetbrains.com/idea/.

Accessing Object Fields: The object oriented paradigm encourages encapsulation, in order to make sure that "sensitive" data is hidden from users. Thus, every class should provide public getters and setters. However, the overhead caused by often calling getters and setters can increase both the execution time and energy consumption. Thus, the use of a get/set method is an energy smell and can be refactored to direct access of the attribute [57].

Java Exceptions: Exceptions are used to manage any unexpected event in the code, while ensuring code readability. When an object is in a condition it cannot handle, it raises an exception to be captured by another object. The JVM searches backward through the call stack to find methods that do can handle the exception. Exception handling is expensive and involves object creation, thus it should be avoided by, for example, the methods returning error codes [57].

4.2 Students Grades

Figure 2 shows the individual grades that students received on the specific question regarding energy smell detection and refactoring the given Java class aiming at improving its energy consumption.

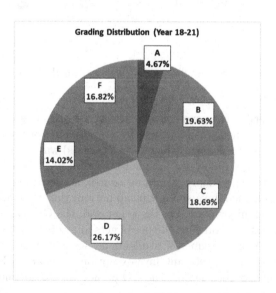

Fig. 2. Green Software Question: Distribution of grades in the last three editions. (Color figure online)

As shown in Fig. 2, a quarter of the students received a very good (19.63%) or excellent (4.67%) grade. On the other end, 16.82% of the students failed in answering this question. Most of these students (60%) also performed poorly in the other questions and did fail in the overall exam (as we can see in Figs. 4, 5, and 6).

The source code of the Java class included in the question contains five energy smells from the (larger) catalog we introduce in the green software module. Figure 3 shows the percentage of students who identified each of the occurring energy smells, in each instance of the course.

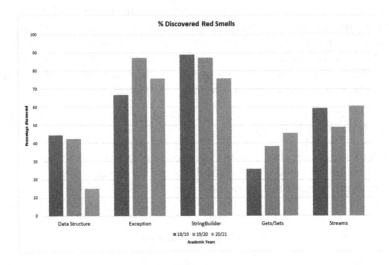

Fig. 3. Percentage of students discovering each red smell (Color figure online)

As we can observe, when we consider the three instances of the exam, the *String Manipulation* smell was identified by roughly 80% of the students, while the *Accessing Object Fields* smell (shown as Gets/Sets) was detected by less than 30%, only. Such a large difference in smell detection has two possible answers: since the very first Java OO programming course, students are taught to avoid the inefficient pre-defined Java string concatenation, thus they are familiar with identifying it and eliminating it. On the other end, the OO paradigm teaches/motivates encapsulation, and thus the use of gets and sets to access the (private) state of an object. As a consequence, students do not find such a refactoring natural. Similarly, replacing the elegant Java exceptions mechanism by the use of an (C-like) error code also goes against the OO paradigm. These students, however, do have a strong background in imperative programming (with the C language) and, thus, are used to this basic style of handling exceptions.

Streams offer an advanced functional style of programming in Java. Although students have a good background in functional programming (in Haskell), most students find it hard to understand the concept of higher-order functions and to adopt it. As a result, only half of the students were able to understand, detect and refactor this Java energy smell. Although the transformation from a stream to a for-loop is simple[15], students are not able to fully understand the functional code and to hand-write such refactoring themselves.

The students also performed poorly in detecting and refactoring Java energy greedy collections: in the three instances less than 40% correctly answer this question. Moreover, in the last instance the grades dropped to approximately 15%. While many of the other energy greed smells taught within the course are relatively straightforward rules (i.e. replacing string concatenation with String-Builders), choosing the most energy efficient data structure is inherently more difficult. This is due to having a wide array of choices between the different collections, which also depends on the needed methods and operations. Adding another requirement, in this case energy efficiency, further raises the complexity. While during the practical lab sessions students had tools and/or lecture slides at their disposal, many chose to not take the lecture material to the exam.

Figures 4, 5 and 6 show the comparison between the overall grade students obtained in the individual exam (represented as bars with the left-axis) and on the green software question (represented as lines with the right-axis), in the three instances completed.

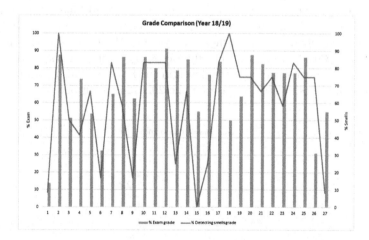

Fig. 4. Comparison between exam grade and red smell detection grade for academic year 2018/2019 (Color figure online)

We can see that only 8 out of 27 obtained a failing score in the 2018/2019 instances. The average score of the full exam is 68.6%, while the average of the green software question is 58.6%. We can also observe in Fig. 4 that students who performed well in the full exam, also received a good make in the green software question. Additionally, during this first instance, two students obtained a perfect score for this question (100% grade).

---

[15] Actually, modern Java IDEs, such as IntelliJ, offer this transformation as a predefined refactoring.

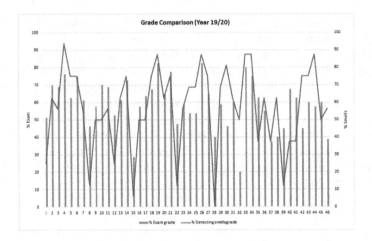

Fig. 5. Comparison between exam grade and red smell detection grade for academic year 2019/2020 (Color figure online)

In the 2019/2020 instance of the course, 11 out of 46 failed answering the exact same green software question. When we compare the scores to the previous instance, we observe that both the average of the exam and the question decreased: 57.6% and 55.7%, respectively. However, we observe the same pattern in the results: students who performed well in the full exam, also performed well in the question. This is also the case for the 2020/2021 edition.

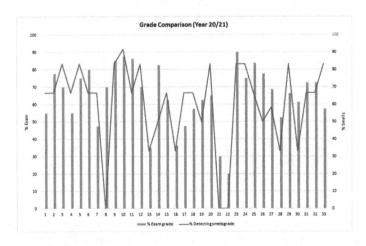

Fig. 6. Comparison between exam grade and red smell detection grade for academic year 2020/2021 (Color figure online)

In the latest instance of the course, 7 out of 33 failed in the green software question. The average scores went up and are similar to the results of the first instance: the exam score is 64.7%, that is also similar to the average of the green software questions 60.1%.

The second instance registered the most number of students in this non-mandatory course, having 70% more students than the first edition, and 40% more than the most recent edition. It is in this second instance that students received the lowest average scores, both in terms of the full exam and the green software question. Since this is a non-mandatory course, the increase in numbers not only influences (negatively) the quality of students, but also makes it harder to teach an advanced course to a larger group of students. We are convinced that this is the main reason for the worsened performance of the students in that instance. In fact, if we consider the results of the 30 best students of 2018/2019, a number similar to the previous/following instance, then the average scores are 66.9% (exam) and 65.4% (question), which in terms of the green software question would the be the best average result to date.

5   Conclusions

This paper presented the module on green software that we introduced as part of the course on software analysis and testing: an advanced course on software engineering. We described in detail the green flavor we incorporated in this well established multi-disciplinary course. Furthermore, we have assessed students in green decision making when developing/optimizing energy efficient software. Our first preliminary results are positive: students acquired the necessary engineering skills to measure and optimize energy consumption of software systems.

Aknowlegments. This work is financed by the ERDF European Regional Development Fund through the Operational Programme for Competitiveness and Internationalisation - COMPETE 2020 Programme within project POCI-01-0145-FEDER-006961, by National Funds through the Portuguese funding agency, FCT - *Fundação para a Ciência e a Tecnologia* within project POCI-01-0145-FEDER-016718 and UID/EEA/50014/2013, and by the Erasmus+ Key Action 2 project *"SusTrainable - Promoting Sustainability as a Fundamental Driver in Software Development Training and Education"*, project No. 2020-1-PT01-KA203-078646.

References

1. Pinto, G., Castor, F.: Energy efficiency: a new concern for application software developers. Commun. ACM **60**(12), 68–75 (2017)
2. Pereira, R., Simão, P., Cunha, J., Saraiva, J.: jStanley: placing a green thumb on java collections. In: Proceedings of the 33rd ACM/IEEE Int. Conference on Automated Software Engineering, ASE 2018, ACM, New York, NY, USA, pp. 856–859 (2018). http://doi.acm.org/10.1145/3238147.3240473
3. Hasan, S., King, Z., Hafiz, M., Sayagh, M., Adams, B., Hindle, A.: Energy profiles of Java collections classes. In: Proceedings of the 38th International Conference on Software Engineering, pp. 225–236. ACM (2016). https://doi.org/10.1145/2884781.2884869

4. Oliveira, W., Oliveira, R., Castor, F., Fernandes, B., Pinto, G.: Recommending energy-efficient Java collections. In: Proceedings of the 16th International Conference on Mining Software Repositories, MSR 2019, pp. 160–170. IEEE Press (2019). https://doi.org/10.1109/MSR.2019.00033

5. Pereira, R., Couto, M., Saraiva, J., Cunha, J., Fernandes, J.P.: The influence of the Java collection framework on overall energy consumption. In: Proceedings of the 5th International Workshop on Green and Sustainable Software, GREENS 2016, pp. 15–21. ACM (2016). https://doi.org/10.1145/2896967.2896968

6. Linares-Vásquez, M., Bavota, G., Bernal-Cárdenas, C., Oliveto, R. Di Penta, M., Poshyvanyk, D.: Mining energy-greedy API usage patterns in android apps: an empirical study. In: Proceedings of the 11th Working Conference on Mining Software Repositories, pp. 2–11. ACM (2014). https://doi.org/10.1145/2597073.2597085

7. Anwar, H., Demirer, B., Pfahl, D., Srirama, S.: Should energy consumption influence the choice of android third-party http libraries? In: Proceedings of the IEEE/ACM 7th International Conference on Mobile Software Engineering and Systems, MOBILESoft 2020, New York, NY, USA, pp. 87–97. Association for Computing Machinery (2020). https://doi.org/10.1145/3387905.3392095

8. Pereira, R., et al.: Energy efficiency across programming languages: how do energy, time, and memory relate? In: Proceedings of the 10th ACM SIGPLAN International Conference on Software Language Engineering, SLE 2017, New York, NY, USA, pp. 256–267. ACM (2017). http://doi.acm.org/10.1145/3136014.3136031

9. Cruz, L., Abreu, R.: Performance-based guidelines for energy efficient mobile applications. In: Proceedings of the 4th International Conference on Mobile Software Engineering and Systems, MOBILESoft 2017, Piscataway, NJ, USA, 2017, pp. 46–57. IEEE Press (2017). https://doi.org/10.1109/MOBILESoft.2017.19

10. Cruz, L., Abreu, R.: Catalog of energy patterns for mobile applications. Empirical Softw. Engg. **24**(4), 2209–2235 (2019). https://doi.org/10.1007/s10664-019-09682-0

11. Li, D., Halfond, W.G.J.: An investigation into energy-saving programming practices for android smartphone app development. In: Proceedings of the 3rd International Workshop on Green and Sustainable Software, GREENS 2014, New York, NY, USA, pp. 46–53. ACM (2014). http://doi.acm.org/10.1145/2593743.2593750

12. Morales, R., Saborido, R., Khomh, F., Chicano, F., Antoniol, G.: EARMO: an energy-aware refactoring approach for mobile apps. IEEE Trans. Software Eng. **44**(12), 1176–1206 (2018). https://doi.org/10.1145/3180155.3182524

13. Couto, M., Saraiva, J., Fernandes, J.P.: Energy refactorings for android in the large and in the wild. In: 2020 IEEE 27th International Conference on Software Analysis, Evolution and Reengineering (SANER), pp. 217–228. IEEE (2020). https://doi.org/10.1109/SANER48275.2020.9054858

14. Rua, R., Couto, M., Saraiva, J.: GreenSource: a large-scale collection of android code, tests and energy metrics. In: 2019 IEEE/ACM 16th International Conference on Mining Software Repositories (MSR), pp. 176–180. IEEE Press (2019). https://doi.org/10.1109/MSR.2019.00035

15. Manotas, I., et al.: An empirical study of practitioners' perspectives on green software engineering. In: Proceedings of the 38th International Conference on Software Engineering, ICSE 2016, New York, NY, USA, pp. 237–248. Association for Computing Machinery (2016). https://doi.org/10.1145/2884781.2884810

16. Pinto, G., Castor, F., Liu, Y.D.: Mining questions about software energy consumption. In: Proceedings of the 11th Working Conference on Mining Software Repositories, pp. 22–31. ACM (2014). https://doi.org/10.1145/2597073.2597110

17. Pang, C., Hindle, A., Adams, B., Hassan, A.E.: What do programmers know about software energy consumption? IEEE Softw. **33**(3), 83–89 (2016). https://doi.org/10.1109/MS.2015.83
18. Cai, Y.: Integrating sustainability into undergraduate computing education. In: Proceedings of the 41st ACM Technical Symposium on Computer Science Education, SIGCSE 2010, New York, NY, USA, pp. 524–528. ACM (2010). https://doi.org/10.1145/1734263.1734439
19. Brundtland, G.H.: Our common future, from one earth to one world - an overview by the world commission on environment and development (1987). https://sustainabledevelopment.un.org/content/documents/5987our-common-future.pdf
20. Harris, J.: Basic principles of sustainable development. In: Bawa, S.K., Seidler, R. (eds.) Dimensions of Sustainable Development, vol. 1, Encyclopedia of Life Support Systems - EOLSS, Oxford, United Kingdom, Ch. 2, pp. 21–40 (2009)
21. Appel, G., Dankelman, I., Kuipers, K.: Disciplinary explorations of sustainable development in higher education. In: Corcoran, P.B., Wals, A.E.J. (eds.) Higher Education and the Challenge of Sustainability, pp. 213–222. Springer, Dordrecht (2004). https://doi.org/10.1007/0-306-48515-X_16
22. Sammalisto, K., Lindhqvist, T.: Integration of sustainability in higher education: a study with international perspectives. Innov. High. Educ. **32**, 221–233 (2008). https://doi.org/10.1007/s10755-007-9052-x
23. Turkin, I., Vykhodets, Y.: Software engineering master's program and green IT: the design of the software engineering sustainability course. In: 2018 IEEE 9th International Conference on Dependable Systems, Services and Technologies, pp. 662–666 (2018)
24. Kaivola, T., Rohweder, L. (eds.): Towards sustainable development in higher education - reflections, no. 2007:6 in Opetusministeriön julkaisuja, Opetusministeriö, koulutus- ja tiedepolitiikan osasto, Finland (2007)
25. Xiong, W., Mok, K.H.: Sustainability practices of higher education institutions in Hong Kong: a case study of a sustainable campus consortium. Sustainability (2), 452 (2020). https://doi.org/10.3390/su12020452
26. Watson, R.T., Corbett, J., Boudreau, M.C., Webster, J.: An information strategy for environmental sustainability. Commun. ACM **55**(7), 28–30 (2012). https://doi.org/10.1145/2209249.2209261
27. Mann, S., Smith, L., Muller, L.: Computing education for sustainability. SIGCSE Bull. **40**(4), 183–193 (2008). https://doi.org/10.1145/1473195.1473241
28. Becker, C., et al.: Venters, sustainability design and software: the Karlskrona manifesto. In: Proceedings of the 37th International Conference on Software Engineering - Volume 2, ICSE 2015, pp. 467–476. IEEE Press (2015)
29. Torre, D., Procaccianti, G., Fucci, D., Lutovac, S., Scanniello, G.: On the presence of green and sustainable software engineering in higher education curricula. In: Proceedings of the 1st International Workshop on Software Engineering Curricula for Millennials, SECM 2017, pp. 54–60. IEEE Press (2017). https://doi.org/10.1109/SECM.2017.4
30. Penzenstadler, B., et al.: Everything is interrelated: teaching software engineering for sustainability. In: Proceedings of the 40th International Conference on Software Engineering: Software Engineering Education and Training, ICSE-SEET 2018, New York, NY, USA, pp. 153–162. Association for Computing Machinery (2018). https://doi.org/10.1145/3183377.3183382

31. Hamilton, M.: Learning and teaching computing sustainability. In: Proceedings of the 2015 ACM Conference on Innovation and Technology in Computer Science Education, ITiCSE 2015, New York, NY, USA, pp. 338. ACM (2015). https://doi.org/10.1145/2729094.2754850

32. Abernethy, K., Treu, K.: Integrating sustainability across the computer science curriculum. J. Comput. Sci. Coll. **30**(2), 220–228 (2014). https://dl.acm.org/doi/10.1145/1734263.1734439

33. Saraiva, J., Zong, Z., Pereira, R.: Bringing green software to computer science curriculum: perspectives from researchers and educators. In: Proceedings of the 26th ACM Conference on Innovation and Technology in Computer Science Education V. 1, ITiCSE 2021, New York, NY, USA, pp. 498–504. ACM (2021). https://doi.org/10.1145/3430665.3456386

34. Pattinson, C.: ICT and green sustainability research and teaching. IFAC-PapersOnLine 50 (1), 12938–12943 (2017). 20th IFAC World Congress. https://doi.org/10.1016/j.ifacol.2017.08.1794

35. Berntsen, K.R., Olsen, M.R., Limbu, N., Tran, A.T., Colomo-Palacios, R.: Sustainability in software engineering - a systematic mapping. In: CIMPS 2016. AISC, vol. 537, pp. 23–32. Springer, Cham (2017). https://doi.org/10.1007/978-3-319-48523-2_3

36. Wolfram, N., Lago, P., Osborne, F.: Sustainability in software engineering. In: Sustainable Internet and ICT for Sustainability (SustainIT) 2017, pp. 1–7 (2017)

37. Calero, C., Piattini, M.: Green in Software Engineering. Springer, Cham (2015). https://doi.org/10.1007/978-3-319-08581-4

38. Luttik, S.P., Visser, E.: Specification of rewriting strategies. In: Proceedings of the 2nd International Conference on Theory and Practice of Algebraic Specifications, Algebraic 1997, Swindon, GBR, p. 9. BCS Learning & Development Ltd. (1997)

39. Lämmel, R., Visser, J.: Typed combinators for generic traversal. In: Krishnamurthi, S., Ramakrishnan, C.R. (eds.) PADL 2002. LNCS, pp. 137–154. Springer, Heidelberg (2002). https://doi.org/10.1007/3-540-45587-6_10

40. Kiczales, G., Hilsdale, E.: Aspect-oriented programming. SIGSOFT Softw. Eng. Notes **26**(5), 313 (2001). https://doi.org/10.1145/503271.503260

41. David, H., Gorbatov, E., Hanebutte, U.R., Khanna, R., Le, C.: RAPL: memory power estimation and capping. In: International Symposium on Low-Power Electronics and Design (ISLPED), 2010 ACM/IEEE, pp. 189–194. IEEE (2010). https://doi.org/10.1145/1840845.1840883

42. Hähnel, M., Döbel, B., Völp, M., Härtig, H.: Measuring energy consumption for short code paths using RAPL. SIGMETRICS Perform. Eval. Rev. **40**(3), 13–17 (2012). https://doi.org/10.1145/2425248.2425252

43. Fowler, M.: Refactoring: Improving the Design of Existing Code. Addison-Wesley Longman Publishing Co., Inc., USA (1999)

44. Mens, T., Tourwé, T.: A survey of software refactoring. IEEE Trans. Softw. Eng. **30**(2), 126–139 (2004). https://doi.org/10.1109/TSE.2004.1265817

45. Allman, E.: Managing technical debt. Commun. ACM **55**(5), 50–55 (2012). https://doi.org/10.1145/2160718.2160733

46. Couto, M., Maia, D., Saraiva, J., Pereira, R.: On energy debt: managing consumption on evolving software. In: Proceedings of the 3rd International Conference on Technical Debt, TechDebt 2020, ACM, New York, NY, USA, pp. 62–66 (2020). https://doi.org/10.1145/3387906.3388628

47. Wong, W.E., Gao, R., Li, Y., Abreu, R., Wotawa, F.: A survey on software fault localization. IEEE Trans. Software Eng. **42**(8), 707–740 (2016). https://doi.org/10.1109/TSE.2016.2521368

48. Abreu, R., Zoeteweij, P., van Gemund, A.J.: On the accuracy of spectrum-based fault localization, in: Testing: Academic and Industrial Conference Practice and Research Techniques - MUTATION, pp. 89–98 (2007)
49. Pereira, R., T. Carção, Couto, M., Cunha, J., Fernandes, J.P., Saraiva, J.: Helping programmers improve the energy efficiency of source code. In: Proceedings of the 39th International Conference on Software Engineering Companion, ICSE-C 2017, Piscataway, NJ, USA, pp. 238–240. IEEE Press (2017). https://doi.org/10.1109/ICSE-C.2017.80
50. Pereira, R., Carção, T., Couto, M., Cunha, J., Fernandes, J.P., Saraiva, J.: Spelling out energy leaks: aiding developers locate energy inefficient code. J. Syst. Software 161 (2020). https://doi.org/10.1016/j.jss.2019.110463
51. Goues, C.L., Pradel, M., Roychoudhury, A.: Automated program repair. Commun. ACM 62(12), 56–65 (2019). https://doi.org/10.1145/3318162
52. Pereira, R., Couto, M., Ribeiro, F., Rua, R., Saraiva, J.: Energyware analysis. In: 7th Workshop on Software Quality Analysis, Monitoring, Improvement, and Applications (SQAMIA), vol. 2217, CEUR Workshop Proceedings (2018)
53. Pereira, R.: Energyware engineering: techniques and tools for green software development, Ph.D. thesis, Universidade do Minho (2018)
54. Saraiva, J., Abreu, R., Cunha, J., Fernandes, J.P.: GreenSoftwareLab: towards an engineering discipline for green software, Impact 2018 (1) (2018). https://doi.org/10.21820/23987073.2018.9
55. Maia, D., Couto, M., Saraiva, J., Pereira, R.: E-Debitum: managing software energy debt. In: Proceedings of the 35th IEEE/ACM International Conference on Automated Software Engineering Workshops, New York, NY, USA, pp. 170–177. ACM (2020). https://doi.org/10.1145/3417113.3422999
56. Kiselyov, O., Biboudis, A., Palladinos, N., Smaragdakis, Y.: Stream fusion, to completeness. In: Proceedings of the 44th ACM SIGPLAN Symposium on Principles of Programming Languages, POPL 2017, New York, NY, USA, pp. 285–299. Association for Computing Machinery (2017). https://doi.org/10.1145/3009837.3009880
57. Longo, M., Rodriguez, A., Mateos, C., Zunino, A.: Reducing energy usage in resource-intensive Java-based scientific applications via micro-benchmark based code refactorings. Comput. Sci. Inf. Syst. 16(2), 541–564 (2019). https://doi.org/10.2298/CSIS180608009L
58. Melfe, G., Fonseca, A., Fernandes, J.P.: Helping developers write energy efficient haskell through a data-structure evaluation. In: 2018 IEEE/ACM 6th International Workshop on Green And Sustainable Software (GREENS), pp. 9–15. IEEE (2018). https://doi.org/10.1145/3194078.3194080
59. Ribeiro, F., Saraiva, J., Pardo, A.: Java stream fusion: adapting FP mechanisms for an OO setting. In: Proceedings of the XXIII Brazilian Symposium on Programming Languages, SBLP 2019, New York, NY, USA, pp. 30–37. ACM (2019). https://doi.org/10.1145/3355378.3355386
60. Mendonça, W.L., et al.: Understanding the impact of introducing lambda expressions in Java programs. J. Software Eng. Res. Dev. 8(1–8), 22 (2020). https://sol.sbc.org.br/journals/index.php/jserd/article/view/744

Utilizing Rail Traffic Control Simulator in Verified Software Development Courses

Štefan Korečko[✉][iD]

Department of Computers and Informatics, Faculty of Electrical Engineering and
Informatics, Technical University of Košice, Košice, Slovakia
stefan.korecko@tuke.sk

Abstract. With the increasing dependency of our society on automated
systems, their correctness is of uttermost importance. Formal methods
for software development, such as the B-Method, belong to rigorous
approaches that may ensure the correctness. They offer mathematical
apparatuses to prove that the software under development meets the
corresponding requirements. But the need to comprehend such apparatus makes formal methods unpopular with students. They may not see
the reasons why to use them. And many formal method courses do not
include executable software development or the software developed is
not used in an appropriate environment. Both problems are addressed
by the TD/TS2JC toolset, described in this chapter. The toolset provides an appropriate virtual railway environment, where verified software controllers can run. The controllers can be developed with any formal method that offers translation to the Java programming language.
The chapter also describes two of several control interfaces the toolset
supports. It also introduces a compact, four to six hour long, course
on verified software development with the B-Method, which utilizes the
toolset.

Keywords: verified software · formal methods · B-Method · virtual
environment · course · teaching · railway

1 Introduction

One of the well-recognized approaches to the development of correct software
systems is the utilization of formal methods (FMs) for their specification and
verification. FMs are rigorous mathematically based techniques for the specification, analysis, development and verification of software and hardware. Rigorous
means that a formal method provides a formal language with unambiguously

This chapter is a result of the implementation of the Erasmus+ Key Action 2 project
No. 2017-1-SK01-KA203-035402: "Focusing Education on Composability, Comprehensibility and Correctness of Working Software".

Z. Porkoláb and V. Zsók (Eds.): CEFP 2019, LNCS 11950, pp. 98–135, 2023.
https://doi.org/10.1007/978-3-031-42833-3_4

defined syntax and semantics and mathematically based means that some mathematical apparatus (formal logic, set theory, etc.) is used to define the language.

The *B-Method* [1, 2, 11, 15] is a state based, model-oriented formal method, intended for verified software development. It is one of the few software-related FMs that is used commonly in industrial practice, primarily in the railway sector. In this area, it is utilized for the safety-critical software behind automated urban metro subway systems [5]. The strength of the B-Method lies in a well-defined development process, which allows to specify a software system as a collection of components, called abstract machines, and to refine such an abstract specification to a concrete, implementable one. The concrete specification can be automatically translated to ADA, C, Java or another programming language. An internal consistency of the abstract specification and correctness of each refinement step are verified by proving a set of predicates, called proof obligations (PObs). The whole development process, including proving, is supported by Atelier B [18], an industrial-strength software tool.

A significant challenge in teaching formal methods for software development, including the B-Method, is to design a corresponding course in such a way that students will be able to develop a working piece of software using the method. The problem is rooted in the limitations of formal method languages. These languages usually cover basic constructs only, such as assignments, compositions, operations and operation calls, conditional statements and loops. The interaction with the user is no supported at all or limited to the console level. The situation gets even more complicated if one wishes to use appropriate examples, clearly showing the benefits of FMs, as advocated in [12–14].

To deal with this challenge, we developed the *TD/TS2JC* software toolset, which provides a virtual environment for programs, developed by students using formal methods. The toolset consists of a modified version of the *Train Director* [17] simulation game and an application, called *TS2JavaConn*, which allows using separately developed software controllers with the game. The controllers are Java programs that control switches and signals in railway scenarios, simulated by the game. The interface of the control programs can be configured, so the toolset is suitable for various formal methods. There is only one requirement the formal method has to fulfill: the existence of a compiler from its language to Java. And because the controllers are in Java, the toolset can be also used in situations that don't involve formal methods at all.

While the previous works [9, 10] presented the toolset and its utilization in B-Method courses in general, here we discuss both of these topics in more depth. Section 2 describes the components of the TD/TS2JC toolset, their communication and usage. Section 3 presents and explains two different controller configurations and corresponding Java controllers. Section 4 presents a compact B-Method course, which utilizes the toolset. The total duration of the course is estimated to four to six hours, so it is ideal for special events, such as summer schools. The chapter concludes with an evaluation of a particular run of the course in Sect. 5.

2   TD/TS2JC Toolset

It is no surprise that rail traffic control systems, primarily those related to signaling [5], are one of the most successful domains of formal methods utilization. This can be attributed to two factors. First, the movement of trains is limited by tracks, which makes an automated control of their operation much easier than, for example, that of the road vehicles. Second, the railway is used to transport large number of passengers and goods at once, so individual accidents may have more severe consequences than those of other types of vehicles. Therefore, methods providing means to ensure the correctness of these control systems should be used. This special position of the rail traffic control systems was the primary reason why we decided to use virtual environments inspired by such systems in our FMs course. The decision was reinforced by the fact that the topic of our course is the B-Method and the B-Method played a key role in the verified development of the railway control software [5].

In order to provide virtual rail traffic control environments, we developed the *TD/TS2JC toolset*, consisting of two software applications. The first one is a modified version of an already existing simulation game, called *Train Director* (*TD*) [17]. The second one is *TS2JavaConn*, a newly developed Java application. The virtual environments are railway scenarios, simulated in TD. Signals and switches in these scenarios are managed by controllers (*control modules*) developed by students in the B-Method and translated to Java. TS2JavaConn serves as a proxy between TD and the control module. It listens to events occurring in the simulated scenario and executes methods of the control module accordingly. Subsequently, it informs TD about changes that should be applied to the scenario. Each control module is accompanied by a configuration file that defines how the events are translated to the method calls.

From the beginning of the toolset development, our goal was to provide a solution that is not limited to the B-Method. This is why we do not deal with formal methods at all in this section. The same is true for Sect. 3, where the control modules are presented on the Java language level only. The utilization in a formal methods course is shown in Sect. 4. The toolset, together with a set of examples, is available at [6].

2.1   Train Director

Train Director (*TD*) is a computer game, which simulates the work of the rail centralized traffic control (CTC). A railway scenario in TD consists of a track layout (track plan) and a train schedule. The player's task is to manipulate the signals and switches in the scenario in such a way that the trains arrive and depart according to the schedule. In TD/TS2JC, which uses the version 3.7 of TD, the task is carried out by the control module. This required several modifications of the simulator.

The first modification was a removal of those control mechanisms that should be implemented in control modules. The removed mechanisms, for example, prevented trains from colliding or entering the same section at once. As the removal enabled train crashes, the next modification was an addition of train collision detection. The most significant change was an update of the communication subsystem of TD. The subsystem included in the version 3.7 of TD allowed to control the simulation remotely by means of messages that emulate user interaction. For example, when a user clicked somewhere in the simulator, a message in the form `click x y`, where x and y are coordinates of the location where he or she clicked, has been sent. Events such as a train entering the layout or waiting for a green signal were not handled at all. The updated version communicates with TS2JC. It sends information about the status of signals and switches and about events triggered by train operation to TS2JC. From TS2JC, it receives new states of signals and switches, computed by the control module. The communication is described in more detail in Sect. 2.3. The last modification was an implementation of a scanning process that creates a list of track sections of the layout. By track sections we mean track segments between signals, switches and entry points. The entry points are places where a train may enter or leave the layout.

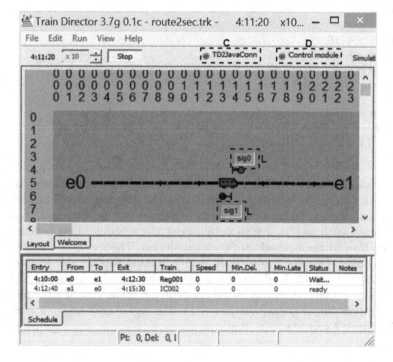

Fig. 1. Modified Train Director during simulation. Features specific to TD/TS2JC are marked with (red) dashed rectangles and labeled by letters C, D and L. (Color figure online)

New features have been also implemented to the GUI of the simulator (Fig. 1). These include the indication of the connection with TS2JC (C in Fig. 1) and presence of the control module (D) and the possibility to show labels (L) with the names of switches and signals in the layout. The scenario shown in Fig. 1 is probably the simplest one that is usable for teaching purposes. It is also utilized in the short course, presented in Sect. 4. The layout of the scenario contains one straight track (the thick black dashed line in Fig. 1) with two entry points (e0, e1) and two signals (sig0, sig1). As with the real railway, the signals guard the entrance to the track ahead of them. Here, sig0 is meant for the trains coming from the west (from e0) and sig1 for the trains coming from the east (from e1). In TD, the trains always obey the corresponding signals. The trains are represented by orange train engine icons. In Fig. 1, a train named Reg001 is passing the signal sig0, which is green. The scanning process mentioned above detects two sections in the layout. The first one is between e0 and the signals and the second one is between the signals and e1. If there are more signals at the same place, the one guarding the section is used to name it. So, the sections in Fig. 1 are (e0, sig1) and (sig0, e1).

Listing 1. Train schedule route2sec.sch.

```
1  #!trdir
2  # no deadlock − delays between trains long enough
3  Start: 4:10
4  Train: Reg001
5    Enter: 04:10,  e0
6           04:12:30, −,  e1
7  .
8  Train: IC002
9    Enter: 04:12:40,  e1
10          04:15:30, −,  e0
11 .
```

The trains operate according to a schedule, given in a form of a text file with the extension sch. The scenario in Fig. 1 uses the schedule shown in Listing 1. Line 1 is mandatory. Other lines starting with the "#" character are regarded as comments, such as line 2 with notes about the schedule. Line 3 defines the simulated time at the beginning of each simulation. The rest of the file contains train schedules. The first train (lines 4–7) is named Reg001 and it enters the layout from e0 at 4:10. It should leave the layout through e1 at 4:12:30. The second train is IC002. It travels in the opposite direction, entering the layout at 4:12:40. Its schedule is defined on lines 8–11. The end of each schedule is marked by a dot (lines 7 and 11).

2.2 TS2JavaConn

The second part of the toolset is a Java application called *TS2JavaConn*. Its name is a shortcut for Train Simulator to Java Connector. TS2JavaConn serves as a middleman between the modified Train Director and control modules.

Control modules are loaded directly to TS2JavaConn, which uses the Java Reflection API to call its methods and process their return values. On the other hand, TS2JavaConn maintains a TCP connection with the updated communication subsystem of TD. The connection is used to receive messages about events occurring in TD during the simulation and to send commands that change the state of track devices in TD. Each message received from TD is translated to a call of a method from the control module. And each command sent to TD is constructed according to the state of the control module. TS2JavaConn allows various styles of control modules and each module has a configuration file that defines how messages from TD are translated to method calls and how to read the state of the control module. Concrete examples of control modules and configuration files are given in Sect. 3 and interaction between the module and TD is explained in detail in Sect. 2.3.

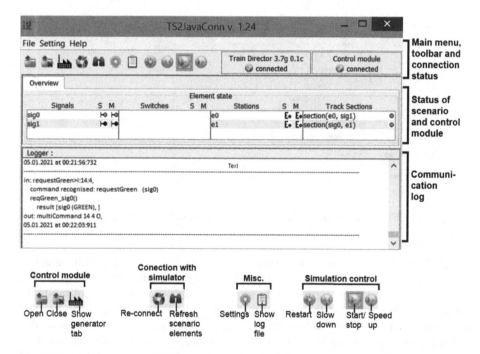

Fig. 2. Primary screen of TS2JavaConn (top) and description of its control panel buttons (bottom).

The primary screen of TS2JavaConn is shown in Fig. 2, which captures the application in the same moment as TD in Fig. 1. The screen is divided into three parts. The first one contains the main menu and toolbar for handling control modules, connection with the simulator and controlling the simulation remotely. It also includes connection status indicators with the same functionality as the ones added to TD (C and D in Fig. 1). The second part lists signals, switches, stations and track sections of the scenario. It also shows the state of these elements in TD (the "S" column) and in the control module (the "M" column). For the track sections, only the state from the control module is shown and it works only if the control module contains corresponding methods (getters). As we can see, the entry points are also treated as stations. The third part is a logger that shows detailed information about the communication between the simulator and the control module. In the case of an incorrect control module or configuration file, it also shows corresponding error messages. All the information shown in this part is saved to a log file, which can be opened from the toolbar. TS2JavaConn can be used with modified versions of two different simulators – Train Director and Open Rails [8]. When TS2JavaConn is opened, it searches for running instances of these simulators and let the user choose the one to connect to. The same thing happens after hitting the "Re-connect" button from the toolbar.

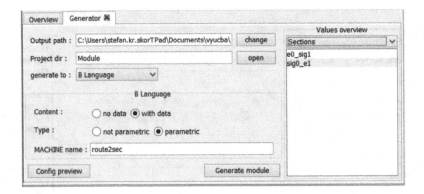

Fig. 3. Control module generator screen of TS2JavaConn.

TS2JavaConn also offers a secondary screen with a control module generator (Fig. 3). The screen is activated by the "Show generator tab" button. The generator can create configuration files and template code for control modules in Java and languages of two formal methods – the B-Method and the Perfect Developer. The template code contains headers of all necessary methods (operations) and may also include variables representing the scenario elements. For Java and the B-Method, two types of control modules are available: parametric and non-parametric. Examples of both are given in Sect. 3.

2.3 Communication with Control Modules

As we will see later, in Sect. 3, each control module contains a *central class* with two types of methods:

- *getters*, which return values of module variables that correspond to states of track elements in the simulated scenario and
- *modifiers*, which are called when an event occurs in the simulated scenario. They may change the values of the module variables.

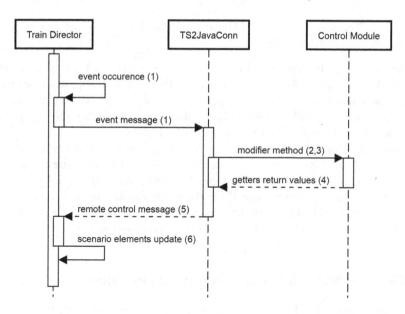

Fig. 4. UML sequence diagram illustrating event handling in TD/TS2JC. The numbers in brackets are numbers of steps in the description of the event handling process.

By *track elements* we mean entry points, signals, switches, stations and track sections. However, it is not necessary to define getters for all of them. In total, there are five types of events:

- A train requests to enter the scenario via an entry point.
- A train stops before a red signal and requests the signal to be cleared.
- A train departs from a station.
- A train leaves a track section.
- A train enters a track section.

TD/TS2JC handles every event in the following way (Fig. 4):

1. After an event occurs, TD composes a message about the event and sends it to TS2JavaConn. The message contains the type of the event and data about involved scenario elements and train.
2. TS2JavaConn reads the event message, received from TD, and identifies the corresponding modifier method of the control module.
3. TS2JavaConn calls the modifier method. Some parts of the method name or the values of its parameters may be composed from the data received from TD.
4. After the call of the modifier method is completed, TS2JavaConn calls all the getters of the control module and composes a remote control message from the values the getters return.
5. TS2JavaConn sends the remote control message to TD.

6. TD reads the message from TS2JavaConn and changes the states of the scenario elements accordingly.

The process of the event handling can be also observed in Fig. 1 and 2, which capture the simulation right after the event "Train Reg001 requests sig0 to be cleared" was handled. In the logger part of TS2JavaConn (Fig. 2), we can see that a modifier method[1] named reqGreen_sig0 was called after the event. And finally, sig0 has been changed to green in TD (Fig. 1).

Communication similar to the event handling also happens when a control module is opened: First, the control module is initiated by creating an instance of its central class. The constructor of the class sets the module variables to their initial values. TS2JavaConn reads these values by calling the getters. As in the case of the events, TS2JavaConn then composes a message from the values and sends the message to TD. Finally, TD sets the scenario elements accordingly and starts the simulation.

3   Control Modules and Configuration Files

When developing the TD/TS2JC toolset, one of the most important objectives was to be able to use outputs of verified software development tools as control modules without any or with minimal modifications. To reach this objective, it was necessary to support various forms of the control module interface, that is of the getters and the modifiers. The form of the interface is defined in a configuration file, accompanying each control module. In this section we present two distinct control modules for the scenario from Fig. 1. Both provide the same functionality but differ significantly in the interface.

The first one is introduced in Sect. 3.1 and is an example of so-called *non-parametric module*. This means that none of its getters and modifiers has input parameters and event data from TD are part of the names of the methods. The second one, in Sect. 3.2, is a fully *parametric module*, where all the event data translate to values of parameters of corresponding methods. It is also possible to create hybrid modules, where some of the data become parts of the method names and other are parameters.

The description of each control module and configuration file is given in the following way. First, the complete source code is presented as a listing. The source codes contain comments marking corresponding parts in terms introduced in Sect. 2.3. The comments start with "//" in the control modules and with "--" in the configuration files. Each listing is followed by a description giving more details about the code, referencing the corresponding code lines.

3.1   Non-parametric Module

From a conventional programmer point of view, it may look irrational to support non-parametric modules. This is because such modules require a separate

---

[1] The control module used in this case is the one from Listing 2 and the method is on lines 49–51.

method for each combination of the event and used data values received from TD. However, the support solves two problems related to the utilization of the toolset in teaching verified software development with formal methods.

First, languages of some formal methods (FMs) may not allow to use input parameters in specification units[2] that translate to the methods of the module. They may only allow units defining simple state transitions, without an external influence, which is usually represented by the input parameters.

Second, even if given formal method (FM) supports input parameters, the ability to use fully functional programs (control modules) without them may come very handy in the teaching process. For example, in an introductory part of a longer course. Or in a short course that teaches only the basics of the corresponding FM, where aspects of the method related to the utilization of input parameters are not tackled at all. The latter is also the case of the course introduced in Sect. 4, where a non-parametric one, similar to the module route2sec, presented here, is used. The complete source code of route2sec in Java can be found in Listing 2.

Listing 2. Non-parametric control module for the scenario from Fig. 1.

```java
 1  public class route2sec {
 2
 3  //Sets defining states of track elements
 4  //(entry points & signals, switches, sections)
 5    public enum ST_SIG {
 6      green(0), red(1);
 7      public final int index;
 8      ST_SIG(int index) { this.index = index; }
 9    }
10    public enum ST_SWCH {
11      switched(0), none(1);
12      public final int index;
13      ST_SWCH(int index) { this.index = index; }
14    }
15    public enum ST_SEC {
16      free(0), occup(1);
17      public final int index;
18      ST_SEC(int index) { this.index = index; }
19    }
20
21  //Variables for entry points, signals and sections
22    private route2sec.ST_SIG e0,e1,sig0,sig1;
23    private route2sec.ST_SEC e0_sig1,sig0_e1;
24
25  //Constructor setting the initial state of the elements
```

---

[2] We use the term "specification unit" as the corresponding parts (units) of formal specifications are named differently in different FMs. For example, they are called operations in the B-Method, events in the Event-B and schemas in the Perfect Developer.

```
26    public route2sec() {
27      e0 = ST_SIG.red; e1 = ST_SIG.red;
28      sig0 = ST_SIG.red; sig1 = ST_SIG.red;
29      e0_sig1 = ST_SEC.free; sig0_e1 = ST_SEC.free;
30    }
31
32  //Getters for entry points and signals
33    public route2sec.ST_SIG getEntry_e0() { return e0; }
34    public route2sec.ST_SIG getEntry_e1() { return e1; }
35    public route2sec.ST_SIG getSig_sig0() { return sig0; }
36    public route2sec.ST_SIG getSig_sig1() { return sig1; }
37
38  //Modifier called when a train requests to enter from e0
39    public void reqGreen_e0() {
40      if (sig1 == ST_SIG.red && e0_sig1 == ST_SEC.free)
41        e0 = ST_SIG.green; }
42
43  //Modifier called when a train requests to enter from e1
44    public void reqGreen_e1() {
45      if (sig0 == ST_SIG.red && sig0_e1 == ST_SEC.free)
46        e1 = ST_SIG.green; }
47
48  //Modifier called when a train requests to clear sig0
49    public void reqGreen_sig0() {
50      if (e1 == ST_SIG.red && sig0_e1 == ST_SEC.free)
51        sig0 = ST_SIG.green; }
52
53  //Modifier called when a train requests to clear sig1
54    public void reqGreen_sig1() {
55      if (e0 == ST_SIG.red && e0_sig1 == ST_SEC.free)
56        sig1 = ST_SIG.green; }
57
58  //Modifiers called when a train enters the corresponding
59  //section from the corresponding direction
60    public void enterNI_e0_sig1() {
61      e0_sig1 = ST_SEC.occup;
62      e0 = ST_SIG.red; sig1 = ST_SIG.red; }
63
64    public void enterIN_sig0_e1() {
65      sig0_e1 = ST_SEC.occup;
66      sig0 = ST_SIG.red; e1 = ST_SIG.red; }
67
68    public void enterNI_e1_sig0() {
69      sig0_e1 = ST_SEC.occup;
70      sig0 = ST_SIG.red; e1 = ST_SIG.red; }
71
72    public void enterIN_sig1_e0() {
73      e0_sig1 = ST_SEC.occup;
74      e0 = ST_SIG.red; sig1 = ST_SIG.red; }
75
```

```
76  //Modifiers called when a train leaves the corresponding
77  //section from the corresponding direction
78    public void leaveNI_e0_sig1() { e0_sig1 = ST_SEC.free; }
79    public void leaveIN_sig1_e0() { e0_sig1 = ST_SEC.free; }
80
81    public void leaveIN_sig0_e1() { sig0_e1 = ST_SEC.free; }
82    public void leaveNI_e1_sig0() { sig0_e1 = ST_SEC.free; }
83
84  }
```

The whole module route2sec is defined in its central class, with the same name. It uses values from enumerated sets for the states of signals (the set ST_SIG), switches (ST_SWCH) and track sections (ST_SEC). The sets[3] are defined on lines 5–19 of the module. The set ST_SWCH (lines 10–14) can be excluded as the layout does not contain switches.

The instance variables, defined on lines 22–23, provide an internal representation of the state of the scenario. Here we have a separate variable for each entry point, signal and section and the variables have the same names as the corresponding elements in the scenario. However, such one-to-one correspondence between the elements and the variables is not mandatory. A programmer is free to choose whatever representation desired as the variables of the module are never accessed directly when communicating with TD. The variables are initialized in the constructor on lines 26–30.

Lines 33–36 contain the getters, returning the states of entry points and signals. These getters are mandatory[4]. The module may also include getters for the track sections, but their only purpose is to display states of the sections in TS2JavaConn.

Lines 39–56 define modifiers called when a train wants to enter the scenario from the corresponding entry point or clear the corresponding signal. All four of them work in the same way: "Check whether the section to be entered is free and closed from the other side. If yes, set the signals and entry points involved accordingly."

The next four modifiers (lines 60–74) respond to the "train entering a section" events. There are four of them, while the scenario contains only two sections. This is because there is a separate method for each direction. The direction to which the method belongs is defined by the order of the track element names in its header. For example, enterNI_e0_sig1 is called when a train enters the section (sig0, e1) from e0 and enterIN_sig1_e0 when it enters the same section from sig1. The letter "N" in method names means "entry point" and "I" means "signal". These shortcuts have been introduced to ensure unambiguity when different types of track elements have the same names. Each of these methods marks the corresponding section as occupied and sets the signals guarding it to red. Similar modifiers for the "train leaving a section" events are defined on lines 78–82.

---

[3] Technically, the enumerated sets are classes, too.

[4] If a scenario contains switches, their getters are mandatory, too.

For TS2JavaConn to understand the control module from Listing 2, the configuration file shown in Listing 3 is needed.

Listing 3. Configuration file of the non-parametric module from Listing 2.

```
 1  mainClassName=route2sec.class
 2
 3  –– Entry point representation and getters
 4  entryState=ST_SIG
 5  entryOpenState=green
 6  entryCloseState=red
 7  getEntryNames=getEntry_%name%
 8  getEntryOut=%ST_SIG%
 9
10  –– Signal representation and getters
11  sigState=ST_SIG
12  signalGreenState=green
13  signalRedState=red
14  getSignalNames=getSig_%name%
15  getSignalOut=%ST_SIG%
16
17  –– Switch representation and getters
18  swchState=ST_SWCH
19  switchOpenState=switched
20  switchCloseState=none
21  getSwitchNames=getSwch_%name%
22  getSwitchOut=%ST_SWCH%
23
24  –– Section representation
25  sectionState=ST_SEC
26  sectionFreeState=free
27  sectionOccupState=occup
28
29  –– Modifiers for train requests to enter the scenario,
30  –– clear a signal and depart a station
31  requestDepartureEntry=reqGreen_%name%
32  requestGreen=reqGreen_%name%
33  requestDepartureStation=%ignore%
34
35  –– Modifiers for section entering and leaving events
36  sectionEnter=
        enter%shortcutAct%%shortcutNxt%_%nameAct%_%nameNxt%
37  sectionLeave=
        leave%shortcutPre%%shortcutAct%_%namePre%_%nameAct%
38
39  –– Track element shortcuts
40  signalShortcut=I
41  switchShortcut=W
42  entryShortcut=N
```

The first line of the file in Listing 3 specifies the filename of the compiled version of the control module central class. Lines 4–27 define how the track elements, namely entry points, signals, switches and sections, are represented and how the corresponding getters look.

For entry points, the representation and getters definition is given on lines 4–8. In this case, the states of the entry points are values from an enumerated set named ST_SIG (line 4). It is also possible to use the integer (value %int%) or the boolean (value %boolean%) type for the state values. Line 5 defines the value for an opened entry point and line 6 for a closed entry point.

The interface of the entry point getters is given on lines 7–8. The name of the getter is specified on line 7 as a combination of a fixed part and the placeholder %name%, which means the corresponding entry point name in the scenario. Two additional placeholders can be used when naming the getters:

- %number% – the numerical part of the element name and
- %shortcut% – a shortcut of the corresponding track element type. The shortcuts are defined on lines 40–42.

It is possible to combine the placeholders. For example, if line 7 in Listing 3 has been defined as

```
7  getEntryNames=get%shortcut%%number%
```

then the getters for the entry points will be

```
33  public  route2sec.ST_SIG getN0() { return e0; }
34  public  route2sec.ST_SIG getN1() { return e1; }
```

The return type of the entry point getters is specified on line 8. If it is an enumerated set, as in this case, its name is enclosed in the percent signs (% ST_SIG%) and only the set already defined for the corresponding state values (line 4) can be used.

In the same way, the representation and getters are defined for signals (lines 11–15) and switches (lines 18–22). As this scenario does not contain switches, lines 18–22 can be omitted. We included them primarily to explain the switch state values, which may not be clear from the names of the corresponding properties. Line 19 defines the value used for a switch set to the diverging track (value switched) and line 20 the value for the straight track. The part for sections (lines 25–27) lacks the properties getSectionNames and getSectionOut as there are no section getters in the control module. These properties are used in the configuration file in Listing 5.

The names of the modifiers are given on lines 30–37. The names of the methods called when a train requests to enter the scenario (line 31) or to clear a signal (line 32) are defined in the same way as for the getters. Line 33 sets the names of modifiers called when a train leaves a station. Our module does not contain any stations. Therefore, we decided to use the %ignore% placeholder to indicate that the module does not handle such events. A rather complicated interface of the modifiers for the section entering (line 36) and section leaving (line 37) events requires six placeholders:

– %shortcutAct% and %nameAct% – the shortcut and name of the scenario element from which the train enters or leaves the track section,
– %shortcutNxt% and %nameNxt% – the shortcut and name of the element from which the train will leave the section it is now entering and
– %shortcutPre% and %namePre% – the shortcut and name of the element from which the train entered the section it is now leaving.

The configuration file ends with the definition of the shortcuts for signals, switches and entry points on lines 40–42. Line 41 is for switches, so it can be omitted.

3.2 Parametric Module

Albeit it is not so obvious in this case, parametric modules offer more compact interface as there is no need for a separate method for each combination of involved scenario elements. The parametric module route2secP (Listing 4) controls the scenario in the same way as the nonparametric route2sec from Listing 2, but there are several differences in the interface and representation of the scenario elements and their states:

– scenario elements are defined as members of the enumerated sets SIGNALS and SECTIONS,
– states of the scenario elements are expressed as integers,
– instance variables are arrays of the scenario elements state values and
– scenario elements related to the getters and modifiers are given as their parameters.

Listing 4. Parametric control module for the scenario from Fig. 1.

```
1  public class route2secP {
2
3  //Sets defining track elements
4  //(entry points & signals, sections)
5    public enum SIGNALS {
6      e0(0), e1(1), sig0(2), sig1(3);
7      public final int index;
8      SIGNALS(int index) {
9        this.index = index; }
10   }
11   public enum SECTIONS {
12     e0_sig1(0), sig0_e1(1);
13     public final int index;
14     SECTIONS(int index) {
15       this.index = index; }
16   }
17
18  //Array variables for entry points & signals and sections
19    private int[] signals = {0,0,0,0}; //entry p. & signals
```

```
20    private int [] sections = {0,0};
21
22 //constructor (empty)
23    public route2secP() {       }
24
25 //Getters for entry points & signals and sections
26    public int getSig(route2secP.SIGNALS sig) {
27      return signals[sig.index]; }
28    public int getSec(route2secP.SECTIONS sec) {
29      return sections[sec.index];}
30
31 //Modifier called when a train requests to enter from e0/e1
32    public void reqEnter(route2secP.SIGNALS sig) {
33      switch (sig) {
34        case e0:
35          if ((signals[SIGNALS.e0.index] == 0   &&
36                signals[SIGNALS.sig1.index] == 0 &&
37                sections[SECTIONS.e0_sig1.index] == 0)) {
38                  signals[SIGNALS.e0.index] = 1;
39          } break;
40        case e1:
41          if ((signals[SIGNALS.e1.index] == 0   &&
42                signals[SIGNALS.sig0.index] == 0 &&
43                sections[SECTIONS.sig0_e1.index] == 0)) {
44                  signals[SIGNALS.e1.index] = 1;
45          } break;
46      }
47    }
48
49 //Modifier called when a train requests to clear sig0/sig1
50    public void reqGreen(route2secP.SIGNALS sig) {
51      switch (sig) {
52        case sig0:
53          if ((signals[SIGNALS.sig0.index] == 0 &&
54                signals[SIGNALS.e1.index] == 0   &&
55                sections[SECTIONS.sig0_e1.index] == 0)) {
56                  signals[SIGNALS.sig0.index] = 1;
57          } break;
58        case sig1:
59          if ((signals[SIGNALS.sig1.index] == 0 &&
60                signals[SIGNALS.e0.index] == 0 &&
61                sections[SECTIONS.e0_sig1.index] == 0)) {
62                  signals[SIGNALS.sig1.index] = 1;
63          } break;
64      }
65    }
66
67 //Modifier called when a train enters a section
68    public void enter(route2secP.SECTIONS sec) {
69      switch (sec) {
```

```
70      case e0_sig1 :
71         sections [SECTIONS . e0_sig1 . index ] = 1;
72         signals [SIGNALS . e0 . index ] = 0;
73         signals [SIGNALS . sig1 . index ] = 0;
74         break ;
75      case sig0_e1 :
76         sections [SECTIONS . sig0_e1 . index ] = 1;
77         signals [SIGNALS . e1 . index ] = 0;
78         signals [SIGNALS . sig0 . index ] = 0;
79         break ;
80      }
81    }
82
83 //Modifier called when a train leaves a section
84   public void leave ( route2secP .SECTIONS sec ) {
85      sections [ sec . index ] = 0;    }
86 }
```

As in the case of route2sec, the parametric module is defined in one class (Listing 4). And again, the code of the class starts with enumerated sets declarations (lines 5–16 in Listing 4). However, the sets SIGNALS and SECTIONS hold scenario elements and not their states. These sets are needed because the elements are parameters of the methods of the module. On the other hand, the element states are integers (0 and 1) here, so no enumerated sets for them are necessary.

Regarding the enumerated sets, there is one more difference between this module and the non-parametric one. In Java, each member of an enumerated set is represented by its name and index. The non-parametric route2sec uses only the values while route2secP relies heavily on the indices. This is because the instance variables (lines 19–20) are arrays that hold values of the scenario elements states on the positions given by the corresponding indices in the enumerated sets (for signals in SIGNALS and for sections in SECTIONS). The variables are initialized when declared, so the constructor (line 23) is empty.

The getters are defined on lines 26–29 and the modifiers occupy the rest of the module. The getter getSig returns states of the entry points and signals and getSec of the track sections. A getter may have only one input parameter, the element which state it returns. The modifier reqEnter is called when a train wishes to enter the scenario via e0 or e1 and reqGreen when it requests to clear sig0 or sig1. All section entering events are handled by the method enter and all section leaving ones by leave. A parametric module may be defined in a different, probably simpler, way. The form presented here has been chosen because it is nearly identical to a parametric module when developed in the B-Method using the template code generated by TS2JavaConn.

The configuration file of the module route2secP can be found in Listing 5 and follows the same structure as the one in Listing 3. Regarding the differences, this file contains additional properties for method parameters and track element representation and the unnecessary properties related to switches are excluded.

A minor difference is also the utilization of the integer type (placeholder %int%) and the values 0 and 1 for the track element states.

Listing 5. Configuration file of the parametric module from Listing 4.

```
 1  mainClassName=route2secP
 2
 3  --- Entry point representation and getters
 4  entryState=%int%
 5  entryOpenState=1
 6  entryCloseState=0
 7  entryIndex=SIGNALS
 8  entryIndexName=%name%
 9  getEntryNames=getSig
10  getEntryParams=%SIGNALS%
11  getEntryOut=%int%
12
13  --- Signal representation and getters
14  sigState=%int%
15  signalGreenState=1
16  signalRedState=0
17  sigIndex=SIGNALS
18  sigIndexName=%name%
19  getSignalNames=getSig
20  getSignalParams=%SIGNALS%
21  getSignalOut=%int%
22
23  --- Section representation and getters
24  sectionState=%int%
25  sectionFreeState=0
26  sectionOccupState=1
27  sectionIndex=SECTIONS
28  sectionIndexName=%west%_%east%
29  getSectionNames=getSec
30  getSectionParams=%SECTIONS%
31  getSectionOut=%int%
32
33  --- Modifiers for train requests to enter the scenario,
34  --- clear a signal and depart a station
35  requestDepartureEntry=reqEnter
36  requestDepartureEntryParams=%SIGNALS%
37  requestGreen=reqGreen
38  requestGreenParams=%SIGNALS%
39  requestDepartureStation=%ignore%
40
41  --- Modifiers for section entering and leaving events
42  sectionEnter=enter
43  sectionEnterParams=%SECTIONS%
44  sectionLeave=leave
45  sectionLeaveParams=%SECTIONS%
```

The properties defining the parameters of the getters and modifiers can be found on lines 10, 20, 30, 36, 38, 43 and 45 in Listing 5. In general, their values are comma-separated lists of placeholders, defining the types of the parameters of the corresponding methods. In this module, all methods have only one parameter, so there is always just one value for each property.

As track elements are now members of enumerated sets, additional properties are required to define them. For the entry points, these can be found on lines 7–8 in Listing 5. Line 7 specifies the name of the enumerated set and line 8 how the names of its members are constructed from the entry points in the scenario. The property on line 8 can use the placeholders %name%, %number% and %shortcut%, in the same way as already discussed in Sect. 3.1. The same properties for signals are on lines 17–18 and for sections on lines 27–28. The section names (line 28) are formed from

- the name of the track element on their west (left) end (placeholder %west%),
- the underscore and
- the name of the track element on their east (right) end (%east%).

How the section names look in the module route2secP can be seen on line 12 in Listing 4.

4   Teaching Verified Software Development in B-Method with TD/TS2JC Toolset

In this section, we describe a course on Software Development with the B-Method, which utilizes the toolset. The course is intended for events such as summer schools and its typical duration is four to six hours. The description provided here covers both the body of knowledge to be given to the course participants and the process of the course, including examples and tasks.

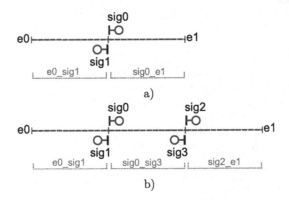

Fig. 5. Track layouts of scenarios used in the course: a straight track with two (a) and three (b) sections.

The language and development process of the B-Method is explained on a control module for a straight track with two sections (Fig. 5 a). The module is equivalent to the one in Listing 2. Within the course, the participants develop a similar control module for a straight track with three sections (Fig. 5 b). Both modules are non-parametric and, except of the class name on line 1, they use the same configuration file as the one in Listing 3.

The course starts with the lecturer informing the participants that the B-Method [1, 2, 11, 15] was originally developed by J.R. Abrial and combines his previous invention, the Z-notation [16], with a minimalistic programming language, based on the language of Guarded commands [4] by E.W. Dijkstra. According to the taxonomy presented in [3], the B-Method belongs to so-called heavyweight formal methods as it involves theorem proving to verify software correctness.

4.1   Software Development Process of B-Method

The highlight of the method is the development process that fully incorporates formal verification. First, a formal specification of a system, consisting of components called abstract machines, is written. An abstract machine, or simply a machine, consists of a set of variables that defines its state and a set of operations that define state transitions. The specification of each machine (which has variables) contains a formula that defines its invariant properties. The B-Method allows to formally prove that these properties hold in every state of the machine. Machines are then developed to implementable components, called implementations.

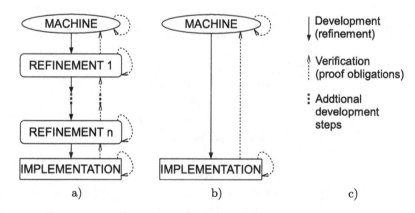

Fig. 6. Development of a specification component in B-Method: in general (a), in the course (b), legend (c).

This development process, which is also called stepwise refinement, consists of one or more steps. Multiple-steps process (Fig. 6 a) involves intermediate components, called refinements. One-step process (Fig. 6 b) goes directly from a machine to an implementation and it is the one chosen for this course. Refinements and implementations are components similar to machines. They contain invariant properties, too. These properties also define a relation between their variables and the variables of components they refine. And, again, it is possible to formally prove that they hold in each state of the component. In this way, it is possible to verify that the properties once defined at the abstract level (machines) still hold in the executable implementation. This is the reason why we can say that the B-Method offers a verified software development process. At each step, the specification may consist of multiple components and the number of components may vary. The number of refinement steps can also be different for each component. In this short course, we develop a control module that consists of one component, refined in one step from a machine to an implementation. Of course, the TD/TS2JC toolset allows for modules developed from multiple components, as it is shown in [9].

4.2   B-Language

The course continues with an explanation of the B-language, a specification language in which the components are written. The B-language can be divided to two parts:

- A *mathematical notation* to write expressions and predicates on data in terms of the Zermelo-Fraenkel set theory.
- The *Generalized Substitution Language (GSL)*, a minimalistic programming language with the formal semantics defined by the weakest pre-condition calculus [4].

Table 1. Selected operators of the mathematical notation of B-language.

Operator	Meaning
&	and (logical conjunction)
not	not (logical negation)
=>	then (logical implication)
<=>	logical equivalence
=	equals
{	start of a set
}	end of a set
:	belongs to (a member to a set)

The mathematical notation is quite complex, fortunately we need just a small portion of it here. This portion is given in Table 1.

The commands of GSL are called *generalized substitutions (GS)* and those relevant to the course are listed in Table 2. The symbols introduced in Table 2 have the following meaning:

Table 2. Selected commands of GSL and their informal meaning.

Command	Meaning
skip	Do nothing
x := e	Assignment of values of expressions e to variables x
S1 ; S2	Sequential composition: do S1, then S2
S1 ‖ S2	Parallel composition: do S1 and S2 at once
PRE E THEN S1 END	If E holds, do S1. Otherwise, do anything
SELECT E THEN S1 END	If E holds, do S1. Otherwise, do not execute
CHOICE S1 OR S2 END	Bounded choice: do S1 or S2
IF E THEN S1 ELSE S2 END	If E holds, do S1. Otherwise, do S2

- x is a comma-separated list of variables,
- e is a comma-separated list of expressions over variables, with the same length as x,
- S1 and S2 are GS (GSL commands) and
- P and E are predicates.

In the case that the ELSE branch is omitted in the IF command, S2 is considered equal to skip. There are two significant omissions in Table 2. The first one is so-called unbounded non-determinism, which is like the bounded choice, but allows to introduce local variables. The second one is a do-while loop, which includes a loop invariant. Both of them, together with other, derived, GSL commands, and the mathematical notation are described in [1,11,15].

The formal semantics of GS is defined in the *weakest pre-condition calculus* of E.W. Dijkstra [4]. The *weakest pre-condition of a GS S1 with respect to a post-condition P* is the predicate (1),

$$[S1]P \tag{1}$$

which is satisfied in exactly all states from which an execution of S1 is guaranteed to terminate in a state satisfying P.

The weakest pre-conditions of the commands from Table 2 can be found in Table 3. The operators are from the mathematical notation and are listed in Table 1. The notation (2)

$$P[x := e] \tag{2}$$

is the predicate P with all free occurrences of variables from x replaced by the corresponding expressions from e.

There are two interesting things one may notice in Table 3. First, the IF command is just a combination of the commands CHOICE and SELECT and it can be written in the form (3).

$$\text{CHOICE SELECT E THEN S1 END OR} \\ \text{SELECT not(E) THEN S2 END END} \tag{3}$$

Table 3. Formal semantics of GSL commands from Table 2.

Command	Weakest pre-condition
[skip]P	P
[x := e]P	P[x := e]
[S1 ; S2]P	[S1]([S2]P)
[PRE E THEN S1 END]P	E & [S1]P
[SELECT E THEN S1 END]P	E =>[S1]P
[CHOICE S1 OR S2 END]P	[S1]P & [S2]P
[IF E THEN S1 ELSE S2 END]P	(E =>[S1]P) & (not(E) =>[S2]P)

Second, the semantics of the parallel composition is not defined here. This is because the simplest case (4) of the parallel composition can be written in the form (5).

$$x1 := e1 \parallel x2 := e2 \tag{4}$$
$$x1,x2 := e1,e2 \tag{5}$$

The B-Method also offers rules to transform more complicated cases of multiple GS to the case (4). These rules are not needed in the course, but an interested reader can find them in [1, 11].

Within the course, the comprehension of this theory can be fortified by Exercise 1.

Exercise 1. Generalized Substitution Syntax and Semantics.

Task

Compute the weakest pre-condition (6).

$$\text{[IF sig1=red \& e0\_sig1=free} \\ \text{THEN e0:=green} \parallel \text{e0\_sig1:=occup END] (e0=green)} \tag{6}$$

Solution

First, we use the semantics of IF from Table 3 and the form (5) of (4) to rewrite (6) to (7).

$$(\text{(sig1=red \& e0\_sig1=free)} => \text{[e0,e0\_sig1:=green,occup](e0=green))} \\ \& (\text{not(sig1=red \& e0\_sig1=free)} => \text{[skip](e0=green))} \tag{7}$$

Applying the semantics of skip and := from Table 3 to (7), we get (8).

$$(\text{(sig1=red \& e0\_sig1=free)} => \text{(green=green))} \\ \& (\text{not(sig1=red \& e0\_sig1=free)} => \text{(e0=green))} \tag{8}$$

The form (8) is equivalent to (9).

$$(\text{(sig1=red \& e0\_sig1=free)} => \text{true)} \\ \& (\text{not(sig1=red \& e0\_sig1=free)} => \text{(e0=green))} \tag{9}$$

According to the definition of the logical conjunction and implication, (9) can be further reduced to (10), and, finally, to (11), which is the final form of (6).

$$\text{true \& (not(sig1=red \& e0\_sig1=free) => (e0=green))} \tag{10}$$

$$\text{not(sig1=red \& e0\_sig1=free) => (e0=green)} \tag{11}$$

(End of Exercise 1)

∎

4.3 Abstract Specification

A development of a software system in the B-Method starts with a formal abstract specification, consisting of (abstract) machines. A typical machine resembles an object in the object oriented programming as it encapsulates a set of variables, defining its state, with a set of operations, defining state transitions.

A machine is defined in a textual form consisting of several clauses. Only one of them, the MACHINE clause, which defines its name and may also list its formal parameters, is mandatory. To cover all purposes a machine can serve and corresponding combinations of clauses is out of the scope of this short course. Therefore, we will limit ourselves to the clauses we need for the control modules to be developed. And we explain them on a particular example of a machine representing a control module for the scenario from Fig. 5 a). But before that, in Exercise 2, we use the Train Director part of the TD/TS2JC toolset to emulate a process of customer requirements analysis, which should result in the invariant properties of the machine.

Exercise 2. From requirements to invariant properties.

Task

1. Launch the version of Train Director that is a part of the TD/TS2JC toolset and open the railway scenario `route2sec.trk`, with the track layout as in Fig. 5 a), in it.
2. Imagine that your task is to develop a control module for this scenario. The control module
   - represents entry points and signals by variables e0, e1 and sig0, sig1 with values green and red,
   - represents track sections by variables e0_sig1, sig0_e1 with values free and occup (occupied),
   - reacts to a request from a train to enter a section by setting the corresponding signal or entry point and
   - assumes that all trains obey the values it sets for the entry points and signals (i.e. a train enters a section only when the corresponding signal (entry point) is green).
3. Specify invariant properties that ensure safety of the trains in the scenario

- informally, in English and
- formally, using the mathematical notation of the B-language and the variables defined above.

Use simulation of the scenario in the Train Director to explore possible situations. You can clear the signals manually by clicking on them and change the train schedule by editing the text file `route2sec.sch`.

Solution
Informally, the invariant properties can be specified as follows:

1. Only one of the signals (entry points) guarding a section can be green.
2. If any of the signals (entry points) guarding a section is green, the section itself must be free.

These statements can be formally expressed in several ways. One of them is given in Listing 6 on lines 12–13 (the first statement) and lines 14–16 (the second statement).

(End of Exercise 2)

■

The machine specifying a non-parametric controller for the scenario from Fig. 5 a) can be found in Listing 6. The interface and functionality of the controller is identical to the Java version from Listing 2 and its final, executable, version will use the same configuration file (Listing 3).

Listing 6. Machine route2sec of a non-parametric module for the two section track from Fig. 5 a).

```
 1 MACHINE route2sec
 2 SETS
 3    ST_SIG={green , red };
 4    ST_SWCH={switched , none };
 5    ST_SEC={free ,occup}
 6
 7 CONCRETE_VARIABLES e0, e1, sig0, sig1, e0_sig1, sig0_e1
 8
 9 INVARIANT
10    e0 : ST_SIG & e1 : ST_SIG & sig0 : ST_SIG & sig1 : ST_SIG &
11    e0_sig1 : ST_SEC & sig0_e1 : ST_SEC &
12    ( e0=green => sig1=red ) & ( sig1=green => e0=red ) &
13    ( e1=green => sig0=red ) & ( sig0=green => e1=red ) &
14    ( e0=green => e0_sig1=free ) & ( sig1=green => e0_sig1=free )
15    &
16    ( e1=green => sig0_e1=free ) & ( sig0=green => sig0_e1=free )
17
18 INITIALISATION
19    e0:=red || e1:=red || sig0:=red || sig1:=red ||
20    e0_sig1 :=free || sig0_e1:=free
```

```
21
22  OPERATIONS
23    ss <—  getSig_sig0  =  BEGIN  ss:=sig0  END;
24    ss <—  getSig_sig1  =  BEGIN  ss:=sig1  END;
25    ss <—  getEntry_e0  =  BEGIN  ss:=e0  END;
26    ss <—  getEntry_e1  =  BEGIN  ss:=e1  END;
27
28    reqGreen_e0  =
29      IF  sig1=red & e0_sig1=free  THEN  e0:=green  END;
30    reqGreen_e1  =
31      IF  sig0=red & sig0_e1=free  THEN  e1:=green  END;
32    reqGreen_sig0  =
33      IF  e1=red & sig0_e1=free  THEN  sig0:=green  END;
34    reqGreen_sig1  =
35      IF  e0=red & e0_sig1=free  THEN  sig1:=green  END;
36
37    enterNI_e0_sig1  =
38      BEGIN  e0_sig1:=occup  ||  e0:=red  ||  sig1:=red  END;
39    enterIN_sig0_e1  =
40      BEGIN  sig0_e1:=occup  ||  sig0:=red  ||  e1:=red  END;
41    enterNI_e1_sig0  =
42      BEGIN  sig0_e1:=occup  ||  sig0:=red  ||  e1:=red  END;
43    enterIN_sig1_e0  =
44      BEGIN  e0_sig1:=occup  ||  e0:=red  ||  sig1:=red  END;
45
46    leaveNI_e0_sig1  =  BEGIN  e0_sig1:=free    END;
47    leaveIN_sig0_e1  =  BEGIN  sig0_e1:=free    END;
48    leaveNI_e1_sig0  =  BEGIN  sig0_e1:=free    END;
49    leaveIN_sig1_e0  =  BEGIN  e0_sig1:=free    END
50
51  END
```

The MACHINE clause with the machine name (route2sec, on line 1 in Listing 6) is followed by the SETS clause on lines 2 to 5. This clause defines three enumerated sets with their members in curly brackets. They are considered types in the B-language. Line 4 can be omitted as the scenario does not contain switches.

The CONCRETE_VARIABLES clause names state variables of the machine. A machine may have two types of state variables. The first one is concrete variables, as in this case. Such variables remain the same in each subsequent refinement or implementation of the component. Therefore, there are certain restrictions on them as they must be implementable, that is automatically translatable to a common programming language. For the second type, we have the ABSTRACT_VARIABLES clause and these variables can be of any type definable in the B-language.

The invariant properties of the machine are specified as a predicate in the INVARIANT clause (lines 9–16). It is divided into the typing invariant (lines 10–11), defining the types of the state variables, and safety properties (lines 12–16) that are those formulated in Exercise 2.

The next clause is INITIALISATION (lines 18–20) with a command in GSL, which assigns initial values to all state variables. It regards all sections as empty and sets all signals and entry points to red.

GSL is also used in the OPERATIONS clause (lines 22–51) with all the operations of the component. The operations are separated by semicolons and their interface and functionality is the same as that of the methods in the Java module in Listing 2. In the B-language, a general form of an operation is (12),

$$y <-- op(x) = \\ PRE\ P\ THEN\ S\ END \tag{12}$$

where y is a comma-separated list of its output parameters, op its name and x a comma-separated list of its input parameters. The predicate P, called the precondition of the operation, defines conditions under which it should be called. In operations with input parameters, it also defines their properties, including types. S is a command (a GS) that forms the body of the operation. For machines, it is required that operations are atomic state transitions without intermediate states. Because of this, they cannot contain the sequential compositions or loops.

If P is true and there are no input parameters, the form (12) is reduced to (13). This is the case of getters in our machine (lines 23–26). Remaining operations do not even have output parameters so they are written in the form (14). If S contains only compositions and assignments, it is common to place it between the keywords BEGIN and END. All operations in Listing 6, except of those in lines 28–35, use these keywords.

$$y <-- op = S \tag{13}$$

$$op = S \tag{14}$$

Verification of Machine. To verify the correctness of a formal specification written in the B-language, one must prove a set of formulas, called proof obligations (PObs), for each machine of the specification. To explain this topic in a concise way, we restrict ourselves to machines like the one in Listing 6. In general, such a machine can be written as in Listing 7.

Listing 7. General form of a machine with clauses as in Listing 6.

```
1  MACHINE M
2  SETS St
3  CONCRETE_VARIABLES v
4  INVARIANT I
5  INITIALISATION T
6  OPERATIONS
7    y <— op(x) =
8      PRE P THEN S END
9  END
```

The PObs for the machine are (15) and (16). The POb (16) must be proved for every operation of the machine.

$$[T]I \tag{15}$$
$$P \ \& \ I => [S]I \tag{16}$$
$$I => [S]I \tag{17}$$

The POb (15) means that the initialisation must establish the invariant and (16) that each operation must preserve it. If P is true, (16) is reduced to (17).

Exercise 3. Proving the proof obligations.
Task
For the machine route2sec from Listing 6, prove (17) for the operation req-Green_e0.

Solution
The POb has the form (18). The letter I represents the invariant of route2sec, that is lines 10–16 from Listing 6.

$$I => [\text{IF } sig1{=}red \ \& \ e0\_sig1{=}free \text{ THEN } e0{:=}green \text{ END}]I \tag{18}$$

After applying the GS semantics (Table 3) to (18), we get (19).

$$I => (\ ((sig1{=}red \ \& \ e0\_sig1{=}free) => [e0{:=}green]I) \ \& \tag{19}$$
$$(not(sig1{=}red \ \& \ e0\_sig1{=}free) => I)) \ )$$

In the rest of the exercise, we use the tautologies (20)–(22) of the propositional logic.

$$(a => (b \ \& \ c)) <=> ((a =>b) \ \& \ (a =>c)) \tag{20}$$
$$(a => (b{=>}c)) <=> ((a \ \& \ b) =>c) \tag{21}$$
$$(a \ \& \ b) \ => \ b \tag{22}$$

Utilizing (20), we can split (19) to (23) and (24).

$$I =>((sig1{=}red \ \& \ e0\_sig1{=}free) => [e0{:=}green]I) \tag{23}$$
$$I =>(not(sig1{=}red \ \& \ e0\_sig1{=}free) => I) \tag{24}$$

Considering (21), the formulas (23) and (24) can be rewritten to (25) and (26).

$$(I \ \& \ (sig1{=}red \ \& \ e0\_sig1{=}free)) => [e0{:=}green]I \tag{25}$$
$$(I \ \& \ not(sig1{=}red \ \& \ e0\_sig1{=}free)) => I \tag{26}$$

According to (22), (26) is true. What remains is to resolve (25). This requires to "dive into" the invariant I of route2sec, which is quite a long formula, consisting of 14 conjuncts. Therefore, in the rest of this solution and starting with (27), we omit those conjuncts that repeat in the same form on both sides of the implication and are not important for the proof.

$$
\begin{aligned}
&(\text{sig1:ST\_SIG \& sig1=red \& e0\_sig1=free}) => \\
&[\text{e0:=green}]\ (\text{e0:ST\_SIG \& (e0=green => sig1=red) \&} \\
&\qquad (\text{sig1=green => e0=red}) \& \\
&\qquad (\text{e0=green => e0\_sig1=free}))
\end{aligned}
\tag{27}
$$

First, we use the semantics of assignment (Table 3) to transform (27) to (28).

$$
\begin{aligned}
&(\text{sig1:ST\_SIG \& sig1=red \& e0\_sig1=free}) => \\
&(\text{green:ST\_SIG \& (green=green => sig1=red) \&} \\
&(\text{sig1=green => green=red}) \& \\
&(\text{green=green => e0\_sig1=free}))
\end{aligned}
\tag{28}
$$

Some of the expressions in (28) can be reduced to true or false, resulting in (29).

$$
\begin{aligned}
&(\text{sig1:ST\_SIG \& sig1=red \& e0\_sig1=free}) => \\
&(\text{true \& (true => sig1=red) \&} \\
&(\text{sig1=green => false}) \& \\
&(\text{true => e0\_sig1=free}))
\end{aligned}
\tag{29}
$$

Considering the definition of logical implication and conjunction, (29) can be further reduced to (30).

$$
\begin{aligned}
&(\text{sig1:ST\_SIG \& sig1=red \& e0\_sig1=free}) => \\
&(\text{sig1=red \&} \\
&\text{not(sig1=green) \&} \\
&\text{e0\_sig1=free})
\end{aligned}
\tag{30}
$$

According to (20), (30) can be split into 3 separate formulas, (31)–(33), to prove.

$$(\text{sig1:ST\_SIG \& sig1=red \& e0\_sig1=free}) => \text{sig1=red} \tag{31}$$

$$(\text{sig1:ST\_SIG \& sig1=red \& e0\_sig1=free}) => \text{not(sig1=green)} \tag{32}$$

$$(\text{sig1:ST\_SIG \& sig1=red \& e0\_sig1=free}) => \text{e0\_sig1=free} \tag{33}$$

Utilizing (22), (31) and (33) can be reduced to true directly as the right-hand side of the implication is one of the conjuncts on the left-hand side in both cases. And because the set ST_SIG consists of only two members, red and green, the right-hand side of (32) follows from the first two conjuncts on the left-hand side.

(End of Exercise 3)

■

B-Method in Atelier B. After getting familiar with the B-language and abstract machines and trying the formal verification in a pen-and-paper way, it is time to get some experience with Atelier B, the development environment and prover for the B-Method. In Exercise 4, we create a new project in Atelier B with the machine from Listing 6, which we type check and prove. This and the following exercises use the archive [7] of support materials and assume that the archive is unpacked into the folder C:/VSD. If one chooses another folder, he or she has to alter the steps accordingly.

Exercise 4. Machine specification and proof in Atelier B.
Instructions

1. Unpack the course package [7] to C:/VSD.
2. If not yet installed, download Atelier B from [18], install and run it. The *primary window* of Atelier B appears. The following steps are carried out in Atelier B.
3. Create a new workspace
   - workspace name: bcourse.
   - workspace database directory: C:/VSD/bdb.
4. Set the "Default project directory" to C:/VSD/Bprojects.
5. Create a new project called route2sec.
6. In the left panel ("Workspaces"), right click on the name of the project and choose "Add Components".
7. In the dialog "Select one or more files to add", locate and open the file C:/VSD/Bprojects/route2sec/route2sec.mch. It contains the machine from Listing 6.
8. In the *main part of the primary window*, which is located right to the "Workspaces" panel, choose "Classical view" from the dropdown menu (if not already chosen). A list of project components appears in the main part. The list contains route2sec.mch only.
9. Double click on the route2sec.mch in the list. This opens the *editor window* of Atelier B.
10. Explore the possibilities of the editor window and close it without saving changes in the file.
11. Right click on the route2sec.mch in the main part of the primary window and choose "Type check". This will check the syntax of the component. Provided that you didn't change anything in the file, this task should finish with success.
12. In the same way as in the previous step, choose "Generate PObs". This will generate the proof obligations of the component. There should be eight of them.
13. In the same way as in the previous step, choose "Proof" and then "Automatic (Force 0)". This will launch the *automatic prover* of Atelier B, which tries to prove the generated PObs of the component. The prover can be launched with different amount of resources (memory and time) allocated. There are four options in the menu - from the least amount ("Force 0") to the greatest amount ("Force 3"). As the PObs of route2sec.mch are simple, Force 0 is sufficient.

14. Choose the "Proof" option, as in the previous step, and then "Interactive Proof". This opens the *interactive prover window* of Atelier B. The interactive prover is used for human-assisted proving when the automatic prover fails.
15. In the part "Situation" of the interactive prover window, double click on route2sec and then on POO. The formula of the corresponding POb appears in the main part of the prover window. Notice the similarity between this formula and the ones we had in Exercise 3.
16. Close the interactive prover window and return to the primary window.
17. Notice that the type checking, POb generation and some of the proof options are also available from the toolbar.
18. If time allows, explore the functionality of Atelier B further. Corresponding documentation can be found in the main menu ("Help" and then "Manuals").

(End of Exercise 4)
∎

4.4   Refinement to Implementation

The B-Method allows for a sophisticated development (refinement) process, with multiple steps and changes in both data representation and functionality of operations. Considering the limited duration of the course, we opted for a minimalistic form of refinement. This consists of only one step, directly from a machine to an implementation. And this step is only necessary because of certain limitations of different types of components in the B-Method. As we mentioned earlier, machine operations must be atomic state transitions, so sequential composition and loops are prohibited. In implementations, only commands compatible with those of sequential imperative programming languages are allowed. This rules out parallel composition and PRE, SELECT and CHOICE in their pure form (IF is allowed). Abstract (unimplementable) variables and constants are forbidden, too. On the other hand, sequential composition and loops can be used. Refinements, as intermediate components, are a mixed bag. They can use both the abstract and concrete data and all commands, except of the loops, are allowed in them. All refinements and the implementation of a machine must have the same interface as the machine. By the interface we mean the list of component parameters and headers of its operations. No operation can be added or removed during the refinement process.

A straightforward implementation of the machine route2sec is the component route2sec_i in Listing 8.

Listing 8. Implementation component, refined from the abstract machine in Listing 6.

```
1  IMPLEMENTATION route2sec_i
2  REFINES route2sec
3
4  INITIALISATION
5    e0:=red; e1:=red; sig0:=red; sig1:=red;
```

```
 6    e0_sig1:= free ; sig0_e1:= free
 7
 8  OPERATIONS
 9    ss <—— getSig_sig0 = BEGIN ss:=sig0 END;
10    ss <—— getSig_sig1 = BEGIN ss:=sig1 END;
11    ss <—— getEntry_e0 = BEGIN ss:=e0 END;
12    ss <—— getEntry_e1 = BEGIN ss:=e1 END;
13
14    reqGreen_e0 =
15      IF sig1=red & e0_sig1=free THEN e0:=green END;
16    reqGreen_e1 =
17      IF sig0=red & sig0_e1=free THEN e1:=green END;
18    reqGreen_sig0 =
19      IF e1=red & sig0_e1=free THEN sig0:=green END;
20    reqGreen_sig1 =
21      IF e0=red & e0_sig1=free THEN sig1:=green END;
22
23    enterNI_e0_sig1 =
24      BEGIN e0_sig1:=occup ; e0:=red ; sig1:=red END;
25    enterIN_sig0_e1 =
26      BEGIN sig0_e1:=occup ; sig0:=red ; e1:=red END;
27    enterNI_e1_sig0 =
28      BEGIN sig0_e1:=occup ; sig0:=red ; e1:=red END;
29    enterIN_sig1_e0 =
30      BEGIN e0_sig1:=occup ; e0:=red ; sig1:=red END;
31
32    leaveNI_e0_sig1 = BEGIN e0_sig1:=free   END;
33    leaveIN_sig0_e1 = BEGIN sig0_e1:=free   END;
34    leaveNI_e1_sig0 = BEGIN sig0_e1:=free   END;
35    leaveIN_sig1_e0 = BEGIN e0_sig1:=free   END
36
37  END
```

There are several differences between the components route2sec and route2sec_i:

- The keyword MACHINE is replaced by IMLEMENTATION (line 1 in Listing 8).
- The clauses SETS and CONCRETE_VARIABLES are not present as the ones already defined in the machine are sufficient.
- The clause INVARIANT is omitted as no new variables are introduced and there is no need to define new properties over the concrete variables from the machine.
- All parallel compositions are replaced by sequential compositions in the INITIALISATION and OPERATIONS clauses.

Verification of Implementation. Refinements and implementations are verified against themselves and components they refine. Again, we will not deal with the most general case but only with a simplified one, as given in Listing 9.

Listing 9. General form of an implementation with clauses as in Listing 8 and INVARI-ANT.

```
1  IMPLEMENTATION  M_i
2  REFINES  M
3  INVARIANT  J
4  INITIALISATION  T1
5  OPERATIONS
6    y <— op(x) =
7      BEGIN  S1  END
8  END
```

The PObs for the implementation are (34) and (35) and (35) must be proved for every operation of the implementation. The PObs of the refinement components have the same form.

$$[T1](not([T] not(J))) \tag{34}$$

$$P \& I \& J => [S1'](not([S] not(J \& y'=y))) \tag{35}$$

While these PObs look rather complicated, their resolution is trivial in the case of route2sec_i. This is because

- the implementation route2sec_i does not contain invariant, so J is true and
- the weakest preconditions of the operation bodies of the machine (S) and the implementation machine (S1) are the same, because the right-hand sides of the assignments do not contain any state variables (that occur on the left-hand sides).

When looking on the general form of machine operation (12), and POb (35), one may wonder why we did not use PRE instead of IF in the machine route2sec (Listing 6). It is true that if we replace all IF keywords with PRE in Listing 6, then such machine can be refined to the implementation from Listing 8 and the verification will go without problems. But, it can also be refined to an implementation that differs from the one in Listing 8 in additional ELSE parts of the IF commands. And it will verify perfectly fine, regardless on what is inside the ELSE parts. In the case that these operations are called from another component in the same specification, it is OK. Because, in such a case it will not be possible to prove any component that calls them outside of their pre-conditions. But the operations of our verified control module will be called from outside of the verified part, where no one cares whether any conditions are met.

Implementation in Atelier B and BKPI Compiler. What remains is to finish the development of our control module in Atelier B and translate it to an executable form that can be run with the TD/TS2JC toolset. This is done in Exercise 5. The exercise requires both Java Runtime Environment and Java Development Kit installed. Similarly to Exercise 4, it assumes that the archive [7] is unpacked to C:/VSD.

Exercise 5. Implementation to executable code in Atelier B and BKPI compiler.
Instructions

1. In Atelier B, open the project route2sec, created in Exercise 4.
2. In the left panel ("Workspaces"), right click on the name of the project and choose "Add Components".
3. In the dialog "Select one or more files to add", locate and open the file C:/VSD/Bprojects/route2sec/route2sec_i.imp. It contains the implementation from Listing 8.
4. Type check, generate and prove PObs of route2sec_i.imp in the same way as for route2sec.mch in Exercise 4.
5. Close Atelier B.
6. Run the BKPI compiler.
   It is the file C:/VSD/BKPICompiler/BKPIcompiler.jar and we will use it to translate route2sec_i.imp to Java.
7. In the the BKPI compiler, right click on route2sec and choose "Generate Java code".
8. In a file manager (e.g. Explorer), navigate to the folder C:/VSD/Bprojects/route2sec/java.
9. Delete MainClass.java and compile route2sec.java. To compile, just run compile.bat.
10. Run Train Director and open the file C:/VSD/scenarios/route2sec.trk in it.
11. Run TS2JavaConn and load (open) the module C:/VSD/Bprojects/route2sec/java/route2sec.class in it.
12. Start the simulation, in Train Director or TS2JavaConn.

(End of Exercise 5)
■

4.5   Three Sections Control Module Development Project

Finally, the course participants may try the verified development process on a control module for the three track sections scenario from Fig. 5 b).

Exercise 6. Development of a control module for the three sections scenario.
Task
Develop a verified control module for the three track sections scenario from Fig. 5 b). The invariant of the machine of the module has to contain safety conditions that prevent collision of trains in the scenario. Use the control module template generator of TS2JavaConn to create an initial form of the module machine in the B-language. Alternatively, you can start with the machine from Listing 10. Follow the TODO comments to modify the machine.

Listing 10. Initial form of the abstract machine route3sec.

```
1 MACHINE route3sec
2 SETS
```

```
 3    ST_SIG={green ,  red };
 4    ST_SWCH={switched ,  none };
 5    ST_SEC={free , occup}
 6
 7  CONCRETE_VARIABLES
 8    e0,  e1,  sig0,  sig1,  sig2,  sig3,
 9    e0_sig1,  sig0_sig3,  sig2_e1
10
11  INVARIANT
12    e0 : ST_SIG  &  e1 : ST_SIG  &
13    sig0 : ST_SIG  &  sig1 : ST_SIG  &  sig2 : ST_SIG  &  sig3 : ST_SIG  &
14    e0_sig1 : ST_SEC  &  sig0_sig3 : ST_SEC  &  sig2_e1 : ST_SEC  &
15    ( e0=green  =>  sig1=red )  &  ( sig1=green  =>  e0=red )
16    /*TODO: finish safety conditions for the relations
17            between signals (entry points)*/
18    &
19    ( e0=green  =>  e0_sig1=free )  &
20    ( sig1=green  =>  e0_sig1=free )
21    /*TODO: finish safety conditions for the relations
22            between signals (entry points) and sections*/
23
24  INITIALISATION
25    e0:=red  ||  e1:=red  ||
26    sig0:=red  ||  sig1:=red  ||  sig2:=red  ||  sig3:=red  ||
27    e0_sig1:= free  ||  sig0_sig3:= free  ||  sig2_e1:= free
28
29  OPERATIONS
30    ss <-- getSig_sig0 = BEGIN ss:=sig0 END;
31    ss <-- getSig_sig1 = BEGIN ss:=sig1 END;
32    ss <-- getSig_sig2 = BEGIN ss:=sig2 END;
33    ss <-- getSig_sig3 = BEGIN ss:=sig3 END;
34    ss <-- getEntry_e0 = BEGIN ss:=e0 END;
35    ss <-- getEntry_e1 = BEGIN ss:=e1 END;
36
37    reqGreen_e0 =
38      IF sig1=red & e0_sig1=free THEN e0:=green END;
39    reqGreen_e1   = skip;
40    reqGreen_sig0 = skip;
41    reqGreen_sig1 = skip;
42    reqGreen_sig2 = skip;
43    reqGreen_sig3 = skip;
44    /*TODO: replace skip in the previous operation
45            with appropriate commands*/
46
47    enterNI_e0_sig1 =
48      BEGIN e0_sig1:=occup || e0:=red || sig1:=red END;
49    enterII_sig0_sig3 =
50      BEGIN sig0_sig3:=occup || sig0:=red || sig3:=red END;
51    enterIN_sig2_e1 =
52      BEGIN sig2_e1:=occup || sig2:=red || e1:=red    END;
```

```
53
54   enterNI_e1_sig2 =
55      BEGIN  sig2_e1:=occup  ||  sig2:=red  ||  e1:=red    END;
56   enterII_sig3_sig0 =
57      BEGIN  sig0_sig3:=occup  ||  sig0:=red  ||  sig3:=red END;
58   enterIN_sig1_e0 =
59      BEGIN  e0_sig1:=occup  ||  e0:=red    ||  sig1:=red END;
60
61   leaveNI_e0_sig1    = BEGIN  e0_sig1:=free    END;
62   leaveII_sig0_sig3  = BEGIN  sig0_sig3:=free END;
63   leaveIN_sig2_e1    = BEGIN  sig2_e1:=free    END;
64   leaveNI_e1_sig2    = BEGIN  sig2_e1:=free    END;
65   leaveII_sig3_sig0  = BEGIN  sig0_sig3:=free END;
66   leaveIN_sig1_e0    = BEGIN  e0_sig1:=free    END
67
68 END
```

Solution

In essence, the process of the control module development is the same as in Exercise 4 and Exercise 5. The parts that must be changed in the machine from Listing 10 can be found in Listing 11. The differences between the machine and its implementation are the same as between the ones in the aforementioned exercises.

Listing 11. Invariant and selected operations of the final form of the machine route3sec from Listing 10.

```
1  INVARIANT
2     e0:ST_SIG & e1:ST_SIG &
3     sig0:ST_SIG & sig1:ST_SIG & sig2:ST_SIG & sig3:ST_SIG &
4     e0_sig1:ST_SEC & sig0_sig3:ST_SEC & sig2_e1:ST_SEC &
5     (e0=green => sig1=red) & (sig1=green => e0=red) &
6     (sig0=green => sig3=red) & (sig3=green => sig0=red) &
7     (e1=green => sig2=red) & (sig2=green => e1=red) &
8     (e0=green    => e0_sig1=free)    &
9     (sig1=green => e0_sig1=free)    &
10    (sig0=green => sig0_sig3=free) &
11    (sig3=green => sig0_sig3=free) &
12    (e1=green    => sig2_e1=free)    &
13    (sig2=green => sig2_e1=free)
14
15 OPERATIONS
16    reqGreen_e1 =
17       IF  sig2=red & sig2_e1=free THEN e1:=green END;
18    reqGreen_sig0 =
19       IF  sig3=red & sig0_sig3=free THEN sig0:=green END;
20    reqGreen_sig1 =
21       IF  e0=red & e0_sig1=free THEN sig1:=green END;
22    reqGreen_sig2 =
```

```
23    IF e1=red & sig2_e1=free THEN sig2:=green END;
24    reqGreen_sig3 =
25      IF sig0=red & sig0_sig3=free THEN sig3:=green END;
```

(End of Exercise 6)

■

5 Conclusion

This chapter presented a compact four-to-six-hour long course on formal verified software development in the B-Method. We do hope that, with additional
materials [6] and [7], the chapter provides enough information for an interested
reader to go through the course by him or herself. The B-Method was chosen
because of the tool support, provided by the freely available Atelier B integrated
development environment and prover, and an impressive track record of industrial utilization. This course has been carried out during the Central European
Functional Programming (CEFP) summer school in June 2019, in Budapest. A
special feature of the course is the utilization of the TD/TS2JC toolset. The cen-
terpiece of the toolset is a modified railway traffic control game, Train Director.
It provides a virtual environment for the software developed during the course by
its participants, that is for railway controllers. The participants use the toolset
at least at the beginning and at the end of the development; at the beginning
to examine the scenario for which the controller will be developed and after the
development to run the controller with the scenario. A questionnaire given to
the participants after the course at the CEFP summer school confirmed the positive impact of the tool set. From 15 participants, 66.7% agreed that the toolset
helped them to understand the importance of formal methods and for 99.3%
it mattered that they had been able to see their formally developed software
running.

The TD/TS2JC toolset had been developed with universality in mind and can
be used with any formal method that provides translation to the Java programming language and, also, directly with Java. The chapter tried to demonstrate
this universality by describing different types of control modules and corresponding configuration files.

The course presented here includes some pen-and-paper exercises dealing
with formal semantics of the B-Method and formal proof. To remind concise,
these exercises do not use the formal system behind the B-Method, but try
to explain the topic in a way understandable for a common programmer. The
course focuses on formulation of the abstract specification and understanding
the importance and process of formal verification by mathematical proof. The
development to implementation is, deliberately, trivial. A more complex scenario with the specification consisting of multiple components and a nontrivial
refinement can be found in [9].

References

1. Abrial, J.R.: The B-Book: Assigning Programs to Meanings. Cambridge University Press, New York (1996)
2. Abrial, J.R.: Modeling in Event-B: System and Software Engineering, 1st edn. Cambridge University Press, New Yor (2010)
3. Almeida, J.B., Frade, M.J., Pinto, J.S., De Sousa, S.M.: Rigorous Software Development: An Introduction to Program Verification. Springer, London (2011). https://doi.org/10.1007/978-0-85729-018-2
4. Dijkstra, E.W.: A Discipline of Programming. Prentice-Hall, Englewood Cliffs (1976)
5. Fantechi, A.: Twenty-five years of formal methods and railways: what next? In: Counsell, S., Núñez, M. (eds.) SEFM 2013. LNCS, vol. 8368, pp. 167–183. Springer, Cham (2014). https://doi.org/10.1007/978-3-319-05032-4_13
6. Korečko, Š.: TD/TS2JavaConn toolset package. https://hron.fei.tuke.sk/korecko/FMInGamesExp/resources/allInOneTDTS2J.zip (2019)
7. Korečko, Š.: Verified software development in B-Method short course package (2019). https://hron.fei.tuke.sk/korecko/cefp19/cefp19BmethodPack.zip
8. Korečko, Š, Sobota, B.: Computer games as virtual environments for safety-critical software validation. J. Inf. Organ. Sci. **41**(2), 197–212 (2017)
9. Korečko, Š., Sorád, J.: Using simulation games in teaching formal methods for software development. In: Queirós, R. (ed.) Innovative Teaching Strategies and New Learning Paradigms in Computer Programming, pp. 106–130. IGI Global (2015)
10. Korečko, Š, Sorád, J., Dudláková, Z., Sobota, B.: A toolset for support of teaching formal software development. In: Giannakopoulou, D., Salaün, G. (eds.) SEFM 2014. LNCS, vol. 8702, pp. 278–283. Springer, Cham (2014). https://doi.org/10.1007/978-3-319-10431-7_21
11. Lano, K.: The B Language and Method: A Guide to Practical Formal Development, 1st edn. Springer, New York (1996). https://doi.org/10.1007/978-1-4471-1494-9
12. Larsen, P., Fitzgerald, J., Riddle, S.: Practice-oriented courses in formal methods using vdm++. Formal Aspects Comput. **21**(3), 245–257 (2009). https://doi.org/10.1007/s00165-008-0068-5
13. Liu, S., Takahashi, K., Hayashi, T., Nakayama, T.: Teaching formal methods in the context of software engineering. SIGCSE Bull. **41**(2), 17–23 (2009). https://doi.org/10.1145/1595453.1595457
14. Reed, J.N., Sinclair, J.E.: Motivating study of formal methods in the classroom. In: Dean, C.N., Boute, R.T. (eds.) TFM 2004. LNCS, vol. 3294, pp. 32–46. Springer, Heidelberg (2004). https://doi.org/10.1007/978-3-540-30472-2_3
15. Schneider, S.: The B-Method: An Introduction. Cornerstones of Computing, Palgrave (2001)
16. Spivey, J.M., Abrial, J.: The Z Notation. Prentice Hall Hemel Hempstead, Englewood Cliffs (1992)
17. Train director homepage (2020). https://www.backerstreet.com/traindir/en/trdireng.php
18. Atelier B homepage (2021). https://www.atelierb.eu/en/

The Role of Functional Programming in Management and Orchestration of Virtualized Network Resources
Part II. Network Evolution and Design Principles

Tihana Galinac Grbac[1]([✉]) [iD] and Nikola Domazet[2]

[1] Juraj Dobrila University of Pula, Zagrebačka 30, 52100 Pula, Croatia
`tihana.galinac@unipu.hr`
[2] Ericsson Nikola Tesla, Krapinska 45, 10000 Zagreb, Croatia
`nikola.domazet@ericsson.com`

Abstract. This is part II of the follow-up lecture notes of the lectures given by the authors at the *Three "CO" (Composability, Comprehensibility, Correctness)* Winter School held in Košice, Slovakia, in January 2018, and Summer School held in Budapest, Hungary, in June 2019. In this part we explain the recent network evolution and the concept of virtualization, focusing on the management and orchestration of virtualized network resources. Network Functions Virtualization (NFV) is a new paradigm for changing the way networks are built and operated. Decoupling software implementation from network resources through a virtualization layer introduces a need for developing sets of NFV management and orchestration (MANO) functions. We discuss how this new point of view is highly inspired by the functional programming concepts. We provide examples and exercises on Open Stack virtual technology, and also discuss the challenges and problems inspired by the telecommunication industry. Focus is on the Reliable operation of Management and Orchestration functions of Virtualized resources. These notes provide an introduction to the subject, with the goal of explaining the necessity for new knowledge and skills in the area of network programming. We introduce students to the main problems and the network design principles, methods, and techniques used for their solution. The worked examples and exercises serve students as the teaching material, from which they can learn how to use functional programming to effectively and efficiently coordinate management and orchestration functions in distributed complex systems using NFV.

Keywords: Network Function Virtualization · Management and orchestration · Complex software systems · OpenStack platform

1 Introduction

This lecture part II belongs to lecture series on the role of functional programming in the management and orchestration of virtualized network resources. In

ⓒ The Author(s), under exclusive license to Springer Nature Switzerland AG 2023
Z. Porkoláb and V. Zsók (Eds.): CEFP 2019, LNCS 11950, pp. 136–164, 2023.
https://doi.org/10.1007/978-3-031-42833-3_5

the previous lectures part I of the follow-up lecture notes of the lectures given by the authors at the *Three "CO" (Composability, Comprehensibility, Correctness)* Winter School held in Košice, Slovakia, in January 2018, we discuss the **system structure for complex systems and design principles**. We provided an introduction to the theory of complex software systems reflecting on examples from telecommunication networks and carefully positioning the considered problems imposed by network evolution and continuous complexity increase. Furthermore, we discussed the main system design principles proposed to cope with complexity such as modularity, abstraction, layering, and hierarchy. Since these are very generic recommendations on how to design such complex systems we further explain in detail the main paradigms such as service orientation and virtualization forcing implementation of such principles. Virtualization is a paradigm frequently used in the management of complex software systems. It implies the introduction of a new abstract layer, a virtual edition of the system layer and its functions, which avoids introducing dependency between system layers.

Here, in this lecture, we go one step further where we discuss **network evolution and design principles for autonomic network management**. We introduce new concepts that are cornerstones for future network evolution and are based on virtualization and service orientation. These are Network Functions Virtualization (NFV) and Software Defined Networking (SDN). Network Functions Virtualization (NFV) decouples network function from physical network resources through a new virtualization layer [8] thus avoiding dependencies among them. However, it introduces a need for developing sets of NFV management and orchestration functions (MANO). Further in this lecture, we describe new challenges arising from the implementation point of view and show students how to use the programming techniques for coordination of management and orchestration functions of virtualized network resources operating in distributed environments.

The problems and challenges of coordination of management and orchestration functions are addressed using the OpenStack platform [12]. It is an open source cloud operating system that integrates a collection of software modules that are necessary to provide a cloud computing layered model. Such technology is necessary for dealing with problems arising from the virtualization paradigm in current networks, and the students' understanding solutions in OpenStack will be able to transfer their knowledge to other existing technologies with the same or similar purpose.

These notes provide an introduction to the subject, with the goal of explaining the problems and the principles, methods and techniques used for their solution. The worked examples and exercises serve students as the teaching material, from which they can learn how the use of functional programming may result in effective and efficient coordination management and orchestration functions in distributed complex systems using NFV.

The methods and techniques explained in these lecture notes and applied to the problems of management and orchestration of network virtualization, are already existing and we claim no originality in that sense. The purpose of these notes is to serve as a teaching material for these methods.

The challenges arising from the new network paradigms, as well as their solutions, are illustrated through practical examples using OpenStack virtual technology and inspired by the problems from the telecommunication industry.

The course is divided into the following main parts:

- Background with reflection to key learnings from previous lectures on a defini-
  tion of complex systems and challenging aspects of their management, system
  design principles, and technologies enforcing design principles, Sect. 2.
- New network technologies which drive network evolution such as Cloud Com-
  puting, Network Function Virtualisation, and Software Defined Network,
  Sect. 3.
- Management and orchestration of virtualized resources and network design
  principles, Sect. 4.
- Introduction to Open stack platform and the main services, Sect. 5.
- Reflections on practical examples on using OpenStack services for developing
  management and orchestration scripts, Sect. 6.
- Reflections on use cases from the industry, Sect. 7.
- Discussion, Sect. 8.
- Conclusion, Sect. 9.

The key learning outcomes of this course lecture are to introduce virtual-ization as one of the design principles for building modern complex systems, to explain the need for automated management and orchestration functions (MANO) in virtualized environments, to understand the challenges of unreli-able MANO functions in virtualized environments, and finally to understand how well-formalized virtualization can help improve reliable operation in net-work environments.

2   Background

Nowadays, all software systems, or more precisely, everything, are interconnected via the Internet-based telecommunication network. This network is distributed and connects various peripheral systems at the edge of the network, intercon-necting a variety of application domains. Many edge systems and their applica-tions are increasingly growing thus forcing the current core network to increase its capacities. Today's networks are already becoming very complex and their management is becoming extremely expensive and inefficient. Therefore, inno-vations are needed to simplify network management and use. System reliability and safety are paramount for the growing number of applications and services. Note that in a telecommunications network, services are provided to users by distributed and complex systems in coordination. **Reliability** is defined as conti-nuity of system functionality and service. **Safety** is defined as a non–occurrence of catastrophic consequences for the environment due to unreliable system oper-ation.

The main problem in current research and practice is that we do not have adequate mathematical models that provide a better understanding of the underlying causes of such complex system behavior and that can model global system properties that produce reliable and secure behavior of modern software systems with increasingly growing complexity [7]. The principles of network and systems engineering must be redesigned to accommodate these innovations. The current knowledge base of software and systems engineering needs to be revised in light of the new challenges [5,10]. In addition, leading software companies (e.g., Google) have recognized these properties as an important specialization of **software and systems engineering** research focused on the reliability and maintainability of large complex software systems and networks [4,15]. This knowledge is seen as important for the next generation of software and systems engineers specializing in network programming. Therefore, these lectures are in complex systems theory, particularly as it relates to complex software systems and their role in telecommunications networks.

To build a complex system, there are numerous possibilities for how to structure the complex system. The way how the system is built is limiting or enables its further evolution and system maintenance. Moreover, when building large–scale complex systems that provide complex functionalities, the functional system composition is enforced as a logical solution. This is especially the case with complex software systems present in the telecommunication network which are constantly evolving and introducing more and more complex system functionalities, and whose entire development follows precise standards and recommendations described and regulated by numerous standardization bodies. All these standards and recommendations define system functionalities, which are achieved by implementing many system functions. Thus, the functional system is already driven by numerous standard bodies.

We have already given an introduction to this topic in the first part of this lecture notes *Part I. System structure for complex systems and design principles*, which we have published as a follow-up to the authors' lectures on the *Three"CO" (Composability, Comprehensibility, Correctness)* Winter School held in Košice, Slovakia, in January 2018 and the Summer School held in Budapest, Hungary, in June 2019. Therefore, in the following we will only briefly recap the main learning and basic understanding necessary to easily follow and understand the more advanced topics in this lecture.

In the previous lecture, we first started with a relevant definition of a complex system from complex systems theory, [3], and applied this definition to a complex *software* system. **The complex software system** is a system in which there are a number of levels of abstraction and in which it is impossible to derive simple rules from local system properties describing the behavior of components to global properties of a system (such as reliability and security). This behavior of software systems can be observed in large systems, such as mission-critical systems that have been developed in an evolutionary manner and are usually very sensitive to reliability and security requirements. These systems are typically developed in a sequence of projects and releases involving several hundred or even thousands of software and systems engineers spread across the globe. The developed product involves more than several thousand lines of code while serving millions of users in collaboration with similar complex systems in a distributed network environment. There are many network nodes within the telecommunication network that share this challenges. In previous lecture we focus and interpret these challenges on mobile switching node that is central node for switching mobile subscribes within telecommunication core network.

Here, the main problem arises from the fact that humans develop these systems, and as these systems grow, the inability of humans to deal with such complexity is recognized as one of the major obstacles to their further evolution. The main tool for managing such software systems is the system structure, which can be used to logically decompose a complex system into a set of system components required to perform the system functions. Such a system structure is used to reason and manage system implementation while providing a link between local and global system properties. Efficient systems use a functional system decomposition that can serve a variety of system functionalities. In such a system, we must control the side effects of changing system functions when implementing new system functions and upgrading existing system functions. The propagation of effects of implementation errors in a large number of system functions can become very costly and time-consuming. In this context, the functional programming paradigm is attracting more and more attention. The main idea behind it is to treat program execution during the operation of system functions as an evaluation of mathematical functions, without affecting the global system state and keeping mutable data across system functions. However, this idea is not easy to realize in such systems.

There are numerous possible candidate structures for building such systems, and the global system behavior and system quality can be seriously influenced by the selected solution. To succeed as much as possible, we have introduced the four main **system design principles**. These are modularity, abstraction, layering, and hierarchy. **Modularity** means building systems as a set of smaller system components that are independent of each other. **Abstraction** is a term that refers to the design of system interfaces and communications in between system components. The main idea is to develop standard interfaces between components that are clearly separated from the internal implementation details of the components. Components are further organized into **hierarchical layered** structure where components with similar functionality are grouped within the system layer and communication follows strict hierarchical rules and only adjacent layers are allowed to communicate with each other. In the previous lecture, we provided an overview of the standard Open Systems Interconnection Model (OSI model), which defines a hierarchical layering of system functions that are present in communication with other systems. The development of such standards has promoted better interconnection within the equipment of different providers and across national borders and regulations.

As the network evolves, the number of potential network users, the variety of technologies connected to the network, and the various services offered by the network continue to grow. The core telecommunication network is continuously evolving and finding new ways to cope with new demands, such as massive data traffic with diverse information content, variety of different users, mobile and fixed, interconnected across geographic and application domains. The main technological trends being implemented in modern telecommunication networks are inspired by two main ideas, **virtualization and service orientation**.

These ideas have been embedded in telecommunication networks from the very beginning. The main motivation for virtualization of physical resources comes along with the first idea of building a common telecommunication infrastructure that provides its services to subscribers. This common infrastructure is shared among subscribers. In the previous lecture, we described in detail how the number of subscribers is multiplexed within a shared physical wire. Multiplexing subscribers was the first abstraction from physical resources to their software representation. To implement reliable management of shared resources, a suitable virtualization function has to be developed. The concept of service orientation has also already been implemented in the network. Nevertheless, as the network evolves, service orientation in the network moves from a manual process to a software process. In a modern telecommunications network, the user dynamically requests network services whenever she or he needs the services, and the network meets the user's needs by executing the user requests in a fully service-oriented computing paradigm. Even more, the network functions provide services to each other in a service-oriented fashion.

Both concepts bring numerous benefits, such as increased capacity that enables rapid innovation.

3   Network Evolution

Telecommunication networks are continuously evolved in generations and implement new concepts that enable them to accomplish their main goal. The main goal during its evolution is to allow interconnection of various technologies by various vendors and at the same time to keep a reasonable balance between costs and performances. Telecommunication networks are used by different classes of users, utilizing different technologies, sometimes with very specific service demands. In such cases, the process of network configuration and management becomes very expensive and time and resource-consuming. Efficient scaling of network resources, enabling innovation, and introducing new services and energy-efficient solutions are hard to implement. The main problem network operators are facing today is how to effectively and efficiently manage the high diversity of numerous users and technologies but at the same time achieve capital efficiency and flexibility for improvements. Recent work is focused on the development of new network architectures that would allow operators to architect their networks more efficiently. In the sequel, we introduce the main ingredients of the new network architecture defined for the fifth-generation (5G) network.

3.1   Cloud Computing Platforms

There is a growing need and interest in consuming computing and storage resources from third-party vendors as a service principle. For software development companies, the service orientation increases opportunities for specialization while leaving hardware management operations out of its business. On the other side, vendor companies can specialize in the hardware management business. Therefore, there is a business-driven need for open and well-standardized Application Platform Interfaces (APIs) over which hardware vendors may offer their services to application service providers, see Fig. 1.

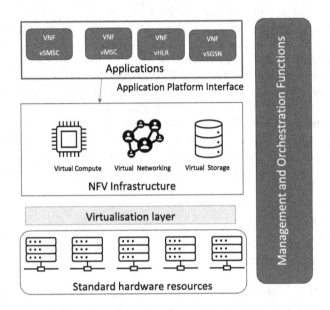

Fig. 1. Open stack virtualisation of network resources

The new paradigm of abstracting resource plane requires huge efforts in the standardization of cloud platforms. An operating system has to be developed for the management of distributed hardware and related software resources and offering them as services over the well-standardized set of interfaces APIs. Note that this is a key difference between the distributed system and the cloud system. Users may approach Cloud resources from a single interface point (e.g. using a command-line interface or Graphical user interface) and use its resources on demand via well standardized APIs. In traditional distributed system architectures all network resources were physical nodes with installed communication software for use on that single physical hardware. However, this paradigm has been changed and now communication software is independent of physical hardware and can be installed on any network node by using a standard set of APIs. This is the main reason why telecommunication systems are progressively moving into virtualized Cloud environments.

With aim of speeding up this standardization process of cloud platforms, there are established numerous initiatives. OpenStack is one such project established jointly by NASA and Rackspace intended to provide an open source cloud platform alternative that would be compatible with Amazon Elastic Compute Cloud (EC2). Furthermore, it should provide run time, reliability, and massive scalability of resources with simple design. Therefore, the project contributed to numerous experts around the globe from various industries. Today, OpenStack becomes widely accepted as an innovation platform for Cloud platform industry [9,13]. Here, in this lecture, all our examples will be provided on OpenStack to provide examples of management functions and their operation in virtual environments. We selected an open-source computing platform OpenStack aiming to simplify exercises execution to a wide community, and especially targeting the audience of graduate students at University Master level of Computing curricula.

3.2   Network Function Virtalisation and Software Defined Network

Network functions virtualisation (NFV) term is referred to abstracting physical networking equipment and related behaviour by creating software representations (including memory and storage resources) of network elements and network operations. In other words, the NFV provides a network service that is decoupled from the physical hardware and offers feature set identical to and consistent to its hardware counterpart. Thus, network functions (hardware and software) are redesigned and offered as a service and following on demand principle and independently of the physical hardware. Network Functions Virtualisation (NFV) is aiming to define virtual network technologies that would allow operators to implement different technologies within its network offerings, for a which a dedicated and specialized device was needed by using common industry standard information technologies (IT), such as servers, switches and storage.

The general framework around the implementation of the NFV concept is defined in [6] consists of the following main layers:

- Network functions virtualization infrastructure (NFVI) is the layer hosting generic COTS-based hardware components like storage, compute, network hardware, etc.
- Virtualized network functions (VNFs) is the layer with functions implemented solely within software reusing benefits of software products like are easy scaling process, simple and fast deploying over multiple hardware, or even combining virtual instances on the same hardware, automation of these processes with licensing.
- Management and orchestration functions (MANO) that need to be developed for managing virtual instances and implementing its autonomous operation as we will discuss further within this lecture. For this purpose, a special working group is defined within the European Telecommunications Standards Institute (ETSI).

Software Defined Networking (SDN) is a new networking paradigm that introduces additional abstractions in networks by separating data and a control plane of network devices. It assumes the control plane to be able to use standardized vertical interfaces to dynamically reconfigure the data plane flows, based on a global network policy. Therefore, many network functions can easily be virtualized using common servers and simple data plane networking devices.

The invention of Software Defined Network (SDN) architecture is motivated by the fact that traditional networking technologies are inadequate to scale to the levels required by today's telecommunication networks. These limits are mainly caused by the complexity of network control and management functions and their distributed implementation logic. Distributed logic works well in medium-sized networks but in today's large and fast-expanding network scenarios it becomes inefficient and too complex to manage and coordinate their scale and growth [15]. Therefore, a centralized network solution is needed. The main characteristics that should be provided by the solution are:

- Network management should be driven by general network objectives and low-level device performance issues should be separated and considered at a lower level of abstraction.
- A global network view should be built and maintained for a comprehensive understanding of network complexity at a higher abstraction level, such as its topology, traffic, and events.
- Devices at the lower level should be controllable through a standardized interface, such that they can be programmed and their behavior changed on the fly, based on actual network demands and governed from the global network view.

The fundamentals of Software Defined Network are the separation of Control and Data planes, simplified SDN devices (forwarding devices without complex distributed management protocols but managed from the control plane), centralized control (all network management is centralized at the control plane that is managing data plane SDN devices with help of an open standard), network automation and virtualization and network openness. Open Networking Foundation (ONF) [11] was established in 2011 by major network operators to promote the adoption of SDN through open standards development. Open standards under consideration are Open Flow and Open Flow Configuration and Management Protocol, both used to communicate control decisions from the control to the data plane. The main idea behind SDN is to provide a programmable network. The main challenges in SDN-based networks are latency, scale, high availability, and security. Latency may be affected by the introduction of a central processing function. It may introduce delays because of numerous requests it has to process. Since the number of users and devices connected to a network is continuously growing the question of scale in this centralized paradigm may be limited with the processing power of the central function. Also, the central function has to be very reliable and highly available not to represent a single point of failure for the whole network. Therefore, a mechanism of high redundancy in processing and data storage may be required. And finally, the central point of control may be a serious issue for security attacks.

4   Management and Orchestration of Virtualized Network Resources

As is already stated in Sect. 2 systems are getting more and more complex. The same situation is happening with telecommunication networks. Networks are transforming from a classical distributed set of interworking nodes to modern distributed interworking functions and services. The management of such a complex system becomes very expensive, asking for higher expertise and higher-skilled personnel in network management and consequences of actions performed are unpredictable. Note that in modern networked complex systems the functions are implemented in different functional blocks, as part of different complex systems, and that we need new knowledge to accomplish reliable operation for management and orchestration functions operating in these distributed environments. Therefore, one of the recognized strategies in evolving telecommunication networks is the way towards its autonomy and self–management. Recent research efforts are devoted to innovation in this field. There is a need for effective mechanisms to automate networks so they may automatically adapt their configurations to new traffic demands and introduce network flexibility and autonomously adapt to new technologies and new vendor equipment. These research efforts are driven by the idea of autonomic computing [16], and further involve research on autonomic communication, autonomic networks, autonomic network management, and self–managed networks. The final level of system autonomy is the level at which the humans only specify business policies and objectives to govern the systems while self–management following these policies is left to the system. Self–management mainly means:

- self–configuration
- self–healing
- self–optimisation
- self–protection

In such new networks, the concept of programming software localized within one node, industry closed standard, and solution for network functions is moved to the concept of programming software for open network functions. The necessity for the new profession of network developer is evident. In that new world of network programming, we start to develop network design principles. In the next section, we open a discussion on that topic.

4.1   Design Principles for Implementing Autonomic Behavior

Autonomic behavior has been developed in many other fields and some general design principles have been recognized across all fields. Concerning network heterogeneity, scalability and distribution the same principles may be valid also for networks. Here we shortly introduce these principles from [1] to motivate students to think about their implementation within examples provided in Sect. 6 of this lecture.

- Living systems inspired design
- Policy based design
- Context awareness design
- Self–similarity
- Adaptive design
- Knowledge based design

Living system inspired design is perspective to system design where inspiration is taken from the functioning of living systems. There is much self–management mechanisms in the functioning of living systems and their interaction with the environment and those ideas are taken as motivators for autonomy design. These concepts are mostly driven by survival instinct and collective behavior. Survival instinct is related to system tension to come back to the original equilibrium state. Collective behavior refers to some spontaneous system reactions that may be derived from collective movement. Note that there is a huge knowledge base derived from observing the individual in respect to collective behavior (like for example in Twitter, Facebook applications) and sometimes it happens that individual information moves collective behavior in some particular state.

Policy based design is a predefined rule that governs the behavior of the system. This design principle has already been implemented widely across the network. However, it does not eliminate human interaction with the system.

Context awareness design is related to the ability of the system to characterize a situation or environment and based on historic behavior decide how to adapt to new conditions. This principle has already been implemented within the computing and networking field. One example is numerous sensing environment case studies.

Self–similarity design principle is related to the characteristic that system organization persists as the system scales and thus guarantees its global properties. This characteristic is also reflected in global system properties that emerge solely from low-level interactions, so low-level interactions do not interfere with global.

Adaptive design is related to the ability of the system to adapt its inner behavior as a reaction to various environmental conditions. Such a system can learn from its experience in operation and react accordingly by adapting its actions based on collected information and knowledge gained.

Knowledge–based design is related to finding the best design of the knowledge gathering process. Since systems are complex, there are numerous possibilities in selecting the appropriate set of properties to measure, designing appropriate data collection procedures, and using appropriate artificial intelligence models to build the appropriate knowledge base. This design is linked to the building of appropriate business goals.

4.2   Current State

Networks are already highly developed and the introduction of automation (by excluding humans) into network management is not an easy and one-step process. The first step in automation is to virtualize its complex infrastructure and provide virtualized network resources. Furthermore, real-time management and orchestration functions have to be developed that operate on these virtual network resources. As already mentioned, currently telecommunication network functions are progressively redesigned (to get virtual) so they can be offered over Cloud. In this process, every network resource gets its virtual image so it may be reinstalled, activated, or deactivated as is needed in network reconfiguration or scaling demands. To automate these installation processes of this complex infrastructure scripts are written which are then called for execution whenever needed during dynamic network management activities. These scripts are written in classical programming languages like is for example Python. Note here that real-time management and orchestration of network functions should secure avoiding the overlapping of management and orchestration processes over the same physical network resource pool. Again, the functional programming-like approach here is of ultimate importance to secure reliable and safe network management and orchestration operations.

5   OpenStack

OpenStack is a software platform that implements the main functionality of providing distributed resources and infrastructure using the 'As a service' paradigm to its users. Furthermore, OpenStack is a modular platform meaning that is designed as a set of standardized units each designed to serve a specific purpose, and these units may be used as needed or may be optional to OpenStack deployment. These units provide services to OpenStack users or other OpenStack units using standardized Application Platform Interfaces (APIs). Table 1 provides a list of services, names of projects, and a short description of its main function. The OpenStack was designed around three logical tiers: Network, Control, and Compute, [13]. The Compute tier is taking over all the logic needed as a hypervisor of virtual resources. For example, it implements agents and services to handle virtual machines. All communication among OpenStack services and with OpenStack users is provided through Application Platform Interface (API) services, web interface, database, and message bus. Numerous services have been implemented so far and a detailed list of services can be found on OpenStack official web page and documentation [12]. In the aforementioned Table 1, we listed just a group of services specialized for the specific purpose that we will also use in the examples in Sect. 6 where we present how they operate together within a running Openstack environment. Furthermore, OpenStack offers communication through a web interface called Horizon or dashboard. The Openstack conceptual architecture is presented in Fig. 2 available from [12] where is depicted interaction among OpenStack services mentioned in Table 1. For communication may be used MySQL, MariaDB, and PostgreSQL databases and RabbitMQ, Opid, and ActiveMQ message buses.

Table 1. OpenStack services and projects

Projects	Services	Short description
Horizon	Dashboard	Web interface for using OpenStack services and manipulating with virtual resources
Keystone	Identity service	Authentification and authorisation functions
Glance	Image service	Image Management services
Neutron	Networking service	Provides services for networking of OpenStack resources to external network
Nova	Compute service	Lifecycle management of virtual resources
Cinder	Block storage service	Provides persistent storage functionality t virtual resources
Swift	Object storage service	Data management over RESTful and HTTP based API's implementing fault tolerant mechanisms for data replication and scaling
Ceilometer	Telemetry services	Collecting measurements and monitoring of resources
Heat	Orchestration service	Coordination of multiple virtual resources within one service provided to user

5.1   Graphical User Interface for Manipulating Virtual Resources

Horizon is a project defined within an Openstack environment for managing virtual resources over a graphical user web interface. A screenshot of Horison GUI called dashboard is presented in Fig. 3. The dashboard is an Openstack component that implements a set of OpenStack services over the user interface. The OpenStack users are given the possibility to manipulate virtual resources over the visual commands provided on the web interface. In the background on the graphical user interface are implemented service calls to the APIs of all officially supported services included within OpenStack. Note that OpenStack also provides programmable access to its services over the APIs that we describe in a sequel. In the exercises, we will more focus on programmable access.

5.2   Authentification and Authorisation Functions

Authentication and authorization of user access to cloud computing resources in OpenStack are managed through Keystone service. Objects that may be subject to keystone management operations are users, tenants, roles, instances (from the catalog of services), and networks (endpoints of the virtual resources running in the OpenStack environment).

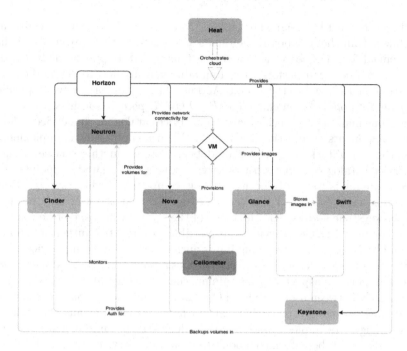

Fig. 2. Open stack conceptual architecture. Source www.openstack.org

Fig. 3. Horison graphical user interface

All objects must be assigned to tenants. Name tenant is used in the command line while within the dashboard the tenant is referred to the project. A role has to be defined for each object assigned to a tenant and its purpose is to restrict actions each object can perform. Even an administrator has to define their role and have to be assigned to the tenant. Actions enabled for roles may be specified within special policy documents, $/etc/PROJECT/policy.json$ files.

Keystone maintains a service register or service catalog for the services offered by the components within the OpenStack. When a component is implemented within the OpenStack cluster it should be registered in this service catalog. The service catalog contains a list of service names and related endpoints. The service endpoint is the URL granted to this component within the OpenStack cluster. The main benefit of this service catalog is that the user only needs to know the keystone address and the name of the service which she or he wants to access. Then the keystone service is responsible to verify the authentification of users and based on its role verifying if it is authorized to access the service. Users never access Openstack services directly, it does always over the keystone service. Another important aspect of maintaining the service catalog is in managing independency between users and local OpenStack implementation so the changes in endpoints are not propagated to all its users. I.e. this means that when a service changes its implementation and is deployed on another endpoint, the end-user does not be informed about that action. Service users will get the correct service endpoint address by asking the keystone service just in time the service is needed.

5.3   Management of Disk Images

Glance is a component within Openstack with the main function to manage disk images. For quick and fast deployment of virtual resources, a pre-installed disk image may be used to boot from. Glance maintains the register of these disk images which are cached to compute node during instantiation of virtual resources and then copied to the ephemeral virtual resource disk location. These images had installed operating system but have removed secure identity elements such as Secure Shell host key (SSH) and network device MAC address that make these images generic and easily transferable to the number of virtual machines without risk of interleaving the processes among them. This host-specific information is transferred at system boot within a cloud-init script.

Disk images may be also made for specific purposes. For example, if there is a multiple need for a specific web service, then the pre-installed disk image may contain also web service preinstallation so the deployment process may be fully automated and faster for the number of instances. There are available numerous tools for the creation of such disk images with the separated cloud-init script, like for example appliance-creator, Oz, and many others.

5.4   Network Management Functions

The main function of the Neutron component is network management and offers to its users a Networking as A Service (NaaS) functionality. This function is needed for configuring virtual resources to operate within the virtual network environment. OpenStack uses the Open vSwitch plugin to allow software-defined networking of networking infrastructure and it provides several APIs and related services for its management. These include the connection of virtual instances to virtual isolated networks, virtual routers, interconnection of virtual networks via virtual routers, and external networks via external gateways connected to virtual routers. Thus, users may configure their own virtual networks appliances which are interconnected to the external network. Neutron can manage multiple network appliances.

Each instance may be associated with a private or public network and is assigned a private and public IP address range. A private or fixed IP address is assigned to an instance during its creation and is active during the instance lifetime. On the other hand, a public IP address or floating IP address is not dependent on instance lifetime and it may be associated with an instance when the instance is made available for the public and disassociated when an instance is removed from the public. Network Address Translation (NAT) transverse between public and private address spaces during communication flow between these two networks.

5.5   Management of Virtual Instances

Nova is a component responsible for instance management. This includes managing flavors, key pairs, instances, floating IPs, and security groups. Flavors define the number of resources that are allocated to an instance. Before an instance can be launched, the authentification of users should be performed. An authenticated user uses key pair (SSH pair) and a security group to create its virtual instances. It can use its SSH or the SSH generated by the system. The SSH key pairs are not new in the OpenStack environment but it is reused principle from Linux. When a virtual instance is deployed a public key is placed in $authorized_keys$ file and the running instance can be accessed using an SSH connection without a password. The security group is a firewall at the cloud infrastructure layer that should be opened to allow connection to the virtual instance. By default, virtual instances belonging to the same security group may communicate to each other, while the rules should be specified for the Internet Control Message Protocol, SSH, and other connections outside of the security group.

5.6   Management of Persistent Memory

Cinder is a component for the management of block storage. It is used whenever a persistent memory space is needed, not dependent on instance lifetime. Note that disk space associated with an instance at its creation is destroyed at its termination. This is not the case for block storage. Block storage may be requested by users on-demand and may be presented to running instances. It is also used for storing the snapshots of block volumes or of instances that are needed for instance boot.

5.7   Management of Object Storage

Swift is an object storage management component. Files and containers are stored as objects without any metadata and are transferred from a virtual instance to an object store by using client-server communication with minimal overhead to the operating system.

5.8   Performance Measurement Functions

A component within Openstack that is responsible for monitoring Openstack resources and collecting resource measurements is called Ceilometer. Originally it was designed for billing purposes but later it receives much generic purpose to take care of all telemetry within the OpenStack. These include also observation of instance behavior, its availability and performances, and for alarm setting. A very important application of the ceilometer measurement system is the alarm is for autoscaling of OpenStack resources at runtime.

5.9   Orchestration Functions

Openstack has a component responsible for the orchestration of its resources. When multiple resources are intended to be used for the specific purpose and the same user these resources have to be interconnected and tied together so all operations that are available for regular Openstack instances may be also performed on this'orchestrated' instance. For this purpose within a heat component of Openstack, a template file may be used to specify resources that need to be orchestrated, to specify their order and their mutual dependencies, required data that needs to be transferred among them. Heat is also compatible with Amazon Web Service (AWS) Cloud Formation template language.

6   Examples

In this section, we present the examples implementing the design principles presented in Sect. 4 for the management and orchestration of virtual network resources. The key learning objective is to explain to students the need for implementing autonomic behavior in the management and orchestration of virtualized network resources and to understand the role of functional programming for future network evolution. Our examples are based on the use of the OpenStack platform, Sect. 5, which is an open-source platform for the management of virtual resources.

Here, in the examples that follow, the focus is on writing Heat scripts that are used to automate management and orchestration of cloud resources and to order the results on the composite resources. The resources may be virtual instances, floating IP addresses, volumes, security groups, users, or even some advanced functionalities such as high availability, instance autoscaling. Heat supports various template formats and the format we will be using in this tutorial is the HOT (Heat Orchestration Template) format written as YAML files that are declarative template format that implements REST APIs calls to Openstack native services described in Sect. 5. In a declarative sense, the template is used to order what to manage or orchestrate and not how to manage and orchestrate. It belongs to the group of domain-specific languages containing the configuration of instructions with API system calls while keeping the API itself minimalistic. Thus, the HOT scripts are executed with runtime Openstack services calls by the Heat service[1]. The HOT files are readable and writable by humans and can be managed by version control systems. A resource or group of resources created during a HOT deployment is referred to as a stack. We will use the following examples to describe the particulars of writing a HOT template and to show how ORCHESTRATION can be used.

These exercises were developed for the Software Engineering Management course within the Computer Science master study program available at the link[2]. The source files for the examples that follow are available at GitHub[3].

6.1 Example 1

This is a starting Example 1 that presents a simple HOT template. Here we explain the minimum required information for writing a functional HOT template. In the sequel, the specific parts of the HOT script are explained along with their purpose.

Example 1.
```
heat_template_version: 2013-05-23

description: Simple template to deploy a single compute instance

resources:
    my_instance:
        type: OS::Nova::Server
        properties:
            image: ubuntu_cloud14
            flavor: m1.small
            key_name: my_key1
            networks:
                - network: my_net1
```

---

[1] https://wiki.openstack.org/wiki/Heat/DSL.

[2] https://github.com/nikoladom91/ARIKS2016/.

[3] https://github.com/nikoladom91/ARIKS2016/tree/master/Skripte/Heat.

The heat_template_version key is a required field in every HOT template and describes details about the version of the HOT template. The description section is optional and is usually used to describe the purpose and function of the template.

The resources section introduces all the resources that will be part of the resource management strategy described by the HOT template. The resources that can be managed are specific OpenStack resources such as a virtual machine, nova-network, security group, etc. These resources will be subject to creation and configuration during the deployment and resource lifetime. It is required to have at least one resource per template. Each resource must have a type specified. The list of available resource types for OpenStack version Mitaka can be found on the web-page https://docs.openstack.org/heat/mitaka/template_guide/openstack.html. The available resources somewhat differ between Open-Stack versions so the correct one must be referenced when looking for them.

Services might require properties that contain the information required for their successful deployment. Some properties under the properties section are mandatory while others are optional. The properties of a resource are described under its type. Example 1 deploys a stack containing a single VM with hard-coded property values. The resource is identified as "my_instance" and is of type "OS::Nova::Server". Its properties describe what image and flavor will be used in the VM deployment, what security key will be provided to the OS, and to what neutron network the vNIC of the VM will be connected. All the input resources used as properties need to be defined beforehand or the deployment of the stack will not be successful. Example 1 is not meant to be deployed, although it would deploy successfully. We will go over deploying a template after introducing Example 2.

6.2   Example 2

Example 2 deploys a stack similar to Example 1 but, unlike Example 1, it can be passed different values for its deployment. If no new values are given, the specified default values will be used and the stacks from Example 1 and Example 2 will functionally be the same. They will still be separate entities as different UUIDs (Universally Unique Identifier) will be generated for the created resources. Providing different input parameters, VMs with, among other things, different images can be created with functionally different resources.

In this example, we introduce parameters. This section is optional and enables the use of multiple stacks within the same script. Optional parameters are used to allow passing the input values that are needed for stack deployment. Specific parameters are named, similar to specific resources, and are described by attributes. In this example, specific parameters are flavor, key, image. The type attribute is the only mandatory attribute and it defines the type of the value that the parameter represents. The label and description attributes are human-readable parameter names and description and the default attribute describes the value that the parameter takes if no other value is given. There are more optional attributes that are not covered in this example.

Example 2.

```
heat_template_version: 2013-05-23
description: Simple template to deploy a single compute instance
parameters:
    image:
        type: string
        label: Image name or ID
        description: Image to be used for compute instance
        default: ubuntu_cloud14
    flavor:
        type: string
        label: Flavor
        description: Type of instance (flavor) to be used
        default: m1.small
    key:
        type: string
        label: Key name
        description: Name of key-pair to be used for compute instance
        default: my_key1
    private_network:
        type: string
        label: Private network name or ID
        description: Network to attach instance to.
        default: my_net1
resources:
    my_instance:
        type: OS::Nova::Server
        properties:
            image: { get_param: image }
            flavor: { get_param: flavor }
            key_name: { get_param: key }
            networks:
                - network: { get_param: private_network }
outputs:
    instance_ip:
    description: IP address of the instance
    value: { get_attr: [my_instance, first_address] }
```

The resource property uses an input parameter with the syntax

```
"<property name>: { get_param: <parameter name> }".
```

Upon deployment, the resource property will assume the value of the specified parameter. This allows the user to deploy HOT multiple times with different input parameters and create unique stacks. The stacks may share the same blueprint but are separate entities with potentially different functionalities. The outputs section allows for specifying output parameters available to the users once the template has been deployed. We will see its use in later examples. Here we use it to output the IP of the VM we created as the parameter instance_ip. The resource attribute value is retrieved with the following syntax:

```
"{ get_pattr: [<resource name>, <attribute name>] }" .
```

This is used to retrieve resource attributes generated during deployment that can be used as outputs of the stack or as inputs for other resources.

6.3   Example 3

In example 3, we illustrate the automation process of instancing and deploying a VM with an initial working state. This example deploys an instance of VM that generates a *Hello Word* string message.

Example 3.

```
. . .



resources:
   rng:
      type: OS::Heat::RandomString
      properties:
         length: 4
         sequence: digits

   inst_simple:
      type: OS::Nova::Server
      properties:

...



         user_data_format: RAW
         user_data: |
            #!/bin/sh
            echo "Hello, World!" >> hello.txt

     inst_advanced:
        type: OS::Nova::Server
        properties:

...



         user_data_format: RAW
         user_data:
            str_replace:
               params:
                  __name__: { get_param: name }
                  __rnum__:  get_attr: [rng, value]
               template: |
                  #!/bin/sh
```

```
              echo "Hello, my name is __name__. Here is a random
number: __rnum__."
>> hello.txt
```

To automate certain procedures, users can pass blobs of data that the VM can access through the metadata service or config drive. VMs that employ services like cloud-init can use the data in various ways. The blob of data is defined in the resource property "user_data". If given without additional attributes, the value of user_data will be passed. If given the params and template attributes, the targeted text string defined under params is, within the text under the template, replaced with the defined value. Example 3 replaces the "__name__" string with the parameter name while and "__rnum__" replaces it with a randomly generated number.

Here we can see the implementation of the get_attr method where a value of a different resource is used within another resource. In this case, a resource that when deployed represents a randomly generated number is created. The value of that resource is then used as an input for the data blob passed to the VM.

Example 3 HOT when deployed will generate a random number and instantiate two VMs. If the image used to instantiate a VM has the cloud-init service, that VM will execute the shell commands given in the user data as the root user. The inst_simple VM will generate a hello.txt file in the/directory containing the "Hello, World!" string. The inst_advanced VM creates the same file with the difference that the string within it contains the parameter name given as a HOT input and a randomly generated number.

6.4   Example 4

Example 4 depicts a HOT which deploys two interdependent VMs. The first VM is a MySQL server. It is automatically configured during its initialization and when deployed is fully functional. The second VM is a WordPress server that uses the MySQL database as its backend. As the WordPress server requires for the MySQL database to be accessible during its initialization, the MySQL server employs the waiting service. The WordPress VM initialization is therefore not started before the MySQL resource is deployed, as it requires some of its output attributes as its input parameters. Each VM is started within a standalone HOT file which is both used as nested templates within the Example 4 script.

HOT allows for the usage of nested code. This is done by defining the resource type as a batch to a different HOT file. It can be given as the path on the local environment from where the heat command is issued or as an http/https link to a .yaml page accessible online containing the relevant HOT. When a nested HOT resource is defined, the input parameters are passed to that HOT through the resource properties. The output parameters of the nested HOT are accessible as the resource attributes in the parent HOT.

When executing more complicated deployments with custom codes given as user data, Heat cannot natively know if the given code has been executed correctly. The VM is deployed and Heat continues deploying other resources.

Whether or not the code in the user data was successfully executed or how long it took is not taken into account. If other resources depend on the successful execution of the user data code, it is needed to implement a waiting mechanic.

Heat provides two resources for the waiting mechanic. These resorces are the OS::Heat::WaitCondition and the OS::Heat::WaitConditionHandle type resources. The OS::Heat::WaitCondition resource defines the waiting conditions. In the timeout property, it defines how long the execution will wait for the HOT to complete before it is declared as a failed execution. The count property defines how many times a confirmation signal is expected before the execution is considered as successful. The handle property needs a link to the OS::Heat::WaitConditionHandle resource. That link is given by the get_resource method.

The OS::Heat::WaitConditionHandle type resource is used to register the confirmation signal sent from the execution. It does this by defining an address that when curled with the appropriate information registers a confirmation signal. This curl command is inserted into the user data code at the point where we want the confirmation signal to be sent, there can be multiple signals sent, each of which goes towards satisfying the count condition in the OS::Heat::WaitConditionHandle type resource.

7   Use Cases from Industry and Reflection on Design Principles

In this section, we firstly discuss the benefits and drawbacks of virtualizing network functions and explain the relation with design principles provided in Sect. 4. Then in the second use case, we explain how the examples provided in Sect. 6 may be used to implement design principles in management and orchestration of network resources.

7.1   Virtualisation of Mobile Switching Centre

There are huge industry efforts to virtualize network functions that were developed in a closed industry product fashion. Some of the network products are older than forty years and are still active nodes within the current telecommunication network. One example is the Ericsson Mobile Switching Centre node that was used as an example in Part I of this lecture series [2]. In this use case, we elaborate the efforts done by leading telecom industries to implement self-management design principles explained in Sect. 4 and thus increase the level of automation of their products. In this use case, we present an example of automating the *Mobile Switching Centre* function standardized by the 3GPP body as part of the core network.

Mobile Switching Center implements communications switching functions, such as call set-up, release, and routing. It also performs other duties, including routing SMS messages, conference calls, fax, and service billing as well as interfacing with other networks, such as the public switched telephone network

(PSTN). This network function was actively been developed during 2G/3G generation networks. More information about this switching function can be found at the 3GPP standards website (www.3gpp.org).

This product has a large installed base and is still progressively used in many operator networks. Therefore, it is estimated that operators will use 2G/3G networks as fallbacks for a long time to come, so it was decided to virtualize MSC to make it more compatible with modern environments.

There are identified numerous benefits of virtualizing this function. For instance, the virtual appliance of MSC function may be faster deployed and redeployed and thus it can be sold more quickly as only SW is needed for deployment. Both the product and the environment are scalable. The capacity increase is very simple; the capacity of the product is increased by allocating more resources to the VMs or deploying additional VMs, and the capacity increase of the infrastructure itself would require adding more servers to the data center. From here it may be concluded that virtualization enables multiple products to run on the same data center and thus allowing operators more freedom in resource management. On the other hand side, the same data center could be used for multiple products, network functions, and other virtualized instances thus eliminating the need for hardware dedicated to every application domain.

Despite numerous benefits that virtualization of MSC network function may imply there are also numerous potential problems that may arise on the way. In the case of Ericsson MSC, the product is developed in an evolutionary fashion for more than forty years and as such it grows in complexity. The product has numerous functions that enable its long-living but these functions were implemented highly relying on hardware aiming to satisfy very high reliability and safety requirements. To implement such hardware-independent behavior product has to be redesigned. Since the product is very complex because of the number of functions implemented this act would require a lot of expertise and cost. Another very important aspect to understand is that mobile switching function that serves in real-time services such as telephone call has very high-reliability requirements and is usually higher than is the case with standard resources that are getting virtualized. Securing reliable operation of such virtualized MSC requires an additional layer that would secure this requirement. Therefore, Ericsson started developing a new project, its own proprietary network function virtualization infrastructure called Ericsson Cloud Execution Environment CEE. The product is developed by taking OpenStack as a base where proprietary solutions are incorporated to increase service reliability of virtualized products run on it. In Ericsson MSC not only software switching function was hardware related but also this special-purpose hardware is implemented with the special requirement to be reliable. The reliability of this special-purpose hardware is also much higher than is the case with standard equipment. Therefore, an additional solution is to create a specific data center for virtual network function purposes with high demands on performances. There are other open-source ongoing initiatives to produce High Available OpenStack solutions such as for example OPNFV Doctor, OpenStack Freezer, and OpenStack Masakari. All these solutions work on the monitor, detect and correct solutions. However, the implementation solution for the above-stated design principles has to be invented and deployed within these solutions.

7.2 Management Functions for Reliable and Stable Operation

Despite efforts to virtualize network functions there are also numerous efforts devoted to development of reliability and management functions that would enable delivery of better quality products to the Cloud users.

It was recognized by leading industries that there exists some stability patterns and anti-patterns that may have serious consequences for the system in operation and these common sources may lead to more then one failure in the system, [14]. These antipatterns and patterns should be considered while making automation scripts. In Sect. 4 we provide design principles that are motivated from biological systems and there are plenty of cases which may be reused implementing network autonomy and to address the system stability issues. Here we will not elaborate them in detail but will just reflect on some interesting cases to consider while automating the system management and orchestration. Note that scripts provided in the Sect. 6 are actually implementing the cases listed bellow.

One case is that when your product is longer time in production and serving a number of users sometimes it would be recommended to restart this product. This is the case with all technical products because some bugs are not resulting with system failure immediately but are accumulating into wrong state. In such a cases for some products we may have automation scripts that would initiate deployment of new identical machine as the existing one and delete the existing machine. This idea is reused from *living system* principle and survival instinct and the system tension to come back to initial equilibrium state. The script provided as Example 2 in Sect. 6 may be useful for implementing in this case.

Another example is that the existence of automation script allows changing of the resource (product offered in virtual network environment) and needs just update of the automation script in the way to change the product name and start automatic build process of a new machine. The machine with old product could be simply deleted for which you can have automation script as well. In some cases this change should be governed and comply to strict policies that may easily be incorporated into automation script. This would mean the system is *policy based* and has predefined rules that governs the system behaviour.

Furthermore, there may be number of security threats from the environment that when detected may be solved by using automation scripts explained in the previous Sect. 6. Here we implement into the system *context awareness* design principles which impose that system is able to adapt to its environment conditions.

There is also a separate auto-scaling OpenStack function that may be used in automation scripts in cases of large traffic periods to duplicate the instance or when traffic demand decreases to delete one of the instances. This solution would realize the *self–similarity and adaptive* design principles which state that the system organization and global properties persists as systems scales and thus adapt to environmental conditions. For implementing full autonomy of such principle the adequate metric system (e.g. performance measurement functions as explained in Sect. 4) should be incorporated into the automation script so the system may follow the *knowledge–based* principle and may build also appropriate knowledge base.

8 Discussion

From the very beginning, the telecommunication network has been built with the main aim to divide the management of network cables and switches into separate businesses which would provide connection services to its users. At its core, the switching board and network cables have implemented the multiplexing idea. With the help of the switching board, the same user can be involved in a number of connections (i.e., calls from the subscriber's perspective or processes from the processor's perspective) in the time-sharing principle. This main multiplexing principle has been widely applied in every resource which is consumed in the network. During the network evolution, calls/processes are multiplexed over each network cable, over the processors in switching nodes, over the memory in shared memory devices, etc. In the ongoing evolution step, the processes are multiplexed over the shared network resources (not node resources) and even network functions are considered as network resources that users share in the time-sharing principle.

The above-mentioned multiplexing or time-sharing of common resources and providing them as a service is implemented by adding new abstraction layers and new virtualization layers that introduce the need for new management functions securing safe and reliable switching of users on these common resources.

This specialty of switching or multiplexing functions introduces high demands on safe and reliable management. Since common resources are shared among its users in the time-sharing principle, every lost time slot is directly causing inefficiency and money loss. On the other hand, the services provided for each user must be safe and reliable, so that the user does not sense other users using the same shared resource and users do not overlap on the same shared resource at the same time.

Because of this specific characteristic of sharing resources, specific switching programming languages were developed based on the functional programming paradigm. The essence of functional programming is the ability to have functions that would for the given input always generate the same output. Thus, these functions can be easily formally verified by using mathematical logic. This is especially important in complex systems that require high safety and reliable operation. Although in complex time-sharing systems it may be difficult to achieve pure functional programs, any good programmer should strive to get these programs as functional as possible. Here it is clear that functions that may generate different outputs for the same input are useless and introduce complexity into the system.

In the telecom world, there are plenty of programming languages present in the switching domain. During history, these languages evolved, so that functional programming languages, such as Erlang, have also taken dominance in this area. From the system verification point of view, the testers are used to working on a sequence of execution statements to easily follow the program execution. However, in a purely functional world, the failures would be minimized by proper formal methods. Hence, in the fault mining process traveling across huge state machines would be avoided. Therefore, in principle, the more functional our code is, the fewer verification efforts would be needed.

As we have seen, complex software tends to become even more complex. Many software products started without a functional programming paradigm and have become so complex that it would be too expensive and almost impossible to redesign them in a functional programming fashion. However, new developments, especially those in which new abstractions are added and old source code is easily separated from the new code, should aim to move as much as possible to the functional paradigm. As we can see, evolution is just adding new abstractions and new management functions responsible for managing these virtual resources and implementation of these abstractions would be easier with purely functional code.

Introducing automation of management and orchestration of network functions means that we introduced an additional abstract layer for the purpose of network control. Here we allow the use of programming instructions for calling the installation, orchestration deployment operations performed by other tools, packages, even vendors. Although the list of instructions that should be performed may seem simple it is always a problem in overlaps and gaps in their execution. Also, not all combinations work properly together, and still, there is a need for a lot of network engineering work before the automation becomes working and stable. Here in this lecture we presented automation scripts that work with HEAT service and are written in a declarative language. Unfortunately, currently, automation with help of declarative language is limited in possibilities to combine elements these scripts manage and a lot of network engineering work is needed. If all elements were following the pure functional programming paradigm the evolution of the network towards autonomy and self–management would be simpler and the use of declarative programming would enable the opening of complex software systems with help of virtualization to the end-users.

9   Conclusion

In these Part II lectures, as well as in Part I [2], we went through the network evolution from the design principles and technology perspective. In Part I, we introduced the main definition of a complex system, discussed the challenges of their management. We introduced generic design principles for structuring software systems, such as modularity, abstraction, layering, and hierarchy, in order to achieve easier management. Furthermore, we introduced service orientation and virtualization technologies that are used as a tool for implementing these principles. At the end of Part I, we discussed the example of the case study reporting experiences in redesigning existing complex software products with these design principles.

In this Part II, as a continuation of the previous lecture, we introduced new evolutionary changes that are currently implemented within the networks. These are Network Function Virtualisation and Software Defined Networks. The two new concepts could be viewed just as adding new virtualization layers on network resources (hardware and software functions) and introducing more service orientation and computation for each above-mentioned network resource. Therefore, in addition to design principles stated in the previous Part I lectures that are related to the structuring of complex software, we introduced now in Part II the design principles for implementing network autonomic behavior. For the purpose of introducing the students to new technological changes, we provide examples by introducing students to HEAT declarative language for writing automation scripts in the OpenStack platform for managing and orchestrating resources controlled by OpenStack-based Cloud. For that purpose, we provided four examples and explain a set of instructions used for the scripts in the example. Furthermore, we discuss two use cases of virtualization and elaborate management and orchestration benefits and problems that may arise in such an act. Finally, we discuss the use of the examples for implementing management design principles and provide reflections on the importance of functional programming for future network evolution.

Acknowledgements. This work is supported by the ERASMUS+ project "Focusing Education on Composability, Comprehensibility and Correctness of Working Software", no. 2017-1-SK01-KA203-035402 and the research project "Reliability and Safety in Complex Software Systems: From Empirical Principles towards Theoretical Models in View of Industrial Applications (RELYSOFT)" no. HRZZ-IP-2019-04-4216 funded by the Croatian Science Foundation.

References

1. Agoulmine, N.: Autonomic Network Management Principles: From Concepts to Applications, 1st edn. Academic Press Inc., USA (2016)
2. Tihana Galinac Grbac: The Role of Functional Programming in Management and Orchestration of Virtualized Network Resources Part I. System structure for Complex Systems and Design Principles. CoRR abs/2107.12136 (2021)
3. Barabási, A.L.: Network Science. Cambridge University Press, 1st edn. (2016)
4. Beyer, B., Jones, C., Petoff, J., Murphy, N.R.: Site Reliability Engineering: How Google Runs Production Systems, 1st edn. O'Reilly Media Inc. (2016)
5. Denning, P.J.: Software quality. Commun. ACM **59**(9), 23–25 (2016)
6. ETSI Industry Specification Group (ISG) NFV: ETSI GS NFV-MAN 001 v1.1.1: Network Functions Virtualisation (NFV); Management and Orchestration. European Telecommunications Standards Institute (ETSI) (2014). https://www.etsi.org/deliver/etsi_gs/NFV-MAN/001_099/001/01.01.01_60/gs_NFV-MAN001v010101p.pdf. Accessed 1 July 2018

7. Ganchev, I., van der Mei, R.D., van den Berg, H. (eds.): State of the Art and Research Challenges in the Area of Autonomous Control for a Reliable Internet of Services, pp. 1–22. Springer, Cham (2018)
8. Han, B., Gopalakrishnan, V., Ji, L., Lee, S.: Network function virtualization: challenges and opportunities for innovations. IEEE Commun. Mag. **53**(2), 90–97 (2015)
9. Jackson, K.: OpenStack Cloud Computing Cookbook. Packt Publishing (2012)
10. Mangey Ram, J.P.D. (ed.): Tools and Techniques in Software Reliability Modeling, pp. 281–295. Academic Press (2019)
11. Open Networking Foundation. Open Networking Foundation (2018). https://opennetworking.org/. Accessed 1 July 2018
12. OpenStack Cloud Software. OpenStack Foundation (2018). https://www.openstack.org. Accessed 1 July 2018
13. Radez, D.: OpenStack Essentials. Packt Publishing (2015)
14. Michael, T.: Nygard: Release It! Pragmatic Programmers, LLC (2018)
15. Sloss, B.T., Nukala, S., Rau, V.: Metrics that matter. Commun. ACM **62**(4), 88 (2019)
16. Sterritt, R., Bustard, D.: Autonomic computing - a means of achieving dependability? In: Proceedings 10th IEEE International Conference and Workshop on the Engineering of Computer-Based Systems, pp. 247–251 (2003)

Towards Better Tool Support for Code Comprehension

Tibor Brunner[ID], Máté Cserép[ID], Anett Fekete[ID], Mónika Mészáros[ID], and Zoltán Porkoláb[✉][ID]

Eötvös Loránd University, Faculty of Informatics, Budapest, Hungary
{bruntib,gsd}@caesar.elte.hu, {mcserep,afekete,bonnie}@inf.elte.hu

Abstract. In software development, bug fixing and feature development requires a thorough understanding of all details and consequences of the planned changes. For long-existing large software systems, the code-base has been developed and maintained for decades by fluctuating teams, thus original intentions are lost, the documentation is untrustworthy or missing. Most times, the only reliable information is the code itself. Source code comprehension of such large software is an essential, but usually very challenging task. The comprehension process and approach of existing systems is fundamentally different from writing new software, and the usual development tools provide poor support in this area. Throughout the years, different tools have been developed with various complexity and feature set for code comprehension but none of them fulfilled all specific requirements yet. In this paper we discuss the most accepted models for code comprehension, the required feature set for tools supporting the comprehension process and the various approaches of existing solutions. We present CodeCompass – an open source LLVM/Clang based tool to help understanding large legacy software systems – in detail to analyse the required interface, possible design choices and implementation considerations. Based on the LLVM/Clang compiler infrastructure, CodeCompass gives exact information on complex C/C++ language elements such as inheritance, overloading, variable usage, possible function pointer and virtual function calls etc. These are all features for which various existing tools provide only partial support. Although CodeCompass supports mainly the C and C++ programming languages, it has a restricted support for Java and Python languages as well, therefore our investigation is language-independent.

Keywords: static analysis · code comprehension · Clang

1 Introduction

The maintenance of large, long-existing legacy systems is troublesome. During the extended lifetime of a system the code quality is continuously eroding, the original intentions are lost due to the fluctuation among the developers, and the documentation is getting unreliable. Especially in the telecom industry, high

Z. Porkoláb and V. Zsók (Eds.): CEFP 2019, LNCS 11950, pp. 165–201, 2023.
https://doi.org/10.1007/978-3-031-42833-3_6

reliability software products, such as IMS signaling servers [1] are typically in use for 20–30 years [2,3]. The development landscape has the following peculiar characteristics: i) the software needs to comply with large, complex and evolving standards ii) has a multiple-decade long development and maintenance life-cycle iii) is developed in large (100+ heads) development organization iv) which is distributed in multiple countries and v) transfers of development responsibility from one side to the other occasionally.

However, this software development landscape is not unique to the telecom industry and our observations can be applied at other industries, such as finance, IT platforms, or large-scale internet applications, etc.; all areas where large and complex software is developed and maintained for a long time.

It was observed, that in such a design environment, development and maintenance become more and more expensive. Prior to any maintenance activity – new feature development, bug fixing, etc. – programmers first have to locate the place in the system *where* the change applies, have to understand the actual code to see *what* should be extended or modified to execute the task, and have to explore the connections to other parts of the software to decide *how* to interact in order to avoid regression. All these activities require an adequate understanding of the code in question and its certain environment. Although, ideally the executor of the activity has full knowledge about the system, in practice this is rarely the case. In fact, programmers many times have only a vague understanding of the program they're about to modify. A major cost factor of legacy systems is the extra effort of comprehension. Fixing new bugs introduced due to incomplete knowledge about the system is also very expensive, both in terms of development cost *and* time.

Therefore, code comprehension is a key factor of modern software development, exhaustively researched by both the industry and the academy. Various scientific and industrial papers published on the topic in conferences, e.g. in the series of International Conference of Program Comprehension, and in the Intellectual outputs No. O1 and O2 of the Erasmus+ Key Action 2 (Strategic partnership for higher education) project No.2017-1-SK01-KA203-035402: "Focusing Education on Composability, Comprehensibility and Correctness of Working Software" [4,5] among others.

As the documentation is unreliable, and the original design intentions are lost during the years and due to the fluctuation among the developers, the only reliable source of comprehension is the existing codebase.

Development tools are not performing well in the code comprehension process as they are optimized for writing new code, not for effectively browsing existing ones. When writing new code, the programmer spends a longer time working on the same abstraction level: e.g. defining class interfaces, and later implementing these classes with relationships to other classes. When one is going to understand existing code it is necessary to jump between abstraction levels frequently: e.g. starting from a method call into a different class we have to understand the role of that class with its complete interface, where and how that class is used, then we must dig down into the implementation details of another specific method.

Accordingly, when writing new code, a few files are open in parallel in the development tool, while understanding requires precise navigation through a large number of files.

Based on differences, there are specific tools targeting comprehension. These tools offer fast search options, precise code navigation and visualizations on various abstraction levels. We evaluated the major archetypes in Sect. 4, but neither of them was sufficient to apply to our specific requirements.

In this paper, we introduce **CodeCompass** [6] – an LLVM/Clang based open source tool developed by Ericsson and the Eötvös Loránd University, Budapest, to help the code comprehension process of large legacy systems. The tool has been designed to be extremely scalable, seamlessly working with many million lines of code. Fast search options help locate the requested feature by text search, definition or even by emitted log message. Once the feature has been located, precise information on language elements like read and write access for variables, inheritance and aggregation relations of types, and call points of functions (including possible calls on function pointers and virtual functions) are provided by the LLVM/Clang infrastructure. Easy navigation possibilities and a wide range of visualizations extend far more than the usual class and function call diagrams help the user a more complete comprehension.

Code comprehension may not be restricted to existing code-bases. Important architectural information can be gained from the build system, like relations between libraries, binaries and source files. To make the comprehension more extensive, CodeCompass also utilizes version control information, if available; Git commits and branching history, blame view are also visualized. Clang-based static analysis results are also integrated into the tool as well as some quality analytics based on software metrics.

For the sake of easy access for hundreds of developers, CodeCompass has a web-based architecture. The users can use the tool in a standard browser, however, an experimental Eclipse plugin has been also created using the open Thrift interface of CodeCompass. CodeCompass currently supports systems written in C, C++, Java, and Python, but its pluginable infrastructure makes it extensible for new languages, visualizations or interfaces. Having this web-based, pluginable, extensible architecture, the CodeCompass framework is intended to be an open platform for further code comprehension, static analysis and software metrics efforts.

Our paper is organized as follows. We give an overview on software comprehension models in Sect. 2 to review the theoretical background. In Sect. 3, we describe the specific problems which arise as a consequence of long-term, large-scale software development. We make suggestions on how these problems could be addressed from a program comprehension perspective. In Sect. 4, we review the state of the art comprehension tools for large scale software, showing their highlights and pitfalls. We present our tool called CodeCompass in detail in Sect. 5. Typical design and maintenance workflows used in large projects are discussed along with their CodeCompass support in Sect. 6. Our experience regarding the introduction of CodeCompass to the daily work, and the general acceptance of the framework is explained in Sect. 7, supported by usage statistics. Our paper concludes in Sect. 8 including some of our future plans.

2   Model of Code Comprehension

Since software comprehension is an inevitable part of software development, every developer, regardless of the quantity of experience, frequently engages in this activity during the development process, usually not only at the beginning of work but continuously throughout development. Each programmer has their own, occasionally unconscious method of understanding code, often not only one certain process but multiple various techniques that they utilize according to the current situation. There are various models of software comprehension. Multiple excellent papers have collected and classified comprehension models in the past, such as von Mayrhauser in [7], Storey in [8] and O'Brien in [9].

As von Mayrhauser et al. describe [7], there are several common elements in comprehension models, including knowledge related to and independent of the software, mental models with static elements such as plans, chunks, hypotheses etc. and dynamic elements like strategies or cross-referencing. There are also several elements intended to facilitate program comprehension, e.g. beacons, coding conventions, programming plans, algorithm implementations etc. Multiple of these elements can be discovered in every comprehension model.

The most widely known comprehension models revolve around two main approaches: the top-down and the bottom-up model.

2.1   Top-Down Models

In general, the top-down model covers understanding of the software starting from the "surface": the developer obtains a system-level overview from running the software thus recognizing the functionalities of the program. Then they might look into the system documentation and search for the main parts of the code, like functions responsible for controlling the program or main classes.

Brooks [10] builds up his top-down model by focusing on domain knowledge and hypotheses about the program. He says that the developer utilizes domain knowledge to construct the initial hypothesis about the software and this hypothesis induces other refined follow-up hypotheses which are then proved or contradicted by beacons.

Soloway, Adelson and Ehrlich [11] present another approach to the top-down model in their paper. Their model consists of hierarchical goals in understanding, starting from a general vision of comprehending the software. The knowledge is iteratively built up from matching the external representation of the code to various programming plans according to predetermined expectations, moving from top-level to low-level goals that include more and more details about the code. They also say that the top-down model is to be applied when the programmer faces familiar software code and structure.

2.2   Bottom-Up Models

The bottom-up model consists of studying smaller pieces of code first, and gradually moving towards understanding bigger sections of the code.

Pennington [12] separates two mental models in her comprehension model, namely the program model and the situation model. The former one is a preconception about the control flow of the software which is built from the bottom up, grasping the key code fragments. The program model development is done by studying text structure and programming plans. The situation model blends knowledge about the program goals and the data flow abstractions. It is also built from the bottom up but it uses the program domain knowledge that is hierarchically organized. While creating the situation model, the learned new knowledge (high-level plans) may induce changes in the program model or its input.

Shneiderman and Mayer [13] determine a flow of comprehension of the software. By processing the program code and the preexisting high-level concepts, the acquired knowledge travels from the short-term memory to the working memory to the long-term memory. The model also differentiates syntactic and semantic knowledge. Syntactic knowledge covers the understanding of the actual programming language, while semantic knowledge consists of different levels of program abstractions, from high-level (purpose of the software) to low-level (practical details of the code) concepts which altogether build up the program domain.

Levy remarks [14] that the top-down approach is usually applied when the purpose is to understand system architecture or system modules, while the bottom-up approach is mainly used when comprehending smaller pieces of code that build up a certain functionality. These two methods can also be combined during code comprehension, by gradually understanding one subcomponent of a system in a bottom-up fashion and mixing it with top-down elements when trying to incorporate the acquired knowledge into the known information about the software system.

2.3   Other Approaches

Von Mayrhauser et al. [7] constructed their own comprehension model, called integrated metamodel. It is based on the models of Letovsky [15], Pennington [12] and Soloway, Adelson and Ehrlich. They name three major components in the model that is connected to the comprehension process, all of which have already been mentioned in previous models:

- The program model from Pennington's bottom-up model.
- The situation model also derives from Pennington's model.
- Top-down structures (programming plans) described by Soloway, Adelson and Ehrlich.

These constitute the fourth major component, the knowledge base, which bears similar characteristics to Letovsky's knowledge-based model [15]. It contains the knowledge collected by the programmer which is necessary to build the other three models.

2.4   The Role of Concept Location

Concept location [16] is the process of discovering the definition of functionalities and possible changes in the code. According to Rajlich [17], there are two categories of concepts: implicit concepts are not direct implementations of a feature but rather assumptions and abstractions that can be deduced from the actual code; explicit concepts on the other hand cover direct implementation of classes, functions, variables etc.

Although concept location is not tightly related to any specific comprehension model, it is fundamental for any comprehension process. The notion of concept location is based on the pre-existing domain knowledge of the developer that helps locate the known functionalities in the codebase. Usually at the beginning of the comprehension process, the programmer is only aware of some features of the software and is completely new to the code itself.

3   Nature of the Problems

In this section, we overview the challenges of large-software maintenance we experienced at the development process of large software projects and collect the main requirements for a good comprehension tool.

3.1   Growing Complexity

Telecom standards, such as the 3rd Generation Partnership Project (3GPP) IP Multimedia Subsystem (IMS) [18] are large (more than 1000 pages) and complex and continuously evolving, so is the software that implements them. During a twenty years-long development lifespan, the size of the codebase easily grows above ten million lines. With the influx of new features, software bugs are inevitably introduced, that need continuous maintenance. This is typical for other large-scale projects, too. As the size and complexity of the software increases, the amortized cost of bug fixing or adding new features also raises. This cost factor is due to the increased number of software components and dependencies. When a patch is introduced, the programmer needs to be cautious to avoid regressions which is much harder when explicit and invisible, implicit dependencies flood the system.

The business environment often requires an in-service, non-disruptive upgrade, therefore in many cases, software components need to preserve backward compatibility, which also requires extra effort and has a negative impact on the system size.

The prime requirement towards a comprehension tool based on the above is that it should be scalable with regards to parsing and seamlessly work even more than 10 million lines of source code. It should be responsive, i.e. answering within 1 sec even on such a large codebase, since any longer interruption diverts the attention of the programmer.

3.2   Knowledge Erosion

The extended time of development causes serious fluctuation among the development teams' members. Knowledgeable developers who understand product use-cases, dataflow between components, and component dependencies are replaced by newcomers who suffer from the long learning curve to catch up and be near as efficient. In a multinational environment transfer of the development activity from one site to another happens multiple times. At such occasions, the knowledge loss could be dramatic.

A program comprehension tool shall bolster novices in their learning process. The top-down method of knowledge transfer and information catch up is supported by high-level architectural views such as graphical representation of source code structure, packaging structure and organized representation of documentation.

3.3   Multiple Views of the Software Based on Various Information Sources

Different design tasks, such as bug fixing, feature planning, or quality analysis require different views of the same software system. These views could not be created from the source code alone, they are synthesized from several other sources as well, such as *build processes, revision control information, documentations,* and *bug reports.*

While source code view is excellent for searching in the code and navigating the implementation, diagrams are more suitable for analyzing different types of static dependencies between language elements (such as call hierarchies, inheritance, interface usage patterns). Visualizing dependencies between source files, object files and executable libraries can help planning an upgrade procedure of a change.

Also, the history of the project can tell a lot about the evolution of the system. Files regularly coming up together in commits may imply deeper connections. Recent changes in the code may point to the source of freshly reported bugs. If static analysis results are available on the system, they can give hints about the possible issues related to the source under investigation.

The tool should support comprehension from the micro to the macro level. On the micro-level, navigation between symbols, on the macro level, component dependency analysis or visualization of metrics is to be integrated in a single workflow.

3.4   Communication Barriers

The possibility of communication inefficiency between teams located at different offices is quite high in a distributed development environment. When an incoming bug report arrives, a slow negotiation process starts between component development teams, sometimes blaming each other for the reason behind the fault. This inefficient process is partly due to the fact that they do not have a precise understanding about the actual, and the intended behavior of each others' components, and they cannot reason about that behavior efficiently via email or other communication channels.

The comprehension tool shall support knowledge sharing and teamwork, for example designers should be able to share program comprehension flow (e.g. currently examined file, position or diagram) with each other.

3.5   Multiple Programming Languages

Large software systems are rarely implemented in a single programming language. Core functionality, where efficiency is at utmost importance, may be implemented in C or C++. User interface may be written in Java (or even in JavaScript). There are usually service scripts around written in Perl, Python, Bash or other script languages. Third-party open source components are also implemented, increasing the number of different programming languages being used.

Naturally, the comprehension tool should support various languages within the same framework. The interface should be similar, but at the same time language-specific features should also be reflected. This allows an increased level of usability with the user-friendly approach of an established tool in the teams' workflow. It is even better, if the tool supports the *connections* between modules written in different languages. For these reasons, the software comprehension tool should support multiple programming languages and should be extensible with new languages with limited effort.

3.6   Hard to Deploy New Tools

According to our experience, it is difficult to convince developers to use new tools. Especially if the tool requires clumsy configuration or does not have an intuitive and responsive interface, engineers tend to see it as a barrier to their work and give up its usage very soon.

The comprehension tool should have an intuitive and responsive user interface and should be easy to install and use.

3.7   Requirement of Open Extensibility

When a software product is planned for long-term development, domain-specific languages are considered to describe the domain knowledge in a simple and compact manner [19]. DELOS language of the TelORB real-time operating system [20] is one of the DSLs widely used in the telecom industry. The comprehension tool should be easily extensible to parse such DSLs or proprietary languages in a pluginable manner even by third-party developers.

Moreover, it should reveal how artifacts in one language are mapped into other languages. CORBA interface definition language (IDL) [21], for example, is mapped into a client and a server function in the generated (C/C++/Java) code. We were looking for a comprehension tool that can seamlessly follow these mappings from DSL to host or generated code.

3.8 API Usage

Queries, which may not fit in the concept of web GUI can be initiated by external tools via an open-access interface implemented in Apache Thrift [22]. For example, suppose that one would like to refactor a program so the related functions get organized to a separate module. In order to accomplish this, we need to find the functions which are reachable through function calls from a given function. In other words, we would like to find the transitive closure of functions on function call relationship. As you may see, this is not a task strongly related to code comprehension, but can be solved based on the Language API.

```python
1  def compute_transitive_closure(ast_node_id):
2    ref_type = client.getReferenceTypes(ast_node_id)
3    ref_type = ref_type['This calls']
4
5    result = set()
6
7    process = set()
8    process.add(ast_node_id)
9
10   while process:
11     node = process.pop()
12     result.add(node)
13
14     refs = client.getReferences(node, ref_type, None)
15     for ref in refs:
16       if ref.id not in result:
17         process.add(ref.id)
18
19   return result
```

Listing 1.1. Python client script for querying transitive closure on function call relationship.

The code fragment in Python above demonstrates how to collect the function IDs that are reachable from the one given as a parameter. In the 2nd line, we get the possible reference types available on the given AST node ID. If that ID belongs to a function symbol then we can find ''This calls'' among the resulted types. Note that CodeCompass is also capable to return virtual function calls and calls via function pointers by the corresponding reference types. These are dynamic information, that is concretized in run-time, but if we include them in the algorithm, then an upper bound of all the possible calls can be gathered.

4 State of the Art

On the software market there are several tools that aim some kind of source code comprehension. Some of them use static analysis, others examine also the dynamic behavior of the parsed program. These tools can be divided into different archetypes based on their architectures and their main principles. On the one hand, tools have server-client architecture. Generally, these tools parse the project and store all necessary information in a database. The (usually web-based) clients are served from the database. These tools can be integrated into the workflow as nightly CI runs. This way the developers can always browse and analyze the whole, large, legacy code-base. Also, there are client-heavy applications where a smaller part of the code-base is parsed. This is the use case for IDE editors where the frequent modification of the source requires the quick update of the database about analyzed results. In this section, we present some tools used in industrial environment from each category.

Woboq Code Browser [23] is a web-based code browser for C and C++. This tool has extensive features which aim for fast browsing of a software project. The user can quickly find the files and named entities by a search field which provides code completion for easy usability. The navigation in the code-base is enabled through a web page consisting of static HTML files. These files are generated during a parsing process. The advantage of this approach is that the web client will be fast since no "on-the-fly" computation is needed on the server-side while browsing.

Hovering the mouse on a specific function, class, variable, macro, etc. can show the properties of that element. For example, in case of functions one can see its signature, place of its definition and place of usages. For classes, one can check the size of its objects, the class layout and offset of its members and the inheritance diagram. For variables, one can inspect their type and locations where they are written or read.

A frequent problem for software written in C or C++ is that its compilation consists of several steps. The first step is preprocessing which does textual changes in the source code before the compilation phase. Macro expansions result in a valid C/C++ code fragment, but their final value can only be determined after the preprocessing inasmuch they may depend on compiler arguments. In Woboq, the final value of macro expansions can also be inspected.

A very handy feature of the tool is semantic highlighting. By this feature, the different language elements can easily be distinguished: the formatting of local, global or member variables, virtual functions, types, typedefs, classes, macros, etc. are all different.

Woboq can provide the aforementioned features because the information needed is collected in a real compilation phase. The examined project first has to be compiled and parsed by Woboq. The parsing is done by LLVM/Clang infrastructure which makes the whole abstract syntax tree available. This way all pieces of semantic information can be extracted with the same semantics the final program is to have. This also gives a disadvantage of the tool, namely Woboq can only be used for browsing C and C++ projects.

OpenGrok [24] is a fast source code search and cross-reference engine. Contrary to Woboq, this tool doesn't perform deep language analysis, therefore it is not able to provide semantic information about the particular entities. Instead, it uses *Ctags* [25] for parsing the source code only textually, and to determine the type of the specific elements. Simple syntactic analysis enables the distinguishing

of function, variable or class names, etc. The search among these is highly optimized, and therefore very fast even on large code-bases. The search can be
accomplished via compound expressions (e.g. `defs:target`), containing even
wild cards, furthermore, results can be restricted to subdirectories. In addition
to text search, there is an opportunity to find symbols or definitions separately.
The lack of semantic analysis allows Ctags to support several (41) programming
languages. Also, an advantage of this approach is that it is possible to incremen-
tally update the index database. OpenGrok also gives the opportunity to gather
information from version control systems like Mercurial, SVN, CSV, etc.

Understand [26] is not only a code browsing tool, but also a complete IDE.
Its great advantage is that the source code can be edited and the changes of the
analysis can be seen immediately.

Besides code browsing functions already mentioned for previous tools, Understand provides a lot of metrics and reports. Some of these are the lines of code
(total/average/maximum globally or per class), number of coupled/base/derived
classes, lack of cohesion [27], McCabe complexity [28] and many others. *Treemap*
is a common representation method for all metrics. It is a nested rectangular
view where nesting represents the hierarchy of elements, and the color and size
dimensions represent the metric chosen by the user.

For large code-bases, the inspection of the architecture is necessary. Visual
representation is one of the most helpful ways of displaying such structures.
Understand can show dependency diagrams based on various relations such as
function call hierarchy, class inheritance, file dependency, file inclusion/import.
The users can also create their custom diagram type via the API provided by
the tool.

In programming, the core concepts are common across languages, but there
are some concepts which are interpreted differently in a particular language.
Understand can handle $\sim$ 15 languages and can provide language-specific information about the code e.g. function pointer analysis in C/C++ or package hierarchy diagrams in Ada.

Understand builds a database from the code-base. All information can be
gathered via a programmable API. This way the user can query all the necessary
information which are not included in the user interface.

CodeSurfer [29] is similar to Understand in the sense that it is also a thick
client, static analysis application. Its target is understanding C/C++ or x86
machine code projects. CodeSurfer accomplishes deep language analysis which
provides detailed information about the software behavior. For example, it implements pointer analysis to check which pointers may point to a given variable,
lists the statements which depend on a selected statement by impact analysis,
and uses dataflow analysis to pinpoint where a variable was assigned its value,
etc.

The aforementioned tools are mainly designed for code comprehension.
Another application area of static analysis is writing the code itself. This is
a very different way of working in many aspects, which requires another toolset.
Maybe the most widespread IDEs are *IntelliJ*, *NetBeans* and *Eclipse* primarily

for Java projects, and *QtCreator* or *CodeBlocks* mainly for C++ projects. The recent open-source tools tend to be pluginable so their functions can easily be extended according to special needs and domain-specific tasks. The greatest benefit of these tools is the ability of incremental parsing, which means the real-time re-analysis of small deviations in the source code.

5   The CodeCompass Architecture

In this section, we present the high-level architecture of CodeCompass as well as some important use-cases. This tool provides a read-only, searchable and navigable snapshot of the source code, rendered in both textual and graphical formats.

The overall architecture of CodeCompass is shown in Fig. 1. This image can also be considered the diagram of a pipeline from the input data to the clients. There are 5 steps of this pieline: i) The inputs of CodeCompass parser are the source code and the compilation database containing build instructions as described in Sect. 5.1. ii) The parsers gather the data and store them into iii) the database so iv) the service layer can provide these to the webserver towards v) the clients. Besides this vertical architecture there is an orthogonal view, since due to the heavily modular architecture or CodeCompass, each of these layers are

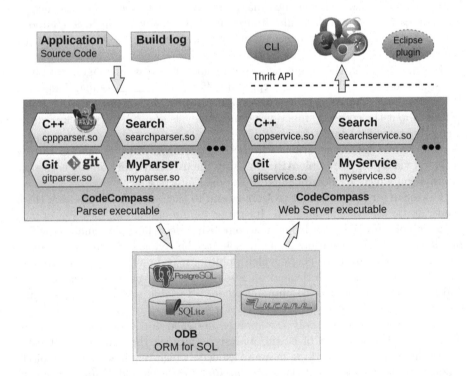

Fig. 1. CodeCompass architecture

extensible with additional plug-ins. The plug-ins provide a specific functionality of CodeCompass. This can be either a programming language, metric, version control data or other source code related operation.

5.1 Layers of the Architecture

Input Compilation Database. Since C and C++ are the most supported languages, we follow the stages of parsing a C++ project, however, other languages require similar introductory steps.

The build process of a C++ program consists of 3 main stages which are also relevant from CodeCompass point of view: preprocessing, compilation and linking. Each compilation action produces binary code from a *translation unit* (TU). A translation unit is made up of a source file and the included header files by #include directive. Some chunks of the source code may vary based on externally defined macro tokens. Conditional compilation is a technique that enables the developers to provide different definitions for certain functions, classes or other constructions. The main benefit of this is that the program can behave differently on specific target architectures or operating systems in order to take the advantage of low-level implementation possibilities of the language.

Suppose that `myprogram.cpp` contains the following lines:

```
1 #include <mylib.h>
2 void operation () {
3 #ifndef X86_64
4   do_this ();
5 #else
6   do_that ();
7 #endif
8 }
```

Listing 1.2. Conditional compilation in C.

The compilation is accomplished by the following command:

```
g++ myprogram.cpp -DX86_64 -I/path/to/my/lib/include ...
```

Depending on the presence of `-DX86_64` flag the `operation()` calls `do_this()` or `do_that()`. The definition of these functions may be located in `mylib.h` header file of which the path is given after the flag `-I`. There are numerous compiler flags which modulate the AST or affect the content of a TU in other ways, such as the ones in the example above. For example `-include` can force the inclusion of a header file as the content of the given TU. This means that the program not only depends on the source text but on external parameters too.

For the precise analysis of a C++ program, all this information is necessary as the previous example illustrates. If the user intends to find all function calls inside the body of `operation()` then we need every compiler flags which influence the build process.

A software project consisting of multiple source files is built traditionally with **make** or another build system. Our goal is to capture all compiler actions with all their build parameters emitted by the build system. We should find a way to catch all compiler invocations during the build process. Under Unix systems the LD_PRELOAD environment variable is available for this purpose.

This variable can be set a *shared object* file which may contain function symbols. When starting an arbitrary process, the content of this object file is searched every time a function symbol is used by the process. The functions defined in the shared object under LD_PRELOAD have priority over the ones under LD_LIBRARY_PATH. If non of them contains the given symbol then the process falls back to the system-level directories. This trick helps us to mock the exec...() system call family as we provide them under LD_PRELOAD. This way we are able to capture all process invocations including its command-line arguments. By pattern matching on the known compiler names, like g++/gcc/clang/clang++/cc, we can log the full compilation to a file and call the original compiler as well.

The output is a JSON file, named the *compilation database* [30]. This file is a list of JSON objects with the following keys:

file The path of the compiled source file. The build action may contain multiple source files, but the action belongs to only one of them which is indicated by this attribute.

directory The current working directory of the build action to which all paths are relative in the compilation arguments.

action The entire build command, including the compiler's name and all its command-line arguments.

Some build systems like CMake can emit the compilation database by adding an extra argument at configuration:

```
cmake -DCMAKE_EXPORT_COMPILE_COMMANDS=ON <source_directory> ...
```

The CodeCompass logger based on the LD_PRELOAD technique is also available by the following command in case our project uses a build system other than CMake and gathering build information is not possible otherwise:

```
CodeCompass_logger \
  -b "<build command>" \
  -o compilation_database.json
```

Parser. CodeCompass parser is a collection of language analyzers, text indexers, version control systems, metric counters, etc. These tools can be installed in the parser infrastructure as shared objects which provide the functions getOptions() to inform the users about the parser-specific command line options and make() to produce a parser object. These objects have to implement the AbstractParser interface with the functions parse(), markModifiedFiles() and cleanupDatabase().

The parsing phase is a time-consuming process. This procedure may contain text indexing, deep language parsing, static analysis, version history iteration, slicing algorithms, pointer analysis, etc. However, the development team might require to see the most up-to-date version of the software. It is obvious to see that the full parsing of a project may be unnecessary if only a few files are modified on a given day. Even if the few hours long parsing phase could be accomplished overnight in the CI system, it doesn't make sense to book the resources in this long period of time.

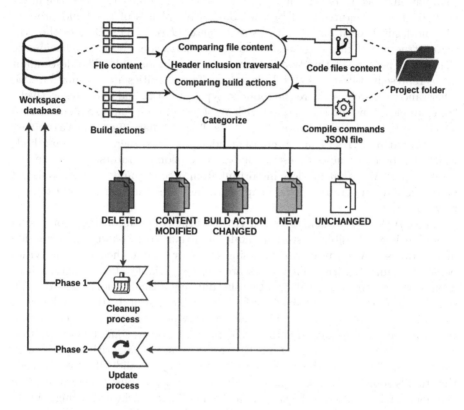

Fig. 2. Incremental parse workflow of CodeCompass

Therefore parsing is consisted of two sub-phases itself: *i*) cleanup and *ii*) update. In the *cleanup sub-phase* first the function markModifiedFiles() compares the workspace database and the project folder to deduce the either directly or indirectly modified (and deleted) files. Source code files usually *include* (or, depending on the language, *import, use*, etc.) other files and they might also include others transitively, thus forming dependency chains. Language-specific plugins can define their own semantic analysis to determine which files are connected this way. If a file was changed, every file depending on its content through direct or transitive includes has to be marked as a modified file. Then the cleanupDatabase() function wipes all outdated content from the workspace database. In the second *update sub-phase* the parse() function can reparse only the new and changed content, the differences between the old and new versions of the source code. This technique is called *incremental parsing* [31] and the workflow of the process is detailed in Fig. 2.

CodeCompass supports several programming languages.

C++ parser uses LLVM/Clang infrastructure which is a C/C++/Objective-C compiler. This is an open-source project that gives control over the entire compilation process. This means that one has the possibility to access the intermediate data structures used by the consecutive phases of the build process. The most substantial one is the *Abstract Syntax Tree* (AST). Besides the syntactic structure of the program, it also encapsulates some lexical and semantic elements. The root of this tree belongs to a translation unit. The descendant nodes represent statements and declarations. These entities are organized in two inheritance hierarchies where the topmost types are `Stmt` and `Decl`, respectively. For example a function is described with an object of type `FunctionDecl` that to which the following inheritance chain leads: `Decl` <: `NamedDecl` <: `ValueDecl` <: `DeclaratorDecl` <: `FunctionDecl`. Under this class, there are also methods which can be constructors, destructors or conversion operators. There are elements in the AST that are less important from a code comprehension point of view, like `MaterializeTemporaryExpr` that indicates the creation of a temporary object.

The C/C++ parser is in essence a visitor of the AST. According to our experiences, it is not feasible to store all nodes and their corresponding information in a database. When users are browsing the source code then most activities belong to named entities. They are searching for variables, type usages, macro expansions, enumeration values, etc. The different visualizations are also presentable using these named symbols: function call diagram, UML class diagram, CodeBites, symbol search, etc. The vast majority of the features can be covered with the collection of named entities. There are, however, some techniques that require a wider set of information. For instance, slicing algorithms work with statements. The goal of this approach is to determine a valid subset of the code that fulfills some criteria. One may use it for impact analysis: what is the set of statements which impacts the value of a given variable (backward slicing)? Or to the other direction: what further statements are impacted by the modification of the current variable or expression (forward slicing)? To answer these questions not only the symbols but the enclosing control structures are also required, since the expressions' values may depend on logical conditions.

Java is similar to C++ in many aspects from a code comprehension point of view. Both of these languages are multipurpose, object-oriented, static typed, imperative languages. There are many common elements like classes, functions (methods), variables, enumerations, modules (inclusion directive), generics (templates), etc. Of course, there are some language-specific features as well, like interfaces in Java.

Python has a dynamic type system. This causes a lot of difficulties in many CodeCompass functionalities. Even in the most simple operation, the definition search of a symbol. The variables are considered references to a value in Python. This way after an assignment the variable may refer to another object even with a different type. When choosing a variable in CodeCompass it is questionable which assignment is considered the definition of it. Lacking any better solution CodeCompass jumps to the last assignment that gave value to the variable if it is determinable at all.

Database. A parser has exclusive competence to determine what kind of information is necessary in order to accomplish its service. It implies that there is no common data structure that would be suitable for all modules. Every module is allowed to choose its database system to use. For example, the text indexer which provides fast text-search abilities is using Apache Lucene engine's storage. The Git version control system has its own database which stores the full history of the project. This is traditionally under .git directory. Furthermore, CodeCompass gives access to a relational SQL database. The parsers are allowed to connect here and create their own tables according to their needs. The modules can use *Object Relational Mapping* (ORM) tools to facilitate its usage. This makes it possible to persist user objects directly by method invocations instead of assembling complex SQL queries.

The drawback of the wide scale of repositories is that it decreases the portability of the system. This is not a negligible circumstance. In a team, there may be build servers that contain a full development environment. In the environment there are compilers, standard and third-party libraries, shared modules and the source code itself. So it is inevitable to run CodeCompass parser in this environment. In ideal cases there will be another environment that runs the CodeCompass service towards the clients. This has to be an accessible environment from outside, i.e. the web ports have to be open for the users for browsing in CodeCompass. The databases have to be transferred to this environment. Fortunately, more advanced SQL databases are also using client-server architecture, thus the parsers can access it on remote machines. However other file-based databases have to be sent to a remote machine either through a network file system or simply by compressing and uploading them.

The C/C++ parser uses ODB which is an ORM tool, in order to persist the collected language elements. Figure 3 displays the main tables of the C/C++ plug-in. The two main tables are CppAstNode and CppEntity.

CppAstNode represents an occurrence of an entity in the program. For example in case of a function there is a row in the table for its definition, declarations and all function calls. Moreover, all references of the symbol are also stored, like an assignment to a function pointer, or passing it to a higher-order function. Besides some other minor data this table stores the location (file, line, column), the (mangled) name, and the textual representation of the node.

CppEntity stores the entities with all their details. In the ORM this table is represented by a class which is the base of the concrete types, like functions, variables, classes, etc.

Service. The job of service the layer is to provide information to the clients from the database. This is implemented by Apache Thrift which enables the

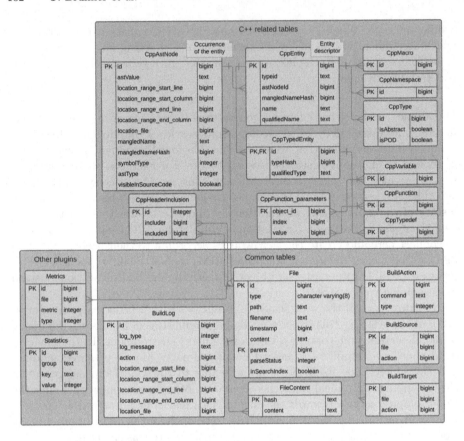

Fig. 3. Simplified database model of CodeCompass

client-side to fetch the data through *Remote Procedure Call* (RPC) mechanism. This means that there is a descriptor language which defines the data structures and methods for communication. These are translated to a stub on a given programming language. Currently, the main server-side stub is written in C++ and the main consumers are web browsers via JavaScript.

There are some common APIs. One is for accessing source files. This is the `project` API that queries source files, directories, file system tree, statistics, build action information, etc.

The other one is **Language** API. Once a new programming language is supported by CodeCompass then its service layer should provide this interface. This way the web-based client can automatically provide the available functionalities to the users, such as symbol information, diagrams (function call diagram, UML class diagram, collaboration diagram, CodeBites, interface diagram among source files and binaries, etc.), symbol references or definition search, Doxygen documentation, syntax highlight.

The additional plug-ins have to deliver their own interfaces to give access for the clients towards their databases. Since there is nothing common in an independent plug-in, all layers are deployed accordingly.

Apache Thrift is a cross-language framework to implement RPC mechanism between the server and the clients. CodeCompass comes with a web GUI written in JavaScript where the users may browse the source code. However, the public CodeCompass API allows the developers to create their own clients in any language in order to query some information that is not necessarily obtainable from the web UI.

Among others, there is a `LanguageAPI`. This provides access to the elements of a parsed source code. As soon as a language plugin provides this API, the web GUI automatically handles all the language-related functionalities (diagrams, Info Tree, CodeBites, etc.). The web interface was originally designed for aiding code comprehension. However, there may be queries that are not related to browsing the source code, but to answer questions on different levels from the high-level architecture to low-level implementation details.

The following procedures are available:

getAstNodeInfo() Returns the most important information about an AST node like its (mangled) name, symbol type, file location, textual representation and tags.

getAstNodeInfoByPosition() This procedure helps to find a node based on its location (file name, line, column). This is a convenient for a GUI to find nodes by clicking on the symbol.

getSourceText() The original source text of the AST node. Depending on the actual context this can be a complete definition of a symbol.

getDocumentation() CodeCompass can process the Doxygen documentation of a symbol. It is useful to store these, since one of the most helpful descriptor information is recoverable from the actual documentations.

getDiagram() Depending on the type of the selected AST node and the selected diagram type, this function returns a visual diagram about the node. This can be either a simple function call diagram or a UML class diagram, etc. The diagram is returned as an SVG image.

getReferences() This function returns the related AST nodes to the selected symbol. It is parameterized with the type of this relationship (definition, call, inheritance, alias, etc.).

getSyntaxHighlight() Sometimes the source code editor library on client side is not that advanced to provide proper syntax highlight. Since on server side we have full knowledge about the symbols, it is possible to provide adequate and different style for distinct language elements: functions, classes, variables, enumerations, etc. can be different. The parser gives precise information to determine their kinds.

Client. Technically it is possible to connect any client to the service layer as long as it can read the REST API provided by the server. Since the interface is specified in the Thrift interface definition language, additional client applications (such as a command-line client or an IDE plugin) can be easily written in more than 15 languages supported by Thrift (including C/C++, Java, Python etc.). Currently, the main CodeCompass client is a web application. The powerful capabilities of a browser make it possible to create various graphical representations and visualizations on the parsed software.

The web client's layout is similar to an IDE tool. At the top of the page there is an input field for textual search. In the left panel there are several information sections. There is a `Project Tree` for file browsing, an *Info Tree* for the presentation of symbol details, a *Query result* list for the search results, a `Similarity Tree` for detecting copy-paste codes, a *Revision Control Navigator* to browse the Git history, and a `Project Information` panel for the generic project information, metrics, symbol catalogs, etc. And lastly the center view presents the source code, the diagrams, and the visualizations that require big space.

It is also possible to use CodeCompass functionality in IDE tools. The drawback of this approach is that CodeCompass was designed to observe a static snapshot of a project. In contrast, the IDE tools are targeting the development of a software which entails the continuous alteration of the code. If the user intends to see the latest version of the source code, then it has to be reparsed after each time it has been edited.

5.2   Web User Interface

In this section, we will give an overview of the features available through the standard GUI. When describing language-specific features, such as listing callers of a method, we will always assume the project's language to be C++ as that has the most advanced support in CodeCompass, but similar features are available for Java and Python.

The web-based UI is organized into a static *top area*, extensible *accordion modules* on the left and also extensible *center modules* on middle-right – see Fig. 5.

The source code and different visualizations are shown in the center, while navigation trees and lists, such as file tree, search results, list of static analysis (CodeChecker) bugs [32], browsing history, code metrics and version control navigation is shown on the left. New center modules and accordion panels can be added by developers.

The top area shows the search toolbar, the currently opened file, the workspace selector, simple navigation history (breadcrumbs) and a generic menu for user guides.

Search. When meeting the code-base for the first time, it is hard for the user to orient himself among the huge amount of files. It is not even trivial to catch which module has to be inspected first in order to fix a bug or to add a new feature. Suppose that a developer has to fix a bug, but the location of the erroneous module to amend is unknown. Many times the only landmark is a log message of the analyzed software which was emitted in run-time. Lacking any further information we just try finding keywords that might be specific to the module. For a code browser tool like CodeCompass it is crucial to have fast search functionality.

The tool provides 4 different types of search possibilities: *full text search, definition search, filename search* and *log search.*

The most basic search method is the simple test search. This helps the user to find any string not only in the source code, string literals and comments, but also in the associated files like documentations, generated files, etc. In *full text search* mode the search phrase is a group of words such as "returns an astnode*". A query phrase matches a text block, if the searched words are next to each other in the source code in that particular order. Wildcards, such as *, or ? can be used, matching any multiple or single character. Logical operators such as AND, OR, NOT can be used to join multiple query phrases at the same time.

CodeCompass is equipped with a more sophisticated search functionality that enables the user to find symbols. This narrows the results on the named entities of the source file. CTags is a fast search indexer which supports a wide range of programming languages. Its goal is to distinguish functions, variables, type names, macros, etc. in various languages without needing a deep parsing or actual compilation. *Definition search* has the same syntax as full text search, but it only queries among symbol definitions. Symbol definitions are recognized for the following languages: Java, C/C++, Perl, JavaScript, Python. Symbol definitions can be further restricted to functions, constants, types, fields, labels or macros.

CodeCompass also provides the so called *Log Search.* Suppose that a run-time log message appears on the screen:

```
(17:32) [ERROR] - Error code (#53) in file hello.cpp
at line 42.
```

The programmer wishes to find the command in the source code that prints this message. Note that this log message contains several dynamically generated parts, such as a timestamp, log level, error code, file name and line number. This message is printed in different ways in different languages:

```
1  printf("(%d:%d) [%s] - Error code (#%d) in file %s at line %d.",
2      hour, minute, logLevel, errorCode, fileName, lineNo);
```

Listing 1.3. Log message in C.

```
1  std::cout
2      << '(' << hour << ':' << minute << ')'
3      << '[' << logLevel << ']'
4      << " - Error code (#" << errorCode << ')'
5      << " in file " << fileName
6      << " at line " << lineNo << '.';
```

Listing 1.4. Log message in C++.

```
1  print("({}:{}) [{}] - Error code (#{}) in file {} at line {}."
2     .format(hour,minute,log_level,error_code,file_name,line_no))
```

Listing 1.5. Log message in Python.

Since there is only a few constant fragments in the message, it is not worth searching only these. However, in CodeCompass it is possible to copy the entire log message in the search bar and use *Log Search*. This is a fuzzy-search possibility that finds the locations in the source code where the message was most probably assembled.

Information About Language Symbols. In the source code view, the user can click on any symbol and get additional information about it or generate a diagram about its usage. The *Info tree* gives the most concise information about a symbol. For an example see the info tree of the void DeekTimerHandler::tick() function in Fig. 4. You can read that the function is called in the DeekTimer.cc file from the dispatcher() function. DeekTimerHandler::tick() is also assigned to a function pointer in CoecuBoardSupport.cc, in line 304.

For C/C++ variables, the tool lists location of reads, writes, and aliases of the variable (references and pointers pointing to the same memory location). For classes, one can query the definition, base classes, derived classes, methods, members, and how the class is used: in a declaration of a local, global, member variable, function parameter, or as return type. Regarding macros, all expansion locations and values can be listed.

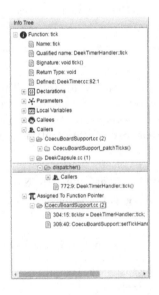

Fig. 4. Info tree of C++ function DeekTimer::tick()

Symbol Level Diagrams. Sometimes a diagram representation of a symbol and its environment can be very helpful for comprehension. CodeCompass provides the interactive *CodeBites* diagram for understanding large call chains (for an example see Fig. 5) and type hierarchies. *Function call* diagram shows all callers and callees of a function in a graph. *UML class inheritance* diagram shows the full inheritance chain up until the root base class and recursively for all derived classes. *Class collaboration* diagram shows base inheritance chain and recursively shows all member classes as nodes. *Pointer aliases* diagram shows all references and pointers (as nodes) that refers to the same memory location as the queried variable.

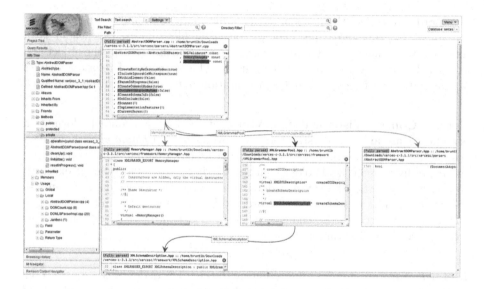

Fig. 5. User interface running in a browser

Architectural Diagrams. Sometimes it is required to observe the high-level overview of a software. For example, in case of a legacy project some refactoring activities are necessary to make the code more concise and thus more maintainable. Suppose that we would like to find the modules which use a certain symbol even indirectly. After collecting these modules we can pinpoint the ones that are located in a distinct region of the code where they are not supposed to be found. Such a situation can be the result of a serial rewriting or negligent architecture organizing. If we manage to determine well-defined boundaries of modules then we may achieve loose coupling principles.

CodeCompass is able to handle source code on file level. Besides symbol information we are storing the source files and their relationships. In case of C++ the code is organized to two file types: *source* and *header*. the translation units are compiled to *object* files that are linked together to *executables*. We may distinguish several relationships between these file types.

include Sources and headers may include other headers. In this case the included header file becomes the part of the given translation unit.

use The file *source.cpp* uses *header.h* if there is a symbol declaration in *header.h* that is used in *source.cpp*.

provide Sources and headers can be considered as implementation and interface respectively. We say that an implementation provides an interface if there is a symbol declaration in the header which is defined in the source.

contain During the build process translation units are compiled to an object file and object files are linked together to other objects or executables. In this case we say that an object contains the source file or the executable contains the object file.

In order to collect the users of a source file we have to find the headers that are *provided by* this source file. Then we collect the files that *use* this header as an interface even transitively. Lastly, the *contain* relationship returns the object and executable files that incorporate these users. This sequence of relations defines a graph structure that is a visual representation of the architecture on file level.

Version Control Visualizations. Visualization of version control information is an important aid to understand software evolution. Git *blame view* shows line-by-line the changes (commits) to a given file. Changes that happened recently are colored lighter green, while older changes are darker red. This view is excellent to review why certain lines were added to a source file. CodeCompass can also show Git commits in a filterable list ordered by the time of commit. This search facility can be used to list changes made by a person or to filter commits by relevant words in the commit message.

Metrics. Software metrics are presenting the characteristics of the source code. There are several well-known metrics that measure the size or the complexity of a program. The simplest one is *Lines Of Code* (LOC) which informs about the size of the software. It can be more precise if we omit the blank lines from the computation. We can also measure the properties of blocked entities, like the average number of statements in a function, or the average number of members in a class. The *McCabe complexity* is one of the most popular software metrics that indicates the complexity of a program. This is also known as *Cyclomatic complexity* which provides the number of branch and loop statements in a file.

Due to the plug-in architecture of CodeCompass it can easily be extended by other static analyzer tools. Clang comes with a bug finder module that aims to catch typical programming errors in compile time. By storing this kind of information we can present metrics on the software quality.

CodeCompass stores these numbers by file granularity. This gives an opportunity to visualize the metrics and to find the complex regions which may need some refactoring. *Treemap* can be an appropriate way of this presentation. This is a rectangular diagram with two dimensions: size and color. These dimensions are assigned to the selected metrics. For example one may setup the diagram so its size indicates the lines of code and the color indicate the number of bugs. The whole rectangle belongs to the selected directory. The inner rectangles represent the subdirectories and files under this folder. The bigger a rectangle is, the more source lines it contains. And the more green the rectangle is, the more programming bugs it has.

CodeChecker Results. Static analysis is the analysis of a program without executing it, usually carried out by an automated tool. Analyzing the Abstract Syntax Tree (AST) and Symbolic execution are the two most powerful static analysis techniques used both in program verification and in bug detection software. CodeChecker is an open-source tool [32] to collect analysis reports from Clang Tidy and Clang Static Analyzer [33] and stores them to the CodeChecker server. However, all static analyzers can produce *false positives* – reporting correct code as error – which have to be detected and filtered out by human experts. This usually requires exploring the code environment of the report, which is especially challenging when the bug path crosses file boundaries [34]. CodeCompass can visualize the bugs identified the Clang Static Analyzer and Clang Tidy by connecting it to a CodeChecker server [32], showing the bug position, and the symbolic execution path that lead to a fault.

AST-Dump. The parser collects only predefined language elements. Data missing from the database have to be collected afterward. Since the compilation commands and the source code itself is stored in the database, there is a possibility to run the parser as a service. This *reparse* functionality is currently implemented in the service layer of the C/C++ plug-in. This enables the visualization even of the entire AST. This is not a so frequent action that would make its persistence necessary, but this functionality helps to understand some weird run-time behavior of the program. For example, the AST contains implicit type conversion nodes or compiler-generated methods [35].

As an example, see how ASt-dump can help to understand CodeChecker reports. In CodeChecker there are hundreds of checker rules of which the violation results in a warning or notification by the compiler. *Memory overlap checker* verifies such a rule. memcpy() function copies raw bytes between specific memory buffers. The *from* and *to* buffer intervals must be disjoint, otherwise the result is unspecified. The *memory overlap checker* emits a report when it experiences a memcpy() function call where the source and target regions overlap. The following code fragment resulted in such a report:

```
1  struct S { int t[10]; };
2  int main() {
3      S s;
4      s = s;
5  }
```

Listing 1.6. Invisible memcpy() call in a compiler-generated assignment operator.

It is not easy to see why Static Analyzer gives a report on this example. The explanation is that in case a structure has an array member, the compiler-generated assignment operator uses `std::memcpy()` to copy this array. To be precise, a built-in version (`__builtin_memcpy()`) is used. Since `main()` function contains a self-assignment, the memory buffers overlap completely. Fortunately the compiler-generated operator prevents this situation, so technically this report is a false positive. Anyway, CodeCompass was a great help in finding why this code fragment results a report on an invisible `memset()` function call, because CodeCompass is able to present the AST to the users. Instead of storing the full AST, the service layer can build it up on-demand. This contains the compiler-generated methods and their bodies, i.e. the assignment operator in question at this example.

Figure 6 shows a screenshot of the AST dump of the previous code fragment. It is visible that the AST also contains the compiler-generated methods like the copy and move constructors and assignment operators. One may also discover the aforementioned `__builtin_memcpy()` call at the middle of the page.

Fig. 6. AST dump of a `struct` with its implicit methods.

Browsing History. De Alwis and Murphy studied why programmers experience disorientation when using the Eclipse Java integrated development environment (IDE) [36]. They use visual momentum [37] technique to identify three factors that may lead to disorientation: i) the absence of connecting navigation context during program exploration, ii) thrashing between displays to view necessary pieces of code, and iii) the pursuit of sometimes unrelated subtasks.

The first factor means that the programmer, during investigating a problem visits several files as follows a call chain, or explores usage of a variable. At the end of a long exploration session, it is hard to remember why the investigation ended up in a specific file. The second reason for disorientation is the frequent change of different views in Eclipse. The third contributor to the problem is that a developer, when solving a program change task, evaluates several hypotheses, which are all individual comprehension subtasks. Programmers tend to suspend a subtask (before finishing it) and switch to another. For example, the programmer investigates how a return value of a function is used, but then changes to a subtask understanding the implementation of the function itself. It was observed that, for a developer, it is hard to remind themselves about a suspended subtask [38].

CodeCompass implements a *browsing history* view which records (in a tree form) the path of navigation in the source code. A new subtask is represented by a new branch of the tree, while the nodes are navigation jumps in the code labeled by the connecting context (such as *jump to the definition of init*). So problem i) and ii) is addressed, by the labeled nodes in the browsing history, while problem iii) is handled by the branches assigned to subtasks.

Namespace and Type Catalogue. CodeCompass processes Doxygen documentation and stores them for the function, type, variable definitions. It also provides a *type catalogue* view that lists types declared in the workspace organized by a hierarchical tree view of namespaces.

5.3   Language Server Protocol

The *Language Server Protocol* (LSP) is a joint project of Microsoft and others to standardize the communication between language tooling and code editors. With LSP defining a new layer between IDEs and language tooling, it enables LSP compliant tooling services and IDEs to communicate in a standard way, thus making them independent of each other. As an advantage of this decoupling the language tooling services can be implemented in any language making it possible to adapt to special needs of these utilities or to optimize the performance. At the same time, since code editors are also independent of the tooling environment, language tooling can be assigned to multiple IDEs and also an IDE can make use of several LSP compliant language tooling utility at the same time [39].

LSP Integration into CodeCompass. As mentioned in the *Services* subsection of Sect. 5.1, the runtime code comprehension functionalities in CodeCompass are organized into services, e.g. CppService. Their public API is served by the webserver component through Thrift protocol. Since LSP requests are cross-compliant with lower-level functions in CodeCompass, we defined a wrapper service named LspService which combines the existing functionalities for LSP [40]. As an example requesting the definition location for a symbol is a single call in LSP, parameterized with the appropriate position consisting of the file path and symbol location (line and column number). Then the position of the definition is returned if found. With the lower-level API of CodeCompass, first the AST node identifier has to be queried for the position and the position of the definition can only be requested afterward, resulting in two calls overall.

Thrift and LSP use different constructions for their requests, therefore a new request handler module named **LspHandler** was also introduced to manage the transformation between LSP messages in JSON format and the strongly-typed inner representation of the program, as shown in Fig. 7.

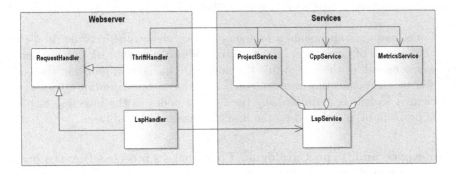

Fig. 7. Class diagram of the LSP integration into CodeCompass

LSP Integration into vs Code. According to the Extension Guide [41] the language tooling in VS Code consists of two components.

- *Language Client* is a normal VS Code extension written in TypeScript.
- *Language Server* is a language analysis tool running in a separate process.

The Language Client provides the user interface inside VS Code and listens for events that require action. When the CodeCompass web service needs to be queried to gather the requested code comprehension information, the Language Client instructs the Language Server to communicate with the CodeCompass server on a separate, background job. CodeCompass can either be executed on the same local machine or on a remote server and in our solution we used this Language Server as a proxy towards it.

As a demonstration, the sequence diagram depicted in Fig. 8 shows the interaction between the language server and client components of VS Code and the LSP components in CodeCompass. First, a component diagram produced by CodeCompass is displayed inside VS Code upon the request of the user, then a real-time incremental parsing in the CodeCompass backend is carried out on the event of saving a modified file inside the code editor.

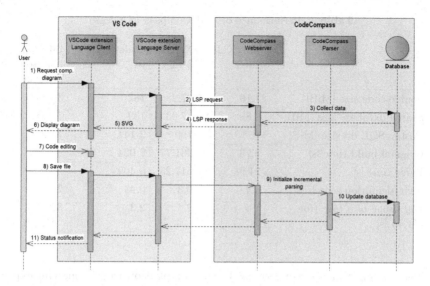

Fig. 8. Interactivity between VS Code and CodeCompass components

1. The request for the diagram is issued by the actor through e.g. a context menu.
2. The Language Server constructs the corresponding LSP request towards the CodeCompass web server.
3. The web server component in CodeCompass processes the request and collects the required data is pulled from the underlying model layer (and ultimately from the workspace database) to build the diagram.
4. The result diagram is returned wrapped in an LSP response message.
5. The SVG diagram is extracted from the response.
6. The requested diagram is displayed to the user.
7. The program code is edited inside VS Code by the user.
8. The changed files are saved and the Language Client triggers a handler on this event. Ultimately the new content of changed files is transferred to the CodeCompass web server.
9. The web server component instructs the parser component of CodeCompass to perform an incremental parsing on the changeset.
10. The workspace database is updated.
11. The user is notified by VS Code (e.g. through an icon) that the source code is in a fully parsed state again.

5.4 Performance

CodeCompass scales well regarding the size of the analyzed code in parsing time, size of the data stored and response times of the webserver.

We demonstrate the results on four different C/C++ applications. Results are summarized in Table 1.

Table 1. Performance of CodeCompass *v4* release

	TinyXML 2.6.2	Xerces 3.1.3	CodeCompass v4	Internal Ericsson product
Source code size [MiB]	1.16	67.28	182	3 344
Search database size [MiB]	0.88	37.93	139	7 168
PostgreSQL db size [MiB]	15	190	2 144	7 729
Original build time [s]	2.73	361.77	2 024	—
Parse time [s]	21.98	517.23	6 409	—
Text/definition search [s]	0.4	0.3	0.43	2
Get usage of a type (for C++) [s]	1.4	2	2.3	3.1

The parsing time is proportional to the compilation time – one can expect the parsing time to be approximately 160% of the original build time.

The disk space needed to store a parsed snapshot is proportional to the number of symbol declarations and references. According to our measurements, the size of a *workspace* (including search database and the relation database) is approximately 5 – 10 times the size of source code.

It can be read from Table 1 that the response times of search and C++ symbol usage query remains low even in case of large (3.2 GiB) source code size.

6   Important Design Workflows

In this section, we show the most common design tasks which emerge during the maintenance and evolution of large programs, and highlight how static program comprehension techniques and specifically CodeCompass helps to solve them.

In [42] the authors collected and categorized typical questions programmers ask during a change task. They identify 4 categories: i) *Finding focus points*: finding locations in the program code implementing a behavior; ii) *Expanding focus points*: exploring relations of interesting types, functions, variables; iii) *Understanding a sub graph*: "How a set of types or functions collaborate in runtime?"; iv) *Questions over groups of sub graphs*: "How parts of the program relate to each other?" We will use these categories to identify the intent of the programmer during the analyzed tasks.

6.1   Bug Investigation

The ultimate goal of the developer is to understand *the minimum amount of code to change that is necessary to solve the bug, but enough not to introduce additional bugs*. This task typically starts by identifying a program location where the problematic behavior was observed [43], then gradually restoring the actual program state and call path leading to the fault. Finally planning code changes, considering how the rewritten program text affects other, non-faulty use-cases. This means that the designer needs to verify how the changed function was called, how a changed type or variable is used in other parts of the system.

A bug investigation process starts based on a trouble report, which is a written description of the unwanted behavior of the program. This textual description can be accompanied by the following additional artifacts: i) In case of a program crash, a full core dump. A core dump contains the full content of the stack and the heap. Thus the full call chain and the values of the variables are known at the point of the crash. ii) In live systems, full core dumps are usually disabled, as it eats up disc space and takes extensive amounts of time to create. A log of the stack state may still be available, which contains the function call chain up to the crash, but not the values of the variables. iii) If none of the above is present, a log may be available which is a sequence of arbitrary printouts from the time period around when the problem occurred.

The developer first identifies the program point when the problematic behavior was observed. If the exact function is known (from the stack trace of core dump), *function definition search* (Sect. 5.2) can be used to locate the function. If only logs are available *log search* can be used to look up the program point where the logs were created (Sect. 5.2).

After locating "focus points", the developer identifies the actual execution flow and values of the variables that lead to the error. To understand complex call chains, *CodeBites* visualization of CodeCompass can be very helpful (see Fig. 5). Function callers (and callees) can be recursively listed, using the *call chain explorer* in the *info tree* (see Sect. 5.2). Analyzing call chains is really difficult using a traditional IDE. Similarly, when one would like to discover the write locations of a variable, and the variable is written through a pointer or a reference, usual IDEs are of little help. It can be really time-consuming for a programmer to discover these non-trivial connections manually, so a comprehension tool can save a considerable amount of time. CodeCompass can detect variable aliasing and also caller identification through virtual functions and function pointers (see Sect. 5.2). Pointer aliasing diagram shows variable aliasing in a graph form (Sect. 5.2). To understand how the involved types are used, CodeCompass can show the types are referred to at various program locations (Sect. 5.2). When navigating among function calls, disorientation is often a problem [36]. CodeCompass organizes browsing track record in a browsing history tree view (Sect. 5.2).

When investigating the reason behind a bug, it is often useful to check version control history, since according to [44] it is likely that the investigated issue is introduced by another, earlier bug fix. Using the *blame view* (described in Sect. 5.2), the programmer can visualize the recent code modifications, that affected the file where the bug occurred.

CodeCompass can show faulty programming constructs (memory leaks, null pointer dereferences, etc.) that Clang Static Analyzer and Clang Tidy detected (see Sect. 5.2) in the current file or in the whole analyzed source code. These are worth checking as the investigated fault may be related to a well known faulty programming pattern.

When planning changes, it is vital to understand the wider context of the change, how the altered parts interact in different usage scenarios. To understand the mapping of domain concepts to implementation, the Doxygen [45] or Javadoc documentation can be of great help (Sect. 5.2). Interactions of classes can be explored on the collaboration diagrams (Sect. 5.2). This visualization is available for a single class, a single header file containing multiple classes, or a directory containing header files. To get wider usage context, directory-level dependency diagrams visualize how C/C++ header files in a directory are implemented or used by files in other directories.

There are some additional static analysis techniques that are useful for a program change task, but currently lack support in CodeCompass. A (backward) slicing feature could help to understand which statements have an effect on the examined program value. A dataflow analysis could show, how a given variable gets its value assigned.

6.2   Feature Development Planning and Estimation

When planning new features, the designer first locates those files, where related features are implemented. CodeCompass provides text search (see Sect. 5.2) for this purpose. In the next step, files are identified, which may be affected by the change. Clustering techniques, such as the mapping metaphor, implemented by CodeSurveyor [46] helps to identify the group of files that are closely related. CodeCompass does not support software maps, but it shows the relationship between files and directories (based on C/C++ symbol usage information) in the internal architecture diagram and interface diagrams.

Binary dependency views can be used to estimate which binaries will be affected by the changes and thus can help in planning an upgrade procedure.

6.3   Refactoring

There are several reasons to refactor an implementation: too complex implementation, circular compilation dependencies, copy-pasted code blocks or performance problems.

There are metrics, such as complexity metrics which indicate that refactoring may be necessary. One, well-known metric is the McCabe Complexity, which can be directly shown by CodeCompass (Sect. 5.2) on file, and aggregated on directory level.

Circular dependencies between files can be shown by analyzing dependencies on the file-level, while architectural compliance violation can be detected from dependencies on the directory level. There is no direct support for these analysis methods in CodeCompass, but could be added, as symbol and file level dependencies are stored in the database.

To estimate the effect of refactoring changes on the overall system, the same features can be used that were described in Sect. 6.1.

6.4 Knowledge Transfer and Newcomers' Catch-Up

When a new engineer joins the team or at knowledge transfer, someone, who is completely new to the code and the domain, needs to acquire knowledge. Domain concepts are best understood from textbooks or articles. However, it is crucial to understand how the domain concepts map down to a particular software's implementation. Design documentation is a useful apparatus for describing this mapping.

According to our experience, there are three important rules that need to be kept to have an up-to-date design documentation for large systems:

- store design documents in the same version control system as the source code
- split design documents in the same modularization as the source code
- use text-based documentation system instead of binary formatting

Design documents that are not stored in the same version control system as the source code tend to get out of sync of the real implementation. Symbol names and file names referred to in these documents change as the code evolves and programmers tend to neglect to patch these in the documentation. Binary formats, such as Microsoft Word documents should be avoided, as it is more convenient for a programmer to apply the same text editors and diff tools for documentation they use for coding.

According to our experience, Doxygen [45] is a versatile tool for documenting source code on function, type, and file level. If the source code is organized into source code level components such as suggested in [47] and in [48] component level documentation can also be written. In CodeCompass we implemented the rendering of symbols, file and component level documentation for Ericsson internal products (see Sect. 5.2).

7 User Acceptance in Real Production

Six months after CodeCompass had been deployed for use with seven products at Ericsson, we conducted a questionnaire poll regarding its usage. We observed that at the products which are above 2 million lines of code, 40% of the developers use CodeCompass at least two times a month and about 15% use it on a day-to-day basis.

OpenGrok was the de-facto comprehension tool used by the teams before CodeCompass was introduced to them.

Figure 9 shows the distribution of the tools used by the respondents to solve specific tasks. In the question, we conducted the investigation of:

- *Function definitions and calls*: this basically means reference-based navigation in the code

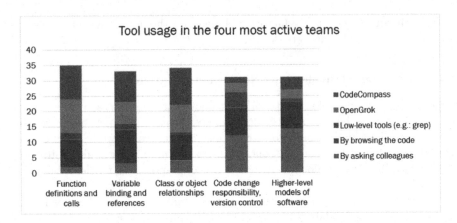

Fig. 9. CodeCompass usage distribution per task

- *Variable binding and references*: like the above, but in the case of variables
- *Class or object relationships*: information clearly visible in higher-level models
- *Code change, responsibility*: version control information
- *Higher-level models of software*: component diagrams, domain-specific archi-
  tecture views, etc.

As the diagram shows, CodeCompass is mostly used to uncover and follow function and variable references, as well as to inspect class relationships; most probably users apply CodeCompass to these tasks because of its thorough static analysis that other tools (e.g. low-level search and OpenGrok) cannot perform. The proportions of "browsing the code" and "asking colleagues" are also worth noting; many employees try to solve complex problems by struggling on the code or by bothering others, rather than taking the right comprehension tool.

8   Conclusion and Future Work

We presented CodeCompass [6], a static analysis tool for comprehension of large-scale software. Having a web-based, pluginable, extensible architecture, the CodeCompass framework can be an open platform to further code compre-hension, static analysis and software metrics efforts.

Initial user feedback and usage statistics suggests that the tool is useful for developers in comprehension activities and it is used besides traditional IDEs and other cross-reference tools.

We would like to further investigate the efficiency of the CodeCompass in software change tasks, based on industrial user group experiment. It is also among our plans to implement efficient data-flow analysis, slicing, and further component visualization techniques for C and C++ languages.

Acknowledgement. This work was supported by the European Union, co-financed by the European Social Fund (EFOP-3.6.3-VEKOP-16-2017-00002)

References

1. Ferraro-Esparza, V., Gudmandsen, M., Olsson, K.: Ericsson telecom server platform 4. Ericsson Rev. **3**, 104–113 (2002)
2. Enderin, M., LeCorney, D., Lindberg, M., Lundqvist, T.: Axe 810-the evolution continues. Ericsson Rev. **4**, 10–23 (2001)
3. Karlsson, E.-A., Taxen, L.: Incremental development for AXE 10. In: Jazayeri, M., Schauer, H. (eds.) ESEC/SIGSOFT FSE -1997. LNCS, vol. 1301, pp. 519–520. Springer, Heidelberg (1997). https://doi.org/10.1007/3-540-63531-9_34
4. Brunner, T.: CodeCompass: an extensible code comprehension framework. Eötvös Loránd University, Faculty of Informatics, Budapest, Tech. Rep. IK-TR1 (2018)
5. Szabó, C.: Programme of the winter school of project no.2017-1-sk01-ka203-035402: "focusing education on composability, comprehensibility and correctness of working software". TUKE Kosice (2018) . Accessed 02 July 2019. https://kpi.fei.tuke.sk/sites/www2.kpi.fei.tuke.sk/files/personal/programme_of_the_first_intensive_programme_for_higher_education_learners_in_the_frame_of_the_project.pdf
6. CodeCompass. https://github.com/Ericsson/CodeCompass
7. Von Mayrhauser, A., Vans, A.M.: Program comprehension during software maintenance and evolution. Computer **28**(8), 44–55 (1995)
8. Storey, M.-A.: Theories, methods and tools in program comprehension: past, present and future. In: 13th International Workshop on Program Comprehension (IWPC2005), pp. 181–191. IEEE (2005)
9. O'brien, M.P.: Software comprehension-a review & research direction. Department of Computer Science & Information Systems University of Limerick, Ireland, Technical Report (2003)
10. Brooks, R.: Towards a theory of the cognitive processes in computer programming. Int. J. Man Mach. Stud. **9**(6), 737–751 (1977)
11. Soloway, E., Adelson, B., Ehrlich, K.: Knowledge and processes in the comprehension of computer programs. The Nature of Expertise, pp. 129–152 (1988)
12. Pennington, N.: Comprehension strategies in programming. In: Empirical Studies of Programmers: Second Workshop, pp. 100–113. Ablex Publishing Corp. (1987)
13. Shneiderman, B., Mayer, R.: Syntactic/semantic interactions in programmer behavior: a model and experimental results. Int. J. Comput. Inf. Sci. **8**(3), 219–238 (1979)
14. Levy, O., Feitelson, D.G.: Understanding large-scale software: a hierarchical view. In: Proceedings of the 27th International Conference on Program Comprehension, pp. 283–293. IEEE Press (2019)
15. Letovsky, S.: Cognitive processes in program comprehension. J. Syst. Softw. **7**(4), 325–339 (1987)
16. Marcus, A., Sergeyev, A., Rajlich, V., Maletic, J.I.: An information retrieval approach to concept location in source code. In: 11th Working Conference on Reverse Engineering, pp. 214–223. IEEE (2004)
17. Rajlich, V., Wilde, N.: The role of concepts in program comprehension. In: Proceedings 10th International Workshop on Program Comprehension, pp. 271–278. IEEE (2002)
18. 3GPP technical specifications. https://www.3gpp.org/specifications/79-specification-numbering
19. Krzysztof, C., Eisenecker, U.W.: Generative Programming: Methods. Addison-Wesley, Tools and Applications (2000)

20. Hennert, L., Larruy, A.: TelORB- the distributed communications operating system. Ericsson Rev.(Engl. Ed.) **76**(3), 156–167 (1999)
21. xxx
22. Apache thrift. https://Thrift.apache.org/
23. Woboq. https://woboq.com/codebrowser.html
24. Opengrok. https://opengrok.github.io/OpenGrok
25. Doxygen. https://ctags.sourceforge.net
26. Ctags. https://www.stack.nl/~dimitri/doxygen/
27. Henderson-Sellers, B.: Object-oriented metrics: measures of complexity. Prentice-Hall Inc. (1995)
28. McCabe, T.J.: A complexity measure. IEEE Trans. Software Eng. **4**, 308–320 (1976)
29. CodeSurfer. https://www.grammatech.com/products/codesurfer
30. The clang JSON compilation database format specification. https://clang.llvm.org/docs/JSONCompilationDatabase.html
31. Fekete, A., Cserép, M.: Incremental parsing of large legacy C/C++ software. In: 21st International Multiconference on Information Society (IS), Collaboration, Software and Services in Information Society (CSS), vol. G, pp. 51–54 (2018)
32. Krupp, D., Orban, G., Horvath, G., Babati, B.: Industrial experiences with the clang static analysis toolset (2015)
33. Horváth, G., Pataki, N.: Clang matchers for verified usage of the c++ standard template library. Ann. Math. Inform. **44**, 99–109 (2015)
34. Horváth, G., Szécsi, P., Gera, Z., Krupp, D., Pataki, N.: [Engineering Paper] Challenges of implementing cross translation unit analysis in clang static analyzer. In: 2018 IEEE 18th International Working Conference on Source Code Analysis and Manipulation (SCAM), pp. 171–176. IEEE (2018)
35. Szalay, R., Porkoláb, Z.: Visualising compiler-generated special member functions of C++ types (2018)
36. De Alwis, B., Murphy, G.C.: Using visual momentum to explain disorientation in the eclipse IDE. In: Visual Languages and Human-Centric Computing (VL/HCC2006), pp. 51–54. IEEE (2006)
37. Woods, D.D.: Visual momentum: a concept to improve the cognitive coupling of person and computer. Int. J. Man Mach. Stud. **21**(3), 229–244 (1984)
38. Herrmann, D., Brubaker, B., Yoder, C., Sheets, V., Tio, A.: Devices that remind (1999)
39. Microsoft Corporation: Language Server Protocol Specification. Tech. Rep. 3.14.0 (2018). https://microsoft.github.io/language-server-protocol/specification
40. Mészáros, M., Cserép, M., Fekete, A.: Delivering comprehension features into source code editors through LSP. In: 2019 42nd International Convention on Information and Communication Technology, Electronics and Microelectronics (MIPRO), pp. 1581–1586. IEEE (2019)
41. Microsoft Corporation. Language Server Extension Guide. https://code.visualstudio.com/api/language-extensions/language-server-extension-guide
42. Sillito, J., Murphy, G.C., De Volder, K.: Asking and answering questions during a programming change task. IEEE Trans. Software Eng. **34**(4), 434–451 (2008)
43. Sillito, J., De Voider, K., Fisher, B., Murphy, G.: Managing software change tasks: an exploratory study. In: 2005 International Symposium on Empirical Software Engineering (2005), p. 10. IEEE (2005)
44. Kim, S., Zimmermann, T., Pan, K., James, E., et al.: Automatic identification of bug-introducing changes. In: 21st IEEE/ACM International Conference on Automated Software Engineering (ASE2006), pp. 81–90. IEEE (2006)

45. Doxygen. https://www.stack.nl/~dimitri/doxygen/
46. Hawes, N., Marshall, S., Anslow, C.: Codesurveyor: mapping large-scale software to aid in code comprehension. In: 2015 IEEE 3rd Working Conference on Software Visualization (VISSOFT), pp. 96–105. IEEE (2015)
47. Darvas, A., Konnerth, R.: System architecture recovery based on software structure model. In: 2016 13th Working IEEE/IFIP Conference on Software Architecture (WICSA), pp. 109–114. IEEE (2016)
48. de Jonge, M.: Build-level components. IEEE Trans. Software Eng. **31**(7), 588–600 (2005)

Balanced Distributed Computation Patterns

Jianhao Li, Yuri Kim, and Viktória Zsók[✉]

Department of Programming Languages and Compilers, Faculty of Informatics,
Eötvös Loránd University, Pázmány Péter sétány 1/C., Budapest 1117, Hungary
`zsv@inf.elte.hu`

Abstract. The state-of-the-art concurrent software development extensively uses various methodologies and approaches to obtain high-speed up. However, parallelism remains one of the most challenging topics, especially in the case of pattern-based programming approaches. The primary purpose of the paper is to explore parallel computation schemes in a new environment by illustrating the appropriateness and applicability in novel distributed computation setups.

The used programming language Go compiles the program into machine code; hence, it does not need extra run-time like virtual machines or interpreters. Additionally, it has powerful built-in concurrency constructs like goroutines and channels. RABBITMQ is a traditional message broker developed for over ten years and well-known for its reliability. Therefore, Go and RABBITMQ were chosen to implement our computation patterns. This paper is a tutorial on concurrent and on distributed programming. The Go introduction and the explanation of concurrent examples provide the reader with necessary background knowledge to understand the distributed programming explorations. The main focus of this paper is the implementation of practical distributed examples that follow existing patterns using Go and RABBITMQ. The patterns are the experience collection of skilled software engineers. By practicing the distributed examples, the readers can gain significant experience in designing and implementing distributed systems.

Keywords: Go · RABBITMQ · Patterns · Concurrent Programming · Distributed Systems

1 Introduction

Nowadays, programs tend to be concurrent and usually need distributed coordination. This paper introduces distributed communication examples following different patterns usually needed in modern distributed systems. The examples are implemented using Go and RABBITMQ. The initial version of the RAB-

This work was supported by the European Union.

BITMQ was released in 2007 and since then it has been adopted by many big companies and organizations like NASA (for Nebula SaaS platform) and New York Times.

The readers are provided with background knowledge of GO programming language essentials and message broker basics via relevant examples, which enables to follow easily the distributed programming patterns. The tutorial offers solutions to problems in several versions following a step-by-step refinement of improvements on concurrency and distribution. Thus, studying the proposed exercises can be done easily. After following the practical aspects of the examples of this paper, the readers gain practical experiences of dealing with parallel communication in a distributed system. The code of all the examples is uploaded to Github [14].

The distributed examples implement existing patterns. The term *pattern* is defined in several software design books, out of which the following was chosen from [3], implemented earlier in [23], and applied also here in examples:

"A pattern for software architecture describes a particular recurring design problem that arises in specific design contexts, and presents a well-proven generic scheme for its solution. The solution scheme is specified by describing its constituent components, their responsibilities and relationships, and the ways in which they collaborate." (p8.)

There are already some practical tutorials of GO and RABBITMQ. In comparison with the courses of the online learning platform [20], this tutorial not only focuses on the GO language essentials and concurrency, but also on practical examples of the distributed computation based on the AMQP. The distributed examples leverage RABBITMQ's built-in mechanisms: the balanced queue mechanism and the exchange routing mechanism. Compared to the tutorials of the RABBITMQ official website [17], which are more focused on the introduction of the basic mechanisms, this tutorial provides more complete and meaningful practical examples of distributed computation.

The process figures of the example in this tutorial follow the Communication Diagrams specification declared in the UNIFIED MODELING LANGUAGE UML 2.0. The rectangle represents an individual participant in the interaction. The small arrow with the sequence number and the message name represents the messages. "The sequence-expression is a dot-separated list of sequence-terms followed by a colon (':'). Each term represents a level of procedural nesting within the overall interaction. The integer represents the sequential order of the message within the next higher level of procedural calling. Messages that differ in one integer term are sequentially related at that level of nesting. Example: Message 3.1.4 follows Message 3.1.3 within activation 3.1" [21].

The code listings contain only source code parts to make it easier to understand and to create a more compact tutorial. Therefore, the error handling and the repeated package import parts are eliminated.

In the following, first we introduce the main GO language elements and different versions of concurrent job processing examples. Next, we present the main concepts of ADVANCED MESSAGE QUEUEING PROTOCOL (AMQP). Afterward, we discuss RABBITMQ basic code and distributed examples following different patterns. Finally, we provide testings, related works, and conclusions.

2   Go Essentials

The programming language Go *is an open-source project to make programmers more productive*, as stated on the website of the language [19]. Go is *expressive, concise, clean, and efficient.* Its concurrency mechanisms make it easy to write programs that get the most benefits of the multicore and networked machines. At the same time, its novel type system enables flexible and modular program construction.

Go also compiles quickly to machine code, and yet it has the convenience of garbage collection and the power of run-time reflection. It is a fast, statically typed, compiled language that feels like a dynamically typed, interpreted language. Famous open-source projects of Go are Docker, Consul, Lantern, Kubernetes, Prometheus, and InfluxDB.

For the installation you can follow the Go download and install instructions [8]. By default, the installation process deals with the system environment variable of the command **go**. Check if you installed Go successfully by using command **go version** in a system command prompt.

2.1   Syntax of Basic Language Elements

Let us start with the classical first example of every programming language: the hello world program. Inside a folder, create a file named **hello.go**. Type in the code of Listing 1.1. Use the command **go run hello.go** to run the program. Only the package named **main** can be executed by the command **go run**. Inside the package **main**, there must be also a function named **main** as the entry point of the program.

```
package main                          1
import "fmt"                          2
func main() {                         3
    fmt.Println("Hello World")        4
}                                     5
```

Listing 1.1. Hello World

After we use the command **go run** to run this program, it prints **Hello World**.

```
go run helloWorld.go                  1
Hello World                           2
```

The whitespaces do not matter in Go; the compiler ignores all of them. Therefore, no worries about the indentation, unlike in PYTHON. Furthermore, the compiler automatically adds a semicolon for you after each statement–accordingly, no concerns about semicolons, unlike in JAVA.

Next, the description of the Go basic elements used in this tutorial is presented; each one is introduced briefly, followed by a practical example using it.

Imports. The keyword **import** is used for importing packages. It is recommended to use a single keyword **import** and parentheses for multiple packages as shown in Listing 1.3.

```
import "fmt"                                                         1
import "strconv"                                                     2
```
Listing 1.2. Import ver.1

```
import (                                                             1
    "fmt"                                                           2
    "strconv"                                                       3
)                                                                   4
```
Listing 1.3. Import ver.2

Constants. Constants can be declared with **const** keyword and = operator inside or outside of a function. Its value can be a character, string, Boolean, or numerical value. After the constant has been initialized with a value, the attempts to modify the value cause errors when compiling the program.

```
const JohnID = 1754                                                 1
```
Listing 1.4. Constant declaration

Variables. A variable statement declares variables with types either at the package or at function level. The keyword **var** initiates a variable declaration. The variable declaration can be done in the format of the keyword **var** then a variable name and the type of the variable. The basic types of Go are: bool, string, int, int8, int16, int32, int64, uint, uint8, uint16, uint32, uint64, uintptr, byte, rune, float32, float64, complex64, and complex128.

```
package main                                                        1
import "fmt"                                                        2
var x, y, z bool            // package level variable               3
func main() {                                                       4
    var i int               // function level variable             5
    fmt.Println(i, x, y, z)                                        6
}                                                                   7
```
Listing 1.5. Variables

Output:

```
0 false false false                                                 1
```

Initializers can be also used during the variable declaration. One initial value is given to each variable to be declared. If an initializer is used, the type can be omitted since the type of the initializer is taken as the type of the variable.

```
package main                                                        1
import "fmt"                                                        2
var i = 1                                                           3
var j int = 2                                                       4
func main() {                                                       5
    var x, y = true, "hello"                                       6
    fmt.Println(i, j, x, y)                                        7
}                                                                   8
```
Listing 1.6. Variables with initializers

Output:

```
1 2 true hello                                                    1
```

It can be made even shorter by using a short assignment, which eliminates the keyword **var** and uses the operator **:=**. The short assignment can be used inside a function. It is not legal to use it to declare a package level variable.

```
package main                                                     1
import "fmt"                                                      2
func main() {                                                    3
    var i = 1                                                    4
    j := 2          // short assignment                         5
    fmt.Println(i, j)                                           6
}                                                                7
```

Listing 1.7. Short variable declarations

Output:

```
1 2                                                             1
```

Functions. A function takes parameters and returns results. The number of parameters and results can be zero or more. The parameters and arguments are different. When you define a function, the input variables are the parameters usually used inside the function block. When you call a function, the variables passed to the function are arguments.

The function **multiplicate** of Listing 1.8 takes two **int** parameters (x and y) and returns one **int** (the product of them). The function **multipAndAdd** takes two **int** parameters (x and y) and returns two **int** results (the product and sum).

```
package main                                                     1
import "fmt"                                                      2
func main() {                                                    3
    fmt.Println(multiplicate(3, 4))                             4
    fmt.Println(multipAndAdd(3, 4))                             5
}                                                                6
func multiplicate(x, y int) int {                               7
    return x * y                                                8
}                                                                9
func multipAndAdd(x, y int) (int, int) {                        10
    return x * y, x + y                                         11
}                                                                12
```

Listing 1.8. Function

Output:

```
12                                                             1
12 7                                                           2
```

Named Return Values. When defining a function, the return values can be also named beside the return types. Values can be assigned to the named return values in the function body because they are treated as variables. After assigning all the named return values, a return statement without arguments can be used to return the named return values.

In Listing 1.9, the function f takes one int parameter x and returns three named return values: a of type int, b of type int, s of type string. In the function body, we assign values for the named return variables and use a return statement without arguments to return them.

```
package main
import "fmt"
func f(x int) (a int, b int, s string) {
    a = 4
    b = x
    s = "apple"
    return
}
func main() {
    fmt.Println(f(5))
}
```

Listing 1.9. Named return values

Output:

```
4 5 apple
```

Variadic Functions. The variadic function has a particular parameter type: ... used to show that it may have many parameters of this type. For example, the parameter nums of function product in Listing 1.10 is of type ...int, which means it matches any number of integers. The nums can be accessed in the function block as a slice of integers (Go slices are introduced in Sect. 2.1). When calling the product function, a different number of integers can be passed.

```
package main
import "fmt"
func main(){
    result1 := product(2,3)
    fmt.Println(result1)
    result2 := product(2,3,4)
    fmt.Println(result2)
}
func product(nums ...int) int {
    result := 1
    for _, num := range nums {
        result *= num
    }
    return result
}
```

Listing 1.10. Variadic function

Output:

```
6
24
```

Defer. The `defer` statement schedules a function call to be run immediately before the function is executing the return statement. The syntax is: `defer` `<function call>`. In Listing 1.11, the `defer` statement is placed in the function `main`. We call the `Println` with the argument `"Last1"`, `"Last2"`, and `"Last3"`. If there is only one defer statement, the `defer` ensures that the related function call runs as the last statement before the function `main` return. If there are multiple defer statements, the first defer statement will be the last statement the function runs. The usage of `defer` statement can also be found in Subsect. 5.1.

```
package main                                1
import "fmt"                                2
func main(){                                3
    fmt.Println("First")                    4
    defer fmt.Println("Last1")              5
    defer fmt.Println("Last2")              6
    defer fmt.Println("Last3")              7
    fmt.Println("Second")                   8
}                                           9
```

Listing 1.11. Defer

Output:

```
First                                       1
Second                                      2
Last3                                       3
Last2                                       4
Last1                                       5
```

Recursion. Go supports recursion, i.e. a function can call itself. As in any other programming language, first we must take care of the terminal condition, then we have to figure out what should be done in each recursive step. In Listing 1.12, we define the multiplication in a recursive way.

```
package main                                1
import "fmt"                                2
func main(){                                3
    fmt.Println(multiplicateR(3,4))         4
}                                           5
func multiplicateR (a int, b int) int{      6
    if a== 0{                               7
        return 0                            8
    }                                       9
    return b + multiplicateR(a-1, b)        10
}                                           11
```

Listing 1.12. Recursion

Output:

```
12                                          1
```

Exported Names. Outside of the imported packages, we can only access the exported names in the imported packages. Exported names must start with a capital letter. In Listing 1.13, we accessed the `IntSize` constant and the `Itoa` method of the `strconv` package.

```
package main                                                      1
import (                                                          2
    "fmt"                                                         3
    "strconv"                                                     4
)                                                                 5
func main() {                                                     6
    fmt.Println(strconv.IntSize)                                  7
    fmt.Println(strconv.Itoa(3))                                  8
}                                                                 9
```

Listing 1.13. Exported names

Output:

```
64                                                               1
3                                                                2
```

Here is another example that includes some commonly used functions of the strconv and strings packages. The function Itoa converts an integer to string. The function Atoi converts a string to an integer. The function ToLower converts all the characters of a string to lower case. The function ToUpper converts all the characters of a string to upper case. The function Contains checks if a string is inside another string. The function Count counts how many times a string that is non-overlapping appears in another string. The function Split splits a string according to a separator.

```
package main                                                      1
import (                                                          2
    "fmt"                                                         3
    "strconv"                                                     4
    "strings"                                                     5
)                                                                 6
func main() {                                                     7
    fmt.Println("strconv-------")                                 8
    s := strconv.Itoa(1)                                          9
    fmt.Println(s)                                                10
    i, err := strconv.Atoi("2")                                   11
    if err != nil {                                               12
        panic(err)                                                13
    }                                                             14
    fmt.Println(i)                                                15
    fmt.Println("strings-------")                                 16
    fmt.Println("ToLower:␣"+strings.ToLower("APPLE"))             17
    fmt.Println("ToUpper:␣"+strings.ToUpper("apple"))             18
    fmt.Println(strings.Contains("apple","pp"))                   19
    fmt.Println(strings.Count("apple","p"))                       20
    fmt.Println(strings.Split("a,p,p,l,e",","))                   21
}                                                                 22
```

Listing 1.14. Commonly used functions of the strconv and strings packages

Output:

```
strconv-------                                                   1
1                                                                2
2                                                                3
strings-------                                                   4
ToLower: apple                                                   5
ToUpper: APPLE                                                   6
true                                                             7
2                                                                8
[a p p l e]                                                      9
```

Type Inference. When declaring a variable without a specified type, the type for the variable is determined by the type of the right-hand side value.

```
var i int                                                          1
j := i // j is an int                                              2
```

Listing 1.15. Type inference without an explicit type

```
i := 42            // int                                          1
f := 3.142         // float64                                      2
g := 0.867 + 0.5i // complex128                                    3
```

Listing 1.16. Type inference with constants

Type Conversions. A type value can be converted by putting it into the parenthesis of a new type: $T(v)$, where T is the new type name to convert into and v is the original value. Go, unlike most other programming languages, requires explicit type conversions.

```
var i int = 42                                                     1
var f float64 = float64(i)                                         2
var u uint = uint(f)                                               3
```

Listing 1.17. Type conversions

For Statement. The syntax of a `for` loop is without parenthesis: between the `for` keyword and the braces, we declare an initialization, a condition, and a final expression.

```
package main                                                       1
import "fmt"                                                       2
func main() {                                                      3
    product := 1                                                   4
    for i := 1; i < 5; i++ {                                       5
        product *= i                                               6
    }                                                              7
    fmt.Println(product)                                           8
}                                                                  9
```

Listing 1.18. For loop

Output:

```
24                                                                 1
```

A `while` loop is expressed with a `for` loop where only a condition is declared.'

```
package main                                                       1
import "fmt"                                                       2
func main() {                                                      3
    i := 1                                                         4
    for i < 5 {                                                    5
        fmt.Println(i)                                             6
        i++                                                        7
    }                                                              8
}                                                                  9
```

Listing 1.19. While loop

Output:

```
1                                                                  1
2                                                                  2
3                                                                  3
4                                                                  4
```

An infinite loop can be created by omitting the loop condition.

```
for {                                                              1
}                                                                  2
```

Listing 1.20. Infinite loop

If Statement. Similar to the `for` loop, there are no parentheses between the `if` keyword and the braces.

```
package main                                                       1
import "fmt"                                                       2
func main() {                                                      3
    x := 2                                                         4
    if x < 0 {                                                     5
        fmt.Println(0)                                             6
    }else{                                                         7
        fmt.Println(x)                                             8
    }                                                              9
}                                                                  10
```

Listing 1.21. Example of if statement

Output:

```
2                                                                  1
```

One short statement can be placed inside of an `if` statement, which is valid until the end of `if`, and it acts like a local declaration of `if`.

```
package main                                                       1
import "fmt"                                                       2
func main() {                                                      3
    if x := -2; x<0 {                                              4
        fmt.Println(x)                                             5
    }                                                              6
}                                                                  7
```

Listing 1.22. Example of if statement with short statement

Output:

```
-2                                                                 1
```

Switch Statement. When using a `switch` statement in Go, break is automatically provided for each cases. `Switch` cases do not need to be constants. The evaluation proceeds from top to bottom and it stops when the case matches. A `switch` without a case is considered as a true match.

```
package main                                                      1
import "fmt"                                                      2
func main() {                                                     3
    lunch:= "apple"                                              4
    switch lunch {                                               5
    case "banana":                                               6
        fmt.Println("My lunch was a banana.")                    7
    case "apple":                                                8
        fmt.Println("My lunch was an apple.")                    9
    case "pear":                                                 10
        fmt.Println("My lunch was a pear.")                      11
    case "tomato":                                               12
        fmt.Println("My lunch was a tomato.")                    13
    default:                                                     14
        fmt.Printf("I did not have lunch.")                      15
    }                                                            16
}                                                                17
```

Listing 1.23. Example of `switch` statement

Output:

```
My lunch was an apple.                                            1
```

Slice. A slice is an array of elements of the same type with dynamic size. It is similar to a list in `Haskell` or to an `ArrayList` in Java. The syntax of slice is: `<SliceName> := [ ]<Type>{ <Elements> }`.

In Listing 1.24, the slice `animals` is created with four initial elements. The built-in function `append` returns a new slice value that contains the new elements. `append` is a variadic function; therefore, more new elements can be appended in one line. A `for range` loop can be used to iterate over the slice, as shown from line 12 to 14. An unneeded index is replaceable by an underscore, as shown in line 15. A declared but not used variable generates compilation error.

The index of a slice starts from zero. We can access the slice elements by putting indexes in the square brackets, as shown from line 18 to 21, `[3]` means the fourth element, `[:3]` means elements from beginning till the fourth element (not included). The `[3:]` means elements from the fourth element (included) till the end and `[2:4]` means elements from the third element (included) till the fifth element (not included). The usage of `slice` can also be found in Sect. 5.5.

```
package main                                                      1
import "fmt"                                                      2
func main() {                                                     3
    animals := []string{                                         4
        "dog",                                                   5
        "cat",                                                   6
        "bird",                                                  7
        "lion",                                                  8
    }                                                            9
    animals = append(animals, "panda")                          10
    animals = append(animals, "tiger", "wolf")                  11
    for index, animal := range animals {                        12
        fmt.Println(index, animal)                              13
    }                                                            14
    for _, animal := range animals {                            15
        fmt.Println(animal)                                     16
    }                                                            17
```

```
    fmt.Println(animals[3])                                        18
    fmt.Println(animals[:3])                                       19
    fmt.Println(animals[3:])                                       20
    fmt.Println(animals[2:4])                                      21
    animals[3] = "SSS"                                             22
    fmt.Println(animals)                                           23
}                                                                  24
```

Listing 1.24. Slice

Output:

```
0 dog                                                              1
1 cat                                                              2
2 bird                                                             3
3 lion                                                             4
4 panda                                                            5
5 tiger                                                            6
6 wolf                                                             7
dog                                                                8
cat                                                                9
bird                                                              10
lion                                                              11
panda                                                             12
tiger                                                             13
wolf                                                              14
lion                                                              15
[dog cat bird]                                                    16
[lion panda tiger wolf]                                           17
[bird lion]                                                       18
[dog cat bird SSS panda tiger wolf]                               19
```

Map. In Listing 1.25, a `map` named `neptunMap` is created and three elements are inserted (line 5 to 7). Using the built-in function `len`, we can get the length of the map. The insertion and the modification of a map share the same syntax.

The built-in function `delete` can be used to delete an element from the map according to the element's key. When you try to get the mapped value of a key in a map, you get two returned values, as shown in line 14 and 16. The first is the value, the second is a Boolean, which shows if this key exists in the map or not. If the key does not exist, this Boolean is false, and the value is the default value of that type value. Additionally, we can iterate over the map with `for range` loop. The syntax is similar to the `for range` loop on a `slice`.
The usage of `map` can also be found in Sect. 5.5.

```
package main                                                       1
import "fmt"                                                       2
func main() {                                                      3
    neptunMap := make(map[string]string)                          4
    neptunMap["AABBCC"] = "Adam"                                  5
    neptunMap["CCBBAA"] = "Ben"                                   6
    neptunMap["BBAACC"] = "Ada"                                   7
    fmt.Println(neptunMap)                                         8
    fmt.Println(len(neptunMap))                                    9
    neptunMap["BBAACC"]  = "CCC"                                  10
    fmt.Println(neptunMap)                                        11
    delete(neptunMap, "BBAACC")                                   12
    fmt.Println(neptunMap)                                        13
    v1, ok1 := neptunMap["CCBBAA"]                                14
    fmt.Println(v1, ok1)                                          15
    v2, ok2 := neptunMap["AAAAAA"]                                16
```

```
    fmt.Println(v2, ok2)                                  17
    for k,v :=range neptunMap {                           18
        fmt.Println(k,v)                                  19
    }                                                     20
}                                                         21
```

Listing 1.25. Map

Output:

```
map[AABBCC:Adam BBAACC:Ada CCBBAA:Ben]                    1
3                                                         2
map[AABBCC:Adam BBAACC:CCC CCBBAA:Ben]                    3
map[AABBCC:Adam CCBBAA:Ben]                               4
Ben true                                                  5
 false                                                    6
AABBCC Adam                                               7
CCBBAA Ben                                                8
```

Struct. The struct is a data structure with collection of fields. The relation between the struct and its typed value is like the relation between the class and the object in Java.

In Listing 1.26, student is the name of the struct and adam is its typed value. We can use dot operator to access a field of a struct when we want to get or modify the field. The struct can be defined inside or outside the function: the student is defined outside the main function, the teacher is defined inside. The struct is also a type that we define. The type of a field in a struct can be another struct: the field named c is of type contact, which is another struct.

```
package main                                              1
import "fmt"                                              2
type student struct {                                     3
    name    string                                        4
    id id                                                 5
    c contact                                             6
}                                                         7
type id string                                            8
type contact struct {                                     9
    email    string                                       10
    mobile string                                         11
}                                                         12
func main() {                                             13
    cont:= contact{"adam@gmail.com","0000"}               14
    adam := student{"Adam",  "abcdef",cont}               15
    fmt.Println(adam)                                     16
    adam.id = "nnnnn"                                     17
    fmt.Println(adam)                                     18
    fmt.Println(adam.name)                                19
    type teacherId string                                 20
    type teacher struct{                                  21
        n string                                          22
        id teacherId                                      23
        c contact                                         24
    }                                                     25
    v:= teacher {"v","a",contact{"v@gmail.com", "1111"}}  26
    fmt.Println(v)                                        27
}                                                         28
```

Listing 1.26. Struct

Output:

```
{Adam abcdef {adam@gmail.com 0000}}                              1
{Adam nnnnn {adam@gmail.com 0000}}                               2
Adam                                                             3
{v a {v@gmail.com 1111}}                                         4
```

Receiver. A receiver sets up methods on the types we created. A method is a function with a receiver. The receiver is like a parameter in a special location. The syntax is: `func (Receiver) functionName (Parameter) returnType {}`.

In Listing 1.27, the two versions of the `getName` function perform the same task, but in different forms. The `getNameR` function passes the `student` as a receiver, the `getNameA` function passes the `student` as a parameter.

```
package main                                                     1
import "fmt"                                                     2
type student struct {                                           3
    name    string                                              4
    id string                                                   5
}                                                               6
func main() {                                                   7
    adam := student{"Adam", "abcdef"}                           8
    fmt.Println(adam.getNameR())                                9
    fmt.Println(getNameA(adam))                                10
}                                                               11
func (s student) getNameR() string {                           12
    return s.name                                              13
}                                                               14
func getNameA(s student) string {                              15
    return s.name                                              16
}                                                               17
```

Listing 1.27. Receiver

Output:

```
Adam                                                             1
Adam                                                             2
```

Pointer. Go is a pass-by-value language. When we call the function and pass the arguments, copies of the arguments are created and then passed to the function. The `struct` follows the default pattern; however, the slice is of reference type, which implies that the references of the slice arguments are passed to the function. If we want to modify the arguments' value instead of just using the copied values, we need to use pointers. The copied value of the slice already contains the pointer, so that we do not need to do the pointer operation to modify the original value.

The operator * has different meanings in different places. As shown in line 22, in the function body, it means dereference a pointer, and it gets the current value the pointer points to. As shown in line 21, when used to declare the type of the parameter, it means the parameter is a pointer. It converts the normal type to the pointer type. The operator & creates a pointer (line 15).

```
package main                                                              1
import "fmt"                                                              2
type student struct {                                                    3
    name    string                                                       4
    id string                                                            5
}                                                                        6
func main() {                                                            7
    animals := []string{                                                 8
        "dog",                                                           9
        "lion",                                                          10
        "panda",                                                         11
    }                                                                    12
    adam := student{"Adam", "abcdef"}                                    13
    fmt.Println(adam)                                                    14
    modifyStudentName(&adam, "Levi")                                     15
    fmt.Println(adam)                                                    16
    fmt.Println(animals)                                                 17
    modifyFirstItem(animals, "cat")                                      18
    fmt.Println(animals)                                                 19
}                                                                        20
func modifyStudentName(pointerToStudent *student, newName string) {      21
    (*pointerToStudent).name = newName                                   22
}                                                                        23
func modifyFirstItem(animals []string, newFirstItem string) {           24
    animals[0] = newFirstItem                                            25
}                                                                        26
```

Listing 1.28. Pointer

Output:

```
{Adam abcdef}                                                            1
{Levi abcdef}                                                            2
[dog lion panda]                                                         3
[cat lion panda]                                                         4
```

Interface. The interface is used for two purposes. The first purpose is to make a more general function with an interface as its parameter, so that all the **struct** implementing this interface can be passed as an argument when the function is called. Therefore, this general function is reused instead of writing similar functions for each specific **struct**. The second purpose is to use the interface to limit the usage of the methods of a **struct** in a function. One **struct** can implement more interfaces, and it may have more methods than the interfaces need. If a function takes the interface as a parameter instead of a **struct**, then in the function body only the methods included in the interface can be used.

Listing 1.29 is an example of Go interface. The **animal** interface contains the **move** and the **breath** methods. The **readThinker** interface contains the **read** and the **think** methods, meaning the **readThinker** function only cares about those two methods. In addition to methods, an interface can also contain other interfaces. The **people** interface contains the **animal** and the **readThinker** interfaces. Therefore, in order to implement the **people** interface, we need to implement all the methods in the **animal** and the **readThinker** interfaces.

The **student** struct implements the **people** interface. The **student** struct can also have other methods that are not related to the **people** interface, like the **study** method. The **dog** struct implements the **animal** interface.

The `moveAndBreath` function takes the `animal` interface as parameter. We can pass the `people` or the `dog` struct as argument when calling this function. This is how to make a general function for multiple structs that have implemented the same interfaces (it contains the same set of related methods).

The `readAndThink` function takes the `readThinker` interface as parameter. We cannot pass the `dog` struct as argument when calling it because the `dog` struct does not implement the `readThinker` interface (does not have the `readAndThink` method). The `people` struct can be passed as argument for this function, but in this function, only the methods related to the `readThinker` interface can be used. For example, we cannot use the `move` method when we pass the `people` struct when calling the function `readAndThink`, even though the `people` struct has implemented the `move` method. When dealing with a struct which implements more interfaces or other methods, we can use the interface to limit the group of methods that can be used by a function. If we want to use the method `move` and `think` in a function, we should pass the "bigger" `people` interface instead of the `readThinker` or `animal` interfaces, as the function `moveAndThink` shows.

```
package main                                            1
import "fmt"                                             2
type animal interface{                                  3
    move() error                                        4
    breath() error                                      5
}                                                       6
type readThinker interface{                             7
    read() error                                        8
    think() error                                       9
}                                                       10
type people interface{                                  11
    animal                                              12
    readThinker                                         13
}                                                       14
type student struct{                                    15
    name string                                         16
}                                                       17
func (s student) move() error{                          18
    fmt.Println(s.name+" move")                         19
    return nil                                          20
}                                                       21
func (s student) breath() error{                        22
    fmt.Println(s.name+" breath")                       23
    return nil                                          24
}                                                       25
func (s student) read() error{                          26
    fmt.Println(s.name+" read")                         27
    return nil                                          28
}                                                       29
func (s student) think() error{                         30
    fmt.Println(s.name+" think")                        31
    return nil                                          32
}                                                       33
func (s student) study() error{                         34
    fmt.Println(s.name+" study")                        35
    return nil                                          36
}                                                       37
type dog struct{                                        38
    name string                                         39
}                                                       40
func (d dog) move() error{                              41
    fmt.Println(d.name+" move")                         42
    return nil                                          43
}                                                       44
```

```
func (d dog) breath() error{                          45
    fmt.Println(d.name+" breath")                     46
    return nil                                        47
}                                                     48
func moveAndBreath(a animal) {                        49
    _ = a.move()                                      50
    _ = a.breath()                                    51
}                                                     52
func readAndThink(r readThinker){                     53
    _ = r.read()                                      54
    _ = r.think()                                     55
}                                                     56
func moveAndThink(p people){                          57
    _ = p.move()                                      58
    _ = p.think()                                     59
}                                                     60
func main(){                                          61
    ol := student{"Olivia"}                           62
    pug := dog{"Bella"}                               63
    moveAndBreath(ol)                                 64
    moveAndBreath(pug)                                65
    readAndThink(ol)                                  66
    moveAndThink(ol)                                  67
}                                                     68
```

Listing 1.29. Interface

Output:

```
Olivia move                                            1
Olivia breath                                          2
Bella move                                             3
Bella breath                                           4
Olivia read                                            5
Olivia think                                           6
Olivia move                                            7
Olivia think                                           8
```

After introducing the basics of Go, next the concurrent constructs are presented and studied via examples.

3   Concurrent Programming

This section introduces several Go language elements related to concurrent programming: goroutine, WaitGroup, mutual exclusion operations, channel, and select. Additionally, the concurrency principles of Go are explained. In the end, a concurrent job processing example is provided with different versions.

3.1   Goroutine

The goroutines are similar to threads in Java; however, they are more lightweight, and neither id nor names are assigned to them. The keyword go is used before a function call to generate a goroutine. The function can be a named function or an anonymous function. The syntax of creating a goroutine with a named function is: go < FunctionName >(Arguments).

In Listing 1.30, line 7 uses go statement to generate a separate goroutine that runs the print() function. The goroutine does not care about the return values of this function; it only cares about what should be executed. Usually, goroutine functions have no return type. In this example, the `printR` function has a return type, while the `print` has not. However, they behave in the same way when they run as goroutines. There are ways to let the goroutine impact the outside world or bring out information. For example, you can mutually exclusively modify a variable outside or use a channel to communicate with other goroutines, see in Subsect. 3.4. When you run a program, the `main` function also runs as a goroutine, which is a special goroutine. Hence, there are three goroutines in the example: the `main` and two goroutines created by the `main`, the `printR` and the `print()`. When the function `main` terminates, all the goroutines it has created are stopped as well. In the example, if we do not let the function `main` to sleep for a while after it started the two goroutines, or the sleeping time is not enough, then it may terminate before the two goroutines finish. In that case, the two goroutines may not have finished their jobs. The sleep prevents the main goroutine from terminating other goroutines before they finish.

```
package main                                    1
import (                                         2
    "fmt"                                        3
    "time"                                       4
)                                                5
func main(){                                      6
    go printR("Hi 1")                            7
    go print("Hi 2")                             8
    time.Sleep(1 * time.Second)                  9
}                                                10
func print(s string) {                           11
    fmt.Println(s)                              '12
}                                                13
func printR(s string) string {                   14
    fmt.Println(s)                               15
    return s                                     16
}                                                17
```

Listing 1.30. Goroutine creation with named function

Output:

```
Hi 1                                             1
Hi 2                                             2
```

The syntax of creating a goroutine with anonymous function is:
`go func (< Parameters_and_their_types >) { } (Arguments)`
where, after the braces, the brackets and the arguments inside them mean that we call anonymous function rather than just defining it (so do not forget these brackets). In Listing 1.31, there are no parameters in the first anonymous function; therefore, the brackets at line 9 are empty. The second anonymous function has a parameter of string type. Accordingly, inside the brackets at the end, we need to put a string as an argument.

```
package main                                    1
import (                                         2
    "fmt"                                        3
    "time"                                       4
)                                                5
func main(){                                      6
```

```
    go func () {                              7
        fmt.Println("Hi␣1")                   8
    }()                                       9
    go func (s string) {                      10
        fmt.Println(s)                        11
    }("Hi␣2")                                 12
    time.Sleep(1 * time.Second)               13
}                                             14
```

Listing 1.31. Goroutine creation with anonymous function

Output:

```
Hi 1                                          1
Hi 2                                          2
```

3.2 WaitGroup

In the previous example, the sleeping time estimation used in goroutines is hard
to decide; 1 second for `Sleep` might be too much for all the goroutines to finish
their job. You may know the `join` method of Java, which lets a thread to wait
until the children threads have finished. Go has a similar construct: `WaitGroup`.
Here is how to use it when applied to wait until the created goroutines finished:

1. `import "sync"` – import the package `sync`.
2. `var < TypedValueName > sync.WaitGroup` – create first a typed value
   of `sync.WaitGroup` type (this value can be used later). There is no need to
   initialize it, the default value is good enough.
3. `< TypedValueName >.Add(1)` – before you start a goroutine, use the `Add`
   method of the `WaitGroup` with argument 1. It means a goroutine is added,
   for which the `WaitGroup` needs to wait.
4. `defer < TypedValueName >.Done()` – use this method of the `WaitGroup` at
   the beginning of a goroutine function body. It means before the goroutine
   terminates, it signals to the `WaitGroup` that its job has finished.
5. `< TypedValueName >.Wait()` – put this method of the `WaitGroup` at a
   place where all the goroutines are awaited.

```
package main                                  1
import (                                       2
    "fmt"                                      3
    "sync"                                     4
)                                              5
func main(){                                   6
    var wg sync.WaitGroup                      7
    for i := 0; i < 5; i++ {                   8
        wg.Add(1)                              9
        go func (a int) {                      10
            defer wg.Done()                    11
            fmt.Println("Hi",a)                12
        }(i)                                   13
    }                                          14
    wg.Wait()                                  15
}                                             16
```

Listing 1.32. WaitGroup

Output:

```
Hi 4                                                                1
Hi 1                                                                2
Hi 0                                                                3
Hi 2                                                                4
Hi 3                                                                5
```

It is normal to have different printing order when executing the code. If the call of `Wait` is deleted at line 15, the output is empty because the `main` function does not wait, it terminates; therefore, all the created goroutines are stopped before they can print the results. If instead of `a` the argument `i` is passed to the `Println` function, then the output is:

```
Hi 5                                                                1
Hi 5                                                                2
Hi 5                                                                3
Hi 5                                                                4
Hi 5                                                                5
```

The previous output is wrong: we do not want the program to print only 5 because `i` is changing at each iteration. Suppose the value of `i` is 3 when we use the `go` keyword to create a goroutine (let us call it goroutine A). After this iteration is over, the `for` loop goes on, `i` is changing and more goroutines are created. At the same time, the created goroutine A is still running. When the goroutine A uses the value of `i` for printing, the value of it is not 3 anymore.

As mentioned before, Go creates a copy of the arguments when calling a function. This copy stores the current value. Therefore, when we deal with a loop (or we need the value at some point, not the currently updated value), we must pass this value as an argument.

3.3 Mutual Exclusion

Mutex. If the goroutines do not access a shared variable mutually exclusive, the race condition occurs. The `sync.Mutex` can be called to create code blocks to be executed with mutual exclusion. Listing 1.33 shows how to use the `Mutex`:

1. `import "sync"` – import the package `sync`.
2. `var < TypedValueName > sync.Mutex` – create `sync.Mutex` type value.
3. `< TypedValueName >.Lock()` – use before accessing the shared resources.
4. `< TypedValueName >.Unlock()` – use after accessing the shared resources.

```
package main                                                        1
import (                                                            2
    "fmt"                                                           3
    "sync"                                                          4
)                                                                   5
func main(){                                                        6
    var mu sync.Mutex                                               7
    var wg sync.WaitGroup                                           8
    var result = 0                                                  9
    for i := 0; i < 1000; i++ {                                    10
        wg.Add(1)                                                  11
        go func (a int) {                                          12
```

```
        defer wg.Done()                              13
        mu.Lock()                                    14
        result += a                                  15
        mu.Unlock()                                  16
    }(i)                                             17
  }                                                  18
  wg.Wait()                                          19
  fmt.Println(result)                                20
}                                                    21
```

Listing 1.33. `Mutex`

The output is the sum of integers from 0 to 999:

```
499500                                                1
```

AddUint. The range of `int` type is platform-dependent. It is 32 bits on a 32-bit system and 64-bits on a 64-bit system. `int64` has larger range than `int32`. The `uint` means unsigned integer. Usually, we use the unsigned integer to count. By ignoring the negative numbers, we can double the size. Therefore, in this example we used the `AddUint64` function instead of the `AddInt32` one.

If a shared variable is an unsigned integer, we use the function `AddUint32` or `AddUint64` for a mutually exclusive addition operation. In this way, no need to handle ourselves the `lock` and `unlock` operations, as Listing 1.34 shows:

1. `import "sync/atomic"` – import the package.
2. `var < TypedValueName > uint64` – declare an `uint64` type variable.
3. `atomic.AddUint64(&< TypedValueName >, Value)` – use in a goroutine to add a value to the shared `uint64`. The first argument is the pointer to the `uint64` variable, while the second is the value to be added, which is of type `uint64`.

```
package main                                          1
import (                                              2
    "fmt"                                             3
    "sync"                                            4
    "sync/atomic"                                     5
)                                                     6
func main(){                                          7
    var result uint64                                 8
    var wg sync.WaitGroup                             9
    for i := 0; i < 1000; i++ {                      10
        wg.Add(1)                                    11
        go func (a int) {                            12
            defer wg.Done()                          13
            u:= uint64(a)                            14
            atomic.AddUint64(&result, u)             15
        }(i)                                         16
    }                                                17
    wg.Wait()                                        18
    fmt.Println(result)                              19
}                                                    20
```

Listing 1.34. `AddUint64`

The output shows that we can use the `AddUint64` in different goroutines to access the shared variable mutually exclusive:

3.4 Channels

Running goroutines can use channels to send and receive messages to each other without worrying about the mutual exclusion problem. A channel *"by default, sends and receives block until the other side is ready. This mechanism allows goroutines to synchronize without explicit locks or condition variables"* [2]. Here is the syntax of `make` when creating a channel:

$< ChannelName >$:= `make` (`chan` $< $`Type`$ >$)
$< ChannelName >$:= `make` (`chan` $< $`Type`$ >$, $< $`BufferSize`$ >$).

There is an initialization process of the channel in Listing 1.36 line 8, where an unbuffered channel of strings is created. The `chan string` means only strings can be sent and received on this channel. If a positive integer is added as second parameter, then it is a buffered channel of that size. The sender can close a channel to indicate that no more values are sent, as shown in Listing 1.35 line 17. Here is the syntax: `close` ($< ChannelName >$).

For the syntax of send and receive, we always use the arrow to the left operator `<-` (or less minus operator). If the channel is on the left-hand side, it is the send operation. If the channel is on the right-hand side, it is the receive operation. The syntax for send is: $< ChannelName > $ `<-` $< Message >$ and for receive is: $< Message > $:= `<-` $< ChannelName >$.

As shown in Listing 1.35, a `for` range loop can be used to iterate over a channel: it receives values from the channel until the channel is closed. The syntax is: `for` $< iterator >$:= `range` $< ChannelName >$ { }.

Next, the difference between the two kinds of channels are given. First, we introduce the buffered channel. As Fig. 1 shows, we have 4 slots for `int`, which is declared in Listing 1.35 line 9 `make(chan int,4)`. At this point the channel is empty. If any goroutine wants to receive, for example, a string from this channel, then it is blocked. If any goroutine wants to send a string to the channel, the string is stored in the buffer. The first, second, third, and fourth sending (insertion) are all successful, but the fifth sending is blocked until some other goroutine is trying to receive (extract) from it.

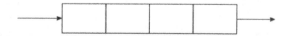

Fig. 1. Buffered channel of size 4

In Listing 1.35, we start two goroutines. The first goroutine tries to send ten integers to the channel c. The second goroutine sleeps 5 seconds before it starts to receive integers from the channel c. When the second goroutine does not start to receive, the first goroutine can only send four integers (because the buffer size is 4); that is why there are only four lines in the output at the beginning.

```
package main                                          1
import (                                              2
    "fmt"                                             3
    "sync"                                            4
    "time"                                            5
)                                                     6
func main() {                                         7
    var wg sync.WaitGroup                             8
    c := make(chan int,4)                             9
    wg.Add(1)                                        10
    go func() {                                      11
        defer wg.Done()                              12
        for i:=0;i<10;i++{                           13
            c<-i                                     14
            fmt.Println("g1 sent ",i)                15
        }                                            16
        close(c)                                     17
    }()                                              18
    wg.Add(1)                                        19
    go func() {                                      20
        defer wg.Done()                              21
        time.Sleep(5*time.Second)                    22
        for r := range c {                           23
            fmt.Println("g2 received ", r)           24
        }                                            25
    }()                                              26
    wg.Wait()                                        27
}                                                    28
```

Listing 1.35. Channel with buffer

In the output, g1 is the first and g2 is the second goroutine. At the beginning g1 sends four messages. After a few seconds, g2 starts to receive, and then g1 sends the rest of the messages:

```
g1 sent  0                                            1
g1 sent  1                                            2
g1 sent  2                                            3
g1 sent  3                                            4
(After a few seconds)                                 5
g2 received 0                                         6
g2 received 1                                         7
g2 received 2                                         8
g2 received 3                                         9
g2 received 4                                        10
g1 sent  4                                           11
g1 sent  5                                           12
g1 sent  6                                           13
g1 sent  7                                           14
g1 sent  8                                           15
g1 sent  9                                           16
g2 received 5                                        17
g2 received 6                                        18
g2 received 7                                        19
g2 received 8                                        20
g2 received 9                                        21
```

Second, we introduce the channel without buffer. The unbuffered channel has the second parameter as 0; there is no buffer for the data, as Fig. 2 shows. Without a sending operation to this channel, the receiving operation is blocked.

Likewise, the sending operation is blocked without a receiving operation. The communication is successful once different goroutine sending and the goroutine receiving. The unbuffered channel leads to the notion of synchronization.

Fig. 2. Channel without buffer.

In Listing 1.36, c is a channel of string without buffer. The first goroutine sends a "Hello" to channel c, the second goroutine receives a string from it.

```
package main                                          1
import (                                              2
    "fmt"                                             3
    "sync"                                            4
)                                                     5
func main() {                                         6
    var wg sync.WaitGroup                             7
    c := make(chan string)                            8
    wg.Add(1)                                         9
    go func() {                                       10
        defer wg.Done()                               11
        s := "Hello"                                  12
        c <- s                                        13
        fmt.Println("g1 sent ",s)                     14
    }()                                               15
    wg.Add(1)                                         16
    go func() {                                       17
        defer wg.Done()                               18
        r := <- c                                     19
        fmt.Println("g2 received ", r)                20
    }()                                               21
    wg.Wait()                                         22
}                                                     23
```

Listing 1.36. Channel without buffer

Output:

```
g1 sent   Hello                                       1
g2 received   Hello                                   2
```

3.5 Select

The select statement enables you to deal with multiple channel operations, channel operations with a timeout, and non-blocking channel operations.

There are a few cases and a possible default inside the select block. There is a channel operating after each keyword case. The select statement checks if those operations are executable (which are not blocked). If there is more than one executable case, select chooses one executable case randomly to execute; If there is no executable case, and there is a default case, then select executes the default case. If there is no executable case, and there is no default case, select blocks and waits until there is at least one executable case.

The function `After` of the package `time` returns a channel. The argument is a duration value. After this duration elapses, the function `After` sends the current time as a message to the returned channel.

Listing 1.37 shows an example of `select` dealing with channel operation with timeout. This example is not executable when `select` checks the first case because the created goroutine is still sleeping. The second case is also not executable because the function `After` only sends a message to the returned channel after 3 s. There is no default case, then `select` blocks and waits. The first case needs 4 s to become executable. The second case only needs 3 s to become executable. After 3 s, the `After` function sends a message to the returned channel, the second case becomes executable, which is the only executable case at that moment. Therefore, the second case is executed.

```
package main                                               1
import (                                                   2
    "fmt"                                                  3
    "time"                                                 4
)                                                          5
func main() {                                              6
    c := make(chan int)                                    7
    go func() {                                            8
        time.Sleep(4 * time.Second)                        9
        c <- 1                                            10
        fmt.Println("g1 sent 1")                          11
    }()                                                   12
    select {                                              13
    case msg := <-c:                                      14
        fmt.Println("Main received ", msg)                15
    case <- time.After(3 * time.Second):                  16
        fmt.Println("Timeout, Quit")                      17
        break                                             18
    }                                                     19
}                                                         20
```

Listing 1.37. Select with timeout

Output:

```
Timeout, Quit                                              1
```

Listing 1.38 shows an example of `select` dealing with continuous multiple channel operations. There are two channels of integers. The first created goroutine sends 5 integers to channel `c1` with a 500 ms interval. The second sends integers to channel `c2`. The `main` function keeps receiving messages from both channels. For every 500 ms, the first two cases become executable nearly simultaneously, so `main` function randomly chooses one of them to execute. After 3 s of `main` receiving all the messages, the timeout case is executed.

```
package main                                               1
import (                                                   2
    "fmt"                                                  3
    "time"                                                 4
)                                                          5
func main() {                                              6
    c1 := make(chan int)                                   7
    c2 := make(chan int)                                   8
    go func() {                                            9
        for i := 0; i < 5; i++ {                          10
```

```
            time.Sleep(500 * time.Millisecond)                    11
            c1 <- i                                               12
            fmt.Println("g1 sent ", i)                            13
        }   }()                                                   14
    go func() {                                                   15
        for i := 0; i < 5; i++ {                                  16
            time.Sleep(500 * time.Millisecond)                    17
            c2 <- i                                               18
            fmt.Println("g2 sent ", i)                            19
        }   }()                                                   20
    L: for {                                                      21
        select {                                                  22
        case msg := <-c1:                                         23
            fmt.Println("Main received ", msg, " from g1")        24
        case msg := <-c2:                                         25
            fmt.Println("Main received ", msg, " from g2")        26
        case <- time.After(3 * time.Second):                      27
            fmt.Println("Timeout , Quit")                         28
            break L                                               29
        }                                                         30
    }                                                             31
}                                                                 32
```

Listing 1.38. Select multiple channel operations

Output:

```
Main received   0   from g1                                       1
Main received   0   from g2                                       2
g1 sent   0                                                       3
g2 sent   0                                                       4
g1 sent   1                                                       5
Main received   1   from g1                                       6
Main received   1   from g2                                       7
g2 sent   1                                                       8
g1 sent   2                                                       9
Main received   2   from g1                                       10
Main received   2   from g2                                       11
g2 sent   2                                                       12
g1 sent   3                                                       13
Main received   3   from g1                                       14
Main received   3   from g2                                       15
g2 sent   3                                                       16
g2 sent   4                                                       17
Main received   4   from g2                                       18
Main received   4   from g1                                       19
g1 sent   4                                                       20
Timeout , Quit                                                    21
```

The **select** with default case is also known as the non-blocking channel operation. Listing 1.39 shows an example of **select** dealing with non-blocking channel operation. The created goroutine sleeps two seconds, then tries to send 1 to channel c. When running the program for the first four iterations, the first case is not executable because the created goroutine is sleeping. The **select** executes the default case. At the fifth iteration, the first case becomes executable.

```
package main                                                      1
import (                                                          2
    "fmt"                                                         3
    "time"                                                        4
)                                                                 5
func main() {                                                     6
    c := make(chan int)                                           7
    go func() {                                                   8
        time.Sleep(2000 * time.Millisecond)                       9
```

```
            c <- 1                                            10
            fmt.Println("g1␣sent␣1")  }()                     11
     L: for {                                                 12
          select {                                            13
          case msg := <-c:                                    14
              fmt.Println("Main␣received␣", msg)              15
              break L                                         16
          default:                                            17
              time.Sleep(500 * time.Millisecond)              18
              fmt.Println("Default")                          19
          }                                                   20
       }                                                      21
   }                                                          22
```

Listing 1.39. Select default

Output:

```
Default                                                        1
Default                                                        2
Default                                                        3
Default                                                        4
Main received   1                                             5
```

3.6 Concurrency Principles

The Go language follows the principle of *"do not communicate by sharing memory; instead, share memory by communicating"* [9].

Communication by Sharing Memory. Sharing memory involves multiple threads accessing or modifying the data simultaneously. To guarantee the security and visibility of the data, we need synchronization mechanisms, like lock or semaphore. However, this increases the code complexity. Even more, if multiple locks are used, then deadlocks may occur.

Share Memory by Communicating. "Instead of explicitly using locks to mediate access to shared data, Go encourages the use of channels to pass references to data between goroutines" [9]. Go uses channels to synchronize and communicate mutually exclusive. The reference to data is sent as messages through channels. We can consider that we are passing the ownership of the data. The sharing between goroutines is therefore achieved.

3.7 Parallelism

Let us discuss the differences between concurrency and parallelism.

"In programming, concurrency is the composition of independently executing processes, while parallelism is the simultaneous execution of (possibly related) computations. Concurrency is about dealing with lots of things at once. Parallelism is about doing lots of things at once" [5].

In Go, concurrency means we can create lots of independent goroutines dealing with different or similar tasks (see Fig. 3). However, those goroutines may not be running in parallel. Parallelism means the created goroutines share more CPUs (see Fig. 4).

Listing 1.40 shows how we can configure the number of CPUs that can be used by the Go program. NumCPU shows how many CPUs are available, GOMAXPROCS method sets the maximum number of CPUs that the program can use according to the argument. The code also uses the functions of the time package to get the duration of the execution. The function Now is used to get the current local time, Since returns the time elapsed since the argument, between them is the code that you might want to test for duration execution.

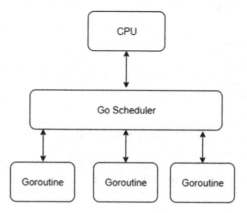

Fig. 3. Concurrency. Go programs only use one CPU by default. The Go scheduler decides which goroutine is running to leverage the core. *Concurrency* means all the created goroutines are independent. However, they might share only one CPU.

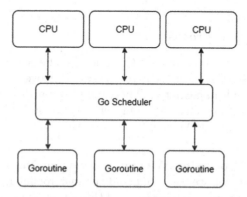

Fig. 4. Parallelism. *Parallelism* means more goroutines run at the same time. In other words, more than one CPU is scheduled between the running goroutines.

```
package main                                           1
import (                                               2
    "fmt"                                              3
    "sync"                                             4
    "time"                                             5
    "runtime"                                          6
)                                                      7
func main(){                                           8
    fmt.Println(runtime.NumCPU())                      9
    _ = runtime.GOMAXPROCS(8)                          10
    start := time.Now()                                11
    var mu sync.Mutex                                  12
    var wg sync.WaitGroup                              13
    var result = 0                                     14
    for i := 0; i < 10000; i++ {                       15
        wg.Add(1)                                      16
        go func (a int) {                              17
            defer wg.Done()                            18
            mu.Lock()                                  19
            result += a                                20
            mu.Unlock()                                21
        }(i)                                           22
    }                                                  23
    wg.Wait()                                          24
    fmt.Println(result)                                25
    duration := time.Since(start)                      26
    fmt.Println("Time: ", duration)                    27
}                                                      28
```

Listing 1.40. CPU

The following outputs show the efficiency difference when setting various CPU numbers. In case of _ = runtime.GOMAXPROCS(8) the output is:

```
16                                                     1
49995000                                               2
Time:   3.1419ms                                       3
```

In case of _ = runtime.GOMAXPROCS(1) the output is:

```
16                                                     1
49995000                                               2
Time:   16.5745ms                                      3
```

3.8 Concurrent Job Processing

This example is inspired by a blog of Castilho [4]. The scenario for this example is handling massive requests sent to servers. Moreover, a request does not need to know the result immediately. This example practices the Go concurrent constructs studied before. There are four versions: Version 1 does not limit the number of goroutines, while Version 2, 3, and 4 show three ways to limit it.

Concurrent Job Processing Without Goroutine Number Limit (Version 1). In this version, we use a buffered channel jobQueue as the job queue (see Fig. 5). The goroutine linkSender and the goroutine workerCreator communicate through the jobQueue. After the linkSender finishes all the sendings, it closes the jobQueue to indicate that there is no more sending. The linkSender goroutine sends jobs to the job queue and does not need responses. The slice `links` contains all the links that are sent to the workers. The `workerCreator` goroutine receives jobs from the `jobQueue` until it is closed. For each received job, the `workerCreator` generates a `worker` to process the job. Once the `jobQueue` is full, the sending operations to the `jobQueue` that are done by the `linkSender` are blocked. Once the `jobQueue` is empty, the receiving operations from the `jobQueue` that are done by the `workerCreator` are blocked.

The main goroutine waits until all the goroutines finish using the `WaitGroup` of the `sync` package and prints out the maximum number of existing goroutines and the running duration. The `goroutineCounter` goroutine gets the number of goroutines that currently exist for every 50 ms. If the current value is greater than the original maximum value, the `goroutineCounter` updates the maximum number of goroutines `maxGo` using the function `StoreUint64`. The `worker` goroutine checks the link using the function `linkTest`. Since the usage of the functions in the package `net/http` causes the generation of more goroutines, the `linkTest` only sleeps 500 ms and randomly returns a check result.

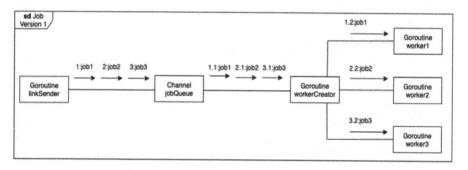

Fig. 5.   Concurrent job processing without goroutine number limit.   The `linkSender` goroutine sends jobs to the `jobQueue` sequentially in `1:job1`, `2:job2`, `3:job3` order. The `workerCreator` goroutine generates a worker for each job received from the `jobQueue` channel (the receiving order is `1.1:job1`, `2.1:job2`, `3.1:job3`. The `workerCreator` sequentially distributes jobs to workers in the order of `1.2:job1`, `2.2:job2`, `3.2:job3` and the workers process them concurrently.

If we use a list here as the job queue, we need to handle sharing memory among threads. Instead, the channel automatically handles the mutual exclusion problem of multiple accesses from different threads. If the processing speed is higher than the request sending speed, the buffered channel does not have the sending job blocking problem. When the processing speed reduces, the requests are stored in the buffer, and the request sending is not blocked until the buffer is full. When the processing speed recovers, it clears the requests in the buffer. Since the job sending operations are not blocked, the client does not notice that the processing speed is reduced until the buffer is full. If the processing speed reduces and does not recover, the buffer finally runs out of place, and the client's job sending operation is blocked.

```
package main                                                                    1
import (                                                                        2
    "fmt"                                                                       3
    "math/rand"                                                                 4
    "runtime"                                                                   5
    "sync"                                                                      6
    "sync/atomic"                                                               7
    "time"                                                                      8
)                                                                               9
var jobQueue = make(chan string, 100)                                          10
var maxGo uint64                                                               11
var wg sync.WaitGroup                                                          12
func main() {                                                                  13
    go goroutineCounter()                                                      14
    start := time.Now()                                                        15
    wg.Add(1)                                                                  16
    go linkSender()                                                            17
    wg.Add(1)                                                                  18
    go workerCreator()                                                         19
    wg.Wait()                                                                  20
    fmt.Println("Max goroutine number: ", atomic.LoadUint64(&maxGo))           21
    duration := time.Since(start)                                              22
    fmt.Println("Time: ", duration)                                            23
}                                                                              24
func goroutineCounter() {                                                      25
    for {                                                                      26
        n := runtime.NumGoroutine()                                            27
        u := uint64(n)                                                         28
        if u > maxGo {                                                         29
            atomic.StoreUint64(&maxGo, u)                                       30
        }                                                                      31
        time.Sleep(50 * time.Millisecond)                                      32
    }                                                                          33
}                                                                              34
func linkSender() {                                                            35
    defer wg.Done()                                                            36
    links := []string{}                                                        37
    var numOfLink = 1000                                                       38
    for i := 0; i < numOfLink; i++ {                                           39
        fakeLink := fmt.Sprintf("http://web%d.com", i)                         40
        links = append(links, fakeLink)                                        41
    }                                                                          42
    for _, link := range links {                                              43
        jobQueue <- link                                                       44
    }                                                                          45
    close(jobQueue)                                                            46
}                                                                              47
func workerCreator() {                                                         48
    defer wg.Done()                                                            49
    for link := range jobQueue {                                              50
        wg.Add(1)                                                              51
        go worker(link)                                                        52
    }                                                                          53
}                                                                              54
func worker(l string) {                                                        55
    defer wg.Done()                                                            56
    fmt.Println(linkTest(l))                                                   57
}                                                                              58
func linkTest(link string) string {                                           59
    time.Sleep(500 * time.Millisecond)                                         60
    if rand.Intn(2) == 1 {                                                     61
        return link + ": Good"                                                 62
    } else {                                                                   63
        return link + ": Bad"                                                  64
    }                                                                          65
}                                                                              66
```

Listing 1.41. Concurrent job processing without goroutine number limit

Output:

```
...                                            1
http://web978.com: Good                        2
http://web25.com: Good                         3
http://web173.com: Good                        4
http://web4.com: Good                          5
http://web41.com: Bad                          6
http://web27.com: Bad                          7
http://web6.com: Bad                           8
http://web9.com: Bad                           9
http://web43.com: Bad                          10
http://web42.com: Bad                          11
http://web0.com: Bad                           12
http://web780.com: Bad                         13
Max goroutine number:   1002                   14
Time:  949.4977ms                              15
```

There is no goroutine number limit in this version. Therefore, if we have created too many goroutines for processing the job at the same time, this program may crash because of running out of memory.

Concurrent Job Processing with Goroutine Number Limit (Version 2).
To prevent this program from crashing, we need to limit the worker goroutines generated for processing the requests (see Fig. 6). We create one more buffered channel `workerPool` to simulate the worker pool. Its size defines the maximum number of goroutines for processing requests that can run simultaneously.

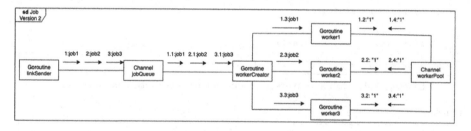

Fig. 6.   Concurrent job processing with goroutine number limit.   The `workerPool` channel is used to constrain the number of concurrently running goroutines. An integer 1 is inserted into the `workerPool` and then a new `worker` goroutine is created. This integer 1 is removed from the `workerPool` before the `worker` goroutine finishes the job.

Before generating a child goroutine, we send 1 to it (any integer can be inserted as a placeholder, 1 is used in this example). After the processing job is done, 1 is removed from it.

If the `workerPool` is full, we cannot send messages to it; therefore, we cannot create new goroutines. For each job received from the `jobQueue`, the `workerCreator` first tries sending 1 to the worker pool, and then it creates a worker to process the received job.

The `defer` statement of Go schedules a function call to be run immediately before the function returns. After the `worker` has done the checking work but before terminates, it removes 1 from the worker pool using the `defer` statement.

```
package main                                          1
import (                                              2
    "fmt"                                             3
    "math/rand"                                       4
    "runtime"                                         5
    "sync"                                            6
    "sync/atomic"                                     7
    "time"                                            8
)                                                     9
var workerPool = make(chan int, 50)                   10
var jobQueue = make(chan string, 100)                 11
var maxGo uint64                                      12
var wg sync.WaitGroup                                 13
func main() { ... }                                   14
func goroutineCounter() { ... }                       15
func linkSender() { ... }                             16
func workerCreator() {                                17
    defer wg.Done()                                   18
    for link := range jobQueue {                      19
        workerPool <- 1                               20
        wg.Add(1)                                     21
        go worker(link)                               22
    }                                                 23
}                                                     24
func worker(link string) {                            25
    defer wg.Done()                                   26
    defer func() { <-workerPool }()                   27
    fmt.Println(linkTest(link))                       28
}                                                     29
func linkTest(link string) string { ... }             30
```

Listing 1.42. Job and Worker concurrent with goroutine number limit

Output:

```
...                                                   1
http://web989.com: Bad                                2
http://web976.com: Bad                                3
http://web991.com: Bad                                4
http://web999.com: Good                               5
http://web997.com: Bad                                6
http://web955.com: Bad                                7
http://web956.com: Bad                                8
Max goroutine number:  54                             9
Time:  10.043942287s                                  10
```

Concurrent Job Processing by Long-Life Workers (Version 3). In version 2, the `workerCreator` keeps receiving a job from the job queue, and it also keeps creating worker goroutines to perform the job.

The `worker` goroutine terminates after the job is done. It only constrains the number of goroutines that run concurrently rather than the number of goroutines that we create.

In version 3, we constrain the number of goroutines we create. Instead of letting the worker terminate after doing the job (short life worker) like in the previous versions for new jobs, we keep several workers alive and continuously work on the jobs (long life worker), as Fig. 7 shows. Additionally, we implement the distribution of the tasks to the workers in a load-balanced way.

In this version, the worker is a **struct** containing the fields **id**, **jobChannel**, **quitChannel**. The **Start** method of the **worker** creates a goroutine that keeps receiving links from its own **jobChannel** until it receives a **q** from the **quitChannel**.

In the **workerCreator** goroutine, first, the long-life worker goroutines are created according to the constant **MaxWorker**; next, for each received link from the **jobQueue**, a worker is selected in a balanced way to check the link; finally, after the **jobQueue** is closed, **q** is sent to all the **worker** goroutines' **quitChannel**.

The **roundRobin** and **randomSelect** functions can be used to select a worker in a balanced way. Once a worker is selected to check the link, the received link is sent to its **jobChannel**.

Listing 1.43 uses **randomSelect**, instead, **roundRobin** can be also applied by commenting the code in line 35 and uncommenting the lines 26 and 34.

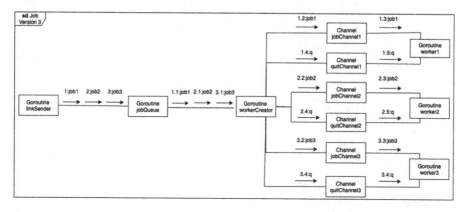

Fig. 7. Concurrent job processing by long-life workers. An unbuffered **jobChannel** is created for each **worker** goroutine to receive a job from the **workerCreator** goroutine. The **workerCreator** goroutine receives jobs from the **jobQueue** channel and sends them to the **jobChannels** of the workers in a balanced round robin manner (or random select manner). The **worker** goroutines process the jobs concurrently. After the **jobQueue** channel is closed, the **workerCreator** goroutine sends a **q** through the **quitChannels** to all the **worker** goroutines. The **worker** goroutine quits after it has received a **q** from the **quitChannel**.

```
package main                                                          1
import (                                                             2
    "fmt"                                                            3
    "math/rand"                                                      4
    "runtime"                                                        5
```

```
        "strconv"                                                    6
        "sync"                                                       7
        "sync/atomic"                                                8
        "time"                                                       9
)                                                                   10
const MaxWorker = 50                                                11
var jobQueue = make(chan string, 100)                              12
var maxGo uint64                                                   13
var wg sync.WaitGroup                                             14
func main() {                                                      15
    ...                                                            16
}                                                                  17
func goroutineCounter() {                                          18
    ...                                                            19
}                                                                  20
func linkSender() {                                                21
    ...                                                            22
}                                                                  23
func workerCreator() {                                             24
    defer wg.Done()                                                25
    //index := 0                                                   26
    workers := []worker{}                                          27
    for i := 0; i < MaxWorker; i++ {                               28
        worker := worker{i, make(chan string), make(chan string)}  29
        worker.Start()                                             30
        workers = append(workers, worker)                          31
    }                                                              32
    for link := range jobQueue {                                   33
        //selectedWorker := roundRobin(workers, &index)            34
        selectedWorker := randomSelect(workers)                    35
        selectedWorker.jobChannel <- link                          36
    }                                                              37
    for _, w := range workers {                                    38
        w.quitChannel <- "q"                                       39
    }                                                              40
}                                                                  41
func roundRobin(l []worker, currentIndex *int) worker {            42
    selected := l[(*currentIndex)]                                 43
    if (*currentIndex) >= len(l)-1 {                               44
        (*currentIndex) = 0                                        45
    } else {                                                       46
        (*currentIndex)++                                          47
    }                                                              48
    return selected                                                49
}                                                                  50
func randomSelect(l []worker) worker {                             51
    lens := len(l)                                                 52
    index := rand.Intn(lens)                                       53
    selected := l[index]                                           54
    return selected                                                55
}                                                                  56
type worker struct {                                               57
    id          int                                                58
    jobChannel  chan string                                        59
    quitChannel chan string                                        60
}                                                                  61
func (w worker) Start() {                                          62
    wg.Add(1)                                                      63
    go func() {                                                    64
        defer wg.Done()                                            65
    L:                                                             66
        for {                                                      67
            select {                                               68
            case link := <-w.jobChannel:                           69
                fmt.Println("Worker ",                             70
                    strconv.Itoa(w.id), ": ",                      71
                    linkTest(link))                                72
            case <-w.quitChannel:                                  73
```

```
            fmt.Println("Worker␣",                              74
                strconv.Itoa(w.id), "Quit")                    75
            break L                                            76
        }                                                      77
    }                                                          78
    }()                                                        79
}                                                              80
func linkTest(link string) string {                            81
    ...                                                        82
}                                                              83
```

Listing 1.43. Concurrent job processing by long-life workers

Output:

```
...                                                            1
Worker  49 :  http://web996.com: Bad                           2
Worker  26 :  http://web992.com: Good                          3
Worker  11 :  http://web997.com: Bad                           4
Worker   7 :  http://web998.com: Good                          5
Worker   7 Quit                                                6
Worker  17 :  http://web988.com: Good                          7
...                                                            8
Worker  27 Quit                                                9
Worker  33 Quit                                                10
Worker  21 Quit                                                11
Worker  18 Quit                                                12
Worker  13 Quit                                                13
Max goroutine number:   54                                     14
Time:   54.164746183s                                          15
```

Concurrent Job Processing Using Goroutine Pool (Version 4). The previous versions implement mechanisms where we limit ourselves the number of goroutines. In this version, the number of goroutines are limited by using the existing goroutine pool library **Tunny** [10].

The size of the goroutine pool is the total number of goroutines in the pool. The goroutine pool creates goroutines on demand until it reaches the size.

Listing 1.44 line 15 declares a global goroutine pool. Line 18 to line 28 creates a goroutine pool with the name **pool** using the **NewFunc** function. The first parameter is the size of the goroutine pool (here the limit of the number of goroutines is 20). The second parameter is the behaviour function of each goroutine of the **pool** which uses the **Done** method of the **WaitGroup**. The **workerCreator** goroutine adds **1** to the **WaitGroup wg** for each link received from the **jobQueue** channel. Using the **Process** method a new worker is created to process the link and to print the result.

```
package main                                                   1
import (                                                       2
    "fmt"                                                      3
    "math/rand"                                                4
    "runtime"                                                  5
    "sync"                                                     6
    "sync/atomic"                                              7
    "log"                                                      8
    "time"                                                     9
    "github.com/Jeffail/tunny"                                 10
)                                                              11
var jobQueue = make(chan string, 100)                          12
var maxGo uint64                                               13
var wg sync.WaitGroup                                          14
```

```go
var pool *tunny.Pool                                            15
func main() {                                                   16
    go goroutineCounter()                                       17
    pool = tunny.NewFunc(20,                                    18
    func(payload interface{}) interface{} {                     19
        var result string                                       20
        s, ok := payload.(string)                               21
        if(!ok){                                                22
            log.Fatalln("type assertion fail")                  23
        }                                                       24
        result = linkTest(s)                                    25
        defer wg.Done()                                         26
        return result                                           27
    })                                                          28
    defer pool.Close()                                          29
    start := time.Now()                                         30
    wg.Add(1)                                                   31
    go linkSender()                                             32
    wg.Add(1)                                                   33
    go workerCreator()                                          34
    wg.Wait()                                                   35
    fmt.Println("Max goroutine number: ",                       36
    atomic.LoadUint64(&maxGo))                                  37
    duration := time.Since(start)                               38
    fmt.Println("Time: ", duration)                             39
}                                                               40
func goroutineCounter() {                                       41
    for {                                                       42
        n := runtime.NumGoroutine()                             43
        u := uint64(n)                                          44
        if u > maxGo {                                          45
            atomic.StoreUint64(&maxGo, u)                       46
        }                                                       47
        time.Sleep(50 * time.Millisecond)                       48
    }                                                           49
}                                                               50
func linkSender() {                                             51
    defer wg.Done()                                             52
    links := []string{}                                         53
    var numOfLink = 100                                         54
    for i := 0; i < numOfLink; i++ {                            55
        fakeLink := fmt.Sprintf("http://web%d.com", i)          56
        links = append(links, fakeLink)                         57
    }                                                           58
    for _, link := range links {                                59
        jobQueue <- link                                        60
    }                                                           61
    close(jobQueue)                                             62
}                                                               63
func workerCreator() {                                          64
    defer wg.Done()                                             65
    for link := range jobQueue {                                66
        wg.Add(1)                                               67
        result := pool.Process(link)                            68
        fmt.Println(result)                                     69
    }                                                           70
}                                                               71
func linkTest(link string) string {                             72
    time.Sleep(50 * time.Millisecond)                           73
    if rand.Intn(2) == 1 {                                      74
        return link + ": Good"                                  75
    } else {                                                    76
        return link + ": Bad"                                   77
    }                                                           78
}                                                               79
```

Listing 1.44. Concurrent job processing using goroutine pool

Output:

```
...                                              1
http://web90.com: Bad                            2
http://web91.com: Bad                            3
http://web92.com: Bad                            4
http://web93.com: Good                           5
http://web94.com: Bad                            6
http://web95.com: Good                           7
http://web96.com: Bad                            8
http://web97.com: Good                           9
http://web98.com: Good                          10
http://web99.com: Bad                           11
Max goroutine number:   23                      12
Time:   6.184s                                  13
```

In this section, four versions of the concurrent job processing example were described. When a smaller task is implemented or when running out of memory does not occur, version 1 may be enough; otherwise, versions 2, 3, or 4 can be used to limit the number of goroutines. The workers of version 2 and 4 are short-life workers, the ones of version 3 are long-life. Version 4 needs extra dependency, while version 3 can customize the way of achieving load balance. Any of the proposed patterns can be chosen based on the needs of the to be implemented problem's scenario.

4   Advanced Message Queueing Protocol (AMQP)

Integrating queues into distributed systems is crucial when dealing with large volumes of continuously generated data traffic. Queueing systems offer parallel execution by allowing multiple workers to process tasks in parallel. In the following sections we introduce RABBITMQ, one of the standard queueing systems.

RABBITMQ mainly specializes in messaging, offering features such as message routing, load distribution, retries, and so on.

Before we dive into the distributed examples, first we introduce AMQP (Advanced Message Queuing Protocol) [1] used by RABBITMQ [22]. AMQP offers messaging and communication, dealing with publishers and consumers.

In the OSI (Open Systems Interconnection) model, which partitions a communication system into seven layers, there is an application layer where IMAP (Internet Message Access Protocol), FTP (File Transfer Protocol), DNS (Domain Name System), SSH (Secure Shell) and IRC (Internet Relay Chat) operate. AMQP is also an application layer protocol.

There are many message broker implementations available for AMQP since it is an open standard, and RABBITMQ is one of such. AMQP offers interoperability between consumers and brokers, which is a crucial feature. AMQP provides solutions for destroying the barriers of communication between different applications designed by different programming languages. Since AMQP is fast, it is a matter of interest to areas where time is valuable, like banks, card companies, real-time programs, and so on. The general structure of the AMQP can be seen in Fig. 8.

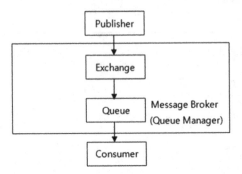

Fig. 8. `AMQP` Structure. The `Publisher` sends messages to the `Exchange`. The `Exchange` routes messages to `Queues`. The `Queue` forwards messages to the `Consumer`.

4.1 `AMQP` Components

Producer (Publisher). The producer is an application that writes messages to queues through the exchanges. In general, it is long-lived and it aims to publish multiple messages while alive. The example of producer can be found in Listing 1.46.

Message Broker (Queue Manager). The message broker is a repository for several one-way channels, typically containing multiple queue nodes. Publishing or consuming messages from a queue is done over a channel, which is a virtual connection that receives messages from publishers then routes them to the specific consumers.

The message broker accepts connections from consumers for message routing and queuing. It either transfers messages to queues that consumers subscribed to, or fetches/pulls messages from queues on demand. The broker gets a notification from a consumer when a message is delivered; then, it removes the message from the queue.

The message brokers can be connected to each other, which is highly common in the case of an overlay network. They are typically built upon a MOM (Message Oriented Middleware), an architecture for a distributed system with lots of internal communication and information or data sharing components. Thus, message brokers are building blocks of MOM.

RABBITMQ is a message broker that also uses MOM implementation, i.e. is a set of routing and queuing patterns, where routing means messages are forwarded to one or more peers, and queuing means messages are held in memory or disk until they can be delivered or acknowledged. `AMQP` is used to specify broker patterns so that an application could rely on uniform behaviour of any `AMQP`-compatible broker.

Consumer (Client). A consumer (or client) processes messages from queues delivered by an exchange. The example of consumer can be found in Listing 1.45.

It receives messages from queues, where the queue contains messages published by a producer. As soon as a new consumer arrives, the delivery is started when a first message enqueues to the queue. If they try to consume messages from a queue that does not exist, it raises a channel-level exception.

Obviously, it is desirable to register a consumer to consume multiple messages, not just a single message. Generally, consumers are long-lived, living throughout a connection or even during the application runs. A consumer may lose its connection to RABBITMQ, which causes stopping the message delivery. Consumers can usually be removed after their connection is lost. They can also publish messages, which means they can be publishers as well.

Queue. In general, a queue is a sequence of the same type of elements that adds new elements at the rear and removes existing elements from the top. This kind of behaviour is called FIFO (First-In First-Out). A queue can store and retrieve one element at a time. Therefore, it is useful when the order of elements is important.

A message queue (MQ) in RABBITMQ is a collection of messages sorted by FIFO, used for receiving and delivering messages. MQ is a mechanism that shares information between processes, threads, or systems. A queue needs to be declared before usage and can be named or automatic name can be given by a broker.

Depending on the durability of a queue, it is categorized as persistent queue and transient queue. Persistent queues are durable queues, which can survive restarts by brokers. Persistent messages are recovered when the broker is backed up, and a queue is re-declared after being taken down. Transient queues are the opposite; they are not durable. Sometimes, we want this type of queues to be short-lived. Consumers can delete queues; however, this is not convenient. Therefore, we suggest automatic queue deletion when the last consumer leaves. This can be done by setting the parameter `autoDelete` to true when declaring the queue.

Exchange. Unlike in most brokers, clients in AMQP publish messages to *exchanges*, not directly to queues. Therefore, in RABBITMQ, producers send messages to *exchanges* not directly to queues, which means producers tend to be unaware if the message is delivered to the queue or not.

If producers send messages to an *exchange*, then the messages are pushed to queues using header attributes, bindings, and routing keys. To route messages, *exchanges* use rules that are called *bindings*. Thus, the *binding* is a relationship between an *exchange* and a *queue*. It can be interpreted as the queue showing interest in the exchange.

Binding may contain routing keys, which are used to pick up certain messages published to an exchange acting as a filter; therefore, they can be routed to the bound queues. When a message fails to be routed to any queue, then it is dropped or returned to the publisher. Whether it is dropped or returned can be determined based on the attributes that the publisher sets. It is possible to have multiple queue bindings with the same binding key. Based on the type of an exchange, it behaves differently. We have four types of exchanges: *Direct exchange, Fanout exchange, Topic exchange* and *Headers exchange*. In Fig. 9 a message with routing key *log_B* is sent to the queue *B* since it has exactly matching binding key as routing key.

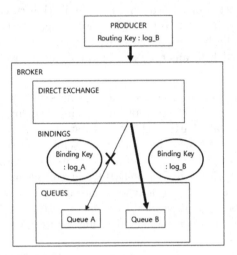

Fig. 9. Direct exchange example. There are two queues: A and B. The binding key between the direct exchange and A is `log_A` and the binding key between the direct exchange and B is `log_B`. When a message is sent to this direct exchange with routing key `log_B`, then the message is sent to the queue B. In the case of A, since the routing key does not match the binding, the message is discarded.

Direct exchange: uses routing keys having the same name as the queue name, and sends messages to only one consumer. It is the default exchange. One of the routing keys is given to the message and the queue has the binding key. These keys are used to identify the queue to exchange. If the routing and the binding keys match (they should completely match), the message can be forwarded to the queue, eventually arriving to the consumer.

The highlight of this exchange is that the messages are load-balanced between consumers, not between queues. Queues can have several possible binding keys and several routing keys. Multiple binding occurs when multiple queues share one binding key. When the exchanges replicate the messages, then each of them are forwarded to multiple consumers. An example of the *Direct exchange* can be seen in Fig. 9 and the code example can be found in Sect. 5.2.

Topic exchange: uses routing and binding keys, but they do not have to match completely. It applies the pattern matching method, i.e. when the routing pattern matches the routing key then messages are delivered to one or more queues.

The routing key consists of word lists delimited by a *period* (.). The routing pattern as well is delimited by a *period*, but instead of a specific word, it may contain an *asterisk* (*) or a *pound* (#), where *asterisk* means any word for that specific position and *pound* means zero or more words. An example of the *Topic exchange* can be seen in Fig. 10.

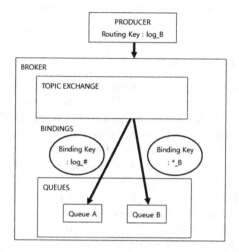

Fig. 10. `Topic exchange example`. A message with routing key `log_B` is sent to both queues `A` and `B`. In case of `A`, it has a binding key `log_#`, where a `pound` (#) can match with any single character, so it matches with the routing key. In case of `B`, it has a binding `*_B`, where an `asterisk` (*) matches with any string. Therefore, both accept the message.

Fanout exchange: does not care about routing keys.

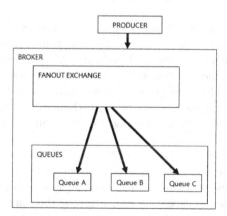

Fig. 11. `Fanout exchange example`. When a message is published to a fanout exchange, then the message is copied and sent to all the queues (`A`, `B` and `C`). `A`, `B` and `C` can be bound to the exchange with any routing key, since the fanout exchange ignores the key. The fanout exchange simply broadcasts to all the queues bound to it.

It copies incoming messages and sends them to all the queues like a broadcasting. Therefore, we cannot expect flexibility in this case.

The *Fanout exchange* is different from the *Direct exchange* or the *Topic exchange* as they use routing keys or pattern matching for bindings. An example of the *Fanout exchange* can be seen in Fig. 11 and the code example can be found in Sect. 5.2.

4.2 Connection and Channel

Connection. When we publish and consume messages using RABBITMQ, we need a connection to the RABBITMQ. A TCP `connection` is the linkage between a client and a broker that can have multiplex over a single TCP connection. AMQP 0-9-1 [1] uses TCP connections between brokers and applications, which is shut down when an application is not in need of them anymore.

RABBITMQ supports the logging of all entering connections that show activity having at least one byte of data sending. We can prevent flooding the logs by not logging connections that do not show any activities. The opening and closing connections rates should be monitored since it is important for the system. Problems can be detected without closing the connections. Unfortunately, this condition makes CPU and RAM nodes heavily used.

High connection churn has a high rate of new connections and closed connections, which means the channels are not long-lived as they were meant to be. Since connections consume a large amount of memory on the client, it is not desirable having too much of them. Therefore, it is recommended to use a single connection for long term rather than opening and closing them frequently.

This is why having one TCP connection with multiple channels is endorsed. Connections may have errors or protocol exceptions, making connections fail or unable to carry consumer's operation. Connection errors are considered 'hard errors', unlike channel errors, which means they can hardly be recovered.

Channel. A virtual connection inside of a TCP connection where the messages travel is called *channel*. When we need multiple connections, we use channels for a single TCP connection instead of multiple TCP connections. Having many TCP connections has shortcuts such as consuming resources and firewall configuration difficulties. Brokers and consumers use an ID for each channel to identify the channel for applying methods to it. Each channel's communication is independent of the other ones. When a connection dies, all the channels living on it die as well.

Messages can be sent or received over channels. To create a channel, we should establish a connection first. After finishing the channel usage, obviously it needs closing. Once a channel is closed, it can no longer be used. If you try to use a closed channel, it raises an exception signaling that the channel is closed. We can close channels by our needs, while it can also be closed by an exception. When it happens, we can often recover it by opening another channel. We can set the number of channels we want to open for a connection. As well as connections, the channel should be carefully monitored to detect some problems such as *channel leaking* or *high channel churn*.

Differences Between Channels and Connections. A connection is an actual TCP connection to the message broker. It can have multiple sessions, whereas a channel is a virtual connection inside that. You can have several channels avoiding overloading the broker with TCP connections. Channels have various lifetimes, while connections are considered relatively stable.

When using a channel, AMQP commands can be sent to the broker, but the channel and the queue do not have one-to-one relation. Of course, it is possible to use only one channel for everything, but it is desirable to have a separate channel for each thread when there are multiple threads.

4.3   Safe Message Delivery in Go

We are interested in safe delivery, that is taking care of situations when message delivery fails for some reason. For safe message delivery, if there is a problem during message delivery, we use acknowledgements, either with Basic.Get (see Fig. 12) or with Basic.Consume (see Fig. 13). We let brokers remove messages when they get acknowledgements. Generally, AMQP offers two options:

1. Removing message from a queue after the broker sends a message to an application (*automatic acknowledgement*).
2. Removing a message from a queue after getting acknowledgement from a consumer (*explicit acknowledgement*).

The first one is sending acknowledgement right after a broker is sending messages to a consumer by using Basic.Deliver or Basic.GetOk. The second one is making consumers send acknowledgements when they receive messages by using Basic.Ack.

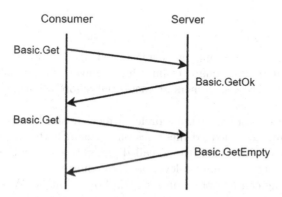

Fig. 12. Acknowledgements with *Basic.Get.* The consumer sends a new request each time it wants to receive a message with Basic.Get, even if there are multiple messages in the queue. If the queue has a message pending when issuing a Basic.Get, RABBITMQ responds with a Basic.GetOk and sends the message. If no messages are pending in the queue, it replies with Basic.GetEmpty, indicating that there are no more messages.

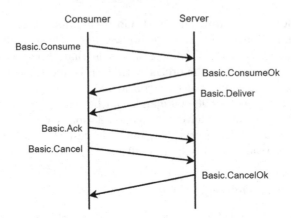

Fig. 13. Acknowledgements with *Basic.Consume*. When a consumer issues a Basic.Consume, RABBITMQ sends messages to it as they become available until the consumer issues a Basic.Cancel.

In the case of *explicit acknowledgement*, we can decide when do we want to send the acknowledgement, which does not have to be necessarily right after receiving messages. Even though a message has reached the consumer, it may not be successfully processed. In that case, the consumer can reject the message and then ask the broker to remove or requeue it. This rejection is called *negative acknowledgement*. If you use Basic.Reject method, you can reject only one message. However, RABBITMQ allows multiple messages rejection by NACK (*negative acknowledgement*). A message is rejected by notifying the broker that the message processing was not successful. A consumer signals to the broker to abandon or requeue the message in case it is rejected.

4.4 Prefetch

Prefetch is the maximum number of unacknowledged messages per consumer. When there is more than one consumer for a queue, the number of messages that can be sent to the consumers at each time before an acknowledgement is specified by the *prefetch.*

It is an extension of the channel prefetch mechanism. It is possible to limit the number of unacknowledged messages on a channel when consuming using the Basic.Qos method. This is the so-called *prefetch count.* In the case of RABBITMQ, it supports only channel-level prefetch count.

Load balancing can be done using this kind of technique. When the number of unacknowledged messages reaches the *prefetch*, RABBITMQ stops delivering messages on that channel until the consumer sends ACKs or NACKs. This means the consumers on that channel no longer can get messages.

We can decide the prefetch count by considering the consumer types. For example, if we have only one fast consumer, then we might set the value high since we might want all the messages to be prefetched, though not too high, so it does not restrict the ability to peeking messages.

In the case of slow consumers, we may set the prefetch count as one and let the RABBITMQ do the job of load balancing. On the other hand, when we have multiple fast consumers, it is recommended to set the value not too low nor too high, like around 20 to 30. If we set the value too low, it can paralyze the consumers since they need to wait. In contrast, it might harm the load balancing if we set it too high.

4.5   AMQP at Network Failures

When network connection failure happens, the message can be lost somewhere in the transit between client and server, or at either side of it, maybe in TCP stack buffer or in the wire. In those cases, messages are not delivered; therefore, we need to transfer them again. Using acknowledgments, we can determine when we need to re-transfer messages.

There are two ways of sending acknowledgments: *consumer acknowledgment* and *publisher confirm*. *Consumer acknowledgment* occurs when the consumer sends acknowledgements to a server, and *publisher confirm* happens when the broker confirms the messages that the consumer published (meaning it is dealt with on the server-side). After any operation that needs to be done with the message has finished, the consumer or the publisher sends acknowledgements.

By using acknowledgements, we guarantee safe message delivery. When failure happens, the acknowledgement is not delivered, then we re-deliver messages by re-queuing them either by RABBITMQ or by consumers. RABBITMQ sets the `redelivered` flag on the failed message; then the consumer can identify if the message is the one that has seen before or not using the flag. In case of consumers are not capable of taking care of the message, the consumer rejects it by `Basic.Reject` or `Basic.Nack`, and it may ask the server to requeue it.

4.6   AMQP Management

After a connection is made, the publisher sends messages to the named exchange. The exchange routes the messages to bound queues according to the routing key and the type of the exchange. Then the consumer takes messages from a queue, or the queue pushes messages to the consumer. Here, named exchange is used so that the publishers and the consumers can recognize each other. You may wonder how a consumer gets the message (which the publisher sends to the exchange) from a queue.

This queue is attached to the exchange, and in most cases, the consumer generates queues then attaches them. The exchange determines which queue the message belongs to by binding. Binding can be seen as a rule that is used to distribute messages from exchanges to queues. Generally, AMQP works like: the publisher sends messages to the consumer, but if the consumer wants to send a reply to the publisher, we can use another queue called `callback`. A message broker ensures that messages from a publisher to a consumer are delivered using exchanges and queues. It means AMQP hides the publisher and the consumer from each other.

Therefore, it allows pervasive decoupling, which means the action between systems does not have to be on the same machine, and it can transact without being connected having flexible infrastructure.

To summarize, the essential feature of AMQP is to deal with the communication between the application and queuing. AMQP grants an application setting up a connection to a queue manager. For bi-directional communication, we can use sessions that are logical grouping of two channels.

4.7 AMQP Advantages

The major benefit of AMQP is that you can readily switch your broker implementation by sending and independently receiving messages to the broker. In addition, adding more servers to handle procedures is easy because of the broker's characteristics.

It also operates trustfully at a distance or poor networks like network loss, bad network connection, network congestion and such. Let us compare AMQP with RPC (Remote Procedure Call) and HTTP (Hypertext Transfer Protocol) with REST (Representational State Transfer) so that AMQP's benefits can be clearly seen.

RPC is a way of building distributed and client-server-based applications extending local procedure calls, which allows the called procedure to be in a different address space as the calling process. REST is an interface that uses HTTP requests to manipulate data with GET, PUT, POST, and DELETE. AMQP and HTTP both run in a heterogeneous and distributed environment. HTTP's nature is synchronous, whereas AMQP is asynchronous, which means publishers and consumers do not have to be active at the same time.

AMQP can make numerous message transactions, all at once, allowing messages to be stored in a queue. It handles a high volume of streams and deals with low-latency data exchange. When AMQP is used, the consumer does not have to process and confirm to the publisher immediately. Instead, consumers gather the messages from the queue when the storage capacity is available. In the meantime, the publisher can work on further tasks. It cannot be stated which one is better than the other, since all have their own advantages. AMQP is really fast, so very cost-effective, and also flexible.

4.8 AMQP Usage

We have been discussing what AMQP offers, how it works and what are the main characteristics. Now, we all can agree AMQP is attractive enough to look at and work with. So, when should we use this exactly? If you want to deliver messages with high-quality and safety between applications, then AMQP is the solution for it. You can assure reliable, fast, ensured message delivery through AMQP.

These features make AMQP valuable in some situations, especially, for example, when you want to distribute a message to multiple consumers or to enable offline consumers to fetch data later, and so on. When there are plenty of requests that should not be lost and needed being processed, it is good to use queues to bridge the sending request and receiving parts.

AMQP focuses on message deliveries to consumers along with broker tracking consumer states. It allows to be ready for new requests and not being locked up by a previous one. Imagine you have a web service that receives order requests simultaneously from customers. It causes problems if the server cannot handle that huge amount of incoming requests. To prevent that kind of situation, we can use RABBITMQ as a solution since it can deal with high throughput situations.

AMQP also shines when connecting different languages since it behaves like a glue between two disconnected components. AMQP creates a common ground allowing interoperability. You may use it when you want to make one component to be changed by a different component, globally sharing the updates. It can also enable the system to fetch data for offline clients, introducing entirely asynchronous functionality for systems.

4.9 AMQP 0.9.1 Model

AMQP 0-9-1 is a network protocol model that is used by RABBITMQ. Version 0-9-1 uses producer, consumer, and broker for each connection, and they do not necessarily have to be on the same machine.

Producers send messages to message brokers; then, they forward the messages to consumers. The brokers handle exchanges and queues to deliver messages from the publisher to consumers.

Exchanges receive messages from publishers, then distribute copies based on bindings to queues. Each exchange has its own rules based on its types (see Sect. 4.1). Therefore, based on those rules, exchanges route messages to queues.

Brokers often use the meta-data of a message specified by publishers, but most attributes are used by the consumers. For example, consumers use acknowledgements to notify brokers when the message is arrived to ensure delivery, just in case the network is poor. We can ensure safe message delivery by allowing brokers to remove a message from a queue when the message acknowledgement is done.

4.10 Go RABBITMQ Client Library

There are several clients of RABBITMQ, and the Go RABBITMQ CLIENT LIBRARY [11] is one of them. As seen in previous sections, an AMQP client publishes messages to exchanges, not to queues, routing via bindings. In this library, replies for each message are received in an RPC manner, which means it is intended to be synchronous. Just like most other client libraries, it copies the actions defined in the AMQP specification, hiding the complexity of the interaction. It allows you to not think of how things work when writing an application. Here are the basic functions of this library; some of their usages can be checked in Subsect. 5.1.

* func Dial(url string) (*Connection, error): connects a RABBITMQ server by getting the url string then returning a new TCP connection.
* func (c *Connection) Channel() (*Channel, error): creates the one and only concurrent server channel that processes AMQP messages.

* `func (ch *Channel) QueueDeclare (name string, durable, autoDelete, exclusive, noWait bool, args Table) (Queue, error)`: a queue is created if it does not exist already, or it is made sure that the existing queue matches parameters. If the queue name field is empty, the server creates unique name for it.
* `func (ch *Channel) Publish (exchange, key string, mandatory, immediate bool, msg Publishing) error`: sends the `Publishing` message to the `Exchange`. `Publishing`s are asynchronous, so when failed to be delivered, they get back to the server. There are two possible scenarios when a message is not deliverable.
  1. `mandatory` field is set as true and no queue is matching the routing key.
  2. `immediate` field is set as true and no consumer of the queue is waiting for the delivery.
* `func (ch *Channel) Consume (queue, consumer string, autoAck, exclusive, noLocal, noWait bool, args Table) (<-chan Delivery, error)`: delivers queued messages until one of the `Connection.Close`, `Channel.Cancel` or `AMQP` exception occurs. The delivery starts immediately and each message needs to be acknowledged. All the unacknowledged messages are requeued to the same queue.
* `func (ch *Channel) ExchangeDeclare (name, kind string, durable, autoDelete, internal, noWait bool, args Table) error`: creates an `Exchange` on the server, if it does not exist.
* `func (ch *Channel) QueueBind (name, key, exchange string, noWait bool, args Table) error`: compares the routing key of the `Publishing` and the `Binding`, then binds an `Exchange` to a queue.
* `func (ch *Channel) Qos (prefetchCount, prefetchSize int, global bool) error`: since it is impossible to keep infinitely many messages on the server, it manages the quantity of messages that the server keeps on the network.
* `func (d Delivery) Ack (multiple bool) error`: consumers call this to acknowledge delivered messages if messages are received successfully.
* `func (d Delivery) Nack (multiple, requeue bool) error`: negatively acknowledges the delivered messages. In this case, we need to decide whether the message is requeued or not.
* `func (d Delivery) Reject (requeue bool) error`: behaves similarly to the `Delivery.Nack`, but this is done through the `Acknowledger` interface.

After studying the RABBITMQ model and its client library, in the next section we practice them with distributed examples implemented in several versions.

5 Distributed Programming

In the previous practical examples, the programs run on the same computer using one or more CPUs. In this section, we discuss how to implement a distributed system in which different computers cooperate to handle the jobs. Go and RABBITMQ are used when implementing our examples.

First, basic examples of the RABBITMQ are presented. Additionally, we introduce three distributed examples implementing existing patterns: distributed job processing (Client-Dispatcher-Server pattern), distributed pipeline (Pipes and Filters pattern), and distributed divide and conquer (Master-Slave pattern). Each example includes several versions from simple to more complex. Instead of focusing only on RABBITMQ essential elements' usage, like the tutorials of the RABBITMQ website [17], our approach emphasizes practical aspects of distributed application implementations.

5.1   RABBITMQ Hello World

This section discusses how to enable programs to communicate in distributed way using RABBITMQ. Here are the installation instructions for a machine with a Windows 10 system:

1. Install GIT: https://git-scm.com/downloads/
2. Install ERLANG: https://www.erlang.org/downloads
   RABBITMQ is an open-source message-broker software written in ERLANG.
3. Install RABBITMQ Server: use `rabbitmq-server-3.8.14.exe` from
   https://www.rabbitmq.com/install-windows.html
4. Start the RABBITMQ service: click on the `RabbitMQ service start` in the Windows Start menu.
5. Create a folder, copy `publisher.go` and `consumer.go` into it.
6. Open the command line window in the created folder. Initialize the Go module by running the command `go mod init` $< NameOfModule >$. Starting from Go `1.13`, a Go program imports packages of other modules and manages the dependencies only through its own module. Thus, create a module for the program in the project folder to import GO RABBITMQ Client Library.
7. Get the GO RABBITMQ Client Library, in the created folder run:
   `go get github.com/streadway/amqp`.
8. First run the `consumer.go`, wait until it prints `"Waiting for msgs"`.
9. Run the `publisher.go`.

The programs are using the methods of the RABBITMQ client library when connecting and communicating to the RABBITMQ server (first install [13] then run it). Before sending (or publishing) and receiving (or consuming), the sender and the receiver both need to connect themselves to the RABBITMQ server. Next, they open an `AMQP` (not GO) channel based on the connection. Then, they declare the exchanges used during the communication, as in Listing 1.45 (from line 17 to 26) and in Listing 1.46 (from line 17 to 26). In Listing 1.45, the receiver declares a queue `jobQueue` and binds it to the `jobExchange` exchange with routing key `jobkey` (as shown from line 39 to line 55). In Listing 1.46, the sender publishes a string as message body to the `jobExchange` exchange with `jobkey` routing key (as shown from line 28 to 39). Afterwards, the receiver uses the `Consume` method to get a GO channel of delivery, as shown from line 45 to 54. The receiver creates a goroutine that keeps receiving messages from the GO channel, as in line 55 to 61. The main goroutine of the receiver waits forever. The receiver has to run first as if no queue is bound to the exchange, the message sent to the exchange is lost.

The introduction of **defer** statement can be found in Sect. 2.1 and the general description of the producer and consumer problem can be found in Sect. 4.1.

```
package main                                                                    1
import (                                                                        2
    "fmt"                                                                       3
    "github.com/streadway/amqp"                                                 4
    "log"                                                                       5
)                                                                               6
func main() {                                                                   7
    //Connection                                                                8
    conn, err := amqp.Dial("amqp://guest:guest@localhost:5672/")                9
    printErrorAndExit(err, "Failed to connect to RabbitMQ")                    10
    defer conn.Close()                                                         11
    //Channel                                                                  12
    ch, err := conn.Channel()                                                  13
    printErrorAndExit(err, "Failed to open a channel")                         14
    defer ch.Close()                                                           15
    //Exchange                                                                 16
    err = ch.ExchangeDeclare(                                                  17
        "jobExchange", // name                                                 18
        "direct",      // type                                                 19
        false,         // durable                                              20
        true,          // auto-deleted                                         21
        false,         // internal                                            22
        false,         // no-wait                                              23
        nil,           // arguments                                            24
    )                                                                          25
    printErrorAndExit(err, "Failed to declare an exchange")                    26
    //Declare and bind queue                                                   27
    q, err := ch.QueueDeclare(                                                  28
        "jobQueue", // name,,empty string let server generate id               29
        false,      // durable                                                 30
        true,       // delete when unused                                      31
        false,      // exclusive                                               32
        false,      // no-wait                                                 33
        nil,        // arguments                                               34
    )                                                                          35
    printErrorAndExit(err, "Failed to declare a queue")                        36
    err = ch.QueueBind(                                                        37
        q.Name,        // queue name                                           38
        "jobkey",      // routing key                                          39
        "jobExchange", // exchange                                             40
        false,                                                                 41
        nil)                                                                   42
    printErrorAndExit(err, "Failed to bind a queue")                           43
    //Consume                                                                  44
    msgs, err := ch.Consume(                                                    45
        q.Name, // queue                                                       46
        "",     // consumer,empty string let server generate id                47
        false,  // auto-ack                                                    48
        false,  // exclusive                                                   49
        false,  // no-local                                                    50
        false,  // no-wait                                                     51
        nil,    // args                                                        52
    )                                                                          53
    printErrorAndExit(err, "Failed to register a consumer")                    54
    go func() {                                                                55
        for d := range msgs {                                                  56
            bodyString := string(d.Body)                                       57
            fmt.Println("Received:", bodyString)                               58
            d.Ack(false)                                                       59
        }                                                                      60
```

```
        }()                                                       61
        fmt.Println("Waiting␣for␣msgs")                           62
        forever := make(chan bool)                                63
        <-forever                                                 64
}                                                                 65
func printErrorAndExit(err error, msg string) {                  66
        if err != nil {                                           67
                log.Fatalln(msg, ":", err)                        68
        }                                                         69
}                                                                 70
```

Listing 1.45. Consumer

```
package main                                                      1
import (                                                          2
        "fmt"                                                     3
        "github.com/streadway/amqp"                               4
        "log"                                                     5
)                                                                 6
func main() {                                                     7
        //Connection                                              8
        conn, err := amqp.Dial("amqp://guest:guest@localhost:5672/")   9
        printErrorAndExit(err, "Failed␣to␣connect␣to␣RabbitMQ")  10
        defer conn.Close()                                       11
        //Channel                                                12
        ch, err := conn.Channel()                                13
        printErrorAndExit(err, "Failed␣to␣open␣a␣channel")       14
        defer ch.Close()                                         15
        //Exchange                                               16
        err = ch.ExchangeDeclare(                                17
                "jobExchange", // name                           18
                "direct",      // type                           19
                false,         // durable                        20
                true,          // auto-deleted                   21
                false,         // internal                       22
                false,         // no-wait                        23
                nil,           // arguments                      24
        )                                                        25
        printErrorAndExit(err, "Failed␣to␣declare␣an␣exchange")  26
        //Send Message                                           27
        body := "Hello,␣World!"                                  28
        err = ch.Publish(                                        29
                "jobExchange", // exchange                       30
                "jobkey",      // routing key                    31
                false,         // mandatory                      32
                false,         // immediate                      33
                amqp.Publishing{                                 34
                        ContentType: "text/plain",               35
                        Body:        []byte(body),               36
                })                                               37
        printErrorAndExit(err, "Failed␣to␣publish␣a␣message")    38
        fmt.Println("Sent:␣", body)                              39
}                                                                40
func printErrorAndExit(err error, msg string) {                 41
        if err != nil {                                          42
                log.Fatalln(msg, ":", err)                       43
        }                                                        44
}                                                                45
```

Listing 1.46. Publisher

We should first run the consumer, which declares and binds the queue. We run the publisher once the consumer is ready to receive.

Otherwise, when the publisher starts first and publishes a message to the exchange, this message will be ignored. Since the exchange can not find a queue bound to this exchange with a matching routing key with the message.
Here is the output after we run the `consumer.go`:

```
go run consumer.go                                          1
Waiting for msgs                                            2
Received: Hello, World!                                     3
```

Here is the output after we run the `publisher.go`:

```
go run publisher.go                                         1
Sent:   Hello, World!                                       2
```

5.2   RABBITMQ Exchange

The exchange is a basic distributed construct maintained at the RABBITMQ server, and it is responsible for routing the messages to queues. "The server MUST implement these standard exchange types: `fanout`, `direct`." [1], this section introduces examples of them.

Fanout Exchange Example. All the messages published through a `fanout exchange` are delivered to all the queues bound to it (see Fig. 11). There are two queues and two consumers in this example (see Fig. 14).

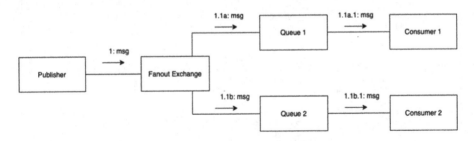

Fig. 14. Fanout exchange example. The publisher sends a message to a `fanout exchange`. After that, the message is routed to the queues bound to this exchange in the `Consumer1` and `Consumer2`.

As it does not consider the routing key, the publish routing key can be any string, as in Listing 1.47 line 17. Also the bounding routing key can be any string, as in Listing 1.48 line 19 and Listing 1.49 line 6. The queue declaration is in Listing 1.48 line 17 and Listing 1.49 line 4. The first argument of the `QueueDeclare` method is the name of the queue, if it as an empty string, the `RabbitMQ` server generates a unique name for the queue. The fourth argument of `QueueDeclare` is the Boolean value `exclusive`. The exclusive queues are only accessible by the connection that declares them. Other connections cannot declare, bind, consume or delete a queue with the same name. We set `exclusive` to true for `Consumer1` and `Consumer2`, thus they have their private queues.

```go
package main                                                              1
import (                                                                  2
    "fmt"                                                                 3
    "github.com/streadway/amqp"                                          4
    "log"                                                                 5
)                                                                         6
func main() {                                                             7
    conn, err := amqp.Dial("amqp://guest:guest@localhost:5672/")         8
    printErrorAndExit(err, "Failed to connect to RabbitMQ")              9
    defer conn.Close()                                                   10
    ch, err := conn.Channel()                                           11
    printErrorAndExit(err, "Failed to open a channel")                  12
    defer ch.Close()                                                    13
    err = ch.ExchangeDeclare("fanoutExchange", "fanout",                14
        false, true, false, false, nil)                                 15
    printErrorAndExit(err, "Failed to declare an exchange")             16
    publishMsg(ch, "fanoutExchange", "anykey1", "msg")                  17
}                                                                        18
func printErrorAndExit(err error, msg string) {                         19
    if err != nil {                                                     20
        log.Fatalln(msg, ":", err)                                      21
    } }                                                                  22
func publishMsg(c *amqp.Channel, ex string, key string, msg string) {   23
    body := msg                                                         24
    err := (*c).Publish(ex, key, false, false,                         25
        amqp.Publishing{                                                26
            ContentType: "text/plain",                                  27
            Body:        []byte(body),                                  28
        })                                                              29
    printErrorAndExit(err, "Failed to publish a message")              30
    fmt.Println("Sent: ", body)                                        31
}                                                                        32
```

Listing 1.47. Fanout exchange example, `Publisher`

```go
package main                                                              1
import (                                                                  2
    "fmt"                                                                 3
    "github.com/streadway/amqp"                                          4
    "log"                                                                 5
)                                                                         6
func main() {                                                             7
    conn, err := amqp.Dial("amqp://guest:guest@localhost:5672/")         8
    printErrorAndExit(err, "Failed to connect to RabbitMQ")              9
    defer conn.Close()                                                   10
    ch, err := conn.Channel()                                           11
    printErrorAndExit(err, "Failed to open a channel")                  12
    defer ch.Close()                                                    13
    err = ch.ExchangeDeclare("fanoutExchange", "fanout",                14
        false, true, false, false, nil)                                 15
    printErrorAndExit(err, "Failed to declare an exchange")             16
    q, err := ch.QueueDeclare("", false, true, true, false, nil)        17
    printErrorAndExit(err, "Failed to declare a queue")                 18
    err = ch.QueueBind(q.Name, "anykey2", "fanoutExchange", false, nil) 19
    printErrorAndExit(err, "Failed to bind a queue")                    20
    msgs, err := ch.Consume(q.Name, "", false, false, false, false, nil) 21
    printErrorAndExit(err, "Failed to register a consumer")             22
    go func() {                                                         23
        for d := range msgs {                                          24
            bodyString := string(d.Body)                               25
            fmt.Println("Received:", bodyString)                       26
            d.Ack(false)                                               27
        }                                                              28
    }()                                                                29
    fmt.Println("Waiting for msgs")                                    30
    forever := make(chan bool)                                         31
```

```
    <-forever                                                        32
}                                                                    33
func printErrorAndExit(err error, msg string) {                      34
    if err != nil {                                                  35
        log.Fatalln(msg, ":", err)                                   36
    }                                                                37
}                                                                    38
```

Listing 1.48. Fanout exchange example, `Consumer1`

```
...                                                                  1
func main() {                                                        2
    ...                                                              3
    q, err := ch.QueueDeclare("", false, true, true, false, nil)     4
    printErrorAndExit(err, "Failed to declare a queue")              5
    err = ch.QueueBind(q.Name, "anykey3", "fanoutExchange", false, nil)  6
    printErrorAndExit(err, "Failed to bind a queue")                 7
    msgs, err := ch.Consume(q.Name, "", false, false, false, false, nil)  8
    printErrorAndExit(err, "Failed to register a consumer")          9
    go func() {                                                      10
        for d := range msgs {                                        11
            bodyString := string(d.Body)                             12
            fmt.Println("Received:", bodyString)                     13
            d.Ack(false)                                             14
        }                                                            15
    }()                                                              16
    fmt.Println("Waiting for msgs")                                  17
    forever := make(chan bool)                                       18
    <-forever                                                        19
}                                                                    20
...                                                                  21
```

Listing 1.49. Fanout exchange example, `Consumer2`

Output of the `Consumer1`:

```
Waiting for msgs                                                     1
Received: msg                                                        2
```

Output of the `Consumer2`:

```
Waiting for msgs                                                     1
Received: msg                                                        2
```

Output of the `Publisher`:

```
Sent:   msg                                                         1
```

Direct Exchange Example. If a message with a publishing routing key is published to a `direct exchange`, all the queues bound to this exchange with the same bounding routing key get this message (see Fig. 9). There are three queues and three consumers in this example (see Fig. 15).

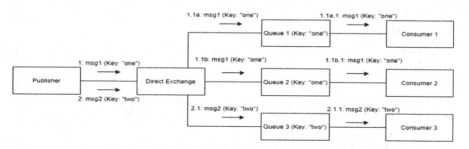

Fig. 15. Direct exchange example. `Queue 1` and `Queue 2` are bound to `Direct Exchange` with key "one", `msg1` is sent with key "one", it is routed to `Queue 1` and `Queue 2`. `Queue 3` is bound to `Direct Exchange` with key "two", `msg2` is sent with key "two". So `Queue 3` gets `msg2`. If `Publisher` sends `msg3` with the key "three", it is ignored because there is no queue bound to this exchange with key "three".

We can also broadcast with the `direct exchange` by binding all the queues to it with the same bounding routing key. However, the `fanout exchange` is faster because it does not compare the keys before routing the messages to queues.

```go
package main                                                           1
import (                                                               2
    "fmt"                                                              3
    "github.com/streadway/amqp"                                        4
    "log"                                                              5
)                                                                      6
func main() {                                                          7
    conn, err := amqp.Dial("amqp://guest:guest@localhost:5672/")       8
    printErrorAndExit(err, "Failed to connect to RabbitMQ")            9
    defer conn.Close()                                                 10
    ch, err := conn.Channel()                                          11
    printErrorAndExit(err, "Failed to open a channel")                 12
    defer ch.Close()                                                   13
    err = ch.ExchangeDeclare("directExchange", "direct",              14
        false, true, false, false, nil)                                15
    printErrorAndExit(err, "Failed to declare an exchange")            16
    publishMsg(ch, "directExchange", "one", "msg1")                    17
    publishMsg(ch, "directExchange", "two", "msg2")                    18
}                                                                      19
func printErrorAndExit(err error, msg string) {                        20
    if err != nil {                                                    21
        log.Fatalln(msg, ":", err)                                     22
    }                                                                  23
}                                                                      24
func publishMsg(c *amqp.Channel, ex string, key string, msg string) {  25
    body := msg                                                        26
    err := (*c).Publish(ex, key, false, false,                         27
        amqp.Publishing{                                               28
            ContentType: "text/plain",                                 29
            Body:        []byte(body),                                 30
        })                                                             31
    printErrorAndExit(err, "Failed to publish a message")              32
    fmt.Println("Sent: ", body)                                        33
}                                                                      34
```

Listing 1.50. Direct exchange example, `Publisher`

```
package main                                                        1
import (                                                            2
    "fmt"                                                           3
    "github.com/streadway/amqp"                                     4
    "log"                                                           5
)                                                                   6
func main() {                                                       7
    conn, err := amqp.Dial("amqp://guest:guest@localhost:5672/")    8
    printErrorAndExit(err, "Failed to connect to RabbitMQ")         9
    defer conn.Close()                                             10
    ch, err := conn.Channel()                                     11
    printErrorAndExit(err, "Failed to open a channel")            12
    defer ch.Close()                                              13
    err = ch.ExchangeDeclare("directExchange", "direct",          14
        false, true, false, false, nil)                           15
    printErrorAndExit(err, "Failed to declare an exchange")       16
    q, err := ch.QueueDeclare("", false, true, true, false, nil)  17
    printErrorAndExit(err, "Failed to declare a queue")           18
    err = ch.QueueBind(q.Name, "one", "directExchange", false, nil) 19
    printErrorAndExit(err, "Failed to bind a queue")              20
    msgs, err := ch.Consume(q.Name, "", false, false, false, false, nil) 21
    printErrorAndExit(err, "Failed to register a consumer")       22
    go func() {                                                   23
        for d := range msgs {                                     24
            bodyString := string(d.Body)                          25
            fmt.Println("Received:", bodyString)                  26
            d.Ack(false)                                          27
        }                                                         28
    }()                                                           29
    fmt.Println("Waiting for msgs")                               30
    forever := make(chan bool)                                    31
    <-forever                                                     32
}                                                                 33
func printErrorAndExit(err error, msg string) {                  34
    if err != nil {                                               35
        log.Fatalln(msg, ":", err)                                36
    }                                                             37
}                                                                 38
```

Listing 1.51. Direct exchange example, Consumer1

```
...                                                                 1
func main() {                                                       2
    ...                                                             3
    q, err := ch.QueueDeclare("", false, true, true, false, nil)   4
    printErrorAndExit(err, "Failed to declare a queue")            5
    err = ch.QueueBind(q.Name, "one", "directExchange", false, nil) 6
    printErrorAndExit(err, "Failed to bind a queue")               7
    msgs, err := ch.Consume(q.Name, "", false, false, false, false, nil) 8
    printErrorAndExit(err, "Failed to register a consumer")        9
    go func() {                                                    10
        for d := range msgs {                                      11
            bodyString := string(d.Body)                           12
            fmt.Println("Received:", bodyString)                   13
            d.Ack(false)                                           14
        }                                                          15
    }()                                                            16
    fmt.Println("Waiting for msgs")                                17
    forever := make(chan bool)                                     18
    <-forever                                                      19
}                                                                  20
...                                                                21
```

Listing 1.52. Direct exchange example, Consumer2

```
...                                                                    1
func main() {                                                          2
    ...                                                                3
    q, err := ch.QueueDeclare("", false, true, true, false, nil)       4
    printErrorAndExit(err, "Failed␣to␣declare␣a␣queue")                5
    err = ch.QueueBind(q.Name, "two", "directExchange", false, nil)    6
    printErrorAndExit(err, "Failed␣to␣bind␣a␣queue")                   7
    msgs, err := ch.Consume(q.Name, "", false, false, false, false, nil) 8
    printErrorAndExit(err, "Failed␣to␣register␣a␣consumer")            9
    go func() {                                                        10
        for d := range msgs {                                          11
            bodyString := string(d.Body)                               12
            fmt.Println("Received:", bodyString)                       13
            d.Ack(false)                                               14
        }                                                              15
    }()                                                                16
    fmt.Println("Waiting␣for␣msgs")                                    17
    forever := make(chan bool)                                         18
    <-forever                                                          19
}                                                                      20
...                                                                    21
```

Listing 1.53. Direct exchange example, Consumer3

Output of the `Consumer1`:

```
Waiting for msgs                                                       1
Received: msg1                                                         2
```

Output of the `Consumer2`:

```
Waiting for msgs                                                       1
Received: msg1                                                         2
```

Output of the `Consumer3`:

```
Waiting for msgs                                                       1
Received: msg2                                                         2
```

Output of the `Publisher`:

```
Sent:   msg1                                                          1
Sent:   msg2                                                          2
```

5.3 RabbitMQ Shared Queue

If more consumers share a queue, the server fairly distributes the deliveries across multiple consumers. "By default, RabbitMQ will send each message to the next consumer, in sequence. On average every consumer will get the same number of messages. This way of distributing messages is called round-robin." [18] There are one queues and two consumers in this example (see Fig. 16).

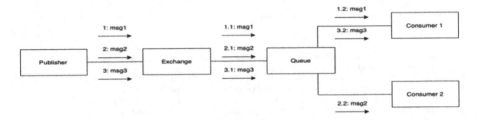

Fig. 16. Shared queue example. The queue is shared by `Consumer1` and `Consumer2`. They consume the messages in the queue in a balanced round-robin manner.

As shown in Listing 1.55 line 17 and Listing 1.56 line 5, the queue is declared with the `SharedQueue` name, which is known by all the consumers. The fourth argument `exclusive` is false so that the consumers can share the queue.

```go
package main                                                                1
import (                                                                    2
    "fmt"                                                                   3
    "github.com/streadway/amqp"                                             4
    "log"                                                                   5
)                                                                           6
func main() {                                                               7
    conn, err := amqp.Dial("amqp://guest:guest@localhost:5672/")           8
    printErrorAndExit(err, "Failed to connect to RabbitMQ")                 9
    defer conn.Close()                                                      10
    ch, err := conn.Channel()                                              11
    printErrorAndExit(err, "Failed to open a channel")                     12
    defer ch.Close()                                                       13
    err = ch.ExchangeDeclare("sharedQExchange", "direct",                  14
        false, true, false, false, nil)                                    15
    printErrorAndExit(err, "Failed to declare an exchange")                16
    publishMsg(ch, "sharedQExchange", "one", "msg1")                       17
    publishMsg(ch, "sharedQExchange", "one", "msg2")                       18
    publishMsg(ch, "sharedQExchange", "one", "msg3")                       19
}                                                                           20
func printErrorAndExit(err error, msg string) {                            21
    if err != nil {                                                        22
        log.Fatalln(msg, ":", err)                                         23
    }                                                                       24
}                                                                           25
func publishMsg(c *amqp.Channel, ex string, key string, msg string) {      26
    body := msg                                                            27
    err := (*c).Publish(ex, key, false, false,                             28
        amqp.Publishing{                                                   29
            ContentType: "text/plain",                                     30
            Body:        []byte(body), })                                  31
    printErrorAndExit(err, "Failed to publish a message")                  32
    fmt.Println("Sent: ", body)                                            33
}                                                                           34
```

Listing 1.54. Shared queue example, `Publisher`

```go
package main                                                                1
import (                                                                    2
    "fmt"                                                                   3
    "github.com/streadway/amqp"                                             4
    "log"                                                                   5
)                                                                           6
func main() {                                                               7
    conn, err := amqp.Dial("amqp://guest:guest@localhost:5672/")           8
```

```
    printErrorAndExit(err, "Failed␣to␣connect␣to␣RabbitMQ")      9
    defer conn.Close()                                           10
    ch, err := conn.Channel()                                    11
    printErrorAndExit(err, "Failed␣to␣open␣a␣channel")           12
    defer ch.Close()                                             13
    err = ch.ExchangeDeclare("sharedQExchange", "direct",        14
        false, true, false, nil)                                 15
    printErrorAndExit(err, "Failed␣to␣declare␣an␣exchange")      16
    q, err := ch.QueueDeclare("SharedQueue",                     17
        false, true, false, false, nil)                          18
    printErrorAndExit(err, "Failed␣to␣declare␣a␣queue")          19
    err = ch.QueueBind(q.Name, "one", "sharedQExchange", false, nil)  20
    printErrorAndExit(err, "Failed␣to␣bind␣a␣queue")             21
    msgs, err := ch.Consume(q.Name, "", false, false, false, false, nil)  22
    printErrorAndExit(err, "Failed␣to␣register␣a␣consumer")      23
    go func() {                                                  24
        for d := range msgs {                                    25
            bodyString := string(d.Body)                         26
            fmt.Println("Received:", bodyString)                 27
            d.Ack(false)                                         28
        }                                                        29
    }()                                                          30
    fmt.Println("Waiting␣for␣msgs")                              31
    forever := make(chan bool)                                   32
    <-forever                                                    33
}                                                                34
func printErrorAndExit(err error, msg string) {                  35
    if err != nil {                                              36
        log.Fatalln(msg, ":", err)                               37
    }                                                            38
}                                                                39
```

Listing 1.55. Shared queue example, `Consumer1`

```
package main                                                     1
...                                                              2
func main() {                                                    3
    ...                                                          4
    q, err := ch.QueueDeclare("SharedQueue",                     5
        false, true, false, false, nil)                          6
    printErrorAndExit(err, "Failed␣to␣declare␣a␣queue")          7
    err = ch.QueueBind(q.Name, "one", "sharedQExchange", false, nil)  8
    printErrorAndExit(err, "Failed␣to␣bind␣a␣queue")             9
    msgs, err := ch.Consume(q.Name, "", false, false, false, false, nil)  10
    printErrorAndExit(err, "Failed␣to␣register␣a␣consumer")      11
    go func() {                                                  12
        for d := range msgs {                                    13
            bodyString := string(d.Body)                         14
            fmt.Println("Received:", bodyString)                 15
            d.Ack(false)                                         16
        }                                                        17
    }()                                                          18
    fmt.Println("Waiting␣for␣msgs")                              19
    forever := make(chan bool)                                   20
    <-forever                                                    21
}                                                                22
...                                                              23
```

Listing 1.56. Shared queue example, `Consumer2`

Output of the `Consumer1`:

```
Waiting for msgs                                                 1
Received: msg1                                                   2
Received: msg3                                                   3
```

Output of the `Consumer2`:

```
Waiting for msgs                                                            1
Received: msg2                                                              2
```

Output of the `Publisher`:

```
Sent:    msg1                                                               1
Sent:    msg2                                                               2
Sent:    msg3                                                               3
```

5.4   Parallel Receive

This section introduces how to receive messages from a channel in a parallel way. The sequential receive example is also given for comparison. The code listings of the sequential and parallel receive examples are in Subsect. A.1.

Listing 1.63 shows the sequential way of receiving messages from the Go channel, which is returned by the method `Consume`. The RABBITMQ channel `chi` is used to declare and bind a queue and consume. The queue is declared with generated name. It is bound to the `pExchange` with `"key"` bounding routing key. The `Consume` method creates a consumer of this queue. The `msgs` is the Go channel returned by the `Consume` method. It is the place where you can get the messages. After the queue is bound to the `pExchange`, you can start publishing messages related to `pExchange` with `"key"` publishing routing key. Here we publish 100 fake links, after that, it sends a message `"END"`. After publishing all the messages, the timer starts. Then, a goroutine is also started to receive messages from the returned Go channel. If the received message is the `"END"`, we use the `Cancel` method to close the Go channel gracefully. Otherwise, the goroutine tests the link, and prints the result. The duration is printed out after this goroutine is finished.

Before `Cancel` actually closes the channel, it waits until all messages received on the network are delivered to the channel. Note that the same RABBITMQ channel must be used as for `Consume` (here `chi` channel is used when calling both `Consume` and `Cancel`). The first argument of `Cancel` is the consumer name. In the sequential receive example, we get the consumer name by accessing the `ConsumerTag` of the received `d`.

In the parallel receive example, multiple goroutines receive and handle messages from the Go channel. Similar to the previous example, the publisher sends a message `"END"` after sending all the links and uses the `Cancel` method to close the Go. After that, all the for range loops of the different goroutines terminate. In the sequential receive example, the consumer name is generated by the RABBITMQ server because we passed empty string as the argument `consumer`. While in the parallel receive example, the method `Consume` is called with a specific consumer name `"linkConsumer"`. Thus, `Cancel` is also called with consumer name `"linkConsumer"`. The output shows that the parallel receive example is faster than the sequential one.

Output of the sequential receive:

```
...                                                                        1
goroutine http://web94.com:Bad                                             2
goroutine http://web95.com:Good                                            3
goroutine http://web96.com:Bad                                             4
goroutine http://web97.com:Good                                            5
goroutine http://web98.com:Good                                            6
goroutine http://web99.com:Bad                                             7
Time:   10.2949749s                                                        8
```

Output of the parallel receive:

```
...                                                                        1
goroutine 15 http://web95.com:Good                                         2
goroutine 3 http://web93.com:Bad                                           3
goroutine 1 http://web94.com:Good                                          4
goroutine 6 http://web97.com:Bad                                           5
goroutine 11 http://web98.com:Good                                         6
goroutine 8 http://web96.com:Good                                          7
goroutine 12 http://web99.com:Bad                                          8
Time:   741.4254ms                                                         9
```

5.5   Distributed Job Processing

The distributed job processing example follows the general idea of the Client-Dispatcher-Server pattern. The context of the pattern is described as: "A software system integrating a set of distributed servers, with the servers running locally or distributed over a network" [3].

In this example, the job-sender is the client, the worker is the server, the RABBITMQ server is the intermediate layer between clients and servers.

The job-senders send independent tasks to the workers, and from version 2, they also receive results from different workers. The workers receive jobs from job-senders and send back the results.

Distributed Job Processing Without Response From Workers (Version 1). The worker does not respond to the jobSender, it only receives tasks from it and prints the result (see Fig. 17). The jobSender and the worker both have declarations of connection, channel and exchange (as in the example of Subsect. 5.1).

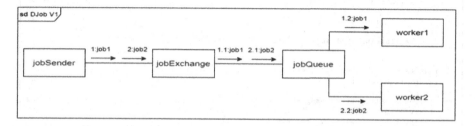

Fig. 17. Distributed job processing without response from workers. The jobQueue is RABBITMQ queue instead of Go queue. The jobSender sends jobs to the jobQueue through the jobExchange sequentially. The workers consume jobs from the jobQueue in a balanced round-robin way.

In Listing 1.58, the string slice `links` contains all the links that the `jobSender` sends to the RABBITMQ server. In Listing 1.57, we declare the queue `jobQueue` and bind it to the `jobExchange` with the routing key `jobkey`. Afterwards, the `worker` consumes the links from the `jobQueue` and checks all the received links using the function `linkTest`.

First the `workers` have to run. If no `worker` binds a queue to the `jobExchange`, the messages sent to the `jobExchange` by the `jobSender` are lost. Several `workers` can run, as they share the same queue, they consume and check all the links in a round-robin way. The introduction of `slice` can be found in Sect. 2.1.

```go
package main                                                                    1
import (                                                                        2
    "fmt"                                                                       3
    "github.com/streadway/amqp"                                                 4
    "log"                                                                       5
    "net/http"                                                                  6
    "time"                                                                      7
)                                                                               8
func main() {                                                                   9
    conn, err := amqp.Dial("amqp://guest:guest@localhost:5672/")                10
    failOnError(err, "Failed to connect to RabbitMQ")                           11
    defer conn.Close()                                                          12
    chi, err := conn.Channel()                                                  13
    failOnError(err, "Failed to open a channel")                               14
    defer chi.Close()                                                           15
    err = chi.ExchangeDeclare("jobExchange", "direct",                          16
        false, true, false, false, nil)                                         17
    failOnError(err, "Failed to declare an exchange")                          18
    queueIn, err := chi.QueueDeclare("jobQueue",                                19
        false, true, false, false, nil)                                         20
    failOnError(err, "Failed to declare a queue")                              21
    err = chi.QueueBind(queueIn.Name, "jobkey", "jobExchange", false, nil)      22
    failOnError(err, "Failed to bind a queue")                                 23
    inputMsgs, err := chi.Consume(queueIn.Name, "",                             24
        false, false, false, false, nil)                                        25
    failOnError(err, "Failed to register a consumer")                          26
    go func() {                                                                 27
        for d := range inputMsgs {                                              28
            fmt.Println(linkTest(string(d.Body)))                               29
            d.Ack(false)                                                        30
        }                                                                       31
    }()                                                                         32
    fmt.Println("Waiting for jobs")                                             33
    forever := make(chan bool)                                                  34
    <-forever                                                                   35
}                                                                               36
func linkTest(link string) string {                                            37
    client := http.Client{                                                      38
        Timeout: 3 * time.Second,                                               39
    }                                                                           40
    _, err := client.Get(link)                                                  41
    if err != nil {                                                             42
        resultString := link + " status: might down"                           43
        return resultString                                                    44
    }                                                                           45
    resultString := link + " status: up. "                                     46
    return resultString                                                        47
}                                                                               48
func failOnError(err error, msg string) {                                       49
    if err != nil {                                                             50
        log.Fatalf("%s: %s", msg, err)                                          51
    }                                                                           52
}                                                                               53
```

Listing 1.57. Distributed job and worker example version 1, `worker`

```go
package main                                                          1
import (                                                             2
    "fmt"                                                           3
    "github.com/streadway/amqp"                                    4
    "log"                                                          5
)                                                                   6
func main() {                                                        7
    links := []string{                                             8
        "http://google.com",                                       9
        "http://facebook.com",                                     10
        "http://stackoverflow.com",                                11
        "http://golang.org",                                       12
        "http://amazon.com",                                       13
    }                                                               14
    var numOfLink = 10                                             15
    for i := 0; i < numOfLink; i++ {                               16
        fakeLink := fmt.Sprintf("http://web%d.com", i)             17
        links = append(links, fakeLink)                            18
    }                                                               19
    conn, err := amqp.Dial("amqp://guest:guest@localhost:5672/")   20
    failOnError(err, "Failed to connect to RabbitMQ")              21
    defer conn.Close()                                             22
    cho, err := conn.Channel()                                     23
    failOnError(err, "Failed to open a channel")                   24
    defer cho.Close()                                              25
    err = cho.ExchangeDeclare("jobExchange", "direct",             26
        false, true, false, false, nil)                           27
    failOnError(err, "Failed to declare an exchange")              28
    for _, link := range links {                                   29
        err := cho.Publish("jobExchange", "jobkey", false, false,  30
            amqp.Publishing{                                       31
                ContentType: "text/plain",                         32
                Body:        []byte(link),                         33
            })                                                      34
        failOnError(err, "Failed to publish a message")            35
        fmt.Println("Published " + link)                           36
    }                                                               37
}                                                                   38
func failOnError(err error, msg string) {                           39
    if err != nil {                                                40
        log.Fatalf("%s: %s", msg, err)                             41
    }                                                               42
}                                                                   43
```

Listing 1.58. Distributed job and worker example version 1, `jobSender`

Run the first **worker**, the output is:

```
go run worker.go                                                    1
Waiting for jobs                                                    2
http://google.com status: up.                                      3
http://stackoverflow.com status: up.                               4
http://amazon.com status: up.                                      5
http://web1.com status: might down                                 6
http://web3.com status: might down                                 7
http://web5.com status: up.                                        8
http://web7.com status: up.                                        9
http://web9.com status: might down                                10
```

Run the second `worker`, the output is:

```
go run worker.go                                          1
Waiting for jobs                                          2
http://facebook.com status: up.                           3
http://golang.org status: up.                             4
http://web0.com status: up.                               5
http://web2.com status: up.                               6
http://web4.com status: might down                        7
http://web6.com status: up.                               8
http://web8.com status: might down                        9
```

Run the `jobSender`, the output is:

```
go run jobSender.go                                       1
Published http://google.com                               2
Published http://facebook.com                             3
Published http://stackoverflow.com                        4
Published http://golang.org                               5
Published http://amazon.com                               6
Published http://web0.com                                 7
Published http://web1.com                                 8
Published http://web2.com                                 9
Published http://web3.com                                 10
Published http://web4.com                                 11
Published http://web5.com                                 12
Published http://web6.com                                 13
Published http://web7.com                                 14
Published http://web8.com                                 15
Published http://web9.com                                 16
```

Distributed Job Processing with Shared Response Queue (Version 2).
In the previous version, the `jobSender` does not care about the result of the jobs. In this version, the `jobSender` sends jobs to the `worker` and receive responses from it (see Fig. 18). The `worker` receives jobs from the `jobSender` and sends the responses back to the `jobSender`. The `jobSender` and the `worker` use different connections to `Consume` and to `Publish` messages, so that publishing does not affect the ability of consuming messages.

The `jobSender` sends links as messages to the `jobExchange` exchange. The exchange routes the message to the `jobQueue` queue, which is bound to the `jobExchange`. Each `worker` receives jobs from this queue as a consumer. There is a round-robin balanced work distribution between all the workers. The `jobSender` receives response from the `worker`. We can have multiple `jobSender`s, each of them keeps a map called `jobCorr` to map a unique correlation `Id` to a job. Before each `jobSender` acknowledges by `ack` the response, they check if this correlation `Id` is in their map, if it is not in the map, then we reject and requeue the response, i.e. to transfer to other customers (`jobSender`s). Before publishing the job, the `jobSender` should create a separate goroutine receiving responses, which prevent the loss of the message. The code listings are in Subsect. A.2. The introduction of `map` can be found in Sect. 2.1.

As shown in `jobSender.go`, Listing 1.66, the `jobSender1` and `jobSender2` have different contents in the `linksToSend` slice. We can start them by giving different command line arguments when running the `jobSender.go`. They share the same response queue `responseQueue`, and bind the queue with `responsekey` to `responseExchange` (as shown from line 54 to 58). We create a string-to-string map to link each task to a unique `CorrelationId`, as shown in line 63. As shown from line 64 to 76, Listing 1.66, for each link, we generated a unique `corrId` before publishing the message (we used a globally unique id generator as in [12] (see from line 92 to 95).

Differently from the previous version, the message to be sent has two more fields: `CorrelationId` and `ReplyTo`. The `CorrelationId` matches the link sent by the `jobSender` with the response for this link sent by the worker. The value of the `CorrelationId` is the unique `corrId` created. The `ReplyTo` specifies the bounding routing key of the response queue.

As shown from line 77 to 88, Listing 1.66, we receive responses in a separate goroutine. Once the `jobSender` receives a response, it checks if this response is related to itself; if so, it acknowledges by `ack` the reply message; if not, it negatively acknowledges by `nack` the response and requeues this response to let another `jobSender` to receive it. The `worker`, as shown from line 29 to 42, Listing 1.65, for each received link, the checking is done, and then the result is published according to the `ReplyTo` using the same `correlationId`. After the response is published, we acknowledge by `ack` the received link message.

Distributed Job Processing with Private Response Queue (Version 3). In version 2, all the workers send responses with the same routing key. Each job sender requeues messages that are not related to them. If we have many job senders, there are too many requeueing operations, which affects the efficiency.

Each job sender has a separate queue for the responses in this version (see Fig. 19). As a result, the job sender does not receive irrelevant messages. Therefore, no requeueing operation is needed. The code listings of this example are in Subsect. A.3.

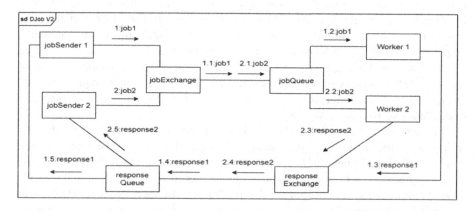

Fig. 18. Distributed job processing with shared response queue. The workers send their responses to the `responseExchange` and then to the `responseQueue`. All the `jobSenders` share one `responseQueue`.

We use different routing keys (their own generated queue name) for each job sender to reduce the message redirection, as in Listing 1.67 from line 4 to 6. When sending each job, it sets ReplyTo value to this queue name, as in line 14.

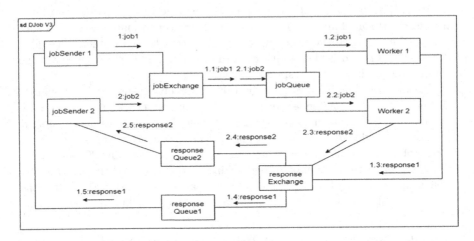

Fig. 19. Distributed job processing with private response queue. Instead of sharing one responseQueue, each jobSender has its own queue to receive the responses.

Distributed Job Processing with Worker Generator (Version 4). To test this program on more computers, each computer may need to run several workers. The previous version needs to manually run workers many times on each computer. In this version, workers are generated on each computer automatically by a worker generator. The organizer sends messages to the generators to run a worker on a specific computer. Hence no need to start and run workers manually anymore (see Fig. 20). The code listings are in Subsect. A.4.

As shown in Listing 1.69 and Listing 1.70, the organizer publishes four messages of "1" to the RABBITMQ server, each one stands for a request to create a worker. Each generator receives them in a round-robin way and runs the exec.Command to start a worker.

The worker is the same as the previous version. The jobSender is different, it does not run forever. The jobSender prints out the duration time after it has received all the responses. By using the WaitGroup, the main goroutine waits until the response received is goroutine finish. As in Listing 1.68, line 47 to 50, after it has handled each response, the jobSender checks if the map jobCorr is empty, which means all the jobs got their responses. If it is empty, we use Cancel to clearly close the msgs Go channel, after that the for range loop is finished. From the timing result, we can see that for the same tasks' list, the distributed version is faster than the sequential one.

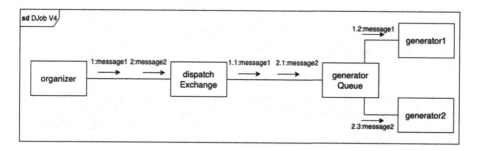

Fig. 20. Worker generator. The **organizer** sends messages to the **dispatch** exchange. Then the messages are routed to the **generator Queue**. Each message means one worker needs to be created by the generator. After **message1** is received, **generator1** generates a worker. At the same time, after receiving **message2**, **generator2** generates another worker; therefore, only two workers are generated in this figure.

5.6   Distributed Pipeline

In this section, we implement a distributed pipeline example. The distributed pipeline is an implementation of the Pipes and Filters pattern. This pattern is described as: "It provides a structure for systems that process a stream of data. Each processing step is encapsulated in a filter component. Data is passed through pipes between adjacent filters. Recombining filters allows you to build families of related systems" [3].

In this example, the workers are the Filters, the Pipes are the connections between the workers, which are achieved with RABBITMQ. The pipeline is valuable when many tasks need to go through a few, same processes. There are three versions, a next version solves some problems occurred in the previous ones.

Distributed Pipeline Without Connection Confirmation (Version 1). In this first version, we have only three workers in the pipeline, each one only knows the information (the exchange name and routing key) about the next worker (see Fig. 21).

When we run the first, the second, and the third worker in order, we find messages that the second and third worker has not received. For example, the second worker may not have received the 0 and 1 sent by the first worker. Likewise, the third worker may not have received the 4 and 6 sent by the second worker. However, the previous worker indeed has sent it. This is because when the previous worker publishes the first few messages, the next worker still has not yet bound the queue to the corresponding exchange. The message is lost if it is sent to the exchange to which there is no queue bound yet. Therefore, the workers should run in reverse order: worker 3, 2, and 1. One second of sleeping time is added to each task to slow down the speed.

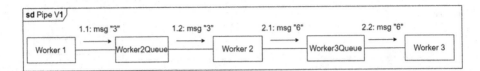

Fig. 21. Distributed pipeline without connection confirmation. The first worker produces numbers and sends them to the second worker. The second worker receives and multiplies them by 2, then sends them to the third worker. The third worker receives the numbers and prints them.

As shown in Listing 1.59 line 20 to 31, `worker 1` publishes 10 integers to the next worker. In Listing 1.60. line 35 to 51, `worker 2` multiplies each received integer by 2 and publishes the result to the next worker. In Listing 1.61, line 28 to 33, `worker 3` receives the messages and prints them out.

```
package main                                                          1
import (                                                              2
    "fmt"                                                             3
    "github.com/streadway/amqp"                                       4
    "log"                                                             5
    "strconv"                                                         6
    "time"                                                            7
)                                                                     8
func main() {                                                         9
    conn, err := amqp.Dial("amqp://guest:guest@localhost:5672/")     10
    failOnError(err, "Failed to connect to RabbitMQ")                11
    defer conn.Close()                                               12
    ch, err := conn.Channel()                                        13
    failOnError(err, "Failed to open a channel")                    14
    defer ch.Close()                                                 15
    err = ch.ExchangeDeclare("pipelineExchangeV1", "direct",        16
        false, true, false, false, nil)                              17
    failOnError(err, "Failed to declare an exchange")               18
    go func() {                                                      19
        for x := 0; x < 11; x++ {                                    20
            body := strconv.Itoa(x)                                  21
            err = ch.Publish("pipelineExchangeV1", "KeyA",           22
                false, false,                                        23
                amqp.Publishing{                                     24
                    ContentType: "text/plain",                      25
                    Body:        []byte(body),                       26
                })                                                   27
            failOnError(err, "Failed to publish a message")        28
            fmt.Println("Worker 1 sent", body)                      29
            time.Sleep(1000 * time.Millisecond)                     30
        }                                                           31
    }()                                                             32
    forever := make(chan bool)                                      33
    <-forever                                                       34
}                                                                   35
func failOnError(err error, msg string) {                           36
    if err != nil {                                                 37
        log.Fatalf("%s: %s", msg, err)                              38
    }                                                               39
}                                                                   40
```

Listing 1.59. Distributed pipeline without connection confirmation, `worker 1`

```go
package main                                                           1
import (                                                               2
    "fmt"                                                              3
    "github.com/streadway/amqp"                                        4
    "log"                                                              5
    "strconv"                                                          6
    "time"                                                             7
)                                                                      8
func main() {                                                          9
    conn1, err := amqp.Dial("amqp://guest:guest@localhost:5672/")     10
    failOnError(err, "Failed to connect to RabbitMQ")                 11
    defer conn1.Close()                                               12
    conn2, err := amqp.Dial("amqp://guest:guest@localhost:5672/")     13
    failOnError(err, "Failed to connect to RabbitMQ")                 14
    defer conn2.Close()                                               15
    cho, err := conn1.Channel()                                       16
    failOnError(err, "Failed to open a channel")                     17
    defer cho.Close()                                                 18
    chi, err := conn2.Channel()                                      19
    failOnError(err, "Failed to open a channel")                     20
    defer chi.Close()                                                21
    err = chi.ExchangeDeclare("pipelineExchangeV1", "direct",        22
        false, true, false, false, nil)                             23
    failOnError(err, "Failed to declare an exchange")               24
    q, err := chi.QueueDeclare("Worker2Queue",                      25
        false, true, false, nil)                                    26
    failOnError(err, "Failed to declare a queue")                   27
    err = chi.QueueBind(q.Name, "KeyA", "pipelineExchangeV1",       28
        false, nil)                                                 29
    failOnError(err, "Failed to bind a queue")                     30
    msgs, err := chi.Consume(q.Name, "",                            31
        false, false, false, false, nil)                           32
    failOnError(err, "Failed to register a consumer")              33
    go func() {                                                     34
        for d := range msgs {                                      35
            var numberString = string(d.Body)                      36
            number, _ := strconv.Atoi(numberString)                37
            var doubleNumber = number * 2                          38
            body := strconv.Itoa(doubleNumber)                     39
            err = cho.Publish("pipelineExchangeV1", "KeyB",        40
                false, false,                                      41
                amqp.Publishing{                                   42
                    ContentType: "text/plain",                     43
                    Body:        []byte(body),                     44
                })                                                 45
            failOnError(err, "Failed to publish a message")        46
            fmt.Println("Worker 2 received ", numberString,        47
                "sent", body)                                      48
            time.Sleep(1000 * time.Millisecond)                    49
            d.Ack(false)                                           50
        }                                                          51
    }()                                                            52
    fmt.Println("Waiting for jobs")                                53
    forever := make(chan bool)                                     54
    <-forever                                                      55
}                                                                  56
func failOnError(err error, msg string) {                         57
    if err != nil {                                                58
        log.Fatalf("%s: %s", msg, err)                            59
    }                                                              60
}                                                                 61
```

Listing 1.60. Distributed pipeline without connection confirmation, worker 2

```
package main                                                        1
import (                                                            2
    "fmt"                                                           3
    "github.com/streadway/amqp"                                     4
    "log"                                                           5
    "time"                                                          6
)                                                                   7
func main() {                                                       8
    conn, err := amqp.Dial("amqp://guest:guest@localhost:5672/")    9
    failOnError(err, "Failed to connect to RabbitMQ")              10
    defer conn.Close()                                             11
    ch, err := conn.Channel()                                      12
    failOnError(err, "Failed to open a channel")                   13
    defer ch.Close()                                               14
    err = ch.ExchangeDeclare("pipelineExchangeV1", "direct",       15
        false, true, false, false, nil)                            16
    failOnError(err, "Failed to declare an exchange")              17
    q, err := ch.QueueDeclare("Worker3Queue",                      18
        false, true, false, false, nil)                            19
    failOnError(err, "Failed to declare a queue")                  20
    err = ch.QueueBind(q.Name, "KeyB", "pipelineExchangeV1",       21
        false, nil)                                                22
    failOnError(err, "Failed to bind a queue")                     23
    msgs, err := ch.Consume(q.Name, "",                            24
        false, false, false, false, nil)                           25
    failOnError(err, "Failed to register a consumer")              26
    go func() {                                                     27
        for d := range msgs {                                      28
            var numberString = string(d.Body)                      29
            fmt.Println("Worker 3 received", numberString)         30
            time.Sleep(1000 * time.Millisecond)                    31
            d.Ack(false)                                           32
        }                                                          33
    }()                                                            34
    fmt.Println("Waiting for jobs")                                35
    forever := make(chan bool)                                     36
    <-forever                                                      37
}                                                                  38
func failOnError(err error, msg string) {                          39
    if err != nil {                                                40
        log.Fatalf("%s: %s", msg, err)                             41
    }                                                              42
}                                                                  43
```

Listing 1.61. Distributed pipeline without connection confirmation, worker 3

Run the worker3, the output is:

```
go run worker3.go                                                   1
Waiting for jobs                                                    2
Worker 3 received 0                                                 3
Worker 3 received 2                                                 4
Worker 3 received 4                                                 5
Worker 3 received 6                                                 6
Worker 3 received 8                                                 7
Worker 3 received 10                                                8
Worker 3 received 12                                                9
Worker 3 received 14                                               10
Worker 3 received 16                                               11
Worker 3 received 18                                               12
Worker 3 received 20                                               13
```

Run the `worker2`, the output is:

```
go run worker2.go                                    1
Waiting for jobs                                     2
Worker 2 received  0 sent 0                           3
Worker 2 received  1 sent 2                           4
Worker 2 received  2 sent 4                           5
Worker 2 received  3 sent 6                           6
Worker 2 received  4 sent 8                           7
Worker 2 received  5 sent 10                          8
Worker 2 received  6 sent 12                          9
Worker 2 received  7 sent 14                         10
Worker 2 received  8 sent 16                         11
Worker 2 received  9 sent 18                         12
Worker 2 received  10 sent 20                        13
```

Run the `worker1`, the output is:

```
go run worker1.go                                    1
Worker 1 sent 0                                      2
Worker 1 sent 1                                      3
Worker 1 sent 2                                      4
Worker 1 sent 3                                      5
Worker 1 sent 4                                      6
Worker 1 sent 5                                      7
Worker 1 sent 6                                      8
Worker 1 sent 7                                      9
Worker 1 sent 8                                     10
Worker 1 sent 9                                     11
Worker 1 sent 10                                    12
```

Distributed Pipeline with Connection Confirmation (Version 2). The previous version had loss of data problem, this version solves this issue (see Fig. 22). There are three types of workers in this example. The `Start worker`'s job is to generate and send messages to the next. The `Start worker`'s queue initially contains all the tasks. Next, the `Mid workers` receive messages, process them, and pass them to the next worker. Finally, the `End worker` receives messages and prints them. The code listings are in Subsect. A.5.

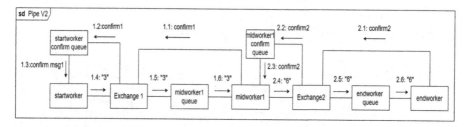

Fig. 22. `Distributed pipeline with connection confirmation`. The workers send messages only after receiving the confirmation message (which shows they are ready to receive) from the next ones.

As shown in Listing 1.72, line 46 to 56, the `Worker` is an struct which contains the methods `ConnectPrevious` and `WaitNext`. The `Worker` struct is embedded in `startWorker`, `midWorker` and `endWorker` structs. Therefore, `startWorker`, `midWorker` and `endWorker` can also call the methods `ConnectPrevious` and `WaitNext`.

In Listing 1.72, line 84 to 109, in the `WaitNext` method, every worker has a queue that receives confirm messages from the previous worker. After the previous worker starts, it waits for the confirmation message from the next worker. Then, the worker prints the bounding routing key of the confirm message queue. In Listing 1.72, line 57 to 83, in the `ConnectPrevious` method, the worker declares a queue for receiving task messages and send the bounding routing key of this queue as a confirmation message to the previous worker.

As shown in Listing 1.72, line 9 to 11, each worker has several command line arguments: `workerType` is the type of the worker; `inputConfirmQueue` is the bounding routing key of the confirm message queue of the previous worker, which is printed by the previous worker, and the next worker publishes confirmation message using this routing key. The `function` is the job of the middle worker and used it to process the received tasks.

In Listing 1.73 and in Listing 1.74, the start and middle workers only start to do their work after receiving the confirmation message from the next worker. Unlike the previous version, the worker does not wait forever after they do their job. The start worker sends an `"END"` after sending all the tasks. The middle worker, if has received it, sends it too to the next worker and exits. If the end worker receives `"END"`, it prints a string and exits.

The three workers are started in order, each one knows the information about the previous worker by passing command line arguments. However, when they start, they know nothing about the next ones; thus, they need to wait for the confirmation message from the next worker.

Distributed Pipeline with Worker Generator (Version 3). In the previous version, we need to manually type in the command line arguments for each worker on different computers to set up the pipeline. In this version, we make this setup process automatically, as shown in Fig. 23.

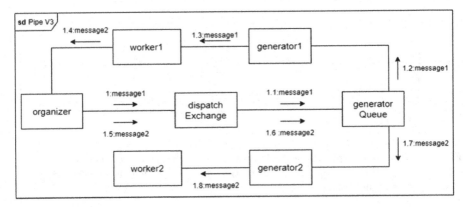

Fig. 23. `Distributed pipeline with worker generator`. The organizer sends the messages with command line arguments of the workers to the generator queue and receives messages from the generated worker. The generators consume messages from the generator queue and generate workers.

The code listings are in Subsect. A.6. As shown in Listing 1.78, line 33 to 45, the generator keeps receiving messages with command line arguments of a worker. The generator for each message generates a worker on a computer in a round-robin way.

In Listing 1.79, the organizer sends messages, including the command line arguments for a worker to the generator. Furthermore, it waits from the generated worker for the command line arguments of the next worker. In the organizer, we can set up the number of workers, the command line arguments for the first worker, and the function for each mid worker. The workers include one starter worker, one end worker, and a few middle workers. From line 55 to line 69, the organizer publishes the command line arguments of the start worker. From line 72 to line 101, the organizer waits for messages containing command line arguments and creates middle workers and end worker.

As shown in Listing 1.76, instead of printing the command line arguments for the next worker, like in previous version, here the worker sends those command line arguments to the organizer before printing them.

As shown in Listing 1.79 line 103 to line 109, the organizer waits for an end message before printing the elapsed time and terminates. The end worker sends this end message to the organizer after it receives the end message from a middle worker, as shown in Listing 1.77.

5.7   Distributed Divide and Conquer

In this section, we implement a distributed divide and conquer example, the quick sort algorithm (see Fig. 24). The version using the merge sort algorithm can be found in the Appendix Sect. B.

The distributed divide and conquer example is an implementation of the Master-Slave pattern. This pattern is described as: "A master component distributes work to identical slave components and computes a final result from the results these slaves return" [3].

In this example, the starter acts as master, the worker acts as both master and slave. The worker receives tasks and may distribute tasks to the generated workers. The generator generates workers after receiving command line arguments for the workers. Those command line arguments come from not only the starter but also from the workers.

The divide condition is that the length of the received list is greater than 4, if the length is less or equal to it, this worker does not divide anymore; it does the sorting and gives back the result to its parent.

Instead of manually running the worker, we use the generator to create the workers on each computer. The generator receives command line arguments from the workers to generate the new workers. The code listings are in Subsect. A.7.

The starter holds the list to be sorted, and it also declares a queueForConfirm, which is the queue to get the confirmation message from the child worker, as shown in Listing 1.83, line 37 to 38. The confirm message means the child worker has already bound the queueIn to the exchange and is ready to receive tasks from the parent worker, as shown in Listing 1.81, line

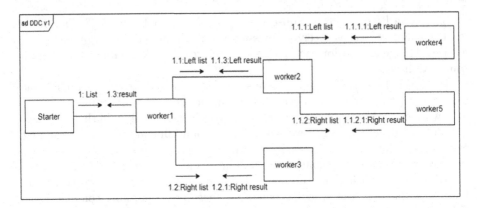

Fig. 24. Distributed Divide and Conquer. The starter sends the list to be sorted to worker1. The size of the list sent from the starter reaches the threshold of the divide; therefore, worker1 receives it and divides into two, and then it sends them to worker2 and worker3. The size of the list sent to worker2 still reaches the threshold of the divide, so it also has to divide the tasks to worker4 and worker5. The size of the list sent to worker3 is less than or equal to the threshold of the divide, so it sorts the sublist and sends back the result.

37 to 41. We use this confirmation message as a routing key to send tasks to the child. The starter declares a queueForResult, it is the queue to receive the result of a child. The child uses the name of queueForResult as a routing key when sending back the result to the parent worker.

Each worker has two command line arguments. One of them is the outputKey, that is the routing key the worker uses when sending back the result to the parent. Another one is the confirmKey, which is the routing key the worker uses when sending the confirmation message. The confirm message is the name of the queue that is used to receive tasks (queueIn.Name).

As shown in Listing 1.81 from line 37 to line 54, each worker first declares the queueIn and it sends a confirm message with the confirmKey as the routing key. In line 61 to 74, if the length of the received list is less or equal to 4, the worker sorts the list and sends back the result with the routing key outputKey. In line 75 to 233, if the length of the received list is greater than 4, the worker divides the received list into two sublists. Then, the worker sends two messages to the generator to create two more children workers. After that, the worker separately gets confirmation and the result from the child worker. In the end, the worker gets the final result and sends it back to the parent worker.

6   Testing Performances

In this section, we picked up one concurrent example from Subsect. 3.8 and one distributed example from Sect. 5.5 to illustrate the test of the performances.

Testing Concurrent Job and Worker Example. Measurements are done for `Concurrent job processing by long-life workers (version 3)` code, introduced in Subsect. 3.8 (see Fig. 25, Fig. 26, Fig. 27 and Fig. 28). For testing purposes, the number of CPUs the program could use was 16 (for descriptions see Subsect. 3.7). Additionally, we eliminated the print about quit. Finally, by changing the constant variable `MaxWorker`, the number of workers could be changed.

```
...                                                          1
const MaxWorker = 4                                          2
...                                                          3
func main() {                                                4
    fmt.Println(runtime.NumCPU())                            5
    _ = runtime.GOMAXPROCS(16)                               6
...                                                          7
            //fmt.Println("Worker ",                         8
            //strconv.Itoa(w.id), "Quit")                    9
...                                                          10
```

Listing 1.62. Test of concurrent job and worker example

The computer used in the test has the following configuration: processor, AMD Ryzen 7 5800H with Radeon Graphics 3.20 GHz. RAM, 16G. Cores, 8. Logical processors, 16.

The speed-up in the following figures is the ratio between the one-worker running time and the tested running time with multiple workers.

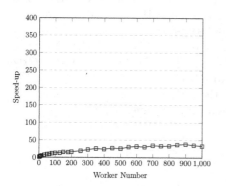

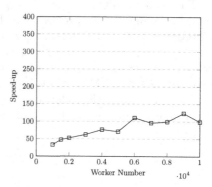

Fig. 25. Parallel job processing by long-life workers test, part 1/4. As the number of workers increases between 2 and 1000, the speed-up has tended to increase.

Fig. 26. Parallel job processing by long-life workers test, part 2/4. As the number of workers increases between 1000 and 10000, the speed-up increases.

Fig. 27. Parallel job processing by long-life workers test, part 3/4. As the number of workers increases between 10000 and 100000, the speed-up increases until 90000.

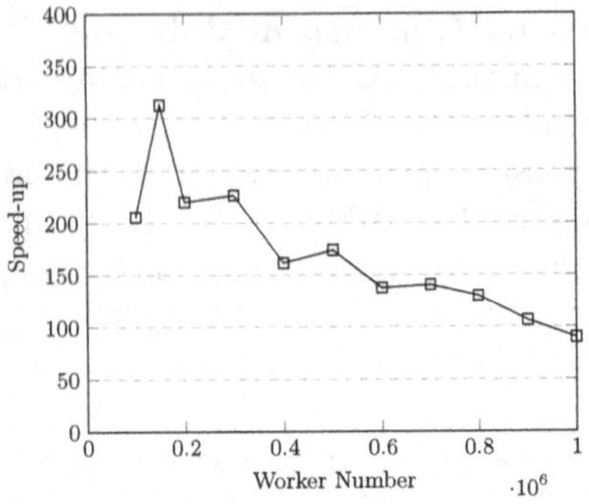

Fig. 28. Parallel job processing by long-life workers test, part 4/4. As the number of workers increases between 100000 and 1000000, the speed-up decreases.

Testing Distributed Job and Worker Example. We have done measurements for the Distributed job processing with worker generator (version 4) example introduced in Sect. 5.5 (see Fig. 29).

The server computer runs the organizer and the job sender and it has the following configuration: processor, AMD Ryzen 7 5800H with Radeon Graphics 3.20 GHz. RAM, 16G. Cores, 8. Logical processors, 16.

The slave computers run the generator and the workers and they have the following configuration: processor, Intel(R) Core(TM) i5-7400 CPU @ 3.00 GHz 3.00 GHz. RAM, 16G. Cores, 4. Logical processors, 4.

The speed-up in the following figure is the ratio between the sequential version running time and the tested distributed running time.

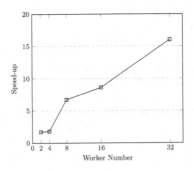

Fig. 29. Distributed job processing with worker generator test.   Each slave computer runs a worker. The speed-up increases as the number of workers increase from 2 till 32.

After testing the concurrent example on 16 available CPUs, we found that the speed-up tends to increase until around 90000 workers (which may also be limited by the long-life style design and the straightforward load balance algorithm of the example).

In this example, with one worker (goroutine), the program needs 510.45 s to process the 1000 tasks. While with 90000 workers (goroutines), the program only needs 1.42 s, which is a significant improvement. Additionally, we found that Go can efficiently deal with a very large number of goroutines.

After testing the distributed example on 32 computers (each computer runs a worker), we found that the speed-up tends to increase until 32 workers. The speed-up is 16.0 with 32 distributed workers, which is also a noteworthy improvement. RABBITMQ was very stable during the testing processes.

7 Related Work

RABBITMQ is open-source message-broker software that is developed by Pivotal Software company, and it is implemented in the ERLANG language. In addition, there is a similar software called KAFKA which is highly used, similarly to the RABBITMQ.

Dobbelaere, Ph. et al. [7] compared RABBITMQ and KAFKA based on the core functionality of publish/subscribe systems. RABBITMQ has better options for routing messages in complex topologies, while KAFKA has a simple routing approach. For example, RABBITMQ supports message delivery based on their priority, while KAFKA always delivers messages in order. RABBITMQ is capable of handling high throughput, especially background jobs. KAFKA is a message bus, which is used to handle high-ingress data streams and replay. RABBITMQ is suitable for traditional messaging while KAFKA is used mainly for streaming. There are limits when KAFKA is used for MQ. Therefore, we chose RABBITMQ for the implementations of this paper.

Madhu, M. P. et al. [15] conducted research about distributing messages using RABBITMQ with advanced message exchanges. It describes how RABBITMQ integrates with systems painlessly, the usefulness of distributing messages, and the guaranteed delivery of messages using AMQP. We acknowledge the benefits RABBITMQ brings on message delivery. RABBITMQ is primarily used for communication and integration between applications with message queues. It is a message broker generally used that supports reliable background jobs and long-running tasks. Message delivery can be either synchronous or asynchronous. RABBITMQ supports various message routing styles for returning data to a consumer, and we demonstrated how they are differently implemented with detailed examples.

NSQ [16] is another alternative message queue tool. It is implemented in Go language; however, it is different from RABBITMQ as NSQ has no brokers. Additionally, it supports distributed topologies without a single point of failure.

8   Conclusion

This tutorial explains all the concurrent and distributed constructs with practical examples. After an introduction to the basics of Go language, we have illustrated the Go concurrent constructs: goroutine, `WaitGroup`, `Mutex`, `AddUint`, channel, select. Afterward, we presented concurrent examples showing three ways to limit the number of goroutines. Next, we introduced several examples with different RABBITMQ mechanisms: fanout exchange, direct exchange, shared queue, parallel receive. Additionally, we introduced a series of distributed examples implementing existing patterns step-by-step: distributed job processing example (Client-Dispatcher-Server pattern), distributed pipeline example (Pipes and Filters pattern), distributed divide and conquer example (Master-Slave pattern). In the end, to illustrate how to test the examples, we measured the speed-up performances of a concurrent example and a distributed example. As it can be seen in Sect. 6, the concurrency (with multiple CPUs) and the distribution brought us significant speed-up.

After practicing the examples of this tutorial, the reader gets familiar with how to use Go and RABBITMQ to implement a distributed system. Throughout the examples of this tutorial, we can observe that Go has robust, stable, and user-friendly concurrent constructs.

Moreover, Go can manage tons of goroutines. We can deal with communications among goroutines without worrying about the mutual exclusion problems of the concurrent constructs. Also, RABBITMQ provides reliable and efficient distributed mechanisms. We can use the mechanisms to organize the distributed nodes into different distribution patterns by defining how they cooperate and communicate.

A   Code Listings and Outputs

A.1   Parallel Receive

The explanation of this example is in Subsect. 5.4.

```
package main                                                          1
import (                                                             2
    "fmt"                                                            3
    "log"                                                            4
    "math/rand"                                                      5
    "sync"                                                           6
    "time"                                                           7
    "github.com/streadway/amqp"                                      8
)                                                                   9
func main() {                                                       10
    conn1, err := amqp.Dial("amqp://guest:guest@localhost:5672/")   11
    failOnError(err, "Failed to connect to RabbitMQ")               12
    defer conn1.Close()                                             13
    conn2, err := amqp.Dial("amqp://guest:guest@localhost:5672/")   14
    failOnError(err, "Failed to connect to RabbitMQ")               15
    defer conn2.Close()                                             16
    cho, err := conn1.Channel()                                     17
    failOnError(err, "Failed to open a channel")                    18
    defer cho.Close()                                               19
```

```
chi, err := conn2.Channel()                                      20
failOnError(err, "Failed␣to␣open␣a␣channel")                     21
defer chi.Close()                                                22
err = cho.ExchangeDeclare("pExchange", "direct",                 23
    false, true, false, false, nil)                              24
failOnError(err, "Failed␣to␣declare␣an␣exchange")                25
q, err := chi.QueueDeclare("", false, true, false, false, nil)   26
failOnError(err, "Failed␣to␣declare␣a␣queue")                    27
err = chi.QueueBind(q.Name, "key", "pExchange", false, nil)      28
failOnError(err, "Failed␣to␣bind␣a␣queue")                       29
msgs, err := chi.Consume(q.Name, "",                             30
    false, false, false, false, nil)                             31
failOnError(err, "Failed␣to␣register␣a␣consumer")                32
for i := 0; i < 100; i++ {                                       33
    fakeLink := fmt.Sprintf("http://web%d.com", i)               34
    err = cho.Publish("pExchange", "key", false, false,          35
        amqp.Publishing{                                         36
            ContentType: "text/plain",                           37
            Body:        []byte(fakeLink),                       38
        })                                                       39
    failOnError(err, "Failed␣to␣publish")                        40
    fmt.Println("Published␣job:" + fakeLink)                     41
}                                                                42
err = cho.Publish("pExchange", "key", false, false,              43
    amqp.Publishing{                                             44
        ContentType: "text/plain",                               45
        Body:        []byte("END"),                              46
    })                                                           47
failOnError(err, "Failed␣to␣publish")                            48
fmt.Println("Published␣END")                                     49
var wg sync.WaitGroup                                            50
start := time.Now()                                              51
wg.Add(1)                                                        52
go func() {                                                      53
    for d := range msgs {                                        54
        s := string(d.Body)                                      55
        if s == "END" {                                          56
            err = chi.Cancel(d.ConsumerTag, false)               57
            failOnError(err, "Failed␣to␣cancel␣a␣consumer")      58
        } else {                                                 59
            result := linkTest(s)                                60
            fmt.Println("goroutine", result)                     61
        }                                                        62
        d.Ack(false)                                             63
    }                                                            64
    wg.Done()                                                    65
}()                                                              66
wg.Wait()                                                        67
duration := time.Since(start)                                    68
fmt.Println("Time:␣", duration)                                  69
}                                                                70
func failOnError(err error, msg string) {                        71
    if err != nil {                                              72
        log.Fatalf("%s:␣%s", msg, err)                           73
    }                                                            74
}                                                                75
func linkTest(link string) string {                              76
    time.Sleep(100 * time.Millisecond)                           77
    if rand.Intn(2) == 1 {                                       78
        return link + ":Good"                                    79
    } else {                                                     80
        return link + ":Bad"                                     81
    }                                                            82
}                                                                83
```

Listing 1.63. Sequential Receive

```
package main                                                             1
import (                                                                 2
    "fmt"                                                                3
    "log"                                                                4
    "math/rand"                                                          5
    "runtime"                                                            6
    "sync"                                                               7
    "time"                                                               8
    "github.com/streadway/amqp"                                          9
)                                                                       10
func main() {                                                           11
    conn1, err := amqp.Dial("amqp://guest:guest@localhost:5672/")       12
    failOnError(err, "Failed to connect to RabbitMQ")                   13
    defer conn1.Close()                                                 14
    conn2, err := amqp.Dial("amqp://guest:guest@localhost:5672/")       15
    failOnError(err, "Failed to connect to RabbitMQ")                   16
    defer conn2.Close()                                                 17
    cho, err := conn1.Channel()                                         18
    failOnError(err, "Failed to open a channel")                       19
    defer cho.Close()                                                   20
    chi, err := conn2.Channel()                                         21
    failOnError(err, "Failed to open a channel")                       22
    defer chi.Close()                                                   23
    err = cho.ExchangeDeclare("pExchange", "direct",                    24
        false, true, false, false, nil)                                 25
    failOnError(err, "Failed to declare an exchange")                  26
    q, err := chi.QueueDeclare("", false, true, false, false, nil)      27
    failOnError(err, "Failed to declare a queue")                      28
    err = chi.QueueBind(q.Name, "key", "pExchange", false, nil)         29
    failOnError(err, "Failed to bind a queue")                         30
    msgs, err := chi.Consume(q.Name, "linkConsumer",                    31
        false, false, false, false, nil)                                32
    failOnError(err, "Failed to register a consumer")                  33
    for i := 0; i < 100; i++ {                                          34
        fakeLink := fmt.Sprintf("http://web%d.com", i)                  35
        err := cho.Publish("pExchange", "key", false, false,            36
            amqp.Publishing{                                            37
                ContentType: "text/plain",                             38
                Body:        []byte(fakeLink),                         39
            })                                                          40
        failOnError(err, "Failed to publish")                          41
        fmt.Println("Published job:" + fakeLink)                        42
    }                                                                   43
    err = cho.Publish("pExchange", "key", false, false,                 44
        amqp.Publishing{                                                45
            ContentType: "text/plain",                                 46
            Body:        []byte("END"),                                47
        })                                                              48
    failOnError(err, "Failed to publish")                              49
    fmt.Println("Published END")                                        50
    var wg sync.WaitGroup                                               51
    start := time.Now()                                                 52
    for i := 0; i < runtime.NumCPU(); i++ {                             53
        wg.Add(1)                                                       54
        go func(index int) {                                           55
            for d := range msgs {                                      56
                s := string(d.Body)                                    57
                if s == "END" {                                        58
                    err = chi.Cancel("linkConsumer", false)            59
                    failOnError(err, "Failed to cancel a consumer")    60
                } else {                                                61
                    result := linkTest(s)                              62
                    fmt.Println("goroutine", index, result)            63
                }                                                       64
                d.Ack(false)                                           65
            }                                                           66
            wg.Done()                                                   67
```

```
        }(i)                                                        68
    }                                                              69
    wg.Wait()                                                      70
    duration := time.Since(start)                                 71
    fmt.Println("Time:␣", duration)                               72
}                                                                  73
func failOnError(err error, msg string) {                         74
    if err != nil {                                               75
        log.Fatalf("%s:␣%s", msg, err)                            76
    }                                                              77
}                                                                 78
func linkTest(link string) string {                               79
    time.Sleep(100 * time.Millisecond)                            80
    if rand.Intn(2) == 1 {                                        81
        return link + ":Good"                                     82
    } else {                                                      83
        return link + ":Bad"                                      84
    }                                                              85
}                                                                 86
```

Listing 1.64. Parallel Receive

A.2   Distributed Job Processing with Shared Response Queue, Version2

The explanation of this example is in Sect. 5.5.

```
...                                                                1
func main() {                                                      2
    conn1, err := amqp.Dial("amqp://guest:guest@localhost:5672/") 3
    failOnError(err, "Failed␣to␣connect␣to␣RabbitMQ")             4
    defer conn1.Close()                                           5
    conn2, err := amqp.Dial("amqp://guest:guest@localhost:5672/") 6
    failOnError(err, "Failed␣to␣connect␣to␣RabbitMQ")             7
    defer conn2.Close()                                           8
    cho, err := conn1.Channel()                                   9
    failOnError(err, "Failed␣to␣open␣a␣channel")                  10
    defer cho.Close()                                             11
    chi, err := conn2.Channel()                                   12
    failOnError(err, "Failed␣to␣open␣a␣channel")                  13
    defer chi.Close()                                             14
    err = cho.ExchangeDeclare("jobExchange", "direct",           15
        false, true, false, false, nil)                          16
    failOnError(err, "Failed␣to␣declare␣an␣exchange")            17
    err = chi.ExchangeDeclare("responseExchange", "direct",      18
        false, true, false, false, nil)                          19
    failOnError(err, "Failed␣to␣declare␣an␣exchange")            20
    q, err := chi.QueueDeclare("jobQueue",                       21
        false, true, false, false, nil)                          22
    failOnError(err, "Failed␣to␣declare␣a␣queue")                23
    err = chi.QueueBind(q.Name, "jobkey", "jobExchange", false, nil) 24
    failOnError(err, "Failed␣to␣bind␣a␣queue")                   25
    msgs, err := chi.Consume(q.Name, "",                         26
        false, false, false, false, nil)                         27
    failOnError(err, "Failed␣to␣register␣a␣consumer")            28
    go func() {                                                  29
        for d := range msgs {                                    30
            var result = linkTest(string(d.Body))               31
            fmt.Println(result)                                  32
            var err = cho.Publish("responseExchange", d.ReplyTo, 33
                false, false,                                    34
                amqp.Publishing{                                 35
                    ContentType:   "text/plain",                36
                    CorrelationId: d.CorrelationId,             37
```

```
            Body:                []byte(result),          38
        })                                                39
        failOnError(err, "Failed to publish a message")   40
        d.Ack(false)                                      41
    }                                                     42
}()                                                       43
fmt.Println("Waiting for jobs")                           44
forever := make(chan bool)                                45
<-forever                                                 46
}                                                         47
..•                                                       48
```

Listing 1.65. Distributed job processing with shared response queue, worker

```
package main                                                      1
import (                                                          2
    "fmt"                                                         3
    "github.com/rs/xid"                                           4
    "github.com/streadway/amqp"                                   5
    "log"                                                         6
    "os"                                                          7
)                                                                 8
func main() {                                                     9
    links := []string{                                           10
        "http://google.com",                                     11
        "http://golang.org",                                     12
    }                                                            13
    var numOfLink = 10                                           14
    for i := 0; i < numOfLink; i++ {                             15
        fakeLink := fmt.Sprintf("http://web%d.com", i)           16
        links = append(links, fakeLink)                          17
    }                                                            18
    links2 := []string{                                          19
        "http://facebook.com",                                   20
        http://amazon.com",                                      21
    }                                                            22
    var numOfLink2 = 20                                          23
    for i':= 11; i < numOfLink2; i++ {                           24
        fakeLink := fmt.Sprintf("http://web%d.com", i)           25
        links2 = append(links2, fakeLink)                        26
    }                                                            27
    var linksToSend []string                                     28
    arg := os.Args[1]                                            29
    switch arg {                                                 30
    case "1":                                                    31
        linksToSend = links                                      32
    case "2":                                                    33
        linksToSend = links2                                     34
    }                                                            35
    conn1, err := amqp.Dial("amqp://guest:guest@localhost:5672/") 36
    failOnError(err, "Failed to connect to RabbitMQ")            37
    defer conn1.Close()                                          38
    conn2, err := amqp.Dial("amqp://guest:guest@localhost:5672/") 39
    failOnError(err, "Failed to connect to RabbitMQ")            40
    defer conn2.Close()                                          41
    cho, err := conn1.Channel()                                  42
    failOnError(err, "Failed to open a channel")                 43
    defer cho.Close()                                            44
    chi, err := conn2.Channel()                                  45
    failOnError(err, "Failed to open a channel")                 46
    defer chi.Close()                                            47
    err = cho.ExchangeDeclare("jobExchange", "direct",           48
        false, true, false, false, nil)                          49
    failOnError(err, "Failed to declare an exchange")            50
    err = chi.ExchangeDeclare("responseExchange", "direct",      51
        false, true, false, false, nil)                          52
    failOnError(err, "Failed to declare an exchange")            53
```

```
q, err := chi.QueueDeclare("responseQueue",                          54
    false, true, false, false, nil)                                  55
failOnError(err, "Failed␣to␣declare␣a␣queue")                        56
err = chi.QueueBind(q.Name, "responsekey", "responseExchange",       57
    false, nil)                                                      58
failOnError(err, "Failed␣to␣bind␣a␣queue")                           59
msgs, err := chi.Consume(q.Name, "",                                 60
    false, false, false, false, nil)                                 61
failOnError(err, "Failed␣to␣register␣a␣consumer")                    62
var jobCorr = make(map[string]string)                                63
for _, link := range linksToSend {                                   64
    var corrId = randomString()                                      65
    err := cho.Publish("jobExchange", "jobkey", false, false,        66
        amqp.Publishing{                                             67
            ContentType:    "text/plain",                            68
            CorrelationId:  corrId,                                  69
            ReplyTo:        "responsekey",                           70
            Body:           []byte(link),                            71
        })                                                           72
    failOnError(err, "Failed␣to␣publish␣a␣message")                  73
    fmt.Println("Published␣" + link)                                 74
    jobCorr[corrId] = link                                           75
}                                                                    76
go func() {                                                          77
    for d := range msgs {                                            78
        if _, ok := jobCorr[d.CorrelationId]; ok {                   79
            delete(jobCorr, d.CorrelationId)                         80
            d.Ack(false)                                             81
            fmt.Println("Get␣result:␣" + string(d.Body))             82
        } else {                                                     83
            fmt.Println("Nacked␣a␣response")                         84
            d.Nack(false, true)                                      85
        }                                                            86
    }                                                                87
}()                                                                  88
forever := make(chan bool)                                           89
<-forever                                                            90
}                                                                    91
func randomString() string {                                         92
    guid := xid.New()                                                93
    return guid.String()                                             94
}                                                                    95
...                                                                  96
```

Listing 1.66. Distributed job processing with shared response queue, `jobSender`

Run the first worker, the output is:

```
go run worker.go                                                     1
Waiting for jobs                                                     2
http://google.com status: up.                                        3
http://web0.com status: up.                                          4
http://web2.com status: up.                                          5
http://web4.com status: might down.                                  6
http://web6.com status: up.                                          7
http://web8.com status: might down.                                  8
(after the second job sender run)                                    9
http://facebook.com status: up.                                      10
http://web11.com status: up.                                         11
http://web13.com status: might down.                                 12
http://web15.com status: up.                                         13
http://web17.com status: might down.                                 14
http://web19.com status: up.                                         15
```

Run the second worker, the output is:

```
go run worker.go                                              1
Waiting for jobs                                              2
http://golang.org status: up.                                 3
http://web1.com status: might down.                           4
http://web3.com status: might down.                           5
http://web5.com status: up.                                   6
http://web7.com status: up.                                   7
http://web9.com status: might down.                           8
(after the second job sender run)                             9
http://amazon.com status: up.                                 10
http://web12.com status: up.                                  11
http://web14.com status: up.                                  12
http://web16.com status: might down.                          13
http://web18.com status: might down.                          14
```

Run the first job sender, the output is:

```
go run jobSender.go 1                                         1
Published http://google.com                                   2
Published http://golang.org                                   3
Published http://web0.com                                     4
Published http://web1.com                                     5
Published http://web2.com                                     6
Published http://web3.com                                     7
Published http://web4.com                                     8
Published http://web5.com                                     9
Published http://web6.com                                     10
Published http://web7.com                                     11
Published http://web8.com                                     12
Published http://web9.com                                     13
Get result: http://google.com status: up.                    14
Get result: http://web0.com status: up.                       15
Get result: http://web2.com status: up.                       16
Get result: http://golang.org status: up.                     17
Get result: http://web1.com status: might down.               18
Get result: http://web3.com status: might down.               19
Get result: http://web4.com status: might down.               20
Get result: http://web6.com status: up.                       21
Get result: http://web8.com status: might down.               22
Get result: http://web5.com status: up.                       23
Get result: http://web7.com status: up.                       24
Get result: http://web9.com status: might down.               25
(after the second job sender run)                             26
Nacked a response                                             27
Nacked a response                                             28
Nacked a response                                             29
Nacked a response                                             30
Nacked a response                                             31
Nacked a response                                             32
Nacked a response                                             33
Nacked a response                                             34
Nacked a response                                             35
Nacked a response                                             36
Nacked a response                                             37
```

Run the second job sender, the output is:

```
go run jobSender.go 2                                         1
Published http://facebook.com                                 2
Published http://amazon.com                                   3
Published http://web11.com                                    4
Published http://web12.com                                    5
Published http://web13.com                                    6
Published http://web14.com                                    7
Published http://web15.com                                    8
```

```
Published http://web16.com                                          9
Published http://web17.com                                         10
Published http://web18.com                                         11
Published http://web19.com                                         12
Get result: http://facebook.com status: up.                        13
Get result: http://web11.com status: up.                           14
Get result: http://web13.com status: might down.                   15
Get result: http://amazon.com status: up.                          16
Get result: http://web15.com status: up.                           17
Get result: http://web12.com status: up.                           18
Get result: http://web14.com status: up.                           19
Get result: http://web17.com status: might down.                   20
Get result: http://web19.com status: up.                           21
Get result: http://web16.com status: might down.                   22
Get result: http://web18.com status: might down.                   23
```

A.3   Distributed Job Processing with Private Response Queue, Version3

The explanation of this example is in Sect. 5.5.

```
...                                                                 1
func main() {                                                       2
    ...                                                             3
    q, err := chi.QueueDeclare("", false, true, false, false, nil) 4
    ...                                                             5
    err = chi.QueueBind(q.Name, q.Name, "responseExchange", false, nil) 6
    ...                                                             7
    for _, link := range linksToSend {                             8
        var corrId = randomString()                                9
        err := cho.Publish("jobExchange", "jobkey", false, false,  10
            amqp.Publishing{                                        11
                ContentType:    "text/plain",                      12
                CorrelationId:  corrId,                            13
                ReplyTo:        q.Name,                            14
                Body:           []byte(link),                     15
            })                                                     16
        failOnError(err, "Failed␣to␣publish")                     17
        fmt.Println("Published␣" + link)                          18
        jobCorr[corrId] = link                                     19
    }                                                              20
    ...                                                            21
}                                                                  22
...                                                                23
```

Listing 1.67. Distributed job processing with private response queue, jobSender

Run the first worker, the output is:

```
go run worker.go                                                    1
Waiting for jobs                                                    2
http://google.com status: up.                                       3
http://web0.com status: up.                                         4
http://web2.com status: up.                                         5
http://web4.com status: might down.                                 6
http://web6.com status: up.                                         7
http://web8.com status: might down.                                 8
(after the second job sender run)                                   9
http://facebook.com status: up.                                    10
http://web11.com status: up.                                       11
http://web13.com status: might down.                               12
http://web15.com status: up.                                       13
http://web17.com status: might down.                               14
http://web19.com status: up.                                       15
```

Run the second worker, the output is:

```
go run worker.go                                          1
Waiting for jobs                                          2
http://golang.org status: up.                             3
http://web1.com status: might down.                       4
http://web3.com status: might down.                       5
http://web5.com status: up.                               6
http://web7.com status: up.                               7
http://web9.com status: might down.                       8
(after the second job sender run)                         9
http://amazon.com status: up.                             10
http://web12.com status: up.                              11
http://web14.com status: up.                              12
http://web16.com status: might down.                      13
http://web18.com status: might down.                      14
```

Run the first job sender, the output is:

```
go run jobSender.go 1                                     1
Published http://google.com                               2
Published http://golang.org                               3
Published http://web0.com                                 4
Published http://web1.com                                 5
Published http://web2.com                                 6
Published http://web3.com                                 7
Published http://web4.com                                 8
Published http://web5.com                                 9
Published http://web6.com                                 10
Published http://web7.com                                 11
Published http://web8.com                                 12
Published http://web9.com                                 13
Get result: http://google.com status: up.                14
Get result: http://web0.com status: up.                  15
Get result: http://golang.org status: up.                16
Get result: http://web1.com status: might down.          17
Get result: http://web3.com status: might down.          18
Get result: http://web2.com status: up.                  19
Get result: http://web4.com status: might down.          20
Get result: http://web6.com status: up.                  21
Get result: http://web8.com status: might down.          22
Get result: http://web5.com status: up.                  23
Get result: http://web7.com status: up.                  24
Get result: http://web9.com status: might down.          25
```

Run the second job sender, the output is:

```
go run jobSender.go 2                                     1
Published http://facebook.com                             2
Published http://amazon.com                               3
Published http://web11.com                                4
Published http://web12.com                                5
Published http://web13.com                                6
Published http://web14.com                                7
Published http://web15.com                                8
Published http://web16.com                                9
Published http://web17.com                                10
Published http://web18.com                                11
Published http://web19.com                                12
Get result: http://facebook.com status: up.              13
Get result: http://web11.com status: up.                  14
Get result: http://web13.com status: might down.          15
Get result: http://web15.com status: up.                  16
Get result: http://amazon.com status: up.                 17
Get result: http://web12.com status: up.                  18
Get result: http://web14.com status: up.                  19
Get result: http://web17.com status: might down.          20
Get result: http://web19.com status: up.                  21
```

A.4   Distributed Job Processing with Worker Generator, Version4

The explanation of this example is in Sect. 5.5.

```go
package main                                                         1
import (                                                            2
    "fmt"                                                           3
    "github.com/rs/xid"                                             4
    "github.com/streadway/amqp"                                     5
    "log"                                                           6
    "sync"                                                          7
    "time"                                                          8
)                                                                  9
func main() {                                                      10
    startTime := time.Now()                                        11
    links := []string{}                                            12
    var numOfLink = 50                                             13
    for i := 0; i < numOfLink; i++ {                              14
        fakeLink := fmt.Sprintf("http://web%d.com", i)             15
        links = append(links, fakeLink)                            16
    }                                                              17
    ...                                                            18
    msgs, err := chi.Consume(q.Name, "responseConsumer",          19
        false, false, false, false, nil)                           20
    failOnError(err, "Failed␣to␣register␣a␣consumer")              21
    var jobCorr = make(map[string]string)                          22
    for _, link := range links {                                   23
        var corrId = randomString()                                24
        err := cho.Publish("jobExchange", "jobkey", false, false,  25
            amqp.Publishing{                                       26
                ContentType:   "text/plain",                       27
                CorrelationId: corrId,                             28
                ReplyTo:       q.Name,                             29
                Body:          []byte(link),                       30
            })                                                     31
        failOnError(err, "Failed␣to␣publish")                      32
        fmt.Println("Published␣" + link)                           33
        jobCorr[corrId] = link                                     34
    }                                                              35
    var wg sync.WaitGroup                                          36
    wg.Add(1)                                                      37
    go func() {                                                    38
        for d := range msgs {                                      39
            if _, ok := jobCorr[d.CorrelationId]; ok {             40
                delete(jobCorr, d.CorrelationId)                   41
                fmt.Println("Get␣result:␣" + string(d.Body))       42
            } else {                                               43
                fmt.Println("Got␣a␣not␣related␣msg")               44
            }                                                      45
            d.Ack(false)                                           46
            if len(jobCorr) == 0 {                                 47
                err = chi.Cancel("responseConsumer", false)        48
                failOnError(err, "Failed␣to␣cancel␣a␣consumer")    49
            }                                                      50
        }                                                          51
        wg.Done()                                                  52
    }()                                                            53
    wg.Wait()                                                      54
    elapsed := time.Since(startTime)                               55
    fmt.Println("Time:␣" + elapsed.String())                       56
}                                                                  57
...                                                                58
```

Listing 1.68. Distributed job processing with worker generator, `jobSender`

```
package main                                                          1
import (                                                              2
    "fmt"                                                             3
    "github.com/streadway/amqp"                                       4
    "log"                                                             5
    "os/exec"                                                         6
)                                                                     7
func main() {                                                         8
    conn, err := amqp.Dial("amqp://guest:guest@localhost:5672/")      9
    defer conn.Close()                                               10
    ch, err := conn.Channel()                                       11
    err = ch.ExchangeDeclare("dispatch",                            12
    "direct", false, true, false, false, nil)                       13
    queueArg, err := ch.QueueDeclare("generatorQueue",              14
    false, true, false, false, nil)                                 15
    err = ch.QueueBind(queueArg.Name,                               16
    "generator", "dispatch", false, nil)                            17
    msg, err := ch.Consume(queueArg.Name,                           18
    "", false, false, false, false, nil)                            19
    go func() {                                                     20
        for d := range msg {                                       21
            cmd := exec.Command("cmd", "/C", "start",              22
            "go", "run", "../worker/worker.go",                    23
            "../worker/amqpClient.go")                             24
            err = cmd.Run()                                        25
            fmt.Println("generated one worker")                    26
            d.Ack(false)                                           27
        }                                                          28
    }()                                                            29
    forever := make(chan bool)                                     30
    <-forever                                                      31
}                                                                  32
...                                                                33
```

Listing 1.69. Distributed job processing with worker generator, `generator`

```
package main                                                          1
import (                                                              2
    "fmt"                                                             3
    "github.com/streadway/amqp"                                       4
    "log"                                                             5
)                                                                     6
func main() {                                                         7
    numWorkers := 4                                                   8
    conn, err := amqp.Dial("amqp://guest:guest@localhost:5672/")      9
    defer conn.Close()                                               10
    cho, err := conn.Channel()                                      11
    err = cho.ExchangeDeclare("dispatch", "direct",                 12
        false, true, false, false, nil)                             13
    for i := 0; i < numWorkers; i++ {                               14
        msg := "1"                                                  15
        err = cho.Publish("dispatch", "generator", false, false,    16
            amqp.Publishing{                                        17
                ContentType: "text/plain",                         18
                Body:        []byte(msg),                          19
            })                                                     20
        failOnError(err, "Failed to publish a message")            21
        fmt.Printf("Organizer Published %s\n", string(msg))        22
    }                                                              23
}                                                                  24
...                                                                25
```

Listing 1.70. Distributed job processing with worker generator, `organizer`

```
package main                                                        1
import (                                                            2
    "fmt"                                                           3
    "net/http"                                                      4
    "time"                                                          5
)                                                                  6
func main() {                                                       7
    startTime := time.Now()                                        8
    links := []string{}                                            9
    var numOfLink = 50                                             10
    for i := 0; i < numOfLink; i++ {                              11
        fakeLink := fmt.Sprintf("http://web%d.com", i)            12
        links = append(links, fakeLink)                           13
    }                                                             14
    for _, link := range links {                                 15
        result := linkTest(link)                                 16
        fmt.Println(result)                                      17
    }                                                             18
    elapsed := time.Since(startTime)                             19
    fmt.Printf("Time:␣%s␣\n", elapsed)                           20
}                                                                 21
...                                                               22
```

Listing 1.71. Distributed job processing with worker generator, `sequential`

On the first computer, we run the first generator, the output is:

```
go run generator.go                                                1
Wait for messages from organizer                                   2
generated one worker                                               3
generated one worker                                               4
```

After running the organizer, the first generator generates two workers on the first computer. The output of the first worker generated by the first generator:

```
Waiting for jobs                                                   1
http://web1.com status: might down.                               2
http://web5.com status: up.                                       3
http://web9.com status: might down.                               4
http://web13.com status: might down.                              5
http://web17.com status: might down.                              6
http://web21.com status: up.                                      7
http://web25.com status: up.                                      8
http://web29.com status: might down.                              9
http://web33.com status: up.                                     10
http://web37.com status: might down.                             11
http://web41.com status: up.                                     12
http://web45.com status: up.                                     13
http://web49.com status: might down.                             14
```

The output of the second worker generated by the first generator is:

```
Waiting for jobs                                                   1
http://web0.com status: up.                                       2
http://web4.com status: might down.                               3
http://web8.com status: might down.                               4
http://web12.com status: up.                                      5
http://web16.com status: might down.                              6
http://web20.com status: might down.                              7
http://web24.com status: might down.                              8
http://web28.com status: up.                                      9
http://web32.com status: up.                                     10
http://web36.com status: might down.                             11
http://web40.com status: up.                                     12
http://web44.com status: up.                                     13
http://web48.com status: up.                                     14
```

On the second computer, we run the second generator, the output is:

```
go run generator.go                                              1
Wait for messages from organizer                                 2
generated one worker                                             3
generated one worker                                             4
```

After running the organizer, the first generator generates two workers on the first computer. The output of the first worker generated by the second generator:

```
Waiting for jobs                                                1
http://web2.com status: up.                                     2
http://web6.com status: up.                                     3
http://web10.com status: up.                                    4
http://web14.com status: up.                                    5
http://web18.com status: might down.                            6
http://web22.com status: might down.                            7
http://web26.com status: up.                                    8
http://web30.com status: up.                                    9
http://web34.com status: up.                                    10
http://web38.com status: might down.                            11
http://web42.com status: up.                                    12
http://web46.com status: might down.                            13
```

The output of the second worker generated by the second generator is:

```
Waiting for jobs                                                1
http://web3.com status: might down.                             2
http://web7.com status: up.                                     3
http://web11.com status: up.                                    4
http://web15.com status: up.                                    5
http://web19.com status: up.                                    6
http://web23.com status: might down.                            7
http://web27.com status: might down.                            8
http://web31.com status: up.                                    9
http://web35.com status: might down.                            10
http://web39.com status: might down.                            11
http://web43.com status: might down.                            12
http://web47.com status: might down.                            13
```

The output of the organizer is:

```
go run organizer.go                                             1
Organizer Published 1                                           2
Organizer Published 1                                           3
Organizer Published 1                                           4
Organizer Published 1                                           5
```

The output of the job sender is:

```
go run jobSender.go                                             1
Published http://web0.com                                       2
Published http://web1.com                                       3
Published http://web2.com                                       4
Published http://web3.com                                       5
Published http://web4.com                                       6
Published http://web5.com                                       7
...                                                             8
Published http://web42.com                                      9
Published http://web43.com                                      10
Published http://web44.com                                      11
Published http://web45.com                                      12
Published http://web46.com                                      13
Published http://web47.com                                      14
Published http://web48.com                                      15
Published http://web49.com                                      16
```

```
Get result: http://web3.com status: might down.          17
Get result: http://web1.com status: might down.          18
Get result: http://web2.com status: up.                  19
Get result: http://web0.com status: up.                  20
Get result: http://web6.com status: up.                  21
Get result: http://web10.com status: up.                 22
Get result: http://web5.com status: up.                  23
...                                                      24
Get result: http://web39.com status: might down.         25
Get result: http://web44.com status: up.                 26
Get result: http://web43.com status: might down.         27
Get result: http://web48.com status: up.                 28
Get result: http://web46.com status: might down.         29
Get result: http://web49.com status: might down.         30
Get result: http://web47.com status: might down.         31
Time: 19.5084314s                                        32
```

The output of the sequential version is:

```
go run sequential.go                                     1
http://web0.com status: up.                              2
http://web1.com status: might down                       3
http://web2.com status: up.                              4
http://web3.com status: might down                       5
http://web4.com status: might down                       6
http://web5.com status: up.                              7
http://web6.com status: up.                              8
http://web7.com status: up.                              9
http://web8.com status: might down                       10
...                                                      11
http://web45.com status: up.                             12
http://web46.com status: might down                      13
http://web47.com status: might down                      14
http://web48.com status: up.                             15
http://web49.com status: up.                             16
Time: 1m17.1356748s                                      17
```

A.5   Distributed Pipeline with Connection Confirmation (Version 2)

The explanation of this example is in Sect. 5.6.

```
package main                                              1
import (                                                 2
    "log"                                                3
    "os"                                                 4
    "fmt"                                                5
    "github.com/streadway/amqp"                          6
)                                                        7
func main() {                                            8
    const exchangeName = "pipeExchangeV2"                9
    workerType := os.Args[1]                             10
    inputConfirmQueue := os.Args[2]                      11
    function := os.Args[3]                               12
    conn1, err := amqp.Dial("amqp://guest:guest@localhost:5672/")  13
    failOnError(err, "Failed to connect to RabbitMQ")    14
    defer conn1.Close()                                  15
    conn2, err := amqp.Dial("amqp://guest:guest@localhost:5672/")  16
    failOnError(err, "Failed to connect to RabbitMQ")    17
    defer conn2.Close()                                  18
    conn3, err := amqp.Dial("amqp://guest:guest@localhost:5672/")  19
    failOnError(err, "Failed to connect to RabbitMQ")    20
    defer conn3.Close()                                  21
    conn4, err := amqp.Dial("amqp://guest:guest@localhost:5672/")  22
    failOnError(err, "Failed to connect to RabbitMQ")    23
    defer conn4.Close()                                  24
```

```
if workerType == "startworker" {                                   25
    w := startWorker{Worker{conn1, conn2, conn3, conn4, nil, nil, nil, 26
        exchangeName, inputConfirmQueue, function}}                27
    w.WaitNext()                                                   28
    w.Work()                                                       29
} else if workerType == "midworker" {                              30
    w := midWorker{Worker{conn1, conn2, conn3, conn4, nil, nil, nil, 31
        exchangeName, inputConfirmQueue, function}}                32
    w.ConnectPrevious()                                            33
    w.WaitNext()                                                   34
    w.Work()                                                       35
} else {                                                           36
    w := endWorker{Worker{conn1, conn2, conn3, conn4, nil, nil, nil, 37
        exchangeName, inputConfirmQueue, function}}                38
    w.ConnectPrevious()                                            39
    w.Work()                                                       40
}                                                                  41
forever := make(chan bool)                                         42
<-forever                                                          43
}                                                                  44
type Worker struct{                                                45
    conn1              *amqp.Connection                            46
    conn2              *amqp.Connection                            47
    conn3              *amqp.Connection                            48
    conn4              *amqp.Connection                            49
    inputMsgs          <-chan amqp.Delivery                        50
    confirmMsgs        <-chan amqp.Delivery                        51
    localchos          *amqp.Channel                               52
    exchangeName       string                                      53
    inputConfirmQueue  string                                      54
    function           string                                      55
}                                                                  56
func (w *Worker) ConnectPrevious() {                               57
    //channel send confirm to inputExchange                        58
    chis, err := w.conn1.Channel()                                 59
    failOnError(err, "Failed to open a channel")                   60
    //channel receive from inputExchange                           61
    chir, err := w.conn2.Channel()                                 62
    failOnError(err, "Failed to open a channel")                   63
    //declare queue and bind to inputExchange                      64
    queueForMsgs, err := chir.QueueDeclare("",                     65
        false, false, true, false, nil)                            66
    failOnError(err, "Failed to declare a queue")                  67
    err = chir.QueueBind(queueForMsgs.Name, queueForMsgs.Name,      68
        w.exchangeName, false, nil)                                69
    failOnError(err, "Failed to bind a queue")                     70
    w.inputMsgs, err = chir.Consume(queueForMsgs.Name, "",          71
        false, false, false, false, nil)                           72
    failOnError(err, "Failed to register a consumer")              73
    //send confirms with routekey as inputConfirmQueue             74
    confirmMessage := queueForMsgs.Name                            75
    err = chis.Publish(w.exchangeName,                             76
        w.inputConfirmQueue, false, false,                         77
        amqp.Publishing{                                           78
            ContentType: "text/plain",                             79
            Body:        []byte(confirmMessage),                   80
        })                                                         81
    failOnError(err, "Failed to publish a message")               82
}                                                                  83
func (w *Worker) WaitNext() {                                       84
    //channel for receiving confirms from output channel           85
    chor, err := w.conn3.Channel()                                 86
    failOnError(err, "Failed to open a channel")                   87
    //channel for sending to output channel                        88
    chos, err := w.conn4.Channel()                                 89
    w.localchos = chos                                             90
    failOnError(err, "Failed to open a channel")                   91
    err = chos.ExchangeDeclare(w.exchangeName, "direct",           92
```

```
        false, false, false, false, nil)                                93
    failOnError(err, "Failed␣to␣declare␣an␣exchange")                    94
    //declare confirm queue                                             95
    queueForConfirm, err := chor.QueueDeclare("",                       96
        false, false, true, false, nil)                                 97
    failOnError(err, "Failed␣to␣declare␣a␣queue")                       98
    err = chor.QueueBind(queueForConfirm.Name, queueForConfirm.Name,    99
        w.exchangeName, false, nil)                                     100
    failOnError(err, "Failed␣to␣bind␣a␣queue")                          101
    w.confirmMsgs, err = chor.Consume(queueForConfirm.Name, "",         102
        false, true, false, false, nil)                                 103
    failOnError(err, "Failed␣to␣register␣a␣consumer")                   104
    //print out the confirm queue for next worker                       105
    fmt.Println(                                                         106
        "The␣input␣confirm␣queue␣(2nd␣cmd␣line␣arg␣for␣the␣next␣worker):", 107
        queueForConfirm.Name)                                           108
}                                                                       109
func failOnError(err error, msg string) {                               110
    if err != nil {                                                     111
        log.Fatalf("%s:␣%s", msg, err)                                  112
    }                                                                   113
}                                                                       114
```

Listing 1.72. Distributed pipeline with connection confirmation, `worker`

```
package main                                                            1
import (                                                                2
    "fmt"                                                               3
    "github.com/streadway/amqp"                                         4
    "strconv"                                                           5
    "time"                                                              6
)                                                                       7
type startWorker struct {                                               8
    Worker                                                              9
}                                                                       10
func (w *startWorker) Work() {                                          11
    //block when waiting confirms                                       12
    nextWorkerQueue := <-w.confirmMsgs                                  13
    nextWorkerQueueName := string(nextWorkerQueue.Body)                 14
    go func() {                                                         15
        for x := 0; x < 10; x++ {                                       16
            msg := strconv.Itoa(x)                                      17
            err := w.localchos.Publish(w.exchangeName,                  18
                nextWorkerQueueName,false, false,                       19
                amqp.Publishing{                                        20
                    ContentType: "text/plain",                         21
                    Body:        []byte(msg),                          22
                })                                                      23
            failOnError(err, "Failed␣to␣publish␣a␣message")             24
            fmt.Println("Start␣worker␣published", msg)                  25
            time.Sleep(1000 * time.Millisecond)                         26
        }                                                               27
        msg := "END"                                                    28
        err := w.localchos.Publish(w.exchangeName,                      29
            nextWorkerQueueName,false, false,                           30
            amqp.Publishing{                                            31
                ContentType: "text/plain",                             32
                Body:        []byte(msg),                              33
            })                                                          34
        failOnError(err, "Failed␣to␣publish␣a␣message")                 35
        fmt.Println("Start␣worker␣published", msg)                      36
        fmt.Println("Start␣worker␣finished")                            37
    }()                                                                 38
}                                                                       39
```

Listing 1.73. Distributed pipeline with connection confirmation, `startWorker`

```
package main                                                        1
import (                                                            2
    "fmt"                                                           3
    "github.com/streadway/amqp"                                     4
    "strconv"                                                       5
    "time"                                                          6
)                                                                   7
type midWorker struct {                                            8
    Worker                                                          9
}                                                                  10
func (w *midWorker) Work() {                                       11
    //block when waiting confirms                                 12
    nextWorkerQueue := <-w.confirmMsgs                            13
    nextWorkerQueueName := string(nextWorkerQueue.Body)           14
    go func() {                                                    15
        for d := range w.inputMsgs {                              16
            var numberString = string(d.Body)                     17
            if numberString == "END" {                            18
                msg := "END"                                      19
                err := w.localchos.Publish(w.exchangeName,        20
                    nextWorkerQueueName,false, false,             21
                    amqp.Publishing{                              22
                        ContentType: "text/plain",               23
                        Body:        []byte(msg),                 24
                    })                                            25
                failOnError(err, "Failed␣to␣publish␣a␣message")   26
                fmt.Println("Mid␣worker␣received", numberString,  27
                    "Published", msg)                             28
                fmt.Println("Mid␣worker␣finished")                29
                break                                             30
            }                                                     31
            number, _ := strconv.Atoi(numberString)              32
            var changedNumber int                                33
            switch w.function {                                  34
            case "+2":                                           35
                changedNumber = number + 2                       36
            case "*2":                                           37
                changedNumber = number * 2                       38
            }                                                    39
            msg := strconv.Itoa(changedNumber)                  40
            err := w.localchos.Publish(w.exchangeName,          41
                nextWorkerQueueName,false, false,               42
                amqp.Publishing{                                43
                    ContentType: "text/plain",                 44
                    Body:        []byte(msg),                   45
                })                                              46
            failOnError(err, "Failed␣to␣publish␣a␣message")    47
            fmt.Println("Mid␣worker␣received", numberString,   48
                "Published", msg)                              49
            time.Sleep(1000 * time.Millisecond)                50
            d.Ack(false)                                       51
        }                                                      52
    }()                                                        53
}                                                              54
```

Listing 1.74. Distributed pipeline with connection confirmation, `midWorker`

```
package main                                                    1
import (                                                        2
    "fmt"                                                       3
    "time"                                                      4
)                                                               5
type endWorker struct {                                        6
    Worker                                                      7
}                                                               8
func (w *endWorker) Work() {                                    9
```

```
    go func() {                                                         10
        for d := range w.inputMsgs {                                    11
            var numberString = string(d.Body)                           12
            fmt.Println("End worker received", numberString)            13
            if numberString == "END" {                                  14
                fmt.Println("End worker finished")                      15
                break                                                   16
            }                                                           17
            time.Sleep(1000 * time.Millisecond)                         18
            d.Ack(false)                                                19
        }                                                               20
    }()                                                                 21
}                                                                       22
```

Listing 1.75. Distributed pipeline with connection confirmation, `endWorker`

Here is the command to build the worker (it generates the `worker.exe`):

```
go build worker.go startWorker.go endWorker.go midWorker.go          1
```

Run the `Start` worker with the `startworker`, `null`, and `null` parameters.

```
worker.exe startworker null null                                       1
The input confirm queue (2nd cmd line arg for the next worker):        2
amq.gen-8tyPS4Olout44SH8-AXAFg                                         3
Start worker published 0                                               4
Start worker published 1                                               5
Start worker published 2                                               6
Start worker published 3                                               7
Start worker published 4                                               8
Start worker published 5                                               9
Start worker published 6                                              10
Start worker published 7                                              11
Start worker published 8                                              12
Start worker published 9                                              13
Start worker published END                                            14
Start worker finished                                                 15
```

Run the `Mid` worker with the following parameters:
`midworker amq.gen-8tyPS4Olout44SH8-AXAFg +2`. The output is:

```
worker.exe midworker amq.gen-8tyPS4Olout44SH8-AXAFg +2                 1
The input confirm queue (2nd cmd line arg for the next worker):        2
amq.gen-so-TcH3UqBMOXy9vtP02eQ                                        3
Mid worker received 0 Published 2                                      4
Mid worker received 1 Published 3                                      5
Mid worker received 2 Published 4                                      6
Mid worker received 3 Published 5                                      7
Mid worker received 4 Published 6                                      8
Mid worker received 5 Published 7                                      9
Mid worker received 6 Published 8                                     10
Mid worker received 7 Published 9                                     11
Mid worker received 8 Published 10                                    12
Mid worker received 9 Published 11                                    13
Mid worker received END Published END                                 14
Mid worker finished                                                   15
```

Run the `End` worker with the following parameters:
`endworker amq.gen-so-TcH3UqBMOXy9vtP02eQ null`. The output is:

```
worker.exe endworker amq.gen-so-TcH3UqBMOXy9vtP02eQ null               1
End worker received 2                                                  2
End worker received 3                                                  3
End worker received 4                                                  4
End worker received 5                                                  5
```

```
End worker received 6                                          6
End worker received 7                                          7
End worker received 8                                          8
End worker received 9                                          9
End worker received 10                                         10
End worker received 11                                         11
End worker received END                                        12
End worker finished                                            13
```

A.6   Distributed Pipeline with Worker Generator (Version 3)

The explanation of this example is in Sect. 5.6.

```
...                                                            1
func (w *Worker) WaitNext() {                                  2
    ...                                                        3
    //send and print out the confirm queue for next worker    4
    err = chos.Publish("dispatch", "resp",                    5
        false, false,                                          6
        amqp.Publishing{                                       7
            ContentType: "text/plain",                         8
            Body:        []byte(queueForConfirm.Name),         9
        })                                                     10
    failOnError(err, "Failed␣to␣publish␣a␣message")            11
    fmt.Println("Worker␣published␣input␣confirm␣queue",        12
                queueForConfirm.Name)                          13
}                                                              14
```

Listing 1.76. Distributed pipeline with worker generator, `worker`

```
...                                                                   1
func (w *endWorker) Work() {                                          2
    go func() {                                                       3
        for d := range w.inputMsgs {                                  4
            var numberString = string(d.Body)                         5
            fmt.Println("End␣worker␣received", numberString)          6
            if numberString == "END" {                                7
                c, err := w.conn3.Channel()                           8
                failOnError(err, "Failed␣to␣create␣a␣channel")        9
                msg := "END"                                          10
                err = c.Publish("dispatch", "end",                    11
                    false, false,                                     12
                    amqp.Publishing{                                  13
                        ContentType: "text/plain",                    14
                        Body:        []byte(msg),                     15
                    })                                                16
                failOnError(err, "Failed␣to␣publish␣a␣message")       17
                fmt.Println("End␣worker␣Published␣to␣dispather:", msg) 18
                fmt.Println("End␣worker␣finished")                    19
                break                                                 20
            }                                                         21
            time.Sleep(1000 * time.Millisecond)                       22
            d.Ack(false)                                              23
        }                                                             24
    }()                                                               25
}                                                                     26
```

Listing 1.77. Distributed pipeline with worker generator, `endWorker`

```
package main                                                   1
import (                                                       2
    "encoding/json"                                            3
    "fmt"                                                      4
```

```
        "log"                                                           5
        "os/exec"                                                       6
                                                                        7
        "github.com/streadway/amqp"                                     8
)                                                                       9
type workerArg struct {                                                 10
      WorkerType          string                                        11
      InputConfirmQueue   string                                        12
      Function            string                                        13
}                                                                       14
func main() {                                                           15
      conn, err := amqp.Dial("amqp://guest:guest@localhost:5672/")      16
      failOnError(err, "Failed to connect to RabbitMQ")                 17
      defer conn.Close()                                                18
      ch, err := conn.Channel()                                         19
      failOnError(err, "Failed to open a channel")                      20
      err = ch.ExchangeDeclare("dispatch", "direct",                    21
          false, true, false, false, nil)                               22
      failOnError(err, "Failed to declare an exchange")                 23
      queueArg, err := ch.QueueDeclare("generatorQueue",                24
          false, true, false, false, nil)                               25
      failOnError(err, "Failed to declare a queue")                     26
      err = ch.QueueBind(queueArg.Name, "generator", "dispatch",        27
          false, nil)                                                   28
      failOnError(err, "Failed to bind a queue")                        29
      argMsgs, err := ch.Consume(queueArg.Name, "",                     30
          false, false, false, false, nil)                              31
      failOnError(err, "Failed to register a consumer")                 32
      go func() {                                                       33
          for d := range argMsgs {                                      34
              arg := workerArg{}                                        35
              json.Unmarshal(d.Body, &arg)                              36
              fmt.Println(arg)                                          37
              cmd := exec.Command("cmd", "/C", "start", "../worker.exe",38
                  arg.WorkerType, arg.InputConfirmQueue, arg.Function)  39
              err = cmd.Run()                                           40
              failOnError(err, "Failed to generate worker")            41
              fmt.Println("generated one worker")                       42
              d.Ack(false)                                              43
          }                                                             44
      }()                                                               45
      forever := make(chan bool)                                        46
      <-forever                                                         47
}                                                                       48
func failOnError(err error, msg string) {                               49
      if err != nil {                                                   50
          log.Fatalf("%s: %s", msg, err)                                51
      }                                                                 52
}                                                                       53
```

Listing 1.78. Distributed pipeline with worker generator, **generator**

```
package main                                                            1
import (                                                                2
      "fmt"                                                             3
      "log"                                                             4
      "time"                                                            5
      "encoding/json"                                                   6
      "github.com/streadway/amqp"                                       7
)                                                                       8
type workerArg struct {                                                 9
      WorkerType          string                                        10
      InputConfirmQueue   string                                        11
      Function            string                                        12
}                                                                       13
func main() {                                                           14
      startTime := time.Now()                                           15
```

```
conn1, err := amqp.Dial("amqp://guest:guest@localhost:5672/")      16
failOnError(err, "Failed␣to␣connect␣to␣RabbitMQ")                  17
defer conn1.Close()                                                18
conn2, err := amqp.Dial("amqp://guest:guest@localhost:5672/")      19
failOnError(err, "Failed␣to␣connect␣to␣RabbitMQ")                  20
defer conn2.Close()                                                21
conn3, err := amqp.Dial("amqp://guest:guest@localhost:5672/")      22
failOnError(err, "Failed␣to␣connect␣to␣RabbitMQ")                  23
defer conn3.Close()                                                24
cho, err := conn1.Channel()                                        25
failOnError(err, "Failed␣to␣open␣a␣channel")                       26
chi1, err := conn2.Channel()                                       27
failOnError(err, "Failed␣to␣open␣a␣channel")                       28
chi2, err := conn3.Channel()                                       29
failOnError(err, "Failed␣to␣open␣a␣channel")                       30
err = cho.ExchangeDeclare("dispatch", "direct",                    31
    false, true, false, false, nil)                                32
failOnError(err, "Failed␣to␣declare␣an␣exchange")                  33
//resp                                                             34
queueResp, err := chi1.QueueDeclare("", false, true, true, false, nil) 35
failOnError(err, "Failed␣to␣declare␣a␣queue")                      36
err = chi1.QueueBind(queueResp.Name, "resp", "dispatch", false, nil) 37
failOnError(err, "Failed␣to␣bind␣a␣queue")                         38
respMsgs, err := chi1.Consume(queueResp.Name, "",                  39
    false, true, false, false, nil)                                40
failOnError(err, "Failed␣to␣register␣a␣consumer")                  41
//end                                                              42
queueEnd, err := chi2.QueueDeclare("", false, true, true, false, nil) 43
failOnError(err, "Failed␣to␣declare␣a␣queue")                      44
err = chi2.QueueBind(queueEnd.Name, "end", "dispatch", false, nil) 45
failOnError(err, "Failed␣to␣bind␣a␣queue")                         46
endMsgs, err := chi2.Consume(queueEnd.Name, "",                    47
    false, true, false, false, nil)                                48
failOnError(err, "Failed␣to␣register␣a␣consumer")                  49
////send args                                                      50
//start worker index 1                                             51
numWorkers := 10                                                   52
indexWorker := 1                                                   53
//start worker                                                     54
startArgP := &workerArg{                                           55
    WorkerType:          "startworker",                            56
    InputConfirmQueue: "null",                                     57
    Function:             "null",                                  58
}                                                                  59
startArgB, err := json.Marshal(startArgP)                          60
failOnError(err, "Failed␣to␣encode")                               61
err = cho.Publish("dispatch", "generator", false, false,           62
    amqp.Publishing{                                               63
        ContentType: "text/plain",                                 64
        Body:        startArgB,                                    65
    })                                                             66
failOnError(err, "Failed␣to␣publish␣a␣message")                    67
fmt.Println("Organizer␣Published:")                                68
fmt.Println(string(startArgB))                                     69
//block consume from queueResp                                     70
//mid and end workers                                              71
for d := range respMsgs {                                          72
    indexWorker++                                                  73
    //2~numWorkers                                                 74
    workerType := "midworker"                                      75
    function := "+2"                                               76
    if indexWorker == numWorkers {                                 77
        workerType = "endworker"                                   78
        function = "null"                                          79
    }                                                              80
    //publish args for mid worker                                  81
    midArgP := &workerArg{                                         82
        WorkerType:          workerType,                           83
```

```
         InputConfirmQueue: string(d.Body),                    84
         Function:             function,                       85
    }                                                          86
    midArgB, _ := json.Marshal(midArgP)                        87
    err = cho.Publish("dispatch", "generator", false, false,   88
        amqp.Publishing{                                       89
            ContentType: "text/plain",                         90
            Body:        midArgB,                              91
        })                                                     92
    failOnError(err, "Failed␣to␣publish␣a␣message")            93
    fmt.Println("Organizer␣Published:")                        94
    fmt.Println(string(midArgB))                               95
    d.Ack(false)                                               96
    //limit number                                            97
    if indexWorker == numWorkers {                             98
        break                                                 99
    }                                                          100
}                                                              101
//wait for the end message                                   102
for d := range endMsgs {                                      103
    d.Ack(false)                                               104
    break                                                     105
}                                                              106
//print the time                                             107
elapsed := time.Since(startTime)                             108
fmt.Println("Time:", elapsed)                                109
}                                                              110
func failOnError(err error, msg string) {                     111
    if err != nil {                                           112
        log.Fatalf("%s:␣%s", msg, err)                        113
    }                                                          114
}                                                              115
```

Listing 1.79. Distributed pipeline with worker generator, `organizer`

```
package main                                                  1
import (                                                      2
    "fmt"                                                     3
    "strconv"                                                 4
    "time"                                                    5
)                                                             6
func main() {                                                 7
    startTime := time.Now()                                   8
    for x := 0; x < 10; x++ {                                 9
        num := x                                              10
        time.Sleep(1000 * time.Millisecond)                  11
        for i := 0; i < 8; i++ {                             12
            num = num + 2                                     13
            time.Sleep(1000 * time.Millisecond)              14
        }                                                     15
        fmt.Println("number␣is:", strconv.Itoa(num))         16
        time.Sleep(1000 * time.Millisecond)                  17
    }                                                         18
    elapsed := time.Since(startTime)                          19
    fmt.Println("Time:", elapsed)                            20
}                                                             21
```

Listing 1.80. Distributed pipeline with worker generator, `sequential`

Here is the command to build the worker (it generates the `worker.exe`):

```
go build worker.go startWorker.go midWorker.go endWorker.go    1
```

Run the first generator, the output is:

```
go run generator.go                                              1
{startworker null null}                                          2
generated one worker                                             3
{midworker amq.gen-86pYPjSd2QSY5efSJjquZw +2}                    4
generated one worker                                             5
{midworker amq.gen-9kxyU5n_V2FLKoiqwJb6ew +2}                    6
generated one worker                                             7
{midworker amq.gen-p_sRRJky_SE4sPqxodY5MQ +2}                    8
generated one worker                                             9
{midworker amq.gen-aNnfj8wPheEcI__1D_uqUA +2}                   10
generated one worker                                            11
```

Run the second generator, the output is:

```
go run generator.go                                              1
{midworker amq.gen-rYOLDr7IWIfFee9I8v_Euw +2}                    2
generated one worker                                             3
{midworker amq.gen-ZJrwqf9I2RVb8J9EmFKprw +2}                    4
generated one worker                                             5
{midworker amq.gen-fzbT18IpiwuM8NW28o6GEQ +2}                    6
generated one worker                                             7
{midworker amq.gen-z3iFrZH5cNp2FLceJxwbOg +2}                    8
generated one worker                                             9
{endworker amq.gen-_bYXpjzTT5Y1PULzNHq9Hg null}                 10
generated one worker                                            11
```

Run the organizer, the output is:

```
go run organizer.go                                                                1
Organizer Published:                                                               2
{"WorkerType":"startworker","InputConfirmQueue":"null","Function":"null"}          3
Organizer Published:                                                               4
{"WorkerType":"midworker","InputConfirmQueue":                                     5
"amq.gen-rYOLDr7IWIfFee9I8v_Euw","Function":"+2"}                                   6
Organizer Published:                                                               7
{"WorkerType":"midworker","InputConfirmQueue":                                     8
"amq.gen-86pYPjSd2QSY5efSJjquZw","Function":"+2"}                                   9
Organizer Published:                                                              10
{"WorkerType":"midworker","InputConfirmQueue":                                    11
"amq.gen-ZJrwqf9I2RVb8J9EmFKprw","Function":"+2"}                                  12
Organizer Published:                                                              13
{"WorkerType":"midworker","InputConfirmQueue":                                    14
"amq.gen-9kxyU5n_V2FLKoiqwJb6ew","Function":"+2"}                                  15
Organizer Published:                                                              16
{"WorkerType":"midworker","InputConfirmQueue":                                    17
"amq.gen-fzbT18IpiwuM8NW28o6GEQ","Function":"+2"}                                  18
Organizer Published:                                                              19
{"WorkerType":"midworker","InputConfirmQueue":                                    20
"amq.gen-p_sRRJky_SE4sPqxodY5MQ","Function":"+2"}                                  21
Organizer Published:                                                              22
{"WorkerType":"midworker","InputConfirmQueue":                                    23
"amq.gen-z3iFrZH5cNp2FLceJxwbOg","Function":"+2"}                                  24
Organizer Published:                                                              25
{"WorkerType":"midworker","InputConfirmQueue":                                    26
"amq.gen-aNnfj8wPheEcI__1D_uqUA","Function":"+2"}                                  27
Organizer Published:                                                              28
{"WorkerType":"endworker","InputConfirmQueue":                                    29
"amq.gen-_bYXpjzTT5Y1PULzNHq9Hg","Function":"null"}                                30
Time: 11.5553831s                                                                 31
```

The output of the generated `startWorker`:

```
Worker published input confirm queue amq.gen-rYOLDr7IWIfFee9I8v_Euw    1
Start worker published 0                                               2
Start worker published 1                                               3
Start worker published 2                                               4
```

```
Start worker published 3                                    5
Start worker published 4                                    6
Start worker published 5                                    7
Start worker published 6                                    8
Start worker published 7                                    9
Start worker published 8                                   10
Start worker published 9                                   11
Start worker published END                                 12
Start worker finished                                      13
```

The output of the first generated `midWorker`:

```
Worker published input confirm queue amq.gen-86pYPjSd2QSY5efSJjquZw   1
Mid worker received 0 Published 2                                     2
Mid worker received 1 Published 3                                     3
Mid worker received 2 Published 4                                     4
Mid worker received 3 Published 5                                     5
Mid worker received 4 Published 6                                     6
Mid worker received 5 Published 7                                     7
Mid worker received 6 Published 8                                     8
Mid worker received 7 Published 9                                     9
Mid worker received 8 Published 10                                   10
Mid worker received 9 Published 11                                   11
Mid worker received END Published END                                12
Mid worker finished                                                  13
```

The output of the second generated `midWorker`:

```
Worker published input confirm queue amq.gen-ZJrwqf9I2RVb8J9EmFKprw   1
Mid worker received 2 Published 4                                     2
Mid worker received 3 Published 5                                     3
Mid worker received 4 Published 6                                     4
Mid worker received 5 Published 7                                     5
Mid worker received 6 Published 8                                     6
Mid worker received 7 Published 9                                     7
Mid worker received 8 Published 10                                    8
Mid worker received 9 Published 11                                    9
Mid worker received 10 Published 12                                  10
Mid worker received 11 Published 13                                  11
Mid worker received END Published END                                12
Mid worker finished                                                  13
```

The output of the third generated `midWorker`:

```
Worker published input confirm queue amq.gen-9kxyU5n_V2FLKoiqwJb6ew   1
Mid worker received 4 Published 6                                     2
Mid worker received 5 Published 7                                     3
Mid worker received 6 Published 8                                     4
Mid worker received 7 Published 9                                     5
Mid worker received 8 Published 10                                    6
Mid worker received 9 Published 11                                    7
Mid worker received 10 Published 12                                   8
Mid worker received 11 Published 13                                   9
Mid worker received 12 Published 14                                  10
Mid worker received 13 Published 15                                  11
Mid worker received END Published END                                12
Mid worker finished                                                  13
```

The output of the fourth generated `midWorker`:

```
Worker published input confirm queue amq.gen-fzbT18IpiwuM8NW28o6GEQ   1
Mid worker received 6 Published 8                                     2
Mid worker received 7 Published 9                                     3
Mid worker received 8 Published 10                                    4
Mid worker received 9 Published 11                                    5
Mid worker received 10 Published 12                                   6
Mid worker received 11 Published 13                                   7
```

```
Mid worker received 12 Published 14                                    8
Mid worker received 13 Published 15                                    9
Mid worker received 14 Published 16                                    10
Mid worker received 15 Published 17                                    11
Mid worker received END Published END                                  12
Mid worker finished                                                    13
```

The output of the fifth generated `midWorker`:

```
Worker published input confirm queue amq.gen-p_sRRJky_SE4sPqxodY5MQ     1
Mid worker received 8 Published 10                                      2
Mid worker received 9 Published 11                                      3
Mid worker received 10 Published 12                                     4
Mid worker received 11 Published 13                                     5
Mid worker received 12 Published 14                                     6
Mid worker received 13 Published 15                                     7
Mid worker received 14 Published 16                                     8
Mid worker received 15 Published 17                                     9
Mid worker received 16 Published 18                                     10
Mid worker received 17 Published 19                                     11
Mid worker received END Published END                                   12
Mid worker finished                                                     13
```

The output of the sixth generated `midWorker`:

```
Worker published input confirm queue amq.gen-z3iFrZH5cNp2FLceJxwb0g     1
Mid worker received 10 Published 12                                     2
Mid worker received 11 Published 13                                     3
Mid worker received 12 Published 14                                     4
Mid worker received 13 Published 15                                     5
Mid worker received 14 Published 16                                     6
Mid worker received 15 Published 17                                     7
Mid worker received 16 Published 18                                     8
Mid worker received 17 Published 19                                     9
Mid worker received 18 Published 20                                     10
Mid worker received 19 Published 21                                     11
Mid worker received END Published END                                   12
Mid worker finished                                                     13
```

The output of the seventh generated `midWorker`:

```
Worker published input confirm queue amq.gen-aNnfj8wPheEcI__1D_uqUA     1
Mid worker received 12 Published 14                                     2
Mid worker received 13 Published 15                                     3
Mid worker received 14 Published 16                                     4
Mid worker received 15 Published 17                                     5
Mid worker received 16 Published 18                                     6
Mid worker received 17 Published 19                                     7
Mid worker received 18 Published 20                                     8
Mid worker received 19 Published 21                                     9
Mid worker received 20 Published 22                                     10
Mid worker received 21 Published 23                                     11
Mid worker received END Published END                                   12
Mid worker finished                                                     13
```

The output of the eighth generated `midWorker`:

```
Worker published input confirm queue amq.gen-_bYXpjzTT5Y1PULzNHq9Hg     1
Mid worker received 14 Published 16                                     2
Mid worker received 15 Published 17                                     3
Mid worker received 16 Published 18                                     4
Mid worker received 17 Published 19                                     5
Mid worker received 18 Published 20                                     6
Mid worker received 19 Published 21                                     7
Mid worker received 20 Published 22                                     8
Mid worker received 21 Published 23                                     9
Mid worker received 22 Published 24                                     10
```

```
Mid worker received 23 Published 25                                      11
Mid worker received END Published END                                    12
Mid worker finished                                                      13
```

The output of the generated `endWorker`:

```
End worker received 16                                                    1
End worker received 17                                                    2
End worker received 18                                                    3
End worker received 19                                                    4
End worker received 20                                                    5
End worker received 21                                                    6
End worker received 22                                                    7
End worker received 23                                                    8
End worker received 24                                                    9
End worker received 25                                                   10
End worker received END                                                  11
End worker Published to dispather: END                                   12
End worker finished                                                      13
```

The output of the sequential version of the program:

```
go run sequential.go                                                      1
number is: 16                                                             2
number is: 17                                                             3
number is: 18                                                             4
number is: 19                                                             5
number is: 20                                                             6
number is: 21                                                             7
number is: 22                                                             8
number is: 23                                                             9
number is: 24                                                            10
number is: 25                                                            11
Time: 1m40.9130261s                                                      12
```

A.7   Distributed Divide and Conquer

The explanation of this example is in Subsect. 5.7.

```
package main                                                              1
import (                                                                  2
    "encoding/json"                                                       3
    "fmt"                                                                 4
    "log"                                                                 5
    "os"                                                                  6
    "sort"                                                                7
    "github.com/streadway/amqp"                                          8
)                                                                         9
type workerArg struct {                                                  10
    OutputKey  string                                                    11
    ConfirmKey string                                                    12
}                                                                         13
func main() {                                                            14
    //command line args                                                 15
    outputKey := os.Args[1]                                             16
    confirmKey := os.Args[2]                                            17
    conn1, err := amqp.Dial("amqp://guest:guest@localhost:5672/")      18
    failOnError(err, "Failed to connect to RabbitMQ")                   19
    defer conn1.Close()                                                 20
    conn2, err := amqp.Dial("amqp://guest:guest@localhost:5672/")      21
    failOnError(err, "Failed to connect to RabbitMQ")                   22
    defer conn2.Close()                                                 23
    conn3, err := amqp.Dial("amqp://guest:guest@localhost:5672/")      24
    failOnError(err, "Failed to connect to RabbitMQ")                   25
```

```
defer conn3.Close()                                                    26
choc, err := conn1.Channel()                                           27
failOnError(err, "Failed to open a channel")                           28
chor, err := conn2.Channel()                                           29
failOnError(err, "Failed to open a channel")                           30
chi, err := conn3.Channel()                                            31
failOnError(err, "Failed to open a channel")                           32
exchangeName := "conquer"                                              33
err = chi.ExchangeDeclare(exchangeName,"direct",                       34
    false,true,false,false,nil)                                        35
failOnError(err, "Failed to declare an exchange")                      36
queueIn, err := chi.QueueDeclare("",false,true,true,false,nil)         37
failOnError(err, "Failed to declare a queue")                          38
err = chi.QueueBind(queueIn.Name,queueIn.Name,                         39
    exchangeName,false,nil)                                            40
failOnError(err, "Failed to bind a queue")                             41
inputMsgs, err := chi.Consume(queueIn.Name,"",                         42
    false,false,false,false,nil)                                       43
failOnError(err, "Failed to register a consumer")                      44
//send confirm                                                         45
msg := queueIn.Name                                                    46
err = choc.Publish(exchangeName,confirmKey,                            47
    false,false,                                                       48
    amqp.Publishing{                                                   49
        ContentType: "text/plain",                                     50
        Body:        []byte(msg),                                      51
    })                                                                 52
failOnError(err, "Failed to publish a message")                        53
fmt.Println("Published confirm:", msg)                                 54
//receive tasks                                                        55
task := <-inputMsgs                                                    56
list := []int{}                                                        57
json.Unmarshal(task.Body, &list)                                       58
task.Ack(false)                                                        59
fmt.Println("Received:", list)                                         60
if length := len(list); length <= 4 {                                  61
    //do the sort                                                      62
    sort.Ints(list)                                                    63
    //publish with outputKey                                           64
    listB, err := json.Marshal(list)                                   65
    failOnError(err, "Failed to encode")                               66
    err = chor.Publish(exchangeName,outputKey,                         67
        false,false,                                                   68
        amqp.Publishing{                                               69
            ContentType: "text/plain",                                 70
            Body:        listB,                                        71
        })                                                             72
    failOnError(err, "Failed to publish a message")                    73
    fmt.Println("Published:", list)                                    74
} else {                                                               75
    //devide                                                           76
    first := list[0]                                                   77
    res := list[1:]                                                    78
    leftList := Filter(res,                                            79
        func(i int) bool { return i < first })                         80
    rightList := Filter(res,                                           81
        func(i int) bool { return i >= first })                        82
    //new connections and channels                                    83
    conn4, err := amqp.Dial("amqp://guest:guest@localhost:5672/")      84
    failOnError(err, "Failed to connect to RabbitMQ")                  85
    defer conn4.Close()                                                86
    conn5, err := amqp.Dial("amqp://guest:guest@localhost:5672/")      87
    failOnError(err, "Failed to connect to RabbitMQ")                  88
    defer conn5.Close()                                                89
    conn6, err := amqp.Dial("amqp://guest:guest@localhost:5672/")      90
    failOnError(err, "Failed to connect to RabbitMQ")                  91
    defer conn6.Close()                                                92
    conn7, err := amqp.Dial("amqp://guest:guest@localhost:5672/")      93
```

```
failOnError(err, "Failed␣to␣connect␣to␣RabbitMQ")                    94
defer conn7.Close()                                                  95
conn8, err := amqp.Dial("amqp://guest:guest@localhost:5672/")        96
failOnError(err, "Failed␣to␣connect␣to␣RabbitMQ")                    97
defer conn8.Close()                                                  98
conn9, err := amqp.Dial("amqp://guest:guest@localhost:5672/")        99
failOnError(err, "Failed␣to␣connect␣to␣RabbitMQ")                   100
defer conn9.Close()                                                 101
chilc, err := conn4.Channel()                                      102
failOnError(err, "Failed␣to␣open␣a␣channel")                       103
chilr, err := conn5.Channel()                                      104
failOnError(err, "Failed␣to␣open␣a␣channel")                       105
chol, err := conn6.Channel()                                       106
failOnError(err, "Failed␣to␣open␣a␣channel")                       107
chirc, err := conn7.Channel()                                      108
failOnError(err, "Failed␣to␣open␣a␣channel")                       109
chirr, err := conn8.Channel()                                      110
failOnError(err, "Failed␣to␣open␣a␣channel")                       111
chor, err := conn9.Channel()                                       112
failOnError(err, "Failed␣to␣open␣a␣channel")                       113
////bind queue and send args                                       114
//left                                                             115
queueLeftConfirm, err := chilc.QueueDeclare("",                    116
    false,true,true,false,nil)                                     117
failOnError(err, "Failed␣to␣declare␣a␣queue")                      118
err = chilc.QueueBind(queueLeftConfirm.Name,                       119
    queueLeftConfirm.Name, exchangeName,false,nil)                 120
failOnError(err, "Failed␣to␣bind␣a␣queue")                         121
leftConfirmMsgs, err := chilc.Consume(queueLeftConfirm.Name,       122
    "",false,true,false,false,nil)                                 123
failOnError(err, "Failed␣to␣register␣a␣consumer")                  124
queueLeftResult, err := chilr.QueueDeclare("",                     125
    false,true,true,false,nil)                                     126
failOnError(err, "Failed␣to␣declare␣a␣queue")                      127
err = chilr.QueueBind(queueLeftResult.Name,                        128
    queueLeftResult.Name,exchangeName, false,nil)                  129
failOnError(err, "Failed␣to␣bind␣a␣queue")                         130
leftResultMsgs, err := chilr.Consume(queueLeftResult.Name,         131
    "",false,false,false,false,nil)                                132
failOnError(err, "Failed␣to␣register␣a␣consumer")                  133
//right                                                            134
queueRightConfirm, err := chirc.QueueDeclare("",                   135
    false,true,true,false, nil)                                    136
failOnError(err, "Failed␣to␣declare␣a␣queue")                      137
err = chirc.QueueBind(queueRightConfirm.Name,                      138
    queueRightConfirm.Name,exchangeName,false,nil)                 139
failOnError(err, "Failed␣to␣bind␣a␣queue")                         140
rightConfirmMsgs, err := chirc.Consume(                            141
    queueRightConfirm.Name,"",false,true,false,false,nil)          142
failOnError(err, "Failed␣to␣register␣a␣consumer")                  143
queueRightResult, err := chirr.QueueDeclare("",                    144
    false,true,true,false,nil)                                     145
failOnError(err, "Failed␣to␣declare␣a␣queue")                      146
err = chirr.QueueBind(queueRightResult.Name,                       147
    queueRightResult.Name,exchangeName,false,nil)                  148
failOnError(err, "Failed␣to␣bind␣a␣queue")                         149
rightResultMsgs, err := chirr.Consume(                             150
    queueRightResult.Name,"",false,false,false,false,nil)          151
failOnError(err, "Failed␣to␣register␣a␣consumer")                  152
//send args                                                       153
argsLeftP := &workerArg{                                           154
    OutputKey:  queueLeftResult.Name,                              155
    ConfirmKey: queueLeftConfirm.Name,                             156
}                                                                  157
argsLeftB, err := json.Marshal(argsLeftP)                          158
failOnError(err, "Failed␣to␣encode")                              159
err = chol.Publish(exchangeName,"generator",                       160
    false, false,                                                  161
```

```
        amqp.Publishing{                                              162
            ContentType: "text/plain",                                163
            Body:        argsLeftB,                                    164
        })                                                            165
    failOnError(err, "Failed␣to␣publish␣a␣message")                    166
    fmt.Println("Published", string(argsLeftB))                       167
    argsRightP := &workerArg{                                         168
        OutputKey:   queueRightResult.Name,                           169
        ConfirmKey: queueRightConfirm.Name,                           170
    }                                                                 171
    argsRightB, err := json.Marshal(argsRightP)                       172
    failOnError(err, "Failed␣to␣encode")                              173
    err = chor.Publish(exchangeName,"generator",                      174
        false,false,                                                  175
        amqp.Publishing{                                              176
            ContentType: "text/plain",                                177
            Body:        argsRightB,                                   178
        })                                                            179
    failOnError(err, "Failed␣to␣publish␣a␣message")                   180
    fmt.Println("Published", string(argsRightB))                      181
    //receive confirm and send task                                   182
    leftConfirm := <-leftConfirmMsgs                                  183
    leftTargetKey := string(leftConfirm.Body)                         184
    leftConfirm.Ack(false)                                            185
    rightConfirm := <-rightConfirmMsgs                                186
    rightTargetKey := string(rightConfirm.Body)                       187
    rightConfirm.Ack(false)                                           188
    leftListB, err := json.Marshal(leftList)                          189
    failOnError(err, "Failed␣to␣encode")                              190
    err = chol.Publish(exchangeName,leftTargetKey,                    191
        false,false,                                                  192
        amqp.Publishing{                                              193
            ContentType: "text/plain",                                194
            Body:        leftListB,                                    195
        })                                                            196
    failOnError(err, "Failed␣to␣publish␣a␣message")                   197
    fmt.Println("Published:", leftList)                               198
    rightListB, err := json.Marshal(rightList)                        199
    failOnError(err, "Failed␣to␣encode")                              200
    err = chor.Publish(exchangeName,rightTargetKey,                   201
        false,false,                                                  202
        amqp.Publishing{                                              203
            ContentType: "text/plain",                                204
            Body:        rightListB,                                   205
        })                                                            206
    failOnError(err, "Failed␣to␣publish␣a␣message")                   207
    fmt.Println("Published:", rightList)                              208
    //receive left and right result and publish final result          209
    leftResultMsg := <-leftResultMsgs                                 210
    listLeftResult := []int{}                                         211
    json.Unmarshal(leftResultMsg.Body, &listLeftResult)               212
    leftResultMsg.Ack(false)                                          213
    fmt.Println("Left␣result:", listLeftResult)                       214
    rightResultMsg := <-rightResultMsgs                               215
    listRightResult := []int{}                                        216
    json.Unmarshal(rightResultMsg.Body, &listRightResult)             217
    rightResultMsg.Ack(false)                                         218
    fmt.Println("Right␣result:", listRightResult)                     219
    //final result                                                    220
    finalResult := append(listLeftResult, first)                      221
    finalResult = append(finalResult, listRightResult...)             222
    finalResultB, err := json.Marshal(finalResult)                    223
    failOnError(err, "Failed␣to␣encode")                              224
    err = chor.Publish(exchangeName,outputKey,                        225
        false,false,                                                  226
        amqp.Publishing{                                              227
            ContentType: "text/plain",                                228
            Body:        finalResultB,                                 229
```

```
        })                                                    230
        failOnError(err, "Failed␣to␣publish␣a␣message")        231
        fmt.Println("Published:",finalResult)                 232
    }                                                         233
    forever := make(chan bool)                               234
    <-forever                                                235
}                                                            236
func Filter(s []int, fn func(int) bool) []int {             237
    var p []int // == nil                                   238
    for _, i := range s {                                   239
        if fn(i) {                                          240
            p = append(p, i)                                241
        }                                                   242
    }                                                       243
    return p                                                244
}                                                            245
func failOnError(err error, msg string) {                   246
    if err != nil {                                         247
        log.Fatalf("%s:␣%s", msg, err)                      248
    }                                                       249
}                                                            250
```

Listing 1.81. Distributed Divide and Conquer example version 1, `worker`

```
package main                                                 1
import (                                                    2
    "encoding/json"                                         3
    "fmt"                                                   4
    "log"                                                   5
    "os/exec"                                               6
    "github.com/streadway/amqp"                             7
)                                                           8
type workerArg struct {                                     9
    OutputKey   string                                     10
    ConfirmKey  string                                     11
}                                                          12
func main() {                                              13
    conn, err := amqp.Dial("amqp://guest:guest@localhost:5672/")  14
    failOnError(err, "Failed␣to␣connect␣to␣RabbitMQ")     15
    defer conn.Close()                                    16
    ch, err := conn.Channel()                             17
    failOnError(err, "Failed␣to␣open␣a␣channel")          18
    err = ch.ExchangeDeclare("conquer", "direct",         19
        true,false,false,false,nil)                       20
    failOnError(err, "Failed␣to␣declare␣an␣exchange")     21
    queueArg, err := ch.QueueDeclare("generator",         22
        false,true,false,false,nil)                       23
    failOnError(err, "Failed␣to␣declare␣a␣queue")         24
    err = ch.QueueBind(queueArg.Name,"generator","conquer",  25
        false,nil)                                        26
    failOnError(err, "Failed␣to␣bind␣a␣queue")            27
    argMsgs, err := ch.Consume(queueArg.Name,"",          28
        false,false,false,false,nil)                      29
    failOnError(err, "Failed␣to␣register␣a␣consumer")     30
    go func() {                                            31
        for d := range argMsgs {                           32
            arg := workerArg{}                             33
            json.Unmarshal(d.Body, &arg)                   34
            fmt.Println(arg)                               35
            cmd := exec.Command("cmd", "/C", "start", "go", "run",  36
                "../worker.go", arg.OutputKey,arg.ConfirmKey)  37
            err = cmd.Run()                                38
            failOnError(err, "Failed␣to␣generate␣worker")  39
            fmt.Println("Generated␣one␣worker")            40
            d.Ack(false)                                   41
        }                                                 42
    }()                                                   43
```

```
forever := make(chan bool)                              44
<-forever                                               45
}                                                           46
func failOnError(err error, msg string) {                  47
    if err != nil {                                       48
        log.Fatalf("%s:␣%s", msg, err)                    49
    }                                                       50
}                                                           51
```

Listing 1.82. Distributed Divide and Conquer example version 1, `generator`

```
package main                                            1
import (                                                2
    "encoding/json"                                     3
    "fmt"                                               4
    "log"                                               5
    "time"                                              6
    "github.com/streadway/amqp"                         7
)                                                       8
type workerArg struct {                                 9
    OutputKey  string                                   10
    ConfirmKey string                                   11
}                                                           12
func main() {                                            13
    startTime := time.Now()                             14
    //list := []int{3, 4, 7, 2, 5, 7, 8, 4, 6, 8, 6, 3, 66, 432,   15
    //63, 6, 7, 8, 4, 65, 34, 4, 36}                    16
    list := []int{5,7,3,4,1,9,6,2,8}                    17
    conn1, err := amqp.Dial("amqp://guest:guest@localhost:5672/")   18
    failOnError(err, "Failed␣to␣connect␣to␣RabbitMQ")   19
    defer conn1.Close()                                 20
    conn2, err := amqp.Dial("amqp://guest:guest@localhost:5672/")   21
    failOnError(err, "Failed␣to␣connect␣to␣RabbitMQ")   22
    defer conn2.Close()                                 23
    conn3, err := amqp.Dial("amqp://guest:guest@localhost:5672/")   24
    failOnError(err, "Failed␣to␣connect␣to␣RabbitMQ")   25
    defer conn3.Close()                                 26
    cho, err := conn1.Channel()                         27
    failOnError(err, "Failed␣to␣open␣a␣channel")        28
    chic, err := conn2.Channel()                        29
    failOnError(err, "Failed␣to␣open␣a␣channel")        30
    chir, err := conn3.Channel()                        31
    failOnError(err, "Failed␣to␣open␣a␣channel")        32
    exchangeName := "conquer"                           33
    err = cho.ExchangeDeclare(exchangeName,"direct",    34
        false,true,false,false,nil)                     35
    failOnError(err, "Failed␣to␣declare␣an␣exchange")   36
    queueForConfirm, err := chic.QueueDeclare("",       37
        false,true,true,false,nil)                      38
    failOnError(err, "Failed␣to␣declare␣a␣queue")       39
    err = chic.QueueBind(queueForConfirm.Name,          40
    queueForConfirm.Name,exchangeName,false,nil)        41
    failOnError(err, "Failed␣to␣bind␣a␣queue")          42
    confirmMsgs, err := chic.Consume(queueForConfirm.Name,   43
        "",false,true,false,false,nil)                  44
    failOnError(err, "Failed␣to␣register␣a␣consumer")   45
    queueForResult, err := chir.QueueDeclare("",        46
        false,true,true,false,nil)                      47
    failOnError(err, "Failed␣to␣declare␣a␣queue")       48
    err = chir.QueueBind(queueForResult.Name,           49
        queueForResult.Name,exchangeName,false,nil)     50
    failOnError(err, "Failed␣to␣bind␣a␣queue")          51
    resultMsgs, err := chir.Consume(queueForResult.Name,"",   52
        false,false,false,false,nil)                    53
    failOnError(err, "Failed␣to␣register␣a␣consumer")   54
    //send args to generate worker                      55
    argsP := &workerArg{                                56
```

```
        OutputKey:  queueForResult.Name,                    57
        ConfirmKey: queueForConfirm.Name,                   58
    }                                                       59
    argsB, err := json.Marshal(argsP)                       60
    failOnError(err, "Failed␣to␣encode")                    61
    err = cho.Publish(exchangeName,"generator",             62
        false,false,                                        63
        amqp.Publishing{                                    64
            ContentType: "text/plain",                      65
            Body:        argsB,                             66
        })                                                  67
    failOnError(err, "Failed␣to␣publish␣a␣message")         68
    fmt.Println("starter␣Published", string(argsB))         69
    confirm := <-confirmMsgs                                70
    targetKey := string(confirm.Body)                       71
    confirm.Ack(false)                                      72
    listB, err := json.Marshal(list)                        73
    failOnError(err, "Failed␣to␣encode")                    74
    msg := listB                                            75
    err = cho.Publish(exchangeName,targetKey,               76
        false,false,                                        77
        amqp.Publishing{                                    78
            ContentType: "text/plain",                      79
            Body:        msg,                               80
        })                                                  81
    failOnError(err, "Failed␣to␣publish␣a␣message")         82
    fmt.Println("Published:", list)                         83
    result := []int{}                                       84
    resultMsg := <-resultMsgs                               85
    json.Unmarshal(resultMsg.Body, &result)                 86
    fmt.Println("result:", result)                          87
    resultMsg.Ack(false)                                    88
    elapsed := time.Since(startTime)                        89
    fmt.Println("Time:␣", elapsed)                          90
}                                                           91
func failOnError(err error, msg string) {                   92
    if err != nil {                                         93
        log.Fatalf("%s:␣%s", msg, err)                      94
    }                                                       95
}                                                           96
```

Listing 1.83. Distributed Divide and Conquer example version 1, `starter`

Run the first generator, the output is:

```
go run generator.go                                                             1
{amq.gen-20oKBjk7phtISs9KxE_baw amq.gen-qKGRCL_OfaQXdxhHqKbHPg}                 2
Generated one worker                                                            3
{amq.gen-pJ-11vjYRdM_Iir3Mx_TUA amq.gen-AdkocSeFGiFlF3YTOCxm6g}                 4
Generated one worker                                                            5
```

Run the second generator, the output is:

```
go run generator.go                                                             1
{amq.gen-9-L6aMbuVLGkvZxEPRA6iw amq.gen-vl_37LPycPXJy-91rQSevg}                 2
Generated one worker                                                            3
```

Run the `Starter`, the output is:

```
go run starter.go                                                               1
starter Published                                                               2
{"OutputKey":"amq.gen-20oKBjk7phtISs9KxE_baw",                                  3
"ConfirmKey":"amq.gen-qKGRCL_OfaQXdxhHqKbHPg"}                                  4
Published: [5 7 3 4 1 9 6 2 8]                                                   5
result: [1 2 3 4 5 6 7 8 9]                                                      6
Time:  1.3748538s                                                               7
```

The output of the first generated worker:

```
Published confirm: amq.gen-bym_OiYfBIwttUy763zNbQ              1
Received: [5 7 3 4 1 9 6 2 8]                                  2
Published                                                     3
{"OutputKey":"amq.gen-9-L6aMbuVLGkvZxEPRA6iw",                4
"ConfirmKey":"amq.gen-vl_37LPycPXJy-91rQSevg"}                5
Published                                                     6
{"OutputKey":"amq.gen-pJ-11vjYRdM_Iir3Mx_TUA",                7
"ConfirmKey":"amq.gen-AdkocSeFGiFlF3YTOCxm6g"}                8
Published: [3 4 1 2]                                          9
Published: [7 9 6 8]                                          10
Left result: [1 2 3 4]                                        11
Right result: [6 7 8 9]                                       12
Result: [1 2 3 4 5 6 7 8 9]                                   13
```

The output of the second generated worker:

```
Published confirm: amq.gen-d-hdAsiGHNJEs--rTagf1Q             1
Received: [3 4 1 2]                                           2
Published: [1 2 3 4]                                          3
```

The output of the third generated worker:

```
Published confirm: amq.gen-gOQmBFcBWYGVnlm3HEDlng             1
Received: [7 9 6 8]                                           2
Published: [6 7 8 9]                                          3
```

B   Task for Readers

Implement the merge sort version of the divide and conquer problem presented in the Subsect. 5.7.

Solution. As shown in Listing 1.84 from line 75 to line 78, the worker divides the list in a different manner from the quick sort version. As shown from line 207 to line 229, the way to get the final result from the results of the children workers is different. We used the `merge` method defined from line 234 to line 255.

```
package main                                                  1
import (                                                      2
    "encoding/json"                                           3
    "fmt"                                                     4
    "log"                                                     5
    "os"                                                      6
    "sort"                                                    7
    "github.com/streadway/amqp"                               8
)                                                             9
type workerArg struct {                                       10
    OutputKey  string                                         11
    ConfirmKey string                                         12
}                                                             13
func main() {                                                 14
    outputKey := os.Args[1]                                   15
    confirmKey := os.Args[2]                                  16
    conn1, err := amqp.Dial("amqp://guest:guest@localhost:5672/")  17
    failOnError(err, "Failed to connect to RabbitMQ")         18
    defer conn1.Close()                                       19
    conn2, err := amqp.Dial("amqp://guest:guest@localhost:5672/")  20
```

```go
failOnError(err, "Failed␣to␣connect␣to␣RabbitMQ")              21
defer conn2.Close()                                            22
conn3, err := amqp.Dial("amqp://guest:guest@localhost:5672/")  23
failOnError(err, "Failed␣to␣connect␣to␣RabbitMQ")              24
defer conn3.Close()                                            25
choc, err := conn1.Channel()                                   26
failOnError(err, "Failed␣to␣open␣a␣channel")                   27
chor, err := conn2.Channel()                                   28
failOnError(err, "Failed␣to␣open␣a␣channel")                   29
chi, err := conn3.Channel()                                    30
failOnError(err, "Failed␣to␣open␣a␣channel")                   31
exchangeName := "conquer"                                      32
err = chi.ExchangeDeclare(exchangeName,"direct",               33
    false,true,false,false,nil)                                34
failOnError(err, "Failed␣to␣declare␣an␣exchange")              35
queueIn, err := chi.QueueDeclare("",false,true,true,false,nil) 36
failOnError(err, "Failed␣to␣declare␣a␣queue")                  37
err = chi.QueueBind(queueIn.Name,                              38
    queueIn.Name,exchangeName,false,nil)                       39
failOnError(err, "Failed␣to␣bind␣a␣queue")                     40
inputMsgs, err := chi.Consume(queueIn.Name,"",                 41
    false,false,false,false,nil)                               42
failOnError(err, "Failed␣to␣register␣a␣consumer")              43
//send confirm                                                 44
msg := queueIn.Name                                            45
err = choc.Publish(exchangeName,confirmKey,                    46
    false,false,                                               47
    amqp.Publishing{                                           48
        ContentType: "text/plain",                             49
        Body:        []byte(msg),                              50
    })                                                         51
failOnError(err, "Failed␣to␣publish␣a␣message")                52
fmt.Println("Published␣confirm:␣", msg)                        53
//receive tasks                                                54
task := <-inputMsgs                                            55
list := []int{}                                                56
json.Unmarshal(task.Body, &list)                               57
task.Ack(false)                                                58
fmt.Println("Received:", list)                                 59
if length := len(list); length <= 4 {                          60
    //do the sort                                              61
    sort.Ints(list)                                            62
    //publish with outputKey                                   63
    listB, err := json.Marshal(list)                           64
    failOnError(err, "Failed␣to␣encode")                       65
    err = chor.Publish(exchangeName,outputKey,                 66
        false,false,                                           67
        amqp.Publishing{                                       68
            ContentType: "text/plain",                         69
            Body:        listB,                                70
        })                                                     71
    failOnError(err, "Failed␣to␣publish␣a␣message")            72
    fmt.Println("Published:", list)                            73
} else {                                                       74
    //devide                                                   75
    middle := int(len(list) / 2)                               76
    leftList := list[0:middle]                                 77
    rightList := list[middle:]                                 78
    //new channels                                             79
    conn4, err := amqp.Dial("amqp://guest:guest@localhost:5672/")  80
    failOnError(err, "Failed␣to␣connect␣to␣RabbitMQ")          81
    defer conn4.Close()                                        82
    conn5, err := amqp.Dial("amqp://guest:guest@localhost:5672/")  83
    failOnError(err, "Failed␣to␣connect␣to␣RabbitMQ")          84
    defer conn5.Close()                                        85
    conn6, err := amqp.Dial("amqp://guest:guest@localhost:5672/")  86
    failOnError(err, "Failed␣to␣connect␣to␣RabbitMQ")          87
    defer conn6.Close()                                        88
```

```
conn7, err := amqp.Dial("amqp://guest:guest@localhost:5672/")    89
failOnError(err, "Failed to connect to RabbitMQ")                90
defer conn7.Close()                                              91
conn8, err := amqp.Dial("amqp://guest:guest@localhost:5672/")    92
failOnError(err, "Failed to connect to RabbitMQ")                93
defer conn8.Close()                                              94
conn9, err := amqp.Dial("amqp://guest:guest@localhost:5672/")    95
failOnError(err, "Failed to connect to RabbitMQ")                96
defer conn9.Close()                                              97
chilc, err := conn4.Channel()                                    98
failOnError(err, "Failed to open a channel")                     99
chilr, err := conn5.Channel()                                    100
failOnError(err, "Failed to open a channel")                     101
chol, err := conn6.Channel()                                     102
failOnError(err, "Failed to open a channel")                     103
chirc, err := conn7.Channel()                                    104
failOnError(err, "Failed to open a channel")                     105
chirr, err := conn8.Channel()                                    106
failOnError(err, "Failed to open a channel")                     107
chor, err := conn9.Channel()                                     108
failOnError(err, "Failed to open a channel")                     109
////bind queue and send args                                     110
//left                                                           111
queueLeftConfirm, err := chilc.QueueDeclare("",                  112
    false,true,true,false,nil)                                   113
failOnError(err, "Failed to declare a queue")                    114
err = chilc.QueueBind(queueLeftConfirm.Name,                     115
    queueLeftConfirm.Name,exchangeName,false,nil)                116
failOnError(err, "Failed to bind a queue")                       117
leftConfirmMsgs, err := chilc.Consume(                           118
    queueLeftConfirm.Name,"",false,true,false,false,nil)         119
failOnError(err, "Failed to register a consumer")                120
queueLeftResult, err := chilr.QueueDeclare("",                   121
    false,true,true,false,nil)                                   122
failOnError(err, "Failed to declare a queue")                    123
err = chilr.QueueBind(queueLeftResult.Name,                      124
    queueLeftResult.Name,exchangeName,false,nil)                 125
failOnError(err, "Failed to bind a queue")                       126
leftResultMsgs, err := chilr.Consume(queueLeftResult.Name,       127
    "",false,false,false,false,nil)                              128
failOnError(err, "Failed to register a consumer")                129
//right                                                          130
queueRightConfirm, err := chirc.QueueDeclare("",                 131
    false,true,true,false,nil)                                   132
failOnError(err, "Failed to declare a queue")                    133
err = chirc.QueueBind(queueRightConfirm.Name,                    134
    queueRightConfirm.Name,exchangeName,false,nil)               135
failOnError(err, "Failed to bind a queue")                       136
rightConfirmMsgs, err := chirc.Consume(queueRightConfirm.Name,   137
    "",false,true,false,false,nil)                               138
failOnError(err, "Failed to register a consumer")                139
queueRightResult, err := chirr.QueueDeclare("",                  140
    false,true,true,false, nil)                                  141
failOnError(err, "Failed to declare a queue")                    142
err = chirr.QueueBind(queueRightResult.Name,                     143
    queueRightResult.Name,exchangeName,false,nil)                144
failOnError(err, "Failed to bind a queue")                       145
rightResultMsgs, err := chirr.Consume(queueRightResult.Name,     146
    "",false,false,false,false,nil)                              147
failOnError(err, "Failed to register a consumer")                148
//send args                                                      149
argsLeftP := &workerArg{                                         150
    OutputKey:  queueLeftResult.Name,                            151
    ConfirmKey: queueLeftConfirm.Name,                           152
}                                                                153
argsLeftB, err := json.Marshal(argsLeftP)                        154
failOnError(err, "Failed to encode")                             155
err = chol.Publish(exchangeName,"generator",                     156
```

```
                false,false,                                            157
                amqp.Publishing{                                        158
                    ContentType: "text/plain",                         159
                    Body:        argsLeftB,                            160
                })                                                      161
    failOnError(err, "Failed␣to␣publish␣a␣message")                    162
    fmt.Println("Published:", string(argsLeftB))                       163
    argsRightP := &workerArg{                                          164
        OutputKey:  queueRightResult.Name,                             165
        ConfirmKey: queueRightConfirm.Name,                            166
    }                                                                  167
    argsRightB, err := json.Marshal(argsRightP)                        168
    failOnError(err, "Failed␣to␣encode")                              169
    err = chor.Publish(exchangeName,"generator",                       170
        false,false,                                                   171
        amqp.Publishing{                                               172
            ContentType: "text/plain",                                 173
            Body:        argsRightB,                                   174
        })                                                             175
    failOnError(err, "Failed␣to␣publish␣a␣message")                   176
    fmt.Println("Published:", string(argsRightB))                      177
                                                                       178
    //receive confirm and send task                                    179
    leftConfirm := <-leftConfirmMsgs                                   180
    leftTargetKey := string(leftConfirm.Body)                          181
    leftConfirm.Ack(false)                                             182
    rightConfirm := <-rightConfirmMsgs                                 183
    rightTargetKey := string(rightConfirm.Body)                        184
    rightConfirm.Ack(false)                                            185
                                                                       186
    leftListB, err := json.Marshal(leftList)                           187
    failOnError(err, "Failed␣to␣encode")                              188
    err = chol.Publish(exchangeName,leftTargetKey,                     189
        false,false,                                                   190
        amqp.Publishing{                                               191
            ContentType: "text/plain",                                 192
            Body:        leftListB,                                    193
        })                                                             194
    failOnError(err, "Failed␣to␣publish␣a␣message")                   195
    fmt.Println("Published:", leftList)                                196
    rightListB, err := json.Marshal(rightList)                         197
    failOnError(err, "Failed␣to␣encode")                              198
    err = chor.Publish(exchangeName,rightTargetKey,                    199
        false,false,                                                   200
        amqp.Publishing{                                               201
            ContentType: "text/plain",                                 202
            Body:        rightListB,                                   203
        })                                                             204
    failOnError(err, "Failed␣to␣publish␣a␣message")                   205
    fmt.Println("Published:", rightList)                               206
    //receive left and right result and publish final result          207
    leftResultMsg := <-leftResultMsgs                                  208
    listLeftResult := []int{}                                          209
    json.Unmarshal(leftResultMsg.Body, &listLeftResult)               210
    leftResultMsg.Ack(false)                                           211
    fmt.Println("Left␣result:", listLeftResult)                       212
    rightResultMsg := <-rightResultMsgs                                213
    listRightResult := []int{}                                         214
    json.Unmarshal(rightResultMsg.Body, &listRightResult)             215
    rightResultMsg.Ack(false)                                          216
    fmt.Println("Right␣result:", listRightResult)                     217
    //final result                                                     218
    finalResult := Merge(listLeftResult, listRightResult)             219
    finalResultB, err := json.Marshal(finalResult)                    220
    failOnError(err, "Failed␣to␣encode")                              221
    err = chor.Publish(exchangeName,outputKey,                         222
        false,false,                                                   223
        amqp.Publishing{                                               224
```

```
                ContentType: "text/plain",                     225
                Body:           finalResultB,                  226
            })                                                 227
        failOnError(err, "Failed␣to␣publish␣a␣message")       228
        fmt.Println("Result:", finalResult)                   229
    }                                                          230
    forever := make(chan bool)                                231
    <-forever                                                  232
}                                                              233
func Merge(left, right []int) (result []int) {                234
    result = make([]int, len(left)+len(right))                235
    i := 0                                                     236
    for len(left) > 0 && len(right) > 0 {                     237
        if left[0] < right[0] {                               238
            result[i] = left[0]                               239
            left = left[1:]                                   240
        } else {                                              241
            result[i] = right[0]                              242
            right = right[1:]                                 243
        }                                                      244
        i++                                                    245
    }                                                          246
    for j := 0; j < len(left); j++ {                          247
        result[i] = left[j]                                   248
        i++                                                    249
    }                                                          250
    for j := 0; j < len(right); j++ {                         251
        result[i] = right[j]                                  252
        i++                                                    253
    }                                                          254
    return                                                     255
}                                                              256
func failOnError(err error, msg string) {                     257
    if err != nil {                                           258
        log.Fatalf("%s:␣%s", msg, err)                        259
    }                                                          260
}                                                              261
```

Listing 1.84. Task 2 solution, worker

```
package main                                                   1
import (                                                       2
    "encoding/json"                                            3
    "fmt"                                                      4
    "log"                                                      5
    "os/exec"                                                  6
    "github.com/streadway/amqp"                                7
)                                                              8
type workerArg struct {                                        9
    OutputKey   string                                        10
    ConfirmKey  string                                        11
}                                                             12
func main() {                                                 13
    conn, err := amqp.Dial("amqp://guest:guest@localhost:5672/")  14
    failOnError(err, "Failed␣to␣connect␣to␣RabbitMQ")        15
    defer conn.Close()                                        16
    ch, err := conn.Channel()                                17
    failOnError(err, "Failed␣to␣open␣a␣channel")             18
    err = ch.ExchangeDeclare("conquer","direct",             19
        false,true,false,false,nil)                          20
    failOnError(err, "Failed␣to␣declare␣an␣exchange")        21
    queueArg, err := ch.QueueDeclare("generator",            22
        false,true,false,false,nil)                          23
    failOnError(err, "Failed␣to␣declare␣a␣queue")            24
    err = ch.QueueBind(queueArg.Name,"generator","conquer",  25
        false,nil)                                           26
    failOnError(err, "Failed␣to␣bind␣a␣queue")               27
```

```
argMsgs, err := ch.Consume(queueArg.Name,"",            28
    false,false,false,false,nil)                        29
failOnError(err, "Failed␣to␣register␣a␣consumer")       30
go func() {                                             31
    for d := range argMsgs {                            32
        arg := workerArg{}                              33
        json.Unmarshal(d.Body, &arg)                    34
        fmt.Println(arg)                                35
        cmd := exec.Command("cmd", "/C", "start", "go", "run", 36
            "../worker.go", arg.OutputKey,arg.ConfirmKey)  37
        err = cmd.Run()                                 38
        failOnError(err, "Failed␣to␣generate␣worker")   39
        fmt.Println("generated␣one␣worker")             40
        d.Ack(false)                                    41
    }                                                   42
}()                                                     43
forever := make(chan bool)                              44
<-forever                                               45
}                                                       46
func failOnError(err error, msg string) {               47
    if err != nil {                                     48
        log.Fatalf("%s:␣%s", msg, err)                  49
    }                                                   50
}                                                       51
```

Listing 1.85. Task 2 solution, generator

```
package main                                            1
import (                                                2
    "encoding/json"                                     3
    "fmt"                                               4
    "log"                                               5
    "time"                                              6
    "github.com/streadway/amqp"                         7
)                                                       8
type workerArg struct {                                 9
    OutputKey   string                                  10
    ConfirmKey  string                                  11
}                                                       12
func main() {                                           13
    startTime := time.Now()                             14
    //list := []int{3, 4, 7, 2, 5, 7, 8, 4, 6, 8, 6, 3, 15
        //66, 432, 63, 6, 7, 8, 4, 65, 34, 4, 36}       16
    list := []int{5,7,3,4,1,9,6,2,8}                    17
    conn1, err := amqp.Dial("amqp://guest:guest@localhost:5672/") 18
    failOnError(err, "Failed␣to␣connect␣to␣RabbitMQ")   19
    defer conn1.Close()                                 20
    conn2, err := amqp.Dial("amqp://guest:guest@localhost:5672/") 21
    failOnError(err, "Failed␣to␣connect␣to␣RabbitMQ")   22
    defer conn2.Close()                                 23
    conn3, err := amqp.Dial("amqp://guest:guest@localhost:5672/") 24
    failOnError(err, "Failed␣to␣connect␣to␣RabbitMQ")   25
    defer conn3.Close()                                 26
    cho, err := conn1.Channel()                         27
    failOnError(err, "Failed␣to␣open␣a␣channel")        28
    chic, err := conn2.Channel()                        29
    failOnError(err, "Failed␣to␣open␣a␣channel")        30
    chir, err := conn3.Channel()                        31
    failOnError(err, "Failed␣to␣open␣a␣channel")        32
    exchangeName := "conquer"                           33
    err = cho.ExchangeDeclare(exchangeName,"direct",    34
        false,true,false,false,nil)                     35
    failOnError(err, "Failed␣to␣declare␣an␣exchange")   36
    queueForConfirm, err := chic.QueueDeclare("",       37
        false,true,true,false,nil)                      38
    failOnError(err, "Failed␣to␣declare␣a␣queue")       39
    err = chic.QueueBind(queueForConfirm.Name,queueForConfirm.Name, 40
```

```
                exchangeName,false,nil)                                    41
    failOnError(err, "Failed to bind a queue")                            42
    confirmMsgs, err := chic.Consume(queueForConfirm.Name,"",             43
        false,true,false,false,nil)                                       44
    failOnError(err, "Failed to register a consumer")                     45
    queueForResult, err := chir.QueueDeclare("",                          46
        false,true,true,false,nil)                                        47
    failOnError(err, "Failed to declare a queue")                         48
    err = chir.QueueBind(queueForResult.Name,queueForResult.Name,         49
        exchangeName,false,nil)                                           50
    failOnError(err, "Failed to bind a queue")                            51
    resultMsgs, err := chir.Consume(queueForResult.Name,"",               52
        false,false,false,false,nil)                                      53
    failOnError(err, "Failed to register a consumer")                     54
    //send args to generate worker                                        55
    argsP := &workerArg{                                                  56
        OutputKey:  queueForResult.Name,                                  57
        ConfirmKey: queueForConfirm.Name,                                 58
    }                                                                     59
    argsB, err := json.Marshal(argsP)                                     60
    failOnError(err, "Failed to encode")                                  61
    err = cho.Publish(exchangeName,"generator",false,false,               62
        amqp.Publishing{                                                  63
            ContentType: "text/plain",                                    64
            Body:        argsB,                                           65
        })                                                                66
    failOnError(err, "Failed to publish a message")                       67
    fmt.Println("Starter Published", string(argsB))                       68
    confirm := <-confirmMsgs                                              69
    targetKey := string(confirm.Body)                                     70
    confirm.Ack(false)                                                    71
    listB, err := json.Marshal(list)                                      72
    failOnError(err, "Failed to encode")                                  73
    msg := listB                                                          74
    err = cho.Publish(exchangeName,targetKey,false,false,                 75
        amqp.Publishing{                                                  76
            ContentType: "text/plain",                                    77
            Body:        msg,                                             78
        })                                                                79
    failOnError(err, "Failed to publish a message")                       80
    fmt.Println("Published:", list)                                       81
    result := []int{}                                                     82
    resultMsg := <-resultMsgs                                             83
    json.Unmarshal(resultMsg.Body, &result)                              84
    fmt.Println("Result:", result)                                        85
    resultMsg.Ack(false)                                                  86
    elapsed := time.Since(startTime)                                      87
    fmt.Println("Time: ", elapsed)                                        88
}                                                                         89
func failOnError(err error, msg string) {                                 90
    if err != nil {                                                       91
        log.Fatalf("%s: %s", msg, err)                                    92
    }                                                                     93
}                                                                         94
```

Listing 1.86. Task 2 solution, starter

Run the first generator, the output is:

```
go run generator.go                                                      1
{amq.gen-1j1uJpS5Nxl72ai0USRM3A amq.gen-6fEhTrnu0zcBA4vDyABRsA}           2
generated one worker                                                     3
{amq.gen-T9HLttt7ZXKOEMTuHw3zuA amq.gen-YmOX_aOXqvTngM4dtzfzag}           4
generated one worker                                                     5
{amq.gen-1EdvmRNFI1ipow21S-c1eA amq.gen-0Viyg08vuJrNWBD9vGU5vQ}           6
generated one worker                                                     7
```

Run the second generator, the output is:

```
go run generator.go                                                      1
{amq.gen-IiY1K5N1W4HEtukHQv4o0Q amq.gen-ff9nWiuRGpxHINXTV6DcQg}           2
generated one worker                                                     3
{amq.gen-wXucitzkqN1B7t-DKHNNzw amq.gen-5ko0gULSZk5qBEk5EuhaoQ}           4
generated one worker                                                     5
```

Run the **starter**, the output is:

```
go run starter.go                                                        1
Starter Published                                                        2
{"OutputKey":"amq.gen-1j1uJpS5Nxl72ai0USRM3A",                           3
"ConfirmKey":"amq.gen-6fEhTrnu0zcBA4vDyABRsA"}                           4
Published: [5 7 3 4 1 9 6 2 8]                                           5
Result: [1 2 3 4 5 6 7 8 9]                                             6
Time:   1.879547s                                                        7
```

The output of the first generated **worker**:

```
Published confirm:  amq.gen-BwsKlxuZyJjIKG-QbiBbww                        1
Received: [5 7 3 4 1 9 6 2 8]                                           2
Published:                                                              3
{"OutputKey":"amq.gen-IiY1K5N1W4HEtukHQv4o0Q",                           4
"ConfirmKey":"amq.gen-ff9nWiuRGpxHINXTV6DcQg"}                           5
Published:                                                              6
{"OutputKey":"amq.gen-T9HLttt7ZXKOEMTuHw3zuA",                           7
"ConfirmKey":"amq.gen-YmOX_aOXqvTngM4dtzfzag"}                           8
Published: [5 7 3 4]                                                     9
Published: [1 9 6 2 8]                                                   10
Left result: [3 4 5 7]                                                   11
Right result: [1 2 6 8 9]                                                12
Result: [1 2 3 4 5 6 7 8 9]                                             13
```

The output of the second generated **worker**:

```
Published confirm:  amq.gen-jnANBOCyh2Ampgnf_DKjsQ                        1
Received: [1 9 6 2 8]                                                   2
Published:                                                              3
{"OutputKey":"amq.gen-wXucitzkqN1B7t-DKHNNzw",                           4
"ConfirmKey":"amq.gen-5ko0gULSZk5qBEk5EuhaoQ"}                           5
Published:                                                              6
{"OutputKey":"amq.gen-1EdvmRNFI1ipow21S-c1eA",                           7
"ConfirmKey":"amq.gen-0Viyg08vuJrNWBD9vGU5vQ"}                           8
Published: [1 9]                                                         9
Published: [6 2 8]                                                       10
Left result: [1 9]                                                       11
Right result: [2 6 8]                                                    12
Result: [1 2 6 8 9]                                                     13
```

The output of the third generated **worker**:

```
Published confirm:  amq.gen-E7s_E7TEh1Jl1JLELSYjbQ                        1
Received: [5 7 3 4]                                                     2
Published: [3 4 5 7]                                                     3
```

The output of the fourth generated worker:

```
Published confirm:  amq.gen-Oy-rhLgARyYyza7qhn6irQ      1
Received: [6 2 8]                                        2
Published: [2 6 8]                                       3
```

The output of the fifth generated worker:

```
Published confirm:  amq.gen-GpG1uOsYnQU69LLrfFQT6g       1
Received: [1 9]                                          2
Published: [1 9]                                         3
```

References

1. AMQP 0-9-1 complete reference guide. RabbitMQ. https://www.rabbitmq.com/amqp-0-9-1-reference.html. Accessed 13 Jan 2020
2. A Tour of Go. https://tour.golang.org/concurrency/2. Accessed 13 Jan 2020
3. Buschmann, F., Meunier, R., Rohnert, H., Sommerlad, P., Stal, M.: Pattern-Oriented Software Architecture - A System of Patterns. Wiley (1996)
4. Castilho, M.: Handling 1 million requests per minute with Go. http://marcio.io/2015/07/handling-1-million-requests-per-minute-with-golang/. Accessed 13 Jan 2020
5. Concurrency is not parallelism. https://go.dev/blog/waza-talk. Accessed 23 Jan 2020
6. Consumer acknowledgements and publisher confirms. https://www.rabbitmq.com/confirms.html. Accessed 23 Jan 2020
7. Dobbelaere, Ph., Esmaili, K. Sh.: Kafka versus RabbitMQ: a comparative study of two industry reference publish/subscribe implementations: industry paper. In: Proceedings of the 11th ACM International Conference on Distributed and Event-based Systems, DEBS 2017, June 2017, pp. 227–238 (2017)
8. Download and install - The Go programming language. https://golang.org/doc/install. Accessed 13 Jan 2020
9. Gerrand, A.: Share memory by communicating. https://blog.golang.org/share-memory-by-communicating. Accessed 13 Jan 2020
10. GitHub - Jeffail/tunny: A Goroutine Pool for Go. https://github.com/Jeffail/tunny. Accessed 08 Sept 2021
11. GitHub - streadway/amqp: Go client for AMQP 0.9.1. https://github.com/streadway/amqp. Accessed 08 Sept 2021
12. Globally unique ID generator. https://github.com/rs/xid. Accessed 21 Jan 2020
13. Install RabbitMQ server on Windows. https://www.rabbitmq.com/install-windows.html. Accessed 1 Sept 2020
14. Li J., Kim Y., Zsók V.: Balanced distributed computation patterns (2022). https://github.com/lijianhao288/Balanced-Distributed-Computation-Patterns
15. Madhu, M.P., Dixit, S.: Distributing messages using RabbitMQ with advanced message exchanges. Int. J. Res. Stud. Comput. Sci. Eng. 6(2), 24–28 (2019)
16. NSQ: A Realtime Distributed Messaging Platform. https://nsq.io/. Accessed 1 Sept 2020
17. RabbitMQ Tutorials. https://www.rabbitmq.com/getstarted.html. Accessed 1 Sept 2020
18. RabbitMQ tutorial - Work Queues - RabbitMQ. https://www.rabbitmq.com/tutorials/tutorial-two-go.html. Accessed 1 Sept 2020

19. The Go Programming Language. https://golang.org/. Accessed 13 Jan 2020
20. Udemy. https://www.udemy.com/. Accessed 1 Sept 2020
21. UML. https://www.omg.org/spec/UML/2.0/Superstructure/PDF. Accessed 1 Sep 2020
22. Videla, A., Williams, J.J.W.: RabbitMQ in Action: Distributed Messaging for Everyone. Manning Publisher, NY, US (2012)
23. Zsók, Viktória, Hernyák, Zoltán, Horváth, Zoltán: Designing distributed computational skeletons in D-clean and D-box. In: Horváth, Zoltán (ed.) CEFP 2005. LNCS, vol. 4164, pp. 223–256. Springer, Heidelberg (2006). https://doi.org/10.1007/11894100_8

PhD Workshop

Tunnel Parsing

Nikolay Handzhiyski[1,2]([⊠]) (iD) and Elena Somova[2] (iD)

[1] ExperaSoft UG (haftungsbeschränkt), Goldasse 10 St., 77652 Offenburg, Germany
nikolay.handzhiyski@experasoft.com
[2] University of Plovdiv "Paisii Hilendarski", 24 Tzar Assen St.,
4000 Plovdiv, Bulgaria
eledel@uni-plovdiv.bg
https://www.experasoft.com/, https://www.uni-plovdiv.bg/

Abstract. This article describes an effective algorithm for parsing and building of concrete syntax trees for languages defined by context-free grammars without left recursion nor rules that recognize empty words. The different states in which the parsing machine can be are pre-computed into a control layer of objects together with all possible sets of steps (tunnels), that can be executed during the parsing to enable the parsing machine to progress from one state to another. When implemented, all pre-computed data is read-only and can be used by more than one parsing machine at a time. The algorithm (called tunnel parsing) uses the grammars directly without a prior refactoring, and can linearly parse some ambiguous grammars.

Keywords: Parsing · Syntax Analysis · Parser Generator · Statically Typed Concrete Syntax Tree

1 Introduction

The electronic systems often use stored data or receive data from other systems. The data itself is structured according to the formal language chosen for the specific purpose, which will be called hereafter only a **language**. The grammar of the language can be conveniently described by a widely known metasyntax such as Augmented Backus-Naur form (ABNF [5]), which is used to describe grammars in this article.

In order to understand the meaning of a given data for a given language, a recognition process must be performed - **parsing** [3]. The different languages can be divided according to the grammars that describe them, and the most commonly used in practice are the **regular grammars**, with them the data recognition is performed by a **finite automaton** (**deterministic** or not), and the **context-free grammars** [22] where the recognition is performed by a **pushdown automaton** (also deterministic or not, depending on the grammar).

The parsing has two main goals: first, to check if a string of characters [3] (for short **string**) belongs to a given language, and second, to build a syntax tree - a data structure that contains syntactic information about the string.

Z. Porkoláb and V. Zsók (Eds.): CEFP 2019, LNCS 11950, pp. 325–343, 2023.
https://doi.org/10.1007/978-3-031-42833-3_8

There are two types of syntax trees - abstract and concrete. An **abstract syntax tree** may not contain all grammar rules (for short **rules**) that are used during the parsing, and it may not contain some of the recognized characters that are implied from the context (for example, the parentheses around mathematical expressions can be omitted, if the expression between the parentheses has its own subtree [1]). In contrast, a **concrete syntax tree** contains all of the used rules and recognized characters during the parsing and it is the type of tree addressed in this article.

An **empty string** [3] (a sequence of zero characters) is defined as ϵ, and a rule that recognizes ϵ, will be called ϵ-rule. This article describes an effective algorithm for parsing of strings and building concrete syntax trees, by the use of context-free grammars without left recursion nor ϵ-rules. The tunnel parsing algorithm is mainly applicable for parsing domain-specific languages, such as programming languages and structured data. Tunnel Grammar Studio [24] generates parser that operate with the tunnel parsing algorithm.

Section 2 provides an overview of the parsing process and describes some common approaches to realize it. Section 3 introduces basic concepts and parsing issues that are relevant to the article. Section 4 describes the tunnel parsing algorithm. Section 5 contains an example parsing with various changes to the internal state of the parser as part of the **parsing machine** (PM) - an object that performs all recognition steps of the string, such as lexing, parsing, and the eventual build of a syntax tree. The section also contains information for the runtime speed performance of the presented algorithm. Section 6 describes the future development of the algorithm and some of its other features that are not covered by the article.

2   Parsing Overview

The process of finding the meaning of data is as follows:

1. If the input data is encoded, it must be decoded to a string. Common character encoding standards are ASCII, UTF-8 and UTF-16;
2. Optionally, the characters of the string can be grouped into lexemes and then into tokens by the use of a lexical grammar from a lexer. To each token recognized by the lexer is given a name - an abstract symbol [3] that is later used by the parser. The lexical grammar describes the syntax of tokens as formed by characters. The end of this step is a list of tokens. Often the lexical analysis is based on a regular grammar, that is used by a non-deterministic finite automaton directly for the recognition of each token's lexeme, or to be converted to a deterministic finite automaton [18] and then be used. This conversion is often done in practice [20] by the use of the Brzozowski algorithm [6] to create minimal deterministic final automata. During the lexemes recognition from the automaton, the longest possible match is often taken for each character group that is converted to a lexeme. If no lexical analysis is performed, or no lexeme is recognized from the lexer, then each character becomes a token [24] with a name - the character itself;

3. With the use of a parser grammar and a list of tokens, the parsing process is performed. The parser grammar describes the syntax of the language as formed by symbols or directly from tokens [24]. The grammars used in this article are presented in terms of the ABNF metasyntax, and hereafter each ABNF terminal value [5] will constitute a symbol;
4. If a syntax tree is required, it is generated as a part of the result;
5. The process completes successfully or with an error - a string that does not belong to the language.

When it is necessary only to check, whether a given string belongs to a given language (i.e. a syntax tree is not required, because no further analysis is performed), the language grammar can changed without restriction. For example, to remove ε-rules or left recursion during refactoring [17] in order to make the grammar recognition possible by certain algorithms, to reduce the memory usage or the recognition time, provided that the new grammar must describe exactly the same language. If it is necessary to build a syntax tree (to translate one language to another, compile, decompile, or perform a specific analysis of the input data), then any change in the grammar, from the parsing algorithm, in order to obtain certain properties, affects the tree. To enable the developer to predict the final syntax tree easily, the parsing algorithm must not change the grammar.

There are different **syntax tree building algorithms**, as the most common two are:

- **top-down** - the left-most derivation is used first [8]. In practice, the first created tree node is the tree root, then the left sub-node will be created in-depth, and the right-most sub-node will be created last. The tunnel parsing algorithm belongs to this category of algorithms;
- **bottom-up** - from the leaves to the root, as the right-most derivation is used first. In practice, the leaves are first created in a list. Then the right-most are grouped in their parent node. The process is repeated until the last created node is the root.

If we consider a general step-by-step PM that during its progress, it transitions from one step to another, based on its internal state [18] plus a certain number of input symbols, then the necessary symbols for making the decision to move the PM from one step to another will be called **look-ahead** symbols. When the parsing is done on the basis of a deterministic context-free grammar, at most one look-ahead symbol is required from the PM to progress. For some context-free grammars, the number of look-ahead symbols might be greater than one.

As a combination of the parsing direction, from left to right (L), and the syntax tree building direction (L or R), the two common parsing strategies are:

- LL - **Left to right, Left-most derivation**. These types of parsers can be developed manually and automatically [24], often by making each grammar rule directly implemented as a function [4] in the target programming language, and the thread-dedicated stack to be used to recurse into the rules. That is an intuitive way to run a parser as a standard software program [15,19]. The LL parsing makes it easy to add events directly to the grammar (for example, functions to be called when the PM passes through some specific places) that makes it a more appropriate parsing strategy to use. The class of grammars that can be recognized by an LL parser with a maximum of k number of look-ahead symbols are called $LL(k)$ grammars. The tunnel parsing is a left to right parsing algorithm; •

– LR - **Left to right, Right-most derivation**. These types of parsers are difficult to be manually developed, and they are usually generated automatically [13]. During parsing by this type of parsers, a list of syntax tree nodes is usually maintained. The main two operations are: a) move the right-most nodes from the list as sub-nodes to a new node that takes their place in the list of nodes. That operation may reduce the length of the list of nodes, and is called a reduce operation; and b) a new symbol is shifted from the input string to a new single node in the right side of the list of nodes. This is effectively reducing the input with one symbol, and is called a shift operation [2].

There are different parsing algorithms that can be classified by the type of grammars they can use. Of practical interest are the context-free grammars and mostly the deterministic context-free grammars, because different programming languages and structured data are represented with them [10,23,25].

A context-free grammar can be a base for parsing by a non-deterministic pushdown automaton. During parsing, these parsers use a link to a **current** automaton state that is changed at the parsing steps depending on the symbols in the input string and the transitions from the current to the next automaton states. When in the current automaton a reference to another automaton is reached, the current link to an automaton state is added to a stack, then the parsing continues from the start of the referenced automaton with a new linked current state, which is the beginning of the new automaton. When the new automaton is completed, then the previous automaton state is popped from the stack, and the parsing continues after it. This way of parsing also works for deterministic context-free grammars. The used stack will be called a **depth stack**.

It is essential for the user to know how the PM will perform its operations, and more specifically, how much memory will be used and how long it will run. There are many linear algorithms for parsing of different grammar classes [11,21], and with a polynomial time [12].

3   Problem

The purpose of this article is to present an efficient and iterative parsing algorithm, called tunnel parsing. The algorithm checks whether a given string belongs to a given language and builds a statically typed concrete syntax tree mirroring the context-free grammar structure without losing grammar information. The algorithm can also easily be adapted to build abstract syntax trees, when simply some of the available concrete information is not used. The grammars accepted by the algorithm, as defined in the article, are without left recursion nor ϵ-rules. The built statically typed syntax tree can be processed quickly without dynamic checks of the data types stored in the tree and are self-sufficient - the tree contains all of the information in itself, without references to other external data structures. To achieve this purpose, it is necessary:

1. To present the grammar appropriately and preserve all of the available information (such as rule enter/exit, alternative enter/exit, element repetitions and omissions, etc.), so that the parsing runs fast and requires little dynamic memory at runtime. This is the memory that is allocated by the PM at runtime for its own calculations;
2. To make the generator accessible, by not using its own custom grammar syntax to describe a language, but a standardized syntax like ABNF [5];
3. To calculate in advance much data that can be used at runtime by more than one PM;
4. To use a representation of the algorithm in a way that allows it to be intuitively upgraded to enable the generation of PMs from grammars that have ϵ-rules or left recursion;
5. To generate a concrete syntax tree as a part of the result of the parsing that can be used for a direct translation from one language to another.

A context-free grammar is defined by a tuple (N, Σ, R, S), where set N contains all non-terminal symbols [8], set Σ contains all terminal symbols, $N \cap \Sigma = \emptyset$ (empty set), set R contains all rules and S is the start symbol of the grammar, $S \in N$. The subsequent grammars will be described with the ABNF metasyntax, where the definitions have the following meanings (only those used in the article are listed):

- "1" - defines a terminal value in ABNF, but for the purpose of this article defines a terminal symbol (an element of Σ), that will match a token having the same symbol as a name;
- r - defines a non-terminal symbol ($r \in N$): a grammar rule (for short a "rule"), when it is on the left side of the sign = or a grammar reference (for short a "reference") to a rule when it is on the right side;
- x y - concatenated grammar elements (for short "elements");
- (z w) - defines a grammar group (for short a "group") of elements;
- a / b - defines an alternative (logical *or* for the elements);
- n*m A - defines the repetitions of A, where $n \in \mathbb{N}$ is the minimum number of repetitions (if omitted it is considered zero), $m \in \mathbb{N}$ is the maximum number of repetitions (if omitted is considered infinity), and $n <= m$. In this article, only the cases where $n \in (0, 1)$ and $m \in (1, \infty)$ (as $m = \infty$ is only applying to references) will be considered, even though the algorithm supports the full range of values for n and m for any grammar element.

The groups in an ABNF grammar can be seen as rules with a single implicit reference to them at the point of the definition, and therefore below, everything written about the rules will apply to the groups as well. Under a "reference", will be understood the defined reference to a rule in the ABNF syntax, as well as the implicit reference to a group when it is seen as a rule.

All terminal symbols that can be recognized from the beginning of a rule directly or by recursively entering into the referenced rules will be called reachable [14]. Reachable terminal symbols after an element are those that can be recognized after it, without the use of the possible depth stacks to the rule where the element is located. For example, in Fig. 1 that has two linked rules, from the beginning of rule `alpha`, the reachable terminal symbols are "1", "9" and "4".

```
alpha = "1" "7" / beta "8" / 0*1 "9" "4"
beta  = "1"
```

Fig. 1. Linked grammar rules

During the tunnel parsing, a concrete syntax tree can be built from top to bottom, because all the information for its building is available. Data recognition by this algorithm could also be implemented with recursive function calls, like a traditional deep recursive LL parser, but such an implementation has the following disadvantages: a) a stack overflow is likely to occur; b) at each entry in a function that recognizes a rule the input symbol must be compared and some sub-function be called in turn. The selected sub-function will re-check the same input symbol, and so on. Although for each finite, non left recursive grammar, the maximum number of the depth entries is a grammar dependent constant, the search in-depth takes time; and c) the depth stack is not explicitly available, and thus cannot be easily saved and restored. To avoid problem a), the tunnel parsing is defined to be an iterative recognition process. To solve problem b) all grammar places where in-depth token search will occur, are calculated in advance, with a runtime search performed only once for each reachable terminal symbol, and to solve problem c) the depth stack is not the thread-dedicated stack, but a separate stack that is explicitly maintained.

4   Tunnel Parsing Algorithm

The tunnel parsing algorithm represents the information extracted from the grammar in a specific way that allows fast parsing and an **execution stack** (stack that contains information for the progress of the PM) with a size proportional to the number of look-ahead symbols. Later on, a **tunnel** will be a list of operations, for a change in the internal state of the PM, and the relevant syntax tree building commands. To enable a non-deterministic grammars recognition, for each **forward tunnel**[1], there must be a **backward tunnel**[2]. For deterministic grammars, the use of backward tunnels is not necessary.

---

[1] A tunnel that advances the PM to a successful final state.

[2] A tunnel that restores the PM, as it was before the use of a forward tunnel.

To create a PM that is based on the tunnel parsing algorithm, the following steps should be performed:

1. **Designing of automata** - an automaton is created for each rule in the grammar (as in Fig. 2), whose states will be called automaton states or only states. Some of these states will be located at the end of a transition that recognizes a terminal symbol, and they will be called **terminal states**. The remaining transitions which do not recognize a terminal symbol, will recognize ϵ (i.e. no check for a terminal symbol is required to pass through them), and the transition label may indicate a certain operation on the internal state of the PM. Hereafter the "entering" and "exiting" of a rule or an alternative will mean the use of the respective transitions in the automaton build for the rule. In Fig. 2 the labels are: a - enter in rule alpha; b, e and h - enter in first, second and third alternatives; c, f and i - next element; d, g and j - exit from the first, second and third alternatives with a success; k - exit from rule alpha with a success; u - enter in rule beta; v - enter in the first alternative of rule beta; w - exit from the first alternative of rule beta; x - exit from rule beta with a success;

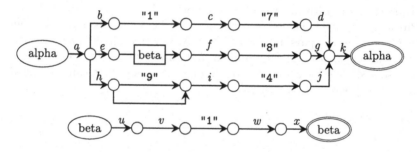

Fig. 2. Automata generated from the grammar in Fig. 1

2. **Extraction of tunnels** - for each rule start state, each state after a reference and each terminal state of each automaton, all transitions to the next reachable terminal states are collected into tunnels in a depth-first search manner. On Fig. 3 the dashed line shows the process of searching for and recording of the tunnels for a terminal symbol "1";

3. **Construction of routers** - all reachable terminal states for all key positions in the automata are collected: at the beginning of each rule, for the automaton states that are after each reference, and for each terminal state. In Fig. 3, the darker automaton states are the reachable terminal states from the beginning of rule alpha. In a proper implementation, this information (the reachable terminal states from a given key position in the automata) is stored sorted in a static read-only memory to speed up the search for a next state of the PM at runtime. The sorting of the terminal states is done by the value of the transition's terminal symbol that led to each terminal state. The object that

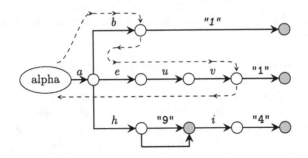

Fig. 3. The search space for reachable terminal states

contains the sorted terminal states reachable from a given key position in the automata will be called a **router** and each of its elements a **path**. Thus, by having the tunnels and the routers before the start of the parsing, there is enough information on how the PM will progress fast from one automaton state to another. The routers for the grammar in Fig. 1 are described below;

4. **Creation of a control layer** - to control the execution of the PM, a set of objects is created, which are using the tunnels and the routers to form a **control layer**, with functionality described below;

5. **Parsing** - a direct parsing is performed (in TGS there is a visual debugger that performs the parsing and builds a syntax tree directly, in forward and backward steps, for a given grammar and an input), or a parser is generated to a source code for a target programming language that can be embedded in other software tools [4,15,24].

4.1   Tunnels

The set of all transitions in automata is defined as E, and the set of the operations that change the depth stack of the PM as O. The set T contains all tunnels $\tau \in T$. A tunnel is defined as $\tau = [e \mid o]$, where the transitions that a tunnel uses are $e = \{e_1, e_2, ...\}, e_i \in E, i \in \mathbb{N}$, and the operations that change the depth stack are $o = \{o_1, o_2, ...\}, o_j \in O, j \in \mathbb{N}$. When $o = \emptyset$, the tunnel will be written as $[e]$. The reverse of x is defined as $\neg x$, where $x \in (E \cup O)$, $\downarrow r$ defines an enter in r and $\uparrow r$ an exit from r after its successful recognition, $r \in \mathbb{N}$, $\downarrow r \in O$, and $\uparrow r \in O$. The tunnels for the grammar in Fig. 1 with automata in Fig. 2 are:

- $\tau_0 = [a, b \mid \downarrow alpha]$ - for an input symbol "1" from the beginning of rule alpha;
- $\tau_1 = [\neg b, e, u, v \mid \downarrow beta]$ - if after τ_0 the parsing is unsuccessful, the PM, by using this tunnel, will recognize "1" in the beginning of rule **beta** whose terminal symbol is also reachable from the beginning of rule **alpha**;
- $\tau_2 = [\neg v, \neg u, \neg e, \neg a \mid \neg \downarrow beta, \neg \downarrow alpha]$ - in case of an unsuccessful recognition after the second reachable terminal symbol "1" from the beginning of rule **alpha**, this tunnel will be used by the PM to change its internal state to the one before the execution of τ_0 and τ_1 tunnels;

- $\tau_3 = [a, h, i \mid \; \downarrow alpha]$ - a tunnel used from the beginning of rule `alpha` when the current input symbol is "4";
- $\tau_4 = [\neg i, \neg h, \neg a \mid \neg \downarrow alpha]$ - in case of an unsuccessful recognition after the use of τ_3, the PM will use this tunnel to restore its internal state to the one before the use of τ_3;
- $\tau_5 = [a, h \mid \; \downarrow alpha]$ - a tunnel used for an input symbol "9" from the beginning of rule `alpha`;
- $\tau_6 = [\neg h, \neg a \mid \neg \downarrow alpha]$ - a tunnel that reverses the effect of τ_5;
- $\tau_7 = [u, v \mid \; \downarrow beta]$ - a tunnel used after a recognized "1" from the beginning of rule `beta`;
- $\tau_8 = [\neg v, \neg u \mid \neg \downarrow beta]$ - a tunnel that reverses the effect of τ_7;
- $\tau_9 = [c]$, $\tau_{10} = [\neg c]$, $\tau_{11} = [f]$, $\tau_{12} = [\neg f]$, $\tau_{13} = [i]$ and $\tau_{14} = [\neg i]$ - forward tunnels after elements and backward tunnels in reverse;
- $\tau_{15} = [d, k \mid \; \uparrow alpha]$, $\tau_{16} = [g, k \mid \; \uparrow alpha]$, $\tau_{17} = [j, k \mid \; \uparrow alpha]$ and $\tau_{18} = [w, x \mid \; \uparrow beta]$ - tunnels that are used in case of a successful recognition of rule `alpha`, from its three alternatives, and a tunnel with a successful recognition of rule `beta` from its single alternative;
- $\tau_{19} = [\neg k, \neg d \mid \neg \uparrow alpha]$, $\tau_{20} = [\neg k, \neg g \mid \neg \uparrow alpha]$, $\tau_{21} = [\neg k, \neg j \mid \neg \uparrow alpha]$ and $\tau_{22} = [\neg x, \neg w \mid \neg \uparrow beta]$ - tunnels used to move the PM internal state back into the three alternatives of rule `alpha` or into the single alternative of rule `beta`.

4.2   Routers

The set of routers in a PM is defined as U, terminal symbol as $s \in \Sigma$, the set of all control states as C, and a control state as $c \in C$. The set of all paths in a router is defined as P, and a path in a router as p like a pair of a terminal symbol and a control state: $s \rightarrow c$. A router is defined then as $r = \langle P \mid c_\epsilon \rangle$, where $r \in U, c_\epsilon \in C$. Here c_ϵ signifies a control state that will be used when a searched terminal symbol in a router is not found in P. A router defined in this way, makes the parsing with a higher priority for a terminal symbol recognition and moving forward in the input. Then, in case of subsequent failure, the last attempt will be the c_ϵ path. For the grammar in Fig. 1 with automata in Fig. 2 the routers are:

- $u_a = \langle$ "1" $\rightarrow c_7$, "4" $\rightarrow c_1$, "9" $\rightarrow c_2 \mid \; \rangle$ - with the reachable terminal states from the beginning of rule `alpha`;
- $u_b = \langle$ "1" $\rightarrow c_3 \mid \; \rangle$ - with the reachable terminal states from the beginning of rule `beta`;
- $u_r = \langle$ "8" $\rightarrow c_5 \mid \; \rangle$ - with the reachable terminal states after the reference to rule `beta` in rule `alpha`;
- $u_0 = \langle$ "7" $\rightarrow c_4 \mid \; \rangle$ - with the reachable terminal states after the recognition of terminal symbol "1" in rule `alpha`;
- $u_1 = \langle \; \mid c_{11} \rangle$ - without reachable terminal symbols, but only a path to exit the rule, after the recognition of "1" in rule `beta`;
- $u_2 = \langle \; \mid c_{10} \rangle$ - only a path to exit the rule, after "4" in rule `alpha`;

- $u_3 = \langle \; | \; c_9 \rangle$ - only a path to exit the rule, after "7" in rule `alpha`;
- $u_4 = \langle \; | \; c_8 \rangle$ - only a path to exit the rule, after "8" in rule `alpha`;
- $u_5 = \langle "4" \rightarrow c_6 \; | \; \rangle$ - a router with the reachable terminal states after terminal symbol "9" in rule `alpha`.

4.3 Segments

A **segment** is an object that exists for each rule reference and has a link to a router with the reachable terminal states after the corresponding reference. The **depth stack** in the tunnel parsing algorithm consists of segments. For the grammar in Fig. 1 there is one segment that uses router u_r. One additional stack exists, to enable the PM to progress backwards to its previous states that is used to archive a portion of the depth stack and will be called a **depth stack archive**. When a PM exits a rule, after its successful recognition, the removed element from the depth stack is not deleted but moved to the archive. To control the backwards progress distance, there is a counter in each element of the execution stack to count how many elements from the depth stack are moved to the archive, so when there is a progress backwards, the PM will restore the depth stack from its archive with as many items as the value of that counter.

4.4 Control Layer

Several types of control objects are distinguished in the control layer. Each object can be in one of several control states (their number depends on the object type), used one after another depending on the input symbols. Each execution stack element uses one control state per an input symbol, and at any given time no more than the maximum look-ahead symbols plus one of elements are needed for the algorithm to operate i.e. for each grammar $LL(k)$ the PM will store at most $k + 1$ elements into the execution stack at runtime. The PM performs the operations required based only on the top of the execution stack. After each execution of the operations defined by a control state the PM may pause, as in practice this is one iterative step. The control objects signify the information to "where" in the automata the PM has reached, and the control states - "which" operations must be performed. In this article, the following control objects and their states are presented:

- **c-origin** - for each rule one control object of this type is created. It contains a link to a router with all reachable terminal symbols from the beginning of the respective rule. The object has only one state: "use". In Table 1, there are two objects of type c-origin, one for each rule `alpha` and `beta`. At the beginning of the parsing, the PM searches for the first input symbol in the router of the c-origin control object for the initial rule S. The path found is then used to progress the PM forward. If a path is not found, the PM will terminate its execution with an error;
- **c-terminal** - a control object if this type is created for each terminal state, and has one control state: "use". The function of this c-object is to perform

a search in a router which contains all reachable terminal symbols from the respective terminal state. When a match is found, a c-token (described below) control object will replace the top of the execution stack, and in the absence of a match, the top of the execution stack is removed. In Table 1 there are six c-terminal control objects for the terminal symbols "1" (two times), "4", "7", "8" and "9";

- **c-token** - the control object exists for each terminal symbol that can be found by a router search. The function of this object is to change the internal state of the PM with one input token forward, and in case of a subsequent unsuccessful recognition, with one token backward. There are two control states: a) "use" - the PM in this state moves with one input symbol forward, replaces the top of the execution stack with the next c-state of this c-object and adds the corresponding c-terminal with its "use" state at the top of the execution stack; and b) "used" - after a subsequently unsuccessful recognition attempt the PM in this c-state performs operations to restore its internal state to the one before the "use" c-state. Additionally the top of the execution stack is replaced with the first control state of the next control object. The control objects for the grammar in Fig. 1 and their relations are shown in Table 1;

- **c-epsilon** - the object is used when there is no reachable terminal symbol for a router, but there is a path to the end of the rule. In the presence of more than one path, the path with the fewer transitions in the automata is used. This makes tunnel parsing an algorithm for a linear and a deterministic recognition of some ambiguous [14] grammars, because from all possible (may be infinite) syntax tree nodes that could be created for the multiple paths leading to the same state, the shortest one is chosen. One c-state is available: "use". The calculations for the shortest path and the ϵ-rules will not be addressed in this article;

- **c-back** - the control object is used after the recognition of one or more identical terminal symbols in a router and has one state "use". If the router that contains this c-object has a c-epsilon path, then after the using of c-back, the c-epsilon will be put on the top of the execution stack, and subsequently used to continue the parsing towards the end of the rule;

- **c-unwind** - a global control object for the entire PM with one state - "use" that is placed on top of the execution stack after the use of c-epsilon. The PM in this c-state removes one element from the depth stack and adds it to the archive depth stack as well as increases by one the exit counter;

- **c-restore** - a global control object for the entire PM with one state - "use", that restores one or more depth stack elements from the depth stack archive and decreases with one the exit counter. The object remains on top of the execution stack until the exit counter reaches zero.

5   Results

The use of tunnels speeds up parsing because all necessary changes to the internal state of the PM are executed at once for each reachable terminal symbol (by the

Table 1. Control objects for the grammar in Fig. 1

Type c-origin

#	Router
19	u_a
20	u_b

Type c-terminal

#	Router
21	u_1
22	u_2
23	u_5
24	u_1
25	u_3
26	u_4
27	u_2
28	u_0

Type c-token

#	Next	c-terminal	Tunnel
0	c_{12}	c_{21}	τ_1
1	c_{13}	c_{22}	τ_3
2	c_{14}	c_{23}	τ_5
3	c_{15}	c_{24}	τ_7
4	c_{16}	c_{25}	τ_9
5	c_{17}	c_{26}	τ_{11}
6	c_{18}	c_{27}	τ_{13}
7	c_0	c_{28}	τ_0

Global c-objects

#	Type
29	c-unwind
30	c-restore

Type c-epsilon

#	Forward	Backward
8	τ_{16}	τ_{19}
9	τ_{15}	τ_{20}
10	τ_{17}	τ_{21}
11	τ_{18}	τ_{22}

Type c-back

#	Tunnel
12	τ_2
13	τ_4
14	τ_6
15	τ_8
16	τ_{10}
17	τ_{12}
18	τ_{14}

use of a tunnel) without in-depth search in the automata by using the thread-dedicated stack. If there is no need to create a syntax tree, then there is no need to store its build information into the tunnels. This further reduces the amount of the generated code and speeds up the parsing.

In tunnel parsing, the number of operations that the PM performs at each iterative step is independent of the number of input symbols. This enables the PM to pause and resume its execution almost instantly. If this is not necessary, a good optimization of the algorithm is to perform several iterative steps in a sequence, before returning the control to the user of the PM. This gives good results described below because less code is executed to control the iteration.

An example of a tunnel parsing algorithm runtime execution, for the grammar in Fig. 1 with automata in Fig. 2, start symbol $S = $ alpha, and two characters for an input ("18") is presented in Table 2. The table contains step-by-step changes on the internal state of the PM in each row. The content of the cells in column "Task" signifies the operation performed by the PM to move from the current row, to the next. An alternative execution of the example is to recognize the first character "1" through the reference to rule beta. That is an alternation in a different order of the reachable terminal symbols in the grammar. The alternation can be in any order, when there are many duplicate reachable terminal symbols in a router. This is correct from the point of view of the defined grammar but is not completely intuitive to the user. If this is ignored, it is possible by profiling the parsing of a large amount of data, to determine which reachable terminal symbols have led to a successful recognition more often. Then the order of the duplicate terminal symbols in the routers can be changed to speed up the parsing of profile-like inputs.

Table 2. Execution of a PM for the grammar in Fig. 1

#	Input	Execution Stack	Depth Stack	Task
1	$\rightarrow$18	$c_{19}\|use$	$\emptyset$	search in u_a and found c_7
2	$\rightarrow$18	$c_7\|use$	$\emptyset$	use of τ_0
3	$\rightarrow$18	$c_7\|use$	$\emptyset$	rule enter
4	$\rightarrow$18	$c_7\|use$	alpha	next token
5	$1\rightarrow$8	$c_7\|use$	alpha	control state change
6	$1\rightarrow$8	$c_7\|used$	alpha	control state addition
7	$1\rightarrow$8	$c_7\|used, c_{28}\|use$	alpha	search in u_0 and not found
8	$1\rightarrow$8	$c_7\|used, c_{28}\|use$	alpha	control state remove
9	$1\rightarrow$8	$c_7\|used$	alpha	next control state
10	$1\rightarrow$8	$c_0\|use$	alpha	use of τ_1
11	$1\rightarrow$8	$c_0\|use$	alpha	rule enter
12	$1\rightarrow$8	$c_0\|use$	alpha,beta	control state change
13	$1\rightarrow$8	$c_0\|used$	alpha,beta	control state addition
14	$1\rightarrow$8	$c_0\|used, c_{21}\|use$	alpha,beta	search in u_1 and found c_{11}
15	$1\rightarrow$8	$c_0\|used, c_{11}\|use$	alpha,beta	use of τ_{18}
16	$1\rightarrow$8	$c_0\|used, c_{11}\|use$	alpha,beta	control object change
17	$1\rightarrow$8	$c_0\|used, c_{29}\|use$	alpha,beta	rule exit
18	$1\rightarrow$8	$c_0\|used, c_{29}\|use$	alpha	search in u_r and found c_5
19	$1\rightarrow$8	$c_0\|used, c_5\|use$	alpha	use of τ_{11}
20	$1\rightarrow$8	$c_0\|used, c_5\|use$	alpha	next token
21	$18\rightarrow$	$c_0\|used, c_5\|use$	alpha	control state change
22	$18\rightarrow$	$c_0\|used, c_5\|used$	alpha	control state addition
23	$18\rightarrow$	$c_0\|used, c_5\|used, c_{26}\|use$	alpha	search in u_4 and found c_8
24	$18\rightarrow$	$c_0\|used, c_5\|used, c_8\|use$	alpha	use of τ_{16}
25	$18\rightarrow$	$c_0\|used, c_5\|used, c_8\|use$	alpha	control state change
26	$18\rightarrow$	$c_0\|used, c_5\|used, c_{29}\|use$	alpha	rule exit
27	$18\rightarrow$	$c_0\|used, c_5\|used, c_{29}\|use$	$\emptyset$	success

An experiment was made with different JavaScript Object Notation (JSON) Data Interchange Format [23] parsers. The grammar has ABNF [5] syntax. The purpose of the experiment is to compare the speed of different PMs with a real world grammar, when they are searching in-depth and are choosing their next internal state from a large number of possible terminal symbols. There is a notable difference between the parser generators that participate in the experiment. Namely, TGS [24] support character matching ranges inside the lexer grammar as well as token matching ranges inside the parser grammar, where ANTLR [4] and JavaCC [9,15] support only character ranges inside the lexer grammar. For this reason two grammars are used in the test: a) the original JSON [23] grammar (only usable by TGS), and b) heavily modified original grammar split in two - lexer and parser grammars, that is translated in the syntax accepted by each parser generator (by one version for TGS, ANTLR, and JavaCC). For the both grammars the presented ambiguity in the original grammar is removed, to make the parsing possible with one token of look-ahead, because the test is not intended to measure the backtracking capabilities of the tools.

All PMs participating in the experiment are compiled by Microsoft®Visual Studio® 2015 Update 3, in C++ for a 64 bit processor, optimized for speed in release, executed in Microsoft®Windows® 10 (64 bit) operation system. The used hardware is Intel®Core™ i7-4790k @4GHz. The measured time values are from the wall clock time, and are made with the high performance profiling [16] API available in Microsoft®Windows®. The experimental input data[3,4] is the same for each PM. Each value in the table is the average of 20 consecutive executions of the executable (containing the compiled PM), which resembles a real work process, when an external program starts a compiler or an interpreter (which have the PM) for many inputs in a row. Before each group of 20 consecutive executions of each PM, there are 2 executions for which no measurement is recorded. The input data is preloaded into the operative memory for each test.

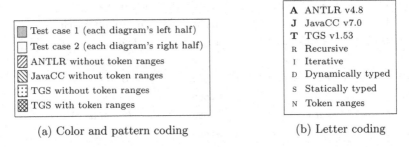

(a) Color and pattern coding   (b) Letter coding

Fig. 4. Figures legend for the experiment

Figures 5, 6, 7, 8, and 9 are displaying the final measurements from the experiment and have a common legend in Fig. 4.

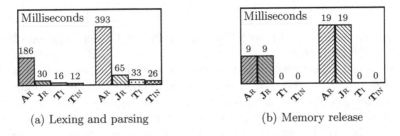

(a) Lexing and parsing   (b) Memory release

Fig. 5. Recognizing without tree generation

---

[3] https://api.nobelprize.org/v1/prize.json - 216670 bytes.
[4] https://api.nobelprize.org/v1/laureate.json - 464980 bytes.

In Fig. 5 are displayed the recognition (lexing and parsing) times of the two inputs as well as the memory release times. The recursive parsers generated by ANTLR and JavaCC require more time to recognize the inputs then the iterative parsers generated by TGS. The best performance is made by the parser with parser grammar ranges ($\mathbf{T}$IN), because each input character becomes a token by itself and then it is quickly processed by the tunnel parsing algorithm. The TGS parsing machine with two grammars ($\mathbf{T}$I) is without token ranges and it is slightly slower at runtime compared to the one with parser grammar ranges, because the lexical analysis creates some overhead. Note that ANTLR and JavaCC (with a combination with JJTree [15] for the generation of the syntax tree) allocate memory proportionally to the input length regardless that the used grammar is deterministic and only one token of look-ahead is enough to recognized it. For larger inputs (hundreds of megabytes) this is not practical. In contrast, TGS releases the unused tokens when they are no longer needed and in this way is practically "streaming" the input. For this reason there is no large memory blocks to be released after the recognition (see Fig. 5b).

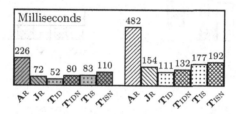

(a) Lexing, parsing and tree building

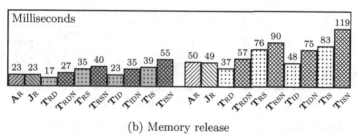

(b) Memory release

Fig. 6. Recognizing with tree generation

In Fig. 6 are the results for the PMs runtime when performing lexing, parsing and tree building as well as the memory release times. The fastest tree to be completed is by an iterative tunnel parsing machine and it is a dynamically typed concrete syntax tree ($\mathbf{T}$ID). The statically typed concrete syntax trees ($\mathbf{T}$IS and $\mathbf{T}$ISN) are slower then the dynamically typed because of the more detailed tree representation. These trees are also the slower to release iteratively, but the developer can use them without dynamic casts and without the worries of a stack overflow occurrence during the release of the tree.

In Fig. 7 are displayed the tree traversal times and in Fig. 8 the times for the conversion of the different trees back to a string.

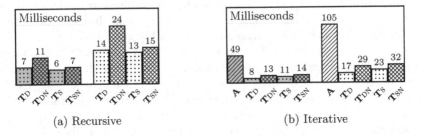

(a) Recursive   (b) Iterative

Fig. 7. Tree traversing

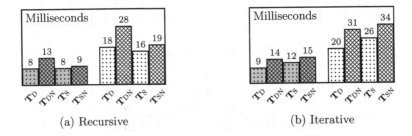

(a) Recursive   (b) Iterative

Fig. 8. Syntax tree to string conversion

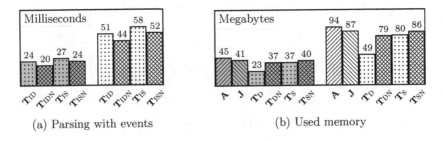

(a) Parsing with events   (b) Used memory

Fig. 9. Other data

In Fig. 9a are displayed the times for the recognition (lexing and parsing) of the inputs when the PM emits only events for the syntax tree building. In TGS the syntax trees builders are using this events to build the relevant trees, but if the input is intended to be processed only one time then the use of this events directly is the best option, because there will be no tree traverse and release after the parsing is complete, but the developer will still receive the tree structure information. The used operative memory from the PMs to perform the lexing, the parsing, and the tree building (all together) is displayed in Fig. 9b.

6   Conclusion

This article presented an algorithm for parsing of data. The data language is defined by a context-free grammar without left recursion nor ϵ-rules. The grammar, for convenience, is described with the ABNF [5] metasyntax and is used directly without a prior refactoring. A part of the parsing result is a statically typed concrete syntax tree that accurately reflects the grammar. In the tunnel parsing algorithm, all processes are iterative to avoid an eventual overflowing of the thread-dedicated stack: the lexing, the parsing, the building of the syntax tree, the tree traversing, the conversion of the syntax tree into a string and the release of the dynamic memory occupied by the tree. A possible future extension is an automatic synchronization [27] of the previously generated trees and reflective printing [26].

A PM based on the algorithm, is using the control objects, their states, the tunnels and the routers to switch from one internal state to another. No in-depth search is performed for the reachable terminal states in the automata. As defined in the article, the algorithm has a linear execution time (relative to the number of input symbols) when operating on the basis of a deterministic context-free grammar, the most commonly used in practice, and with an exponential time at worse for some non-deterministic context-free grammar. The algorithm can also parse certain ambiguous grammars with linear execution time.

The multi-threaded linear parsing [24] (using a separate thread for each parsing module - lexer, parser and builder) could be beneficial when the different PM modules are having heavier tasks to perform. For example, the lexical grammar is more complex or the parser grammar is non-deterministic and the parser module needs more time to process the tokens. These are some of the possible scenarios, but additional study is required to properly show the benefits.

The tunnel parsing algorithm is implemented in TGS [24] that is a parser generator from ABNF [5,7] grammars to a program source code. The generated parsers parse and build a statically or a dynamically typed concrete syntax tree for a given input as instances of object-oriented classes. TGS can also generated parsers that build dynamically typed abstract syntax trees with different levels of abstraction. The software product has a built-in parser for ABNF that is generated by TGS itself.

A subsequent natural development of the current work is the extension of the presented algorithm with the ability to recognize context-free grammars that have ϵ-rules or left recursion.

Author contributions. Nikolay Handzhiyski developed the theory by the supervision and encouragement of Elena Somova, based on his previously existing software implementation in Tunnel Grammar Studio [24]. Nikolay Handzhiyski performed the tests and (along with Elena Somova) verified the results. The authors discussed the theory and the results and contributed to the final article.

References

1. Abstract syntax tree metamodel. https://www.omg.org/spec/ASTM/. Accessed 30 Nov 2019
2. Aho, A.V., Johnson, S.C.: LR parsing. ACM Comput. Surv. **6**, 26 (1974)
3. Aho, A.V.: Compilers: principles, techniques, & tools. Pearson/Addison Wesley (2007)
4. Another tool for language recognition (antlr). https://www.antlr.org/. Accessed 12 Apr 2020
5. Augmented BNF for syntax specifications: ABNF. https://tools.ietf.org/html/rfc5234. Accessed 30 Nov 2019
6. Brzozowski, J.A.: Canonical regular expressions and minimal state graphs for definite events (1962)
7. Case-sensitive string support in ABNF. https://tools.ietf.org/html/rfc7405. Accessed 30 Nov 2019
8. Chomsky, N.: On certain formal properties of grammars. Inf. Control **2**, 137–167 (1959)
9. Copeland, T.: Generating Parsers with JavaCC: an easy-to-use guide tor developers. Centennial Books, 2nd ed. (2007)
10. Extensible markup language (xml). https://www.w3.org/TR/xml/. Accessed 01 Sept 2019
11. Ford, B.: Parsing expression grammars: a recognition-based syntactic foundation. SIGPLAN Not. (2004)
12. Frost, R.A., Hafiz, R.: A new top-down parsing algorithm to accommodate ambiguity and left recursion in polynomial time. SIGPLAN Not. (2006)
13. Grune, D., Jacobs, C.J.H.: Parsing techniques: a practical guide. Ellis Horwood (1990)
14. Hopcroft, J.E., Ullman, J.D.: Introduction to automata theory, languages, and computation. Addison-Wesley Publishing Company (1979)
15. Java Compiler Compiler (JavaCC). https://javacc.org/. Accessed 12 Apr 2020
16. Microsoft windows API: profileapi.h header. https://docs.microsoft.com/en-us/windows/win32/api/profileapi/. Accessed 05 Sept 2020
17. Moore, R.C.: Removing left recursion from context-free grammars. In: Proceedings of the 1st North American Chapter of the Association for Computational Linguistics Conference (2000)
18. Rabin, M.O., Scott, D.: Finite automata and their decision problems. IBM J. Res. Develop. **3**, 114–125 (1959)
19. Parr, T.: Language implementation patterns: create your own domain-specific and general programming languages (pragmatic programmers). Pragmatic Bookshelf (2010)
20. Saraiva, J.: HaLeX: a Haskell library to model, manipulate and animate regular languages. In: Proceedings of the ACM Workshop on Functional and Declarative Programming in Education, University of Kiel Technical Report 0210 (2002)
21. Scott, E., Johnstone, A.: GLL parsing. Electron. Notes Theoret. Comput. Sci. **253**, 177–189 (2010)
22. Sipser, M.: Introduction to the theory of computation. Course Technology, 2nd ed. (2006)
23. The javascript object notation (json) data interchange format. https://tools.ietf.org/html/rfc8259. Accessed 01 Sept 2019

24. Tunnel grammar studio. https://www.experasoft.com/products/tgs/. Accessed 14 Apr 2020
25. Uniform resource identifier (uri): Generic syntax. https://tools.ietf.org/html/rfc3986. Accessed 01 Sept 2019
26. Zhu, Z., Zhang, Y., Ko, H.-S., Martins, P., Saraiva, J., Hu, Z.: Parsing and reflective printing, bidirectionally. In Proceedings of the 2016 ACM SIGPLAN International Conference on Software Language Engineering. ACM (2016)
27. Zhu, Z., Ko, H.-S., Zhang, Y., Martins, P., Saraiva, J., Hu, Z.: Unifying parsing and reflective printing for fully disambiguated grammars. New Generation Computing (2020)

Finding Code Clone Refactoring Techniques by Mapping Clone Context

Simon Baars$^{(\boxtimes)}$ (ID) and Ana Oprescu (ID)

University of Amsterdam, Amsterdam, Netherlands
simon.j.baars@gmail.com, A.M.Oprescu@uva.nl

Abstract. Reducing clones in source code is one of the techniques to improve the maintainability of a software system. Which refactoring technique to use depends on where a clone is found and what the relation between clone instances in a clone class is. We define three influencing factors on how a clone should be refactored: relation, location, and contents. The relation describes the inheritance relation among the clone instances in a clone class. The location describes where a clone instance is found in the source code. The contents describe what a clone instance spans.

Based on experiments on a corpus of open-source Java projects we find that most clones (77%) are in the body of methods or constructors and thus the "Extract Method" refactoring technique applies. What further techniques are required for the refactoring depends on the relation among the clone instances of a clone. We define four relations that require different further refactoring techniques: Common Class, Common Hierarchy, Common Interface, and Unrelated. The closer classes are related, the more favorable refactoring clones by such relations becomes. 37% of clones are in the same class, 24% share an inheritance hierarchy, 24% are unrelated and 15% have a common interface.

Keywords: Code Clones · Mining Software Repositories · Clone Relation · Inheritance · Object-Oriented Programming

1 Introduction

Duplicate code fragments are often considered as bad design [1]. They increase maintenance efforts or cause bugs in evolving software [2]. Changing one occurrence of a duplicated fragment may require changes in other occurrences [3]. Furthermore, duplicated code was shown to account for up to 25% of total system volume [4], entailing more code to be maintained.

Several refactoring techniques can be used to reduce duplication in source code [1]. Which refactoring technique to apply depends on where a clone is located and what the relation is between similar code fragments [5]. Subsequent studies have performed statistical measurements on how many clones fall into these location and relation categories [6,7].

Z. Porkoláb and V. Zsók (Eds.): CEFP 2019, LNCS 11950, pp. 344–357, 2023.
https://doi.org/10.1007/978-3-031-42833-3_9

We extend the state-of-the-art [7] by defining location, relation and contents categories for clones to determine how they should be refactored. The extra categories we provide help to propose a refactoring opportunity that can automatically be applied, rather than merely suggesting the technique that has to be used [7].

We study a large corpus of open-source software systems to determine which relation, location and contents category has the most clones. We find that a significant portion of clones is found in the bodies of constructors and methods, which indicate clones that can be refactored by applying the "Extract Method" refactoring technique. What further techniques apply when refactoring such a clone depends on the relation among its clone instances.

If clone instances share a common class, no further refactoring techniques are required. If they are in the same inheritance hierarchy, the "Pull-Up Method" can be used till the extracted method is in a location accessible by all instances. If the instances share a common interface, some languages allow to move the extracted method there. Otherwise, if the clone instances are not related, we either have to create a superclass/interface abstraction or create a utility class to put the common functionality.

2   Background and Related Work

We use two definitions to argue about code clones [8]:

- **Clone instance**: A single code fragment of which a similar/identical copy exists elsewhere in the codebase.
- **Clone class**: A set of similar/identical clone instances.

To argue about the similarity relation between clone instances in a clone class, several clone type definitions have been proposed [8]:

- **Type 1:** Identical code fragments except for variations in whitespace (may also be variations in layout) and comments.
- **Type 2:** Structurally/syntactically identical fragments except for variations in identifiers, literals, types, layout and comments.
- **Type 3:** Copied fragments with further modifications. Statements can be changed, added or removed in addition to variations in identifiers, literals, types, layout, and comments.

A higher type of clone means that it is harder to detect. It also makes the clone harder to refactor, as more transformations would be required. Higher clone types also become more disputable whether they actually indicate a harmful anti-pattern as not every clone is harmful [9,10].

Next, we outline relevant research to clone refactoring. A significant aspect is the context of clones.

2.1   Clone Context Analysis

Golomingi [5] explores mapping the relation between clone instances to refactoring methods. The author analyses the refactoring methods described by Martin Fowler [11] and analyzes what refactoring methods can be used to refactor clones with what inheritance relations. The identified clone relations are: Ancestor, Common Hierarchy, First Cousin, Same Method, Sibling, Single Class, Superclass and Unrelated. We extend this list with several more fine-grained relations, suitable for automatic refactoring.

Fontana et al. [6, 7] combine the research by Golomingi [5] with clone types 1 and 3 [8]. They use a large corpus [12] on which they perform statistical analysis of clone relations together with clone types. We repeat this research with a different setup, namely we elaborate further in the categories analysed, and thus get results with a finer granularity, and we use a larger dataset, namely the GitHub set of repositories [13].

2.2   Clone Refactoring

Krishnan et al. [14] approach clone refactoring as an optimization problem: how variability between cloned fragments influences the refactoring techniques required and their implications on system design. The main focus of this study is to find out which clones **can** be refactored. We extend this work by looking into which clones **should** be refactored. We propose definitions for refactorable clones together with thresholds to be able to limit their negative impact on system design. We measure which clones improve maintainability when refactored. This results in a set of thresholds that can be used to detect and refactor clones that should be refactored.

For refactoring clones, we took naming the extracted method outside of the scope of the study. To have this not influence the results, the metrics that determine the maintainability of an applied refactoring do not measure the quality of the name of the extracted method.

3   Context Analysis of Clones

The context of a clone determines how it should be refactored [1]. Based on current literature [6, 7], we define the following aspects of a clone as its context:

- **Relation:** The relation of clone instances in a clone class through inheritance.
- **Location:** Where a clone instance occurs in the code.
- **Contents:** The statements/declarations of a clone instance.

3.1   Relation

When merging code clones in object-oriented languages, it is important to consider the relation between clone instances. This relation has a big impact on how a clone should be refactored.

Fontana et al. [7] describe measurements on 50 open source projects on the relation between clone instances in a clone class. To do this, they first define several categories to argue about such relations. These categories are as follows:

- **Same Method**: All instances of the clone class are in the same method.
- **Same Class**: All instances of the clone class are in the same class.
- **Superclass**: All instances of the clone class are in a class that are child or parent of each other.
- **Sibling Class**: All instances of the clone class have the same parent class.
- **Ancestor Class**: All instances of the clone class are superclasses except for the direct superclass.
- **First Cousin Class**: All instances of the clone class have the same grandparent class.
- **Same Hierarchy Class**: All instances of the clone class belong to the same inheritance hierarchy, but do not belong to any of the other categories.
- **Same External Superclass**: All instances of the clone class have the same superclass, but this superclass is not included in the project but part of a library.
- **Unrelated class**: There is at least one instance of the clone class that is not in the same hierarchy.

We added the following categories, to gain more information about clones and be able to suggest a more fine-grained refactoring opportunity:

- **Same Direct Interface**: All instances of the clone class are in a class or interface implement the same interface.
- **Same Indirect Interface**: All instances of the clone class are in a class or interface that have a common interface anywhere in their inheritance hierarchy.
- **No Direct Superclass**: All instances of the clone class are in a class that does not have any superclass.
- **No Indirect Superclass**: All instances of the clone class are in a class that does not have any external classes in its inheritance hierarchy.
- **External Ancestor**: All instances of the clone class are in a class that does not have any external classes in its inheritance hierarchy.

We separate these relations into the following categories, because of their related refactoring opportunities:

- **Common Class**: *Same Method, Same Class*
- **Common Hierarchy**: *Superclass, Sibling Class, Ancestor Class, First Cousin, Same Hierarchy*
- **Common Interface**: *Same Direct Interface, Same Indirect Interface*

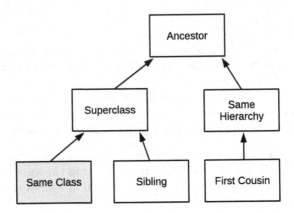

Fig. 1. Abstract figure displaying some relations of clone classes. Arrows represent superclass relations.

- **Unrelated**: *No Direct Superclass, No Indirect Superclass, External Superclass, External Ancestor*

   Every clone class only has a single relation, which is the first relation from the above list that the clone class applies to. For instance: all "Superclass" clones also apply to "Same Hierarchy", but because "Superclass" is earlier in the above list they will get the "Superclass" relation. This is because the items earlier in the above list denote a more favorable refactoring.

Common Class. The *Same method* and *Same class* relations share a common refactoring opportunity. Clones of both these categories, when extracted to a new method, can be placed in the same class. Both of these relations are most favorable for refactoring, as they require a minimal design tradeoff. Furthermore, global variables that are used in the class can be used without having to create method parameters.

Common Hierarchy. Clones that are in a common hierarchy can be refactored by using the "Extract Method" refactoring method followed by "Pull Up Method" until the method reaches a location that is accessible by all clone instances. However, the more often "Pull Up Method" has to be used, the more detrimental the effect is on system design. This is because putting a lot of functionality in classes higher up in an inheritance structure can result in the "God Object" anti-pattern. A god object is an object that knows too much or does too much [1].

Common Interface. Many object-oriented languages know the concept of "interfaces", which are used to specify a behavior that classes must implement. As code clones describe functionality and interfaces originally did not allow for functionality, interfaces did not open up refactoring opportunities for duplicated code. However, many programming languages nowadays support default implementations in interfaces. Since Java 7 and C# 8, these programming languages allow for functionality to be defined in interfaces. Many other object-oriented languages like Python allow this by nature, as they do not have a true notion of interfaces.

The greatest downside on system design of putting functionality in interfaces is that interfaces are per definition part of a classes' public contract. That is, all functionality that is shared between classes via an interface cannot be hidden by stricter visibility. Because of that, we favor all "Common Hierarchy" refactoring opportunities over "Common Interface".

Unrelated. Clones are unrelated if they share no common class or interface in their inheritance structure. These clones are least favorable for refactoring, because their refactoring will almost always have a major impact on system design. We formulated four categories of unrelated clones to look into their refactoring opportunities.

Cloned classes with a *No Direct Superclass* relation mark the opportunity for creating a superclass abstraction and placing the extracted method there. For clone classes with a *No Indirect Superclass* relation, it is possible to create such an abstraction for the ancestor that does not have a parent. Clone classes with an *External Superclass* or *External Ancestor* relation obstruct the possibility of creating a superclass abstraction. In such a case, it is possible to create an interface abstraction to make their relation explicit.

3.2   Location

A paper by Lozano et al. [15] discusses the harmfulness of cloning. The authors argue that 98% are produced at method-level. However, this claim is based on a small dataset and based on human copy-paste behavior rather than static code analysis. We decided to measure the locations of clones through static analysis in our dataset. We chose the following categories:

- **Method/Constructor Level:** A clone instance that does not exceed the boundaries of a single method or constructor (optionally including the declaration of the method or constructor itself).
- **Class Level:** A clone instance in a class, that exceeds the boundaries of a single method or contains something else in the class (like field declarations, other methods, etc.).
- **Interface/Enumeration Level:** A clone that is (a part of) an interface or enumeration.

We check the location of each clone instance for each of its nodes. If any node reports a different location from the others, we choose the location that is lowest in the above list. So for instance, if a clone instance has 15 nodes that denote a *Method Level* location but 3 nodes are *Class Level*, the clone instance becomes *Class Level*.

Method/Constructor Level Clones. Method/Constructor Level clones denote clones that are found in either a method or constructor. A constructor is a special method that is called when an object is instantiated. Most modern clone refactoring studies only focus on clones at method level [16,17]. This is because most clones reside at those places [7,15] and most of those clones can be refactored with a relatively simple set of refactoring techniques [7,18].

Class/Interface/Enumeration Level Clones. Class/Interface/Enumeration Level clone instances are found inside the body of one of these declarations and optionally include the declaration itself. It can also be a clone instance that exceeds the boundaries of a single method. These clone instances can contain fields, (abstract) methods, inner classes, enumeration fields, etc. These types of clones require various refactoring techniques to refactor. For instance, we might have to move fields in an inheritance hierarchy. Or, we might have to perform refactoring on an architectural level, if a large set of methods is cloned.

3.3   Contents

Finally, we looked at what nodes individual clone instances span. We selected a set of categories based on empirical evaluation of a set of clones in our dataset. We selected the following categories to be relevant for refactoring:

- **Full Method/Constructor/Class/Interface/Enumeration:** A clone that spans a full class, method, constructor, interface or enumeration, including its declaration.
- **Partial Method/Constructor:** A clone that spans (a part of) the body of a method/constructor. The declaration itself is not included.
- **Several Methods:** A clone that spans over two or more methods, either fully or partially, but does not span anything but methods (so not fields or anything in between).
- **Only Fields:** A clone that spans only global variables.
- **Other:** Anything that does not match with above-stated categories.

Full Method/Constructor/Class/Interface/Enumeration. These categories denote that a full declaration, including its body, is cloned with another declaration. These categories often denote redundancy and are often easy to refactor: one of both declarations is redundant and should be removed. All usages of the removed declaration should be redirected to the clone instance that was not removed. Sometimes, the declaration should be moved to a location that is accessible by all usages.

Partial Method/Constructor. These categories describe clone instances which are found in the body of a method or constructor. These clones can often be refactored by extracting a new method out of the cloned code.

Several Methods. Several methods cloned in a single class is a strong indication of implicit dependencies between two classes. This increases the chance that these classes are missing some form of abstraction, or their abstraction is used inadequately.

Only Fields. This category denotes that the clone spans over only global variables/fields that are declared outside of a method. This indicates data redundancy: pieces of data have an implicit dependency. In such cases, these fields may have to be encapsulated in a new object. Or, the fields should be somewhere in the inheritance structure where all objects containing the clone can access them.

Other. The "Other" category denotes all configurations of clone contents that do not fall into above categories. Often, these are combinations of the above stated concepts. For instance, a combination of constructors and methods or a combination of fields and methods is cloned. Clones in this category, similarly to "Several Methods", require more architectural-level refactorings. These are often more complicated to refactor, especially when aiming to automate this process.

4   CloneRefactor

To determine the context of clones, we use the tool CloneRefactor [19]. CloneRefactor uses JavaParser [20] to parse the Abstract Syntax Tree (AST) of Java source code. We then find cloned nodes in the syntax tree, of which we map the relation, location, and contents.

CloneRefactor uses this information to propose refactorings for the detected clones. Where clone instances are located in the code has a large impact on how it can be refactored, and what the impact on the design of the code is. In that way, the categorizations that CloneRefactor proposes helps determine which clones are most suitable for refactoring, as opposed to traditional clone detection approaches that do not take clone context into account.

5   Experimental Setup

To find out in which location, relation and contents category most clones are found, we performed measurements on a large corpus of diverse open-source projects.

5.1 The Corpus

For our experiments we use a large corpus of open-source projects assembled by Allamanis et al. [13]. This corpus contains a set of Java projects from GitHub, selected by the number of forks. The projects and files in this corpus were de-duplicated manually. This results in a variety of Java projects that reflect the quality of average open-source Java systems and are thus relevant to study.

Because CloneRefactor requires all dependencies for the projects it analyses, we created a set of scripts [21] to filter the corpus for all projects for which we can obtain all dependencies using Maven.

This procedure results in 2,267 Java projects including all their dependencies[1]. The projects vary in size and quality. The total size of all projects is 14,210,357 lines (11,315,484 when excluding whitespace) over a total of 99,586 Java files. This is an average of 6,268 lines over an average of 44 files per project, 141 lines on average per file. The largest project in the corpus is *VisAD* with 502,052 lines over 1,527 files.

5.2 Tool Validation

We have validated the correctness of CloneRefactor through unit tests and empirical validation. First, we created a set of 57 control projects[2] to verify the correctness in many (edge) cases. These projects test each identified relation, location and contents category (see Sect. 3), to see whether they are correctly identified. Next, we run the tool over the corpus and manually verify samples of the acquired results. This way, we check the correctness of the identified clones and their context.

6 Results

To determine the refactoring methods that can be used to refactor most clones, we perform analysis on the context of clones.

6.1 Relation

Table 1 displays the number of clone classes found for the entire corpus for different relations (see Sect. 3.1).

Our results show that most clones (37%) are in a common class. 24% of clones are in a common hierarchy. Another 24% of clones are unrelated. 15% of clones are in an interface.

---

[1] The full list of projects is in the `SimonBaars/GitHub-Java-Corpus-Scripts` GitHub repository as `filtered_projects.txt`.

[2] Control projects for testing CloneRefactor: https://github.com/SimonBaars/CloneRefactor/tree/master/src/test/resources.

Table 1. Number of clone classes per clone relation.

Category	Relation	Clone Classes	%	Total	%
Common Class	Same Class	22,893	26.8%	31,848	37.2%
	Same Method	8,955	10.5%		
Common Hierarchy	Sibling	15,588	18.2%	20,342	23.8%
	Superclass	2,616	3.1%		
	First Cousin	1,219	1.4%		
	Common Hierarchy	720	0.8%		
	Ancestor	199	0.2%		
Unrelated	No Direct Superclass	10,677	12.5%	20,314	23.7%
	External Superclass	4,525	5.3%		
	External Ancestor	3,347	3.9%		
	No Indirect Superclass	1,765	2.1%		
Common Interface	Same Direct Interface	7,522	8.8%	13,074	15.3%
	Same Indirect Interface	5,552	6.5%		

6.2   Location

Table 2 displays the number of clone instances found for the entire corpus for different location categories (see Sect. 3.2).

Table 2. Amount of clone instances with a per location category.

Category	Clone instances	%
Method Level	232,545	78.43%
Class Level	50,402	17.00%
Constructor Level	10,039	3.39%
Interface Level	2,693	0.91%
cre Enum Level	788	0.27%

We can see from these results that nearly 80% of clones are found at method level. 17% of clones are found at class level, meaning they exceed the boundaries of a single method (or do not span methods at all). Constructors account for approximately 3% of clones. In interfaces, only 1% of clones are found.

6.3   Contents

Table 3 displays the number of clone instances found for the entire corpus for different content categories (see Sect. 3.3).

Table 3. Number of clone instances for clone contents categories

Category	Contents	Clone instances	%	Total	%
Partial	Method Body	219,540	74.05%	229,521	77.42%
	Constructor Body	9,981	3.37%		
Other	Several Methods	22,749	7.67%	53,773	18.14%
	Only Fields	17,700	5.97%		
	Other	13,324	4.49%		
Full	Full Method	12,990	4.38%	13,173	4,44%
	Full Interface	64	0.02%		
	Full Constructor	58	0.02%		
	Full Class	37	0.01%		
	Full Enum	24	0.01%		

From these results, we see that 74% of clones span part of a method body
(77% if we include constructors). 8% of clones span several methods. 6% of clones
span only global variables. Only 4% of clones span a full declaration (method,
class, constructor, etc.).

7   Discussion

Regarding clone context, our results indicate that most clones (37%) are in a
common class. This is favorable for refactoring because the extracted method
does not have to be moved after extraction. 24% of clones are in a common
hierarchy. These refactorings are also often favorable. Another 24% of clones are
unrelated, which is often unfavorable because they often require more comprehensive refactoring. 15% of clones are in an interface.

Regarding clone contents, 74% of clones span part of a method body (77%
if we include constructors). 8% of clones span several methods, which often
require refactorings on a more architectural level. 6% of clones span only global
variables, requiring an abstraction to encapsulate these data declarations. Only
4% of clones span a full declaration (method, class, constructor, etc.).

Comparing our results for the relation categories to the similar study of
Fontana et al. [6,7], we get the percentages stated in. They use a large corpus [12]
on which they perform statistical analyses of clone relations together with clone
types. Table 4 displays the result of this analysis. We added percentages and
ordering to this table for easier comparison with the results of our work (see
Sect. 6.1). We also added the percentages of our work to this table.

Table 4. Clone relation analysis by Fontana et al. [6] measured over the Qualitas Corpus [12].

	Nr. of clones (Fontana et al.)	Percentage (Fontana et al.)	Percentage (Our Work)
Same Class	5,645	32.1%	26.8%
Same External Superclass	4,384	25.0%	20.6%
Unrelated Class	2,758	15.7%	18.4%
Sibling Class	2,721	15.5%	18.2%
Common Hierarchy Class	970	5.5%	0.8%
Same Method	569	3.2%	10.5%
First Cousin Class	416	2.4%	1.4%
Superclass	91	0.5%	3.1%
Ancestor Class	13	0.1%	0.2%

Some of our results differ quite a lot from their results. We think this is mostly accounted due to two differences in their setup:

- Fontana et al. use a corpus consisting of large higher-quality open-source software systems [12] where we use a more varied corpus [13].
- Fontana et al. use clone pairs while we use clone classes.

8   Conclusion

We defined categories to argue about the contextual information of code clones. These categories are:

- **Clone Relation**: The inheritance relation between clone instances in a clone class.
- **Clone Location**: The location of clone instances in the codebase.
- **Clone Contents**: The contents of clone instances in the codebase.

For each category we propose subcategories to get more insight into the number of transformations required for the refactoring and their impact on the maintainability of the software. We measure the distribution of clones over these categories on a corpus of 2,267 open-source systems to determine in which contexts most clones are found.

Regarding the **location** of clones: 78% of clones are found at method-level of which 77% is found in the body of a method or constructor. From this, we conclude that the "Extract Method" refactoring technique is most suitable to refactor most clones.

We also looked at the **relation** of clones. We found that 37% of clones are found in the same class. 24% of clones are in the same inheritance hierarchy. Another 24% of clones are unrelated. The final 15% of clones have the same interface. This implies that most clone refactorings require more transformations than only method extraction to ensure that the extracted method is accessible by all clone instances.

References

1. Fowler, M.: Refactoring: Improving the Design of Existing Code. Addison-Wesley Professional, Second (2018)
2. Heitlager, I., Kuipers, T., Visser, J.: A practical model for measuring maintainability. In: 6th International Conference on the Quality of Information and Communications Technology (QUATIC 2007), pp. 30–39. IEEE (2007)
3. Ostberg J., Wagner, S.: On automatically collectable metrics for software maintainability evaluation. In: 2014 Joint Conference of the International Workshop on Software Measurement and the International Conference on Software Process and Product Measurement, pp. 32–37 (2014). https://doi.org/10.1109/IWSM.Mensura.2014.19
4. Bruntink, M., Van Deursen, A., Van Engelen, R., Tourwe, T.: On the use of clone detection for identifying crosscutting concern code. IEEE Trans. Software Eng. **31**(10), 804–818 (2005)
5. Koni-N'Sapu, G.G.: A scenario based approach for refactoring duplicated code in object oriented systems, Master's thesis, University of Bern (2001)
6. Fontana, F.A., Zanoni, M., Zanoni, F.: Duplicated code refactoring advisor (DCRA): a tool aimed at suggesting the best refactoring techniques of java code clones, Ph.D. dissertation, Universita degli Studi di Milano-Bicocca (2012)
7. Arcelli Fontana, F., Zanoni, M., Zanoni, F.: A duplicated code refactoring advisor. In: Lassenius, C., Dingsøyr, T., Paasivaara, M. (eds.) XP 2015. LNBIP, vol. 212, pp. 3–14. Springer, Cham (2015). https://doi.org/10.1007/978-3-319-18612-2_1
8. Roy, C.K., Cordy, J.R.: A survey on software clone detection research. Queen's Sch. Comput. TR **541**(115), 64–68 (2007)
9. Jarzabek, S., Xue, Y. :Are clones harmful for maintenance? In: Proceedings of the 4th International Workshop on Software Clones, ser. IWSC 2010, New York, NY, USA: ACM, pp. 73–74 (2010). ISBN: 978-1-60558-980-0. https://doi.org/10.1145/1808901.1808911
10. Kapser, C.J., Godfrey, M.W.: "Cloning considered harmful" considered harmful: patterns of cloning in software. Empirical Software Eng. **13**(6), 645–692 (2008)
11. Fowler, M.: Refactoring: improving the Design of Existing Code. Addison- Wesley Professional (1999)
12. Tempero, E.: The qualitas corpus: a curated collection of java code for empirical studies. In: Asia Pacific Software Engineering Conference, pp. 336–345. IEEE (2010)
13. Allamanis, M., Sutton, C.: Mining source code repositories at massive scale using language modeling. In: The 10th Working Conference on Mining Software Repositories, pp. 207–216. IEEE (2013)
14. Krishnan, G.P., Tsantalis, N.: Refactoring clones: an optimization problem. In: 2013 IEEE International Conference on Software Maintenance, pp. 360–363. IEEE (2013)
15. Lozano, A., Wermelinger, M., Nuseibeh, B.: Evaluating the harmfulness of cloning: a change based experiment. In: Fourth International Workshop on Mining Software Repositories (MSR 2007: ICSE) Workshops, pp. 18–18. IEEE (2007)

16. Yue, R., Gao, Z., Meng, N., Xiong, Y., Wang, X., Morgenthaler, J.D.: Automatic clone recommendation for refactoring based on the present and the past. In: 2018 IEEE International Conference on Software Maintenance and Evolution (ICSME), pp. 115–126, IEEE (2018)
17. Yongting, Y., Dongsheng, L., Liping, Z.: Detection technology and application of clone refactoring. In: Proceedings of the 2018 2nd International Conference on Management Engineering, Software Engineering and Service Sciences, pp. 128–133. ACM (2018)
18. Kodhai, E., Kanmani, S.: Method-level code clone modification using refactoring techniques for clone maintenance. Adv. Comput. 4(2), 7 (2013)
19. SimonBaars: Simonbaars/clonerefactor: a tool that automatically refactors duplicate code fragments in java. https://github.com/SimonBaars/CloneRefactor
20. Smith, N., van Bruggen, D., Tomassetti, F.: Javaparser (2018)
21. SimonBaars, Simonbaars/github-java-corpus-scripts: Scripts to prepare a github java corpus for clone analysis. https://github.com/SimonBaars/GitHub-Java-Corpus-Scripts

Code Quality Metrics for Functional Features in Modern Object-Oriented Languages

Bart Zuilhof[1], Rinse van Hees[2], and Clemens Grelck[1(✉)]

[1] University of Amsterdam, Amsterdam, The Netherlands
c.grelck@uva.nl
[2] Info Support BV, Veenendaal, The Netherlands
rinse.vanhees@infosupport.com

Abstract. The evolution of main-stream object-oriented languages such as Java and C# has introduced new code constructs that originate from the functional programming paradigm. We hypothesise that a relationship exists between the usage of these constructs and the error-proneness of code. We define a number of measures specifically focusing on functional programming constructs in the context of object-oriented languages. Based on these measures we define a metric that relates the usage of the functional programming constructs to error-proneness of classes. We validate our metric and confirm our hypothesis using an established methodology for empirical validation of code metrics. Our results presented in this paper grant new insights into the evolution of (increasingly) multi-paradigm programming languages at the cross-roads of the functional and the object-oriented programming paradigms.

1 Introduction

Recent advances in programming language technology have been driven by the cross-pollination of the object-oriented paradigm (OO) and the functional paradigm (FP). Witnesses of this development are the growing popularity of the multi-paradigm language Scala [1] and, even more so, the continuous introduction of functional programming features into main-stream object-oriented (OO) languages such as Java [2] and C# [3].

Taking the example of C#, functions since Version 3.0 are first-class constructs, including support for higher-order functions. So-called lambda-functions introduce the concept of anonymous functions to the world of C#. Pattern matching supports concise and rich syntax for switch-case statements. The concept of lazy evaluation now comes along with a uniform C# query syntax to retrieve data from different sources [4], named Language Integrated Query (LINQ). Previously, lazy evaluation was only possible by using the `Lazy<T>`-keyword [3]. LINQ introduced syntax for list operations such as `map`, `filter` and `sort`, which are basically higher-order functions as known from functional

Z.Porkoláb and V.Zsók (Eds.): CEFP 2019, LNCS 11950, pp. 358–374, 2023.
https://doi.org/10.1007/978-3-031-42833-3_10

languages proper. The LINQ syntax allows for the concise specification of aggregate list operations, as demonstrated by a small example shown in Listing 1.

```
1  Enumerable.Range(1, 10)
2    .Where(i => i % 2 == 0) //filter
3    .Select(i => i * 10) //map
4    .OrderBy(i => -i); //sort
5  // ["100, "80, "60, "40, "20]
```

Listing 1. C# code example using the FP-inspired LINQ library

The increasing integration of object-oriented and functional language features creates new interest into systematic multi-paradigm code evaluation in software evolution. Landkroon has shown that metrics from the OO paradigm and the FP paradigm can be mapped to the multi-paradigm language Scala [5]. However, the integration of OO and FP features introduces artefacts that are neither covered by OO-inspired code metrics nor by FP-inspired code metrics. For example, the usage of mutable class variables in lambda-functions, whose execution might be deferred, potentially leads to issues that are unknown in the pure and side-effect-free world of functional programming. Neither source code metrics proposed for the OO paradigm [6–8] nor their counterparts from the FP paradigm [9–12] are suitable to give a valuable indication of quality regarding the usage of these combined constructs.

Code measures that indicate complexity might have an intuitive relationship with error-proneness. However, this does not have any concrete meaning and usefulness since one cannot substantiate a prediction just by intuition. Therefore, evidence must be provided that a measure is useful. This can be achieved by proving a relationship to an external attribute such as error-proneness.

We adopt the approach of Briand et al. [13], where the term *measure* refers to an assessment on the size of an attribute of the code. The purpose of our research is to explore the relationship between the usage of the FP-inspired constructs and the error-proneness of the classes where these constructs occur. We define measures that cover the usage of these constructs and empirically relate them to the error-proneness of the corresponding class.

The remainder of the paper is organised as follows: In Sect. 2 we provide a more in-depth analysis of functional language features in C# and discuss their impact on traditional measures such as source lines of code and cyclomatic complexity. In Sect. 3 we present our proposed measures on the crossroads of OO and FP. We describe our experimental setup in Sect. 4 and the findings of our experiments in Sect. 5. At last, we discuss potential threats to validity in Sect. 6, sketch out related work in Sect. 7 and draw conclusions in Sect. 8.

2 Problem Analysis

In the following we present two code snippets with the exact same functionality, namely to obtain a list with vehicles starting with 'Red'. For the first implementation shown in Listing 2 we choose a traditional imperative approach. The code has a Source Lines of Code (SLOC) count of 11 and a Cyclomatic Complexity (CC) of 3 since there are two branching points. This is how the general complexity of the snippet translates back into the values returned by the metrics.

```
1   List<string> vehicles = new List<string>()
2    {"Red Car", "Red Plane", "Blue Car"};
3
4   List<string> redVehicles =  new List<string>();
5
6   for (int i = 0; i < vehicles.Count; i++)
7   {
8       if (vehicles[i].StartsWith("Red"))
9       {
10          redVehicles.Add(vehicles[i]);
11      }
12  }
```

Listing 2. C# example code snippet in traditional style

The second implementation shown in Listing 3 uses the LINQ library, which encourages the use of lambda-expressions. The more functional code has a SLOC count of 5 and a cyclomatic complexity of 1 since there are no branching points at all. Even though the functionality and the logical complexity are the same with both snippets, both cyclomatic complexity and SLOC differ drastically.

```
1   List<string> vehicles = new List<string>()
2    {"Red Car", "Red Plane", "Blue Car"};
3
4   List<string> redVehicles = vehicles
5       .Where(t => t.StartsWith("Red"))
6       .ToList();
```

Listing 3. Example of Fig. 2 using the FP-inspired LINQ syntax

3   Candidate Measures

In this section we propose a number of measures that are explicitly geared at FP-inspired language features in object-oriented languages.

3.1   Number of Lambda-Functions Used in a Class (LC)

Lambda-functions in the context of OO languages offer a concise way to write anonymous functions inline. Compared to a regular method, both the parameter type(s) and the return type can be omitted. This might introduce constructs which are harder to understand. An example for this scenario is given in Listing 4. To calculate the value for this measure, we traverse the abstract syntax tree (AST). For each AST node of type *LambdaExpression*, we increment the counter for this measure by one.

```
1   List<int> numbers = new List<int>() { 1, 2, 3 };
2
3   IEnumerable biggerThan2 = numbers.Where(x => x > 2);
```

Listing 4. Example of a lambda-expression in C#

3.2   Source Lines of Lambda (SLOL)

Whereas simple lambda expressions are usually easy to comprehend, more complex lambda-expression may quickly become a challenge. In Listing 5 we give an example of a multi-line lambda-expression. As curly braces are taken into account by the 'source lines of code'-measure [7], we also include these curly braces when calculating the span of the lambda expression. Therefore, the snippet in Listing 5 has a SLOL-count of $1 + 1 + 4 = 6$.

```
1   IEnumerable<int> bla = Enumerable.Range(1, 10)
2       .Where(i => i % 2 == 0)
3       .Select(i => i * 10)
4       .OrderBy(i =>
5           {
6               return -i;
7           });
```

Listing 5. Example of a multi-line lambda-expression in C#

3.3   Lambda Score (LSc)

The density of the usage of lambda functions in a class can give an indication of how functional a class is. Our hypothesis for this measure is that a relationship exists between how functional a class is and the error-proneness of the class. We calculate this lambda density with Eq. 1.

$$LSc = \frac{SLOL}{SLOC} \tag{1}$$

LSc evaluates to 1 if each line of a class is spanned by a lambda-expression and to 0 if no lambda-expression occurs whatsoever.

3.4   Number of Lambda-Functions Using Mutable Field Variables in a Class (LMFV)

Sometimes it is hard to predict when a lambda-function is actually executed. Thus, it becomes likewise hard to reason about what value for the mutable field will be used. An example illustrates this scenario in Listing 6. To calculate the value for this measure, we traverse the AST. For each variable inside a lambda expression, we check if the variable is non-constant and field-scoped by using the semantic data model (SDM) of the class. If this test passes, we increment the counter for this measure.

```
1  class A
2  {
3      int _y = 2;
4      void F()
5      {
6          Func<int, bool> biggerThanY =
7              x => x > _y;
8      }
9  }
```

Listing 6. Example of a C# lambda-expression with a reference to a mutable field variable

3.5   Number of Lambda-Functions Using Mutable Local Variables in a Class (LMLV)

A related scenario is to reason about the concrete value of a mutable local variable inside a lambda-function; we show an example in Listing 7. In order to calculate the value for this measure, we traverse the AST. For each variable inside a lambda-expression we check if the variable is non-constant and locally scoped by using the semantic model of the class. If this test passes, we increase the counter for this measure.

```
1   void F()
2   {
3       int y = 2;
4       Func<int, bool> greaterThanY =
5           x => x > y;
6   }
```

Listing 7. Example of a C# lambda-expression with a reference to a mutable local variable

3.6 Number of Lambda-Functions with Side-Effects Used in a Class (LSE)

We think that the combination of side-effects in lambda-functions with e.g. parallelisation or lazy evaluation is dangerous because it can be hard to reason about when these side-effects effectively occur. We show an example for this scenario in Listing 8. To calculate the value for this measure, we once more traverse the AST of each class. For each variable inside a lambda-expression, we check if local or field variables are being mutated.

```
1   static int _y = 2;
2
3   Func<int, bool> f = x =>
4   {
5       _y++;
6       return x > _y;
7   };
```

Listing 8. Example of a C# lambda-expression with a side-effect to a mutable field variable

3.7 Number of Non-terminated Collection Queries in a Class (UTQ)

By not terminating a collection query, it is hard to reason when the query will be executed. Since these collection queries may contain functions that contain side-effects and use outside scoped variables, the execution at different run-times can yield different and unexpected results. An example for this scenario is given in Listing 9. To calculate the value for this measure we traverse the AST and count how many `IEnumarable<T>` are initiated.

```
1   List<int> nmbs = new List<int>()
2   { 1, 2, 3 };
3   int y = 2;
4   IEnumerable biggerThanY = numbers
5       .Where(x => x > y);
```

Listing 9. Example of a LINQ-query that is not evaluated/terminated

4   Experimental Setup

In this section we explain the various aspects of our experimental setup.

4.1   Methodology

To empirically validate a proposed metric Briand et al. [13] describe three assumptions that should be satisfied, namely:

1. **The internal attribute A_1 is related to the external attribute A_2.** The hypothesised relationship between attribute A_1 and A_2 can be tested if Assumption 2 and Assumption 3 are assumed, by finding a relationship between X_1 and X_2.
2. **Measure X_1 measures the internal attribute A_1.** Measure X_1 measures defined attributes of the code such as mutable external variables used in lambda-functions. This measure X_1 is assumed to measure A_1; A_1 is the internal attribute such as purity of the lambda usages.
3. **Measure X_2 measures the external attribute A_2.** Measure X_2 measures the error-proneness A_2 of a given class. The measure X_2 depends on whether the class contains a bug or not.

4.2   Relating Functional Constructs to Error-Proneness

Investigating the relationship between code metrics and error-proneness is commonly done by creating a prediction model for error-proneness based on code metrics [6,13–15]. The logistic regression classification technique [16] is often used to create such a prediction model [5,6,14,17]. With a logistic regression model trained with the data from our analysis framework, which processes repositories, we explore the relationship between our measured constructs and error-proneness.

Univariate Logistic Regression. With a univariate logistic regression model we can evaluate, in isolation, the prediction model for error-proneness based on the measured constructs. Using Eq. 2 we construct a prediction model.

$$P(faulty = 1) = \frac{e^{\beta_0 + \beta_l X_l}}{1 + e^{\beta_0 + \beta_l X_l}} \tag{2}$$

Her,e $\beta_l X_l$ is the coefficient multiplied with the value of the added measure.

Baseline. To show that our measures are useful for the prediction of error-proneness, their inclusion must yield better results than metrics that are currently used in industry. This set of metrics will define the baseline for our study. We use the union of a set of general code metrics with a set of object-oriented metrics. For general code metrics we take Source Lines of Code (SLOC) [18,19], Cyclomatic Complexity (CC) [8] and Comment Density (CD) [20].

The OO metric suite used for this study was defined by Chidamber and Kemerer [21]. For our baseline, we implement those metrics that showed any significance in Chidamber and Kemerer's study, namely *Weighted Methods per Class (WMC), Depth of Inheritance Tree (DIT), Response for a Class (RFC), Number of Children of a Class (NOC), Coupling between Object Classes (CBO), Lack of Cohesion of Methods (LCOM).*

Multivariate Logistic Regression. Besides looking if our univariate logistic regression model gives an indication of good performance, we can use multivariate logistic regression to test if we can improve the model with the in-place OO metrics. The baseline for the evaluation of the model will be a multivariate logistic regression model based on our baseline set of metrics. To see if we can achieve an increased performance compared to our baseline model, we substitute baseline dependent variables with candidate measures as l.

$$P(faulty = 1) = \frac{e^{\beta_0 + \beta_1 X_i + \beta_2 X_2 + ... + \beta_n X_n + \beta_l X_l}}{1 + e^{\beta_0 + \beta_1 X_i + \beta_2 X_2 + ... + \beta_n X_n + \beta_l X_l}} \tag{3}$$

Model Validation. We choose to validate our model using cross-validation, which is commonly used for the validation of prediction models [22,23]. We use the holdout method for cross-validation. By default, holdout cross-validation separates the data set into a training set and a smaller test set. To compensate for the randomness of the division, we run the model fitting with multiple different selections of the training set, average the results and assess the standard deviation. Based on a classification report created for the holdout set, we assess the performance of the model. We use the F_1-score, which calculates the harmonic mean of the precision and recall (F_1-score) to assess our model performance with Eq. 4.

$$F_1 = 2 * \frac{Precision * Recall}{Precision + Recall} \tag{4}$$

Since our data set is unbalanced, as can be seen in Fig. 1, one could choose to calculate the micro-average between the F_1-scores for the 'faulty-classes'-class and the 'non-faulty-classes'-class, where the support for each class is weighted. However, since we want good prediction performance in both classes we use the macro-average instead which calculates the harmonic mean between the two F_1-scores [24].

4.3   Measuring Functional Constructs

By using the compiler platform SDK 'Roslyn' which is created by the '.NET Foundation' we can derive AST's and SDM's from the classes of a given project. By traversing the AST for each class using Roslyn's implementation of the visitor pattern, we visit each syntax node in depth-first order. Where needed we can request additional data from the semantic data model (SDM) during the traversal, such as: what is the type and the level of scope for a given variable. Using this method we can calculate the values for all of our candidate measures.

4.4   Measuring Error-Proneness

To make an estimation on how error-prone a class is, we make the assumption that if a class during the lifetime of a project was updated by a bug fix, the class is error-prone. Unfortunately, the GitHub API does not provide an easy way to identify bug-fixing commits. From a GitHub repository, we can request all the issues that were created regarding a bug. With this information, we identify all commits that close an issue by searching for issue closing keywords as described in [25].

All commits that mention an issue that was identified as a bug-related issue, are marked as bug-fix commits. We then extract the affected lines from the metadata of the commit. Then we deduce with which classes the affected lines intersect in the parent version of the bug-fix commit by parsing the AST of the updated file. We use the parent version of the bug-fix commit since this is the version where the bug existed. Each of these intersected classes will be marked as error-prone.

4.5   Dataset

For our study we analyse the following complex software projects, all obtained from github:

CLI The .NET Core command-line interface (CLI) is a new cross-platform tool chain for developing .NET applications. The CLI is a foundation upon which higher-level tools, such as Integrated Development Environments (IDEs), editors, and build orchestrators, can rest [26].

ML Machine Learning for .NET is a cross-platform open-source machine learning framework which makes machine learning accessible to .NET developers. ML.NET allows .NET developers to develop their own models and infuse custom machine learning into their applications, using .NET, even without prior expertise in developing or tuning machine learning models [27].

AKK Akka.NET is a community-driven port of the popular Java/Scala framework Akka to .NET. Akka is a toolkit for building highly concurrent, distributed, and resilient message-driven applications. Akka is the implementation of the Actor Model. [28].

ASP ASP.NET Core is an open-source and cross-platform framework for building modern cloud-based Internet-connected applications, such as web applications, internet-of-things (IoT) applications and mobile backends. ASP.NET Core applications can run on .NET Core or on the full .NET Framework [29].

IS4 IdentityServer is a free, open source OpenID Connect and OAuth 2.0 framework for ASP.NET Core [30].

JF Jellyfin is a Free Software Media System that puts you in control of managing and streaming your media [31].

ORA OpenRA is an open source real-time strategy game engine for early Westwood games such as Command & Conquer: Red Alert written in C# using SDL and OpenGL [32].

DNS dnSpy is a debugger and .NET assembly editor. It can be used to edit and debug assembly code even in the absence of source code [33].

ILS ILSpy is the open-source .NET assembly browser and decompiler [34].

HUM Humanizer meets all your .NET needs for manipulating and displaying strings, enums, dates, times, timespans, numbers and quantities [35].

EF EF Core is an object-relational mapper (O/RM) that enables .NET developers to work with a database using .NET objects. It eliminates the need for most of the data access code that developers usually need to write [36].

Our selection of projects covers a wide range of applications from various domains.

5   Experimental Evaluation

In Fig. 1 we show descriptive statistics for the output of our static analysis. We excluded the test projects since they are likely to be modified in a bug-fixing commit to detect the bug should it occur again.

Interestingly, the relationship of bug-fixing commits and faulty classes can be either positive or negative. This can be explained by that a set of the commits are only updating configuration or non-C# code files. Hence, it is possible that the number of bug fixes exceeds the number of faulty classes. Likewise possible is the alternative scenario that one commit modifies multiple classes and, hence, the number of bug fixes is less than the number of faulty classes. The variance in the ratio of $\frac{Classes}{FaultyClasses}$ between projects is also notable. This can be partly attributed to the lifetime of a project. However, some projects contradict this hypothesis, e.g. the ratio for ILSpy is not higher than that of, for instance, the AKKA.NET project, even though the ILSpy project is more than twice as old.

Project	Classes	Bug fixes	Faulty classes
CLI [26]	328	54	24
ML [27]	1404	27	18
AKK [28]	1621	171	199
ASP [29]	3212	99	118
IS4 [30]	331	40	49
JF [31]	1420	81	88
ORA [32]	1990	227	149
DNS [33]	5345	?	159
ILS [34]	1011	95	70
HUM [35]	124	23	10
EF [36]	1432	975	437

Fig. 1. Descriptive statistics (During our research the labels in the repository of dnSpy (DNS) were deleted, leaving us unable to derive the bug-fix count.)

To evaluate the measures in isolation, we fit and evaluate a prediction model using univariate regression. In Fig. 2 we can see the macro-average F1-score for each project in combination with each candidate measure.

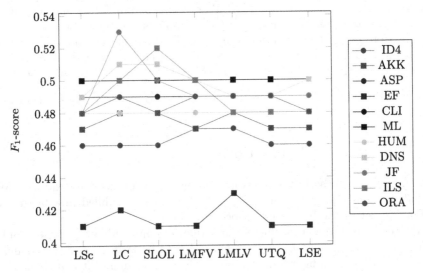

Fig. 2. F_1-score prediction model: univariate regression

In Fig. 2 we see m_1, as described in Sect. 3.1, performs well on the projects ILSpy and JellyFin. The univariate regression models created for the Entity Framework project, perform relatively poorly compared to the other projects. Notably, the SLOC measure performs the best as an isolated measure in the Entity Framework project. Looking at the raw input for the project, we see that only $\frac{1}{5}$ of the classes use lambda-expressions, whereas for other projects, e.g. AKKA.NET, this ratio is $\frac{1}{3}$. The infrequent usage of lambda-expressions could influence the usability of our measures.

The Humanizer project seems to score an almost stable 0.48. When looking into the raw output data from our static analysis we see only $\frac{1}{9}$ classes in this project uses lambda-expressions. Thus, this project might not be functional enough for our measures to perform well.

To evaluate the value of our candidate measures compared to our baseline, we create a multivariate regression model based on K-best features for each of the projects. Figure 3 shows how many out of 11 K-best models include the corresponding measure as a feature.

Measure	# Models
LSc	3
LC	6
SLOL	9
LMLV	4
LMFV	6
LSE	0
UTQ	0

Fig. 3. Inclusion candidate measures K-best model

Most notable is that 9 out of 11 projects include the SLOL-measure as described in Sect. 3.2. The one project where SLOL was excluded in the K-Best, was the Humanizer project. As described earlier, the project does not use a lot of the FP inspired constructs and therefore, is not suitable for our measures. The measure LSE, counting the numbers of side-effects in lambdas, and UTQ, counting the number of unterminated collection queries, both do not seem to yield an interesting result. Even though these FP-inspired constructs do occur in almost all projects, the amount of occurrences is too limited to yield good values.

To do a comparison between our baseline model and the selection of the K-best features model, we plot our results in Fig. 4. We observe that the worst-performing project did not gain improvement in performance, but the first quartile has a performance improvement of 0.02. The best performing project likewise has a 0.02 improvement in performance.

6 Threats to Validity

While we are confident in the correctness of our methodology and the accuracy of our findings, it is good practice to discuss potential threats to validity and the corresponding limitations.

Firstly, our research is focused on the language C# and its ecosystem. The details of the integration of functional features into object-oriented languages

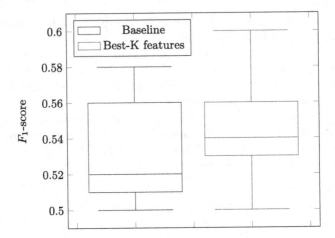

Fig. 4. F_1-score prediction model: multivariate regression

naturally differs slightly from language to language. Hence, it is plausible to expect similar findings from Java or Scala, but we cannot provide evidence for this.

Within the world of C# we only analysed 11 open-source projects. All projects are non-trivial in size, make use of functional language features and represent a wide variety of application domains. Still, we cannot necessarily claim that they are representative for C# projects in general. Including more projects in our analysis would obviously strengthen our findings, but this would require substantial additional resources for research.

We must admit that our methodology for the identification of error-prone classes is merely a best-effort approximation of reality. Unfortunately, github and likewise other publicly available source code repositories lack support for any more educated or direct technique. Our approach, hence, inevitably leads to both false positives as well as false negatives. The size of relevant software projects and the intimate knowledge of each software project required to manually identify error-prone classes prohibits any quantitative estimate on the accuracy of our methodology for the identification of error-prone classes.

We estimate the error-proneness of a class by looking at the number of bug-fixes applied to it. This again is a best-effort approximation. There is no way to guarantee that a class that was never updated by a bug-fix is bug-free. Bugs might have not been identified yet, or maybe bugs that were never fixed by a bug-fix commit were accidentally fixed during a refactoring.

7   Related Work

Uesbeck et al. [37] did a control experiment investigating the impact of lamb-das in C++ on productivity, compilation errors and time to fix said errors. The authors demonstrate that the impact of lambdas, as opposed to iterators, on the number of tasks completed was significant: *"The percentage of time spent on fixing compilation errors was 56.37% for the lambda group while it was 44.2% for the control group with 3.5% of the variance being explained by the group difference."*. The groups consisted of developers with different amount of programming experience. The increased time of fixing compiler error where lambda-functions were used, which seems likely to be the result of lambda-expressions being harder to reason about, which supports our hypothesis.

Finifter et al. [38] show how verifiable purity can be used to verify high-level security properties. By combining determinism with object-capabilities a new class of languages is described that allows purity in largely imperative programs.

Sharma et al. [39] compiled a survey on software metrics from the object-oriented domain. Ryder [9], Ryder and Thompson [10], van den Berg [11] as well as Király and Kitlei [12] developed software metrics specifically geared at the functional domain. Warmuth [40] investigated the validity of software measures for the functional programming language Erlang.

Closer to our own work, Landkroon [5] investigated the suitability of existing suites of software measures proposed in either the object-oriented or the functional context to predict error-proneness of code written in the multi-paradigm language Scala.

We are not aware of any previous work on software metrics or measures that focuses on the introduction of quintessentially functional language features into object-oriented languages, which only has gained popularity and traction in recent years. This paper extends our own preliminary work informally published before [41]. A more in-depth coverage of the subject matter and our findings is available in [42].

8   Conclusion and Discussion

We investigated the evolution of the OO language C# and what features inspired by the FP paradigm are added. The development and introduction of the FP-inspired features seem to be going rapidly and there is no indication of this development slowing down. This new declarative syntax enables more concise code constructions and, thus, enables software engineers to achieve more functionality with less code. However, these constructs are introduced without the constraints that would be present in pure functional languages.

To cover the new type of complexity introduced by these FP-inspired constructs and their usage outside of purely functional contexts, we defined various source code measures that cover the following FP-inspired constructs: closed lambda-expressions, lambda-expressions with mutable field or local variables and lambda-expressions with side-effects. Furthermore, we defined a measure to report unterminated collection queries.

The candidate measure SLOL yields promising results when used in a univariate prediction model for all projects under investigation that actively use FP-inspired constructs. To assess if we can improve our baseline model, we swap the weaker metrics from the baseline model with stronger metrics based on our set of defined measures. We were able to achieve a marginal improvement (F_1-score 0.0–0.02) with respect to different projects. For some projects, we were able to achieve a small improvement+ in the prediction model. On the contrary, the projects where a low amount of FP-inspired constructs were used, the candidate measures do not yield value.

So we did find a correlation between our measures and error-proneness, but the correlation is too uncertain to make claims regarding causality.

As described in the introduction, main-stream OO languages adopt more features from the FP paradigm. Our hypothesis is that the set of FP-inspired features will become more wide-spread and receive a more FP-like syntax. The increase of performance in our prediction models found in this research seems marginal for now. But we hypothesise that their relevance will increase in the future, based on the ongoing evolution of OO languages and the increasing adoption of these FP-inspired features by main-stream developers.

Acknowledgements. We would like to thank the anonymous reviewers for their valuable feedback and the Erasmus+ Strategic Partnership for Higher Education *Focusing Education on Composability, Comprehensibility and Correctness of Working Software (FE3CWS/3COWS)*, project-ID 2017-1-SK01-KA203-035402, for their support.

References

1. Carbonnelle, P.: PYPL. http://pypl.github.io/PYPL.html. Accessed 11 Jan 2019
2. Oracle: Java 8 update notes. https://www.oracle.com/technetwork/java/javase/8-whats-new-2157071.html. Accessed 11 Jan 2019
3. Microsoft: C# update notes. https://docs.microsoft.com/en-us/dotnet/csharp/whats-new/csharp-version-history. Accessed 23 Jan 2019
4. Wagner, B.: Language Integrated Query (LINQ). https://github.com/dotnet/cli (2017)
5. Landkroon, E.: Code quality evaluation for the multi-paradigm programming language Scala. MSc Thesis, University of Amsterdam, Netherlands (2017)
6. Basili, V.R., Briand, L.C., Melo, W.L.: A validation of object-oriented design metrics as quality indicators. IEEE Trans. Softw. Eng. **22**, 751–761 (1996)
7. Heitlager, I., Kuipers, T., Visser, J.: A practical model for measuring maintainability. In: 6th International Conference on Quality of Information and Communications Technology (QUATIC 2007), pp. 30–39. IEEE (2007)
8. McCabe, T.J.: A complexity measure. IEEE Trans. Softw. Eng. **2**, 308–320 (1976)
9. Ryder, C.: Software Measurement for Functional Programming. PhD thesis, University of Kent at Canterbury, United Kingdom (2004)
10. Ryder, C., Thompson, S.J.: Software metrics: measuring Haskell. In: 6th Symposium on Trends in Functional Programming (TFP 2005), pp. 31–46 (2005)
11. van den Berg, K.: Software measurement and functional programming. PhD thesis, University of Twente, Netherlands (1995)
12. Király, R., Kitlei, R.: Application of complexity metrics in functional languages. In: 8th Joint Conference on Mathematics and Computer Science (MaCS 2010), Selected Papers, pp. 267–282 (2010)
13. Briand, L., El Emam, K., Morasca, S.: Theoretical and empirical validation of software product measures. In: International Software Engineering Research Network, Technical Report ISERN-95-03 (1995)

14. Gyimothy, T., Ferenc, R., Siket, I.: Empirical validation of object-oriented metrics on open source software for fault prediction. IEEE Trans. Softw. Eng. **31**, 897–910 (2005)
15. Briand, L.C., Melo, W.L., Wust, J.: Assessing the applicability of fault-proneness models across object-oriented software projects. IEEE Trans. Softw. Eng. **28**, 706–720 (2002)
16. Hosmer, D.W., Jr., Lemeshow, S., Sturdivant, R.X.: Applied Logistic Regression. Wiley, Hoboken (2013)
17. Lanubile, F., Visaggio, G.: Evaluating predictive quality models derived from software measures: lessons learned. J. Syst. Softw. **38**, 225–234 (1997)
18. Nguyen, V., Deeds-Rubin, S., Tan, T., Boehm, B.W.: A SLOC counting standard. In: COCOMO-II Forum, pp. 1–16 (2007)
19. Boehm, B.W., et al.: Software Cost Estimation with COCOMO-II. Prentice-Hall, Upper Saddle River (2000)
20. SonarQube: Metric definitions (2019). https://docs.sonarqube.org/latest/userguide/metric-definitions/
21. Chidamber, S.R., Kemerer, C.F.: A metrics suite for object-oriented design. IEEE Trans. Softw. Eng. **20**, 476–493 (1994)
22. Stone, M.: Cross-validatory choice and assessment of statistical predictions. J. Royal Stat. Soc. Ser. B (Methodol.) **36**, 111–133 (1974)
23. Kohavi, R.: A study of cross-validation and bootstrap for accuracy estimation and model selection. In: 14th International Joint Conference on Artificial Intelligence (IJCAI 1995), pp. 1137–1145. Morgan Kaufmann (1995)
24. Sokolova, M., Lapalme, G.: A systematic analysis of performance measures for classification tasks. Inf. Process. Manag. **45**, 427–437 (2009)
25. GitHub: Closing issues using keywords (2019). https://help.github.com/en/articles/closing-issues-using-keywords
26. https://github.com/dotnet/cli. Version: bf26e7976
27. https://github.com/dotnet/machinelearning. Version: b8d1b501
28. https://github.com/akkadotnet/akka.net. Version: bc5cc65a3
29. https://github.com/aspnet/AspNetCore. Version: 5af8e170bc
30. https://github.com/IdentityServer/IdentityServer4. Version: da143532
31. https://github.com/jellyfin/jellyfin. Version: d7aaa1489
32. https://github.com/OpenRA/OpenRA. Version: 27cfa9b1f
33. https://github.com/0xd4d/dnSpy. Version: 3728fad9d
34. https://github.com/icsharpcode/ILSpy. Version: 72c7e4e8
35. https://github.com/Humanizr/Humanizer. Version: b3abca2
36. https://github.com/aspnet/EntityFrameworkCore. Version: 5df258248
37. Uesbeck, P.M., Stefik, A., Hanenberg, S., Pedersen, J., Daleiden, P.: An empirical study on the impact of C++ lambdas and programmer experience. In: 38th International Conference on Software Engineering (ICSE 2016), pp. 760–771. ACM (2016)
38. Finifter, M., Mettler, A., Sastry, N., Wagner, D.: Verifiable functional purity in Java. In: 15th ACM Conference on Computer and Communications Security (CCS 2008), pp. 161–174. ACM (2008)
39. Sharma, M., Gill, N., Sikka, S.: Survey of object-oriented metrics: focusing on validation and formal specification. ACM SIGSOFT Softw. Eng. Notes **37**, 1–5 (2012)
40. Warmuth, D.: Validation of software measures for the functional programming language Erlang. MSc Thesis, Humboldt-Universität zu Berlin, Germany (2018)

41. Zuilhof, B., van Hees, R., Grelck, C.: Code quality metrics for the functional side of the object-oriented language C#. In: 12th Seminar on Advanced Techniques and Tools for Software Evolution (SATToSE 2019), CEUR Workshop Proceedings, vol. 2510, pp. 31–46 (2019)
42. Zuilhof, B.: Code quality metrics for the functional side of the object-oriented language C#. MSc Thesis, University of Amsterdam, Netherlands (2019)

An Empirical Study on the Energy Efficiency of Matrix Transposition Algorithms

Gonçalo Lopes, João Paulo Fernandes[(✉)], and Luís Paquete

Department of Informatics Engineering, University of Coimbra, CISUC, Coimbra, Portugal
{galopes,jpf,paquete}@dei.uc.pt

Abstract. Energy consumption is becoming a serious concern in the context of software development. Recent works have shown that energy consumption of an algorithm not only depends on its running-time but also on its number of memory accesses. In this work, we empirically analyse several algorithms for matrix transposition with different patterns of low-level cache access, and compare them in terms of energy consumption and running-time with respect to CPU instructions and memory accesses. Our results suggest that different memory access patterns have a strong influence on the energy consumption and on the cache performance of these algorithms.

Keywords: Matrix transposition · Energy efficiency · Cache performance

1 Introduction

The increasing popularity of electronic devices and platforms leads to questions regarding their energy efficiency, which is relevant at several levels. It has impact on the utility of portable devices, e.g. battery life of mobile phones [13], on business costs, e.g. energy consumption of large data centers [4,28], as well as on social aspects, e.g. impact of the energy consumption of electronic devices on global warming [5]. As such, the topic of energy consumption is becoming a growing concern in the context of software development.

In order to deal with energy consumption concerns, hardware manufacturers have been improving lower-level layers of the hardware to reduce energy consumption [10]. However, recent studies [2,15,19] indicate that better results can be achieved by encouraging software developers to participate in the process. For that reason, hardware manufacturers have been designing tools for developers

Supported by the ERDF - European Regional Development Fund through the Operational Programme for Competitiveness and Internationalisation - COMPETE 2020 Programme and by National Funds through the Portuguese funding agency, Fundação para a Ciência e a Tecnologia within project POCI-01-0145-FEDER-016718.

Z. Porkoláb and V. Zsók (Eds.): CEFP 2019, LNCS 11950, pp. 375–391, 2023.
https://doi.org/10.1007/978-3-031-42833-3_11

to understand the energy consumption of their programs. Some CPU manufacturers already provide some measurement tools that collect data from different system interfaces and calculate the energy consumption of their processors, such as PowerTOP, Intel Power Gadget and RAPL [7,8].

It is common folklore that energy consumption depends only on the running-time [29]. This assumption suggests that a faster program is also a more energy-efficient program. However, there are other factors that may play some role on the energy performance of a program [22]. For instance, some works have shown that different algorithm implementations [3,23], different cache architectures and data management choices by the programmers [6,12,17], the choice of the programming language [16,20] or the code practices and data structures used by the programmers [14,18,21], may affect the energy consumption of a program.

Our aim is to understand the energy consumption patterns of certain algorithmic implementations, in particular in the context of linear algebra applications. For this study, we took into consideration the *energy complexity model* proposed by Roy et al. [24], which is based on the parallel memory model [27]. These authors argue that the total energy consumed of an algorithm does not only depends on the time taken by non-I/O operations, but also on the number of memory accesses to a row that contains the required memory word. Therefore, this model indicates that it is possible to minimise energy consumption by improving cache performance. Several techniques exist that optimise cache performance using different patterns of memory accesses, such as *cache-aware algorithms* [1].

This work presents an in-depth empirical analysis of two different algorithms for matrix transposition with the aim of understanding the relation between energy consumption of an algorithm, its running-time and cache performance using different memory access patterns. We describe a thorough experiment with two different algorithms for the matrix transposition operation with two distinct ways of transversing the matrix. Our results suggest that both memory access pattern and cache usage are factors that significantly affect energy consumption.

This article is structured as follows. In Sect. 2, we review the literature concerning energy efficiency, cache efficiency and theoretical models. In Sect. 3, we present the matrix transposition algorithms. The experimental setup and methodology we used is described in Sect. 4. Section 5 discusses the obtained results and, in Sect. 6, we conclude and present ideas for future work.

2   Related Work

In this section, we review some of the most representative empirical and theoretical studies on energy and cache efficiency. In Sect. 2.1, we review the energy complexity model proposed by Roy et al. [24]. Section 2.2 we discuss an empirical study on cache efficiency and, in Sect. 2.3, we discuss empirical studies on energy efficiency.

2.1   Energy Complexity Model

Our work is based on the energy complexity model proposed by Roy et al. [24], in which the energy consumption of an algorithm is modelled as a linear combination of the running-time and the total number of I/O accesses. Their model captures the energy consumed by a modern server for executing an algorithm, focusing exclusively on server power, which includes the power drawn by the processors and the server memory.

Roy et al. model is very closely tied to the memory layout. They assume that memory is divided into a set of P parallel banks, each of which has its own cache. Each bank is also formed by blocks, each of which is formed by B items and B/s strides, where s is the number of items in each stride. Each stride behaves as a cache line, and each cache holds only one block. Therefore, an algorithm can manipulate the items in all caches whenever required. Since an algorithm has at its disposal P banks, the number of Input-Output (I/O) accesses made by the algorithm is the number of parallel I/O made to the P parallel banks. However, blocks needed in parallel are written to different banks, which is ensured by a constraint in the algorithm design. Under these working assumptions, the authors model the energy consumption of an algorithm for a given input as the sum of the work that an algorithm performs on non-I/O instructions, plus the latency times the number of accessed strides. Figure 1 illustrates the architecture of this model for $P = 4$.

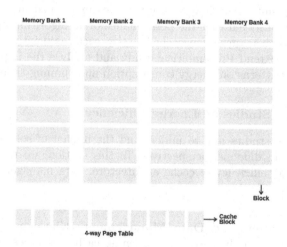

Fig. 1. Memory layout for $P = 4$ under the energy complexity model

The authors proposed algorithms that try to minimize the energy consumption according to the energy consumption model above, and conducted several experiments to validate their findings on several benchmarks [24]. They defined an operating point with a fixed work complexity, i.e., varying the allocation of the data across the banks in a way that an algorithm would have varying degrees of parallelism, and a fixed number of memory accesses. The algorithms require data to set out in memory with a certain degree of parallelism. For this reason, they proposed a generic way to ensure memory parallelism for a given input access pattern or vector. They reported that the energy consumption decreases as the value of P increases and that there is a noticeable difference of energy consumed between the values of P. However, this difference decreases as the value of P gets larger. They also noticed that parallelizing the layout does not lead to energy savings if the auxiliary data structures do not fit into cache.

In our work, we extend their analysis by exploring the relationship between memory accesses and CPU instructions with energy and time and analyse the impact of different memory access patterns and data organisation.

2.2   Empirical Studies on Cache Efficiency

Tsifakis et al. [26] focused on the analysis of the matrix transposition algorithms, cache ignorant, blocked and cache-oblivious and, for each algorithm, they measured hardware performance counters. For their experiment, they used two machines with two different systems: the first system with a 16 KB direct-mapped data cache and the second with a 64 KB 4-way set associative data cache. In the first system, the presented results were similar to the expected, except for slightly higher results for matrices of sizes 2^{12} and 2^{13}. The second system results showed that the use of a data cache with associativity could achieve better results, especially in the previous mentioned matrix sizes. As a conclusion, they observed that the performance of an algorithm may depend of several factors, such as cache size, cache line size, cache associativity and policies. In our work, we extend this empirical study and analyse the impact of similar memory access patterns on energy consumption and running-time.

2.3   Empirical Studies on Energy Efficiency

Several empirical studies aim to understand the impact of software on energy consumption from different perspectives. In this section, we review empirical studies on energy efficiency of cache architecture, data management and algorithm implementations.

Cache Architecture and Data Management. Kim et al. [12] presented an empirical study on the way of partitioning cache resources for energy efficiency. They examined ways of splitting the cache into smaller units, designated *subcaches*, to reduce per-access energy costs and to improve locality behaviour. Moreover, they proposed a *subcache* architecture to improve the cache performance and memory system energy efficiency. They claimed that dynamic energy consumption in the cache could be lowered by reducing the number of accesses to cache. Therefore, they proposed two optimisations for cache energy reduction, *dynamic page remapping* and *subcache prediction*. The obtained results showed that by using *subcaches* configurations and by varying the size of the direct-mapped cache, it is possible to reduce the energy consumption in the memory system from 60% to 83% on average. In conclusion, the results showed that the optimisation at the architecture level, such as *subcache* architectures, is crucial for reducing cache energy costs.

Co et al. [6] analysed the energy efficiency of *trace cache*. Trace cache is a specialised cache that stores the dynamic stream of instructions to increase the fetch bandwidth by storing traces of instructions already fetched. The experiments consisted of evaluating whether concatenating basic blocks, a straight-line code sequence with no branches, improves energy efficiency. They compared trace caches and instructions caches in terms of time, memory and energy. Although trace cache achieved better results than instructions cache, it was the branch prediction that more strongly influenced overall performance and energy. Moreover, results showed that similar performance could be achieved by applying sequential trace caches or instruction cache-based engines.

Liu et al. [17] studied the energy impact of data management choices by programmers, as data organisation or data access patterns, and the interaction between hardware-level energy management and application-level management, for Java. Five programmers choices were analysed: data access pattern, data organisation, data representation, data precision and data I/O strategies. For the data access patterns, they measured the energy consumption when accessing a large array under sequential or random access, considering both read and write operations. As expected, the random accesses consumed much more energy than sequential. Moreover, the energy and performance achieved by read and write instructions were not proportional, which could be explained by the overhead of each hardware instruction.However, energy consumption remained stable at the Dynamic Random Access Memory (DRAM) level. For the data representation and organisation strategies, they measured the impact of using object-oriented arrays and primitive arrays. The results showed that, although object-orientation provides some benefits such as modularity, it does not benefit energy consumption. Finally, for the data precision choices, they analysed the energy consumption of the matrix multiplication operation using different primitive types. The obtained results showed that the matrix of `double` data type consumed 1.45 more energy than `int` and 4.95 more than `short`. The second analysis of Liu et al. [17] was concerned with the interaction between hardware-level energy management and application-level management. Although scaling down the CPU frequency effectively saves power, it may increase the running-time of a program. Therefore, they performed an analysis varying the operation supply voltage of the CPU and the operating frequency. They concluded that downscaling the CPU not only results in a performance loss but also in an increase of energy consumption.

The empirical studies we described so far showed that cache architecture, different types of structures and primitive types, and different CPU frequency significantly affect energy consumption. However, these studies ignored other factors, such as the correlation between the number of cache misses and the primitive types, and the relation between memory accesses and energy consumption. In our work, we analyse the relation between memory accesses, energy consumption and running-time. Moreover, to understand the impact of different memory access patterns on cache performance, we analyse the number of cache references and misses.

Algorithm Implementations. Rashid et al. [23] conducted an experiment to compare the impact of sorting algorithms on energy consumption. The algorithms were implemented in three different programming languages: ARM assembly, C and Java. For each language, algorithm and data set size, they collected the number of instructions per cycle, percentage of cache misses, percentage of branch misses, energy consumed and running-time. They obtained different levels of energy consumption for both different algorithms and languages. In particular, Counting sort exhibited better performance, followed by Quicksort. The most energy-efficient language was ARM assembly. In conclusion, a large part of the energy consumed by the algorithm was determined by the time performance. However, some factors were not considered, such as memory accesses. In our work, we explore this relation between memory accesses, time and energy.

3   Algorithms for Matrix Transposition

Our main goal is to understand the relation between different memory access patterns and energy consumption. For this reason, we considered the operation of transposing a matrix as our case study since it involves many memory accesses and there are multiple approaches that explore different memory access patterns.

In order to transpose a matrix, each element of the matrix must be written and read from memory in different locations. In general, matrices can be represented in row-major or column-major order. As opposed to column-major, adjacent elements within each row are contiguous in memory, in row-major. Therefore, traversing a row-major matrix along rows is much faster than along columns. However, performing a matrix transposition for large matrix sizes can have a tremendous impact on cache performance.

The order in which matrix elements are swapped in a matrix transposition operation has a strong impact in performance, especially on memory, since it uses data elements within relatively close storage locations, exploring spatial locality. For example, when the element [1,1] of the matrix is accessed, it is fetched to the cache line and to the lowest cache level. Therefore, accessing the others elements in the same block of data as [1,1], such as [1,2] through [1,16], has a reduced cost supposing that the cache line carries blocks of data containing sixteen elements. However, each element is written into a column where adjacent elements are separated in memory by a stride equal to the length of the matrix row, which causes cache misses in the first cache level. Consequently, the way the matrix transposition is performed causes the algorithm to either read from the cache line or write new elements to the cache line.

Algorithm 1. Naïve Algorithm for Matrix Transposition

```
1: procedure TRANSPOSE
2:     for i ← 1 to N do
3:         for j ← 1 to N do
4:             Out[j][i] ← In[i][j]
```

Algorithm 2. Cache-Aware Algorithm for Matrix Transposition

```
1: procedure TRANSPOSE
2:     for r ← 1 to N by L do
3:         for c ← 1 to N by L do
4:             rlimit ← min(r + L, N)
5:             climit ← min(c + L, N)
6:             for i ← r to rlimit do
7:                 for j ← c to climit do
8:                     Out[j][i] ← In[i][j]
```

For our experimental analysis, we consider two well-known approaches for matrix transposition, which explore different memory access patterns. The first is the classic algorithm for matrix transposition, named here as the *Naïve algorithm*. Algorithm 1 describes this approach, where In is the original matrix, Out is the transpose of matrix In and N is the number of elements per column. It is a very inefficient algorithm in terms of running time and memory usage. Since it traverses the matrix in row-major order and another in column-major, it gets a cache miss in every step of the column-wise traversal for large matrices.

The second approach is the *Cache-aware algorithm* [1], which uses the knowledge of the memory architecture to achieve a better performance in terms of cache misses. Therefore, it uses the cache line size or other cache sizes of the processor, L, and divides it by the size of the matrix type. Algorithm 2 presents the pseudo-code of the Cache-Aware Algorithm. It is similar to the Naïve Algorithm, but it rearranges the data in order to transfer it to the cache in blocks to minimise the number of cache misses.

4   Methodology and Experimental Setup

The Energy Complexity model described in [24] (see Sect. 2.1) suggests that the total energy consumed by an algorithm A can be modelled as a linear combination of the energy consumed by the Central Processing Unit (CPU) instructions or non-memory accesses and memory accesses. Therefore, in order to model the energy consumed by the two matrix transpositions algorithms described in the previous section, we measured the total amount of running-time and energy consumed by CPU instructions and memory accesses. To accomplish this, we performed two distinct measurements. The first measured the overall energy and time spent with both CPU instructions and memory accesses. The second, explained in more detail in Sect. 4.3, measured the energy and time spent with only the CPU instructions, from which energy and time consumption on memory accesses can be derived by subtracting it from the first measurement.

In the following sections, we provide more details of the experimental methodology that we have followed to compare the implementations of both algorithms described in the previous section.

4.1   Experimental Setup

Our experiments were conducted on a computer with a 6th Generation Intel Core CPU, based on the Skylake architecture (x86-64), which has 8 virtual cores, 4 physical cores, running at 2.6 GHz, and using Ubuntu 18.04.2 LTS. Moreover, the computer was equipped with 16 GB of RAM and 3 cache levels, L1, L2 and L3. More specifically, each physical core is split into two virtual cores, each one with an individual L1 cache connected to a shared L2 cache per each physical core. Moreover, each physical core L2 cache is connected to a shared L3 cache to all of the physical cores. The L1 cache is divided into instructions and data, L1I and L1D, each one with a size of 32KiB and an 8-way associative placement policy. The L2 cache has a size of 256KiB with a 4-way associative placement policy and an exclusive cache inclusion policy. Finally, the L3 cache has a size of 6144KiB with a 12-way associative placement policy and an inclusive cache inclusion policy. Moreover, every cache level has a write-back policy and a Least Recently Used (LRU) replacement policy.

The CPU processor can only refer to data that is accessible in the cache (*cache reference*). If the processor accesses data that is in its cache, a *cache hit* occurs, otherwise, a *cache miss* occurs. In the latter case, the cache needs to evict one of the existing entries and replace it by the new cache entry. Initially, the processor writes only in the cache, but once this block has been replaced by another cache block, it writes the data to the main memory. Each cache level has a P-way associative placement policy where a block of RAM is mapped to a limited number, P, of different memory cache blocks, increasing the change of a cache hit.

Both algorithms described in the previous section were implemented in C++, in particular, using the C++11 standard, and compiled with *clang*++ without optimisation flags. The setup of the matrices and the algorithms for the transposition are implemented using only the C standard library. Moreover, since *clang*++ has been used for intermediate code generation, this compiler was chosen over G++ to maintain coherency in the generated machine code.

We chose data type `int` to represent each element of the matrix. As for the matrix size, we considered square matrices of size $N \times N$ where N starts at 2^{10} and ends at 40960, with jumps of 2^{10}. The source code for each algorithm shares the same *main* function. Moreover, the algorithms perform the transposition from one input matrix to an output matrix. To achieve a better cache performance, we implemented two one-dimensional arrays with $N \times N$ elements with an alignment of 2^6 bytes. This alignment value was chosen after exploring and experimenting with multiple values, such as 2^{12} (cache page size) and 2^6 (cache line size). Note that due to the cache organisation, the best alignment values are always multiples of the cache line size. Furthermore, for the cache-aware in Algorithm 2, we considered $L = 2^4$, 2^6 and 2^8. We have considered other values close to 2^8 in preliminary experiments, but we did not see differences of performance. Finally, we used memset operation to initialise the matrix and to fill the cache levels, since it ensures contiguous memory initialisation.

We used *perf* to collect the performance metrics for each algorithm such as time, energy and memory usage values. Moreover, we analysed the performance of the algorithms without memory access instructions by using LLVM and *clang++* to generate a new executable and collect the performance metrics.

Each algorithm was executed 30 times for each instance to account for slight fluctuations in memory usage performance counters, time and energy values. Note that there are different types of cache misses, i.e. instructions and data. However, in our experiments, we only analyse the data cache misses. To understand more about the collected performance events and the derived values, i.e. the number of cache references at the first level cache, we refer to [11]. Furthermore, to maintain accuracy and reduce disturbances in the collected values, the program executions were made on a light window manager environment (in particular, *i3*) with the screen and networking connections turned off, and with a minimal number of background processes. In order to reduce the noise and interference of other internal processes, we isolated one physical core, two virtual cores. Moreover, to prevent processes migrations between CPUs, we confined the program execution to just one of the isolated virtual cores.

4.2   Performance Counter Measurement Tools

There are generally two ways to measure energy: using the computers *internal sensors* or using hardware connected to the computer as *external sensors*. *External sensors* usually perform measurements at some predetermined time interval (e.g. every second) and measure the entire energy consumed. Therefore, since the level of granularity required for our experiments is too fine, at the instruction level, we have opted to use *internal sensors*. There are a few energy consumption internal sensors, such as PowerTOP, Intel Power Gadget and RAPL [7,8]. However, the first two only measure the instantaneous or actual energy consumption, while RAPL can measure the energy consumed between intervals or during program execution. Therefore, in the context of our experiments and because we were using an Intel architecture, we decided to use RAPL.

Running Average Power Limit (RAPL) interfaces consist of non-architectural Model-Specific Register (MSR), i.e. control registers that are used for debugging, program execution tracing and computer performance monitoring) and it was implemented by Intel to work in SandyBridge architectures and newer [7,8]. RAPL does not directly measure the consumed energy by each processor. Instead, it uses a modelling approach based on 100 different micro-architectural event counters which are after used to model the dynamic energy consumption. Each RAPL domain supports a set of capabilities. One of them is the *Energy Status*, which provides energy consumption information of two main domains: i) *Total package*, which consists of components of the processors involved in instructions execution (PP0 – Core Devices) and devices close to the CPU but not part of the core, such as the GPU and other sub-components such as the L3 cache, the integrated memory controller, etc.(PP1 – Uncore Devices); ii) *DRAM*, which is a type of RAM and the main data component of the processors. The accuracy and validation of RAPL have been analysed in [8], where the authors show that it is capable of providing accurate energy estimates at a fine-grained level, reaching an average error rate of only 1.12%.

On Linux, the RAPL energy measurements can be accessed commonly in three different ways: reading files in the *inter-rapl* directory, using the *perf* tool or reading from the MSR. *Perf* is a standard profiling and performance analysing tool for the Linux kernel that provides a framework for collecting and analysing hardware and software performance counters data, including energy and cache memory usage data. Moreover, it is one of the most commonly used performance counter tools on Linux along with *OProfile*, it has a simpler user interface and allows us to access the energy consumption values. Therefore, since we can collect all the necessary data to our analysis using *perf*, we decided to use it as a benchmarking tool.

To collect a given set of performance events, we used the `perf stat` command. Given a set of performance events and a command to execute, the `stat` command presents a summary of performance events chosen and saves it into a file. For our experiments, we wanted to collect all the available data about energy and cache memory usage. Therefore, the available events in *perf* allow us to gather the energy values for different CPU components, such as Random-Access Memory (RAM), Graphics Processing Unit (GPU), Cores and Package (energy consumed by the GPU and Cores), memory usage performance counters, such as the number of cache misses and stall cycles for the different levels of the memory hierarchy, and other performance counters such as the number of instructions and cycles (see [11]). Moreover, *perf* allows to specify the CPUs to gather the event counters, with flag `-a` to collect from all CPUs and `-cpu=C` from a specific CPU. Furthermore, to measure time, due to the fact that *perf* uses the same approach as `getrusage`, we also decided to use *perf*.

4.3   Intermediate Machine Code Generation Tool

Since it is impossible to measure exclusively the time and energy consumed by the memory accesses, we disabled memory access operations. Therefore, in the context of our experiments and to be able to characterise the performance of the implementation without accessing and storing on memory, we decided to analyse the machine code generated by the compiler and to remove memory access operations, namely, *load* and *store* operations, that refer to matrix transposition instructions.

There are different tools to generate intermediate source code representation. However, due to the familiarity and experience with the library, as well as its popularity, we decided to use the LLVM. LLVM is a collection of libraries and a back-end compiler designed around a language-independent intermediate representation (LLVM IR). Moreover, it can be used to construct, optimise and generate intermediate or binary machine code. To generate the intermediate code representation, we use *clang* as front-end compiler, which is a well-known compiler that is fully compliant with C++11 and uses LLVM as its back-end.

After identifying and removing the intermediate memory access instructions, we compiled the LLVM IR file into assembly language using the `llc` tool from the LLVM library. Then, to create the executable on the generated assembly code, we use the *clang* linker.

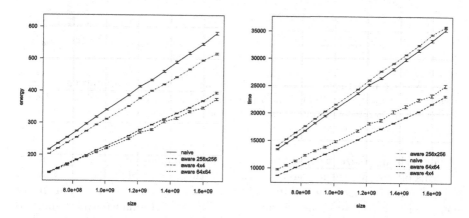

Fig. 2. Average performance of naïve and the three aware implementations in terms of energy consumption in Joules (left plot) and running-time in milliseconds (right plot). 95%-confidence intervals are also shown

5   Experimental Analysis

This section describes an in-depth experimental analysis on the energy consumption of the two matrix transposition algorithms described in Sect. 3 on a wide range of matrices sizes, following the experimental methodology that was introduced in the previous section.

Figure 2 shows the energy consumption (left plot) and running-time (right plot) of all implementations for the input sizes considered. We removed the value for $N = 32768$ from our analysis since we obtained a very large running-time and very low energy consumption as compared with other values of N. We believe that this is due to the multidimensional array sequential access, which can exhibit a poor performance due to poor cache-line utilisation, especially when N is a power of two, leading to cache-line conflicts. Moreover, this can cause several delays because of the distance between the memory address accessed, discontiguous jumps of memory by N, also called *cache contentions*. However, the value of N seems to be dependent of the computer architecture and the CPU cache, and its restrictions, such as cache policies.

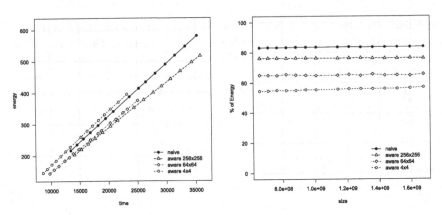

Fig. 3. Average performance of naïve and the three aware implementations in terms of energy consumption in Joules and running-time in milliseconds (left) and average percentage of energy consumption used on memory accesses (right)

For each input size, we also present the 95%-confidence interval for the mean in terms of energy consumption and running-time. Both plots indicate that all implementations take a linear amount of time and consume a linear amount of energy with respect to input size and that a better performance with respect to both energy and running-time is achieved with smaller block sizes.

Noteworthy, the ranking of the implementations with respect to energy consumption and running-time is not the same. In order to improve readability, the caption of each plot follows the ordering of the implementations with respect to the corresponding performance indicator. The plot of Fig. 2 shows that aware 256x256 takes slightly larger running-times than naïve, but the latter consumes a larger amount of energy. A similar observation holds with respect to aware 4x4 and aware 64x64, respectively. This suggests that the energy consumption of an implementation is not solely determined by its running-time.

Similar conclusions can also be taken from the left plot of Fig. 3, which shows the energy consumption and running-time taken by each of the three aware variants and by the naïve implementation. Each point corresponds to an average value of energy consumption and running-time for the same matrix size. The plot indicates a linear relationship between energy consumption and running-time for all the four implementations. However, it also shows that the four implementations present different performance profiles. Moreover, it is possible to see that naïve and aware 256x256 present similar running-times, but the latter consumes less energy. A similar observation applies to aware 64x64 with the aware 4x4, respectively.

The right plot of Fig. 3 shows the average percentage of energy consumption spent on memory accesses. This value is considerably high for naïve and for the aware implementations with larger block sizes, although constant for all implementations over the input size.

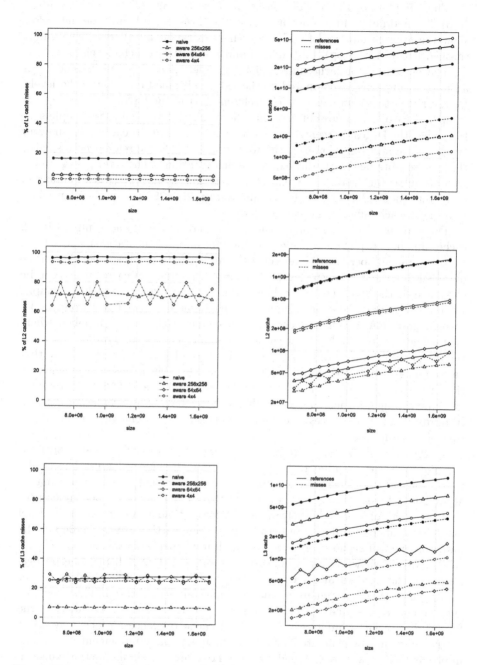

Fig. 4. Percentage of cache misses (left), and number of cache references and cache misses (right) in L1 (top), L2 (middle) and L3 (bottom)

The left plots of Fig. 4 show the average percentage of cache misses in L1 (top), L2 (middle) and L3 (bottom) cache levels, respectively and the right plots show the average number of cache references (straight lines) and cache misses (dashed lines) in L1 (top), L2 (middle) and L3 (bottom) cache levels.

The percentage of cache misses in L1 (top-left plot) is small in general for all implementations as compared to the values obtained on other cache levels. However, the total number of cache references (top-right plot) is very high as compared with the values obtained in other cache levels. The naïve implementation has the largest percentage of cache misses, reaching a cache miss in every five L1 cache accesses. However, the total number of cache references is smaller than those obtained with the aware implementations. The aware 4x4 implementation has the smallest percentage of cache misses and the largest number of cache references. Both aware 64x64 and aware 256x256 present similar values in terms of cache misses and cache references.

Different from the case of L1 cache, the percentage of cache misses in L2 cache (middle-left plot) is considerably high for all implementations, above 60%. However, the number of cache references (middle-right plot) is smaller than those obtained in L1 and L3 cache levels. The large percentage of cache misses can be explained by the L2 cache policy that was used in our experiments. For example, when a cache miss occurs at L1 and L2 caches, the data is fetched from the L3 cache or from RAM. Due to cache policies, such as cache inclusion policy, where all the data in the higher-level cache is also present in the lower-level cache, the majority of blocks are transferred between the L2 and L3 caches. Note that naïve and aware 64x64 exhibit a large percentage of cache misses, which is very close to 100%. The implementations aware 4x4 and aware 256x256 present a lower percentage of cache misses, with the latter having an oscillating pattern. In terms of cache references, the relation between implementations is similar to that of cache misses.

In the case of the L3 cache level, the percentage of cache misses (bottom-left plot) is closely related to that of L1, although slightly larger. The implementations naïve, aware 64x64 and aware 4x4 present similar performance above 20% whereas aware 64x64 is below 10%. The number of cache references (bottom-right plot) is relatively high but lower than those in L1 cache level and with a different ordering of performance. Noteworthy, aware 64x64 has the lowest number of cache references among all implementations.

The results shown in Fig. 4 indicate that aware 256x256 displays better performance than naïve at all cache levels, and it is even able to show better performance than the remaining aware implementations at L3. This may justify the fact that aware 256x256 saves more energy than naïve. However, the former does a large number of L1 and L3 cache references, which may affect the running-time as compared with the remaining aware implementations. The implementations aware 4x4 and aware 64x64 present similar performance in terms of percentage of cache misses for L1 and L3, but the former has a large number of cache references at all cache levels.

6   Conclusion and Future Work

Our work supports the argument that the energy consumed by an algorithm can be modelled as a linear combination of the energy consumed by the CPU instructions and memory accesses and that different memory access patterns can perform distinct energy consumption behaviours. Moreover, it is important that an algorithm takes advantage of the cache to decrease the energy consumption of the memory accesses component.

Our experiments were performed using a specific type of memory hierarchy, considered typical nowadays among CPUs composed of one line of processors [9], which has shown a significant impact on processors market [25]. However, since our experiments show that memory access patterns and organisation have a significant effect on energy consumption, it would also be relevant to perform an in-depth analysis of memory parameters, e.g. cache replacement policies, associative placement policies and different cache sizes. Additionally, it could be relevant to analyse other types of cache misses, such as overall cache misses and instructions cache misses, and consider different memory parameters. Moreover, to accomplish a different analysis, other related linear algebra problems can be placed as a benchmark of our experiments, such as matrix multiplication.

References

1. Aggarwal, A., Vitter, J.S.: The input/output complexity of sorting and related problems. Commun. ACM **31**(9), 1116–1127 (1988)
2. Aggarwal, K., Hindle, A., Stroulia, E.: Greenadvisor: a tool for analyzing the impact of software evolution on energy consumption. In: IEEE International Conference on Software Maintenance and Evolution, ICSME 2015. pp. 311–320 (2015)
3. Albers, S.: Energy-efficient algorithms. Commun. ACM **53**(5), 86–96 (2010)
4. Barroso, L.A.: The price of performance. ACM Queue **3**(7), 48–53 (2005)
5. Bose, B.K.: Global energy scenario and impact of power electronics in 21st century. IEEE Trans. Ind. Electron. **60**(7), 2638–2651 (2013)
6. Co, M., Weikle, D.A.B., Skadron, K.: Evaluating trace cache energy efficiency. ACM Trans. Archit. Code Optim. **3**(4), 450–476 (2006)
7. David, H., Gorbatov, E., Hanebutte, U.R., Khanna, R., Le, C.: RAPL: memory power estimation and capping. In: Proceedings of the 2010 International Symposium on Low Power Electronics and Design, pp. 189–194 (2010)
8. Desrochers, S., Paradis, C., Weaver, V.M.: A validation of DRAM RAPL power measurements. In: Proceedings of the Second International Symposium on Memory Systems, MEMSYS, pp. 455–470 (2016)
9. Gayde, W.: How CPUs are designed and built (2020). https://www.techspot.com/article/1821-how-cpus-are-designed-and-built/
10. Guo, Y., Narayanan, P., Bennaser, M.A., Chheda, S., Moritz, C.A.: Energy-efficient hardware data prefetching. IEEE Trans. VLSI Systems **19**(2), 250–263 (2011)
11. Intel: Intel® 64 and ia-32 architectures - software developer's manual complete (2019). https://software.intel.com/en-us/download/intel-64-and-ia-32-architectures-sdm-combined-volumes-1-2a-2b-2c-2d-3a-3b-3c-3d-and-4

12. Kim, S., Vijaykrishnan, N., Kandemir, M.T., Sivasubramaniam, A., Irwin, M.J.: Partitioned instruction cache architecture for energy efficiency. ACM Trans. Embedded Comput. Syst. **2**(2), 163–185 (2003)
13. Kwon, Y., Tilevich, E.: Reducing the energy consumption of mobile apps. behind the scenes. In: 2013 IEEE International Conference on Software Maintenance, pp. 170–179 (2013)
14. Li, D., Halfond, W.G.J.: An investigation into energy-saving programming practices for android smartphone app development. In: Proceedings of the 3rd International Workshop on Green and Sustainable Software, GREENS 2014, pp. 46–53 (2014)
15. Li, D., Hao, S., Gui, J., Halfond, W.G.J.: An empirical study of the energy consumption of android applications. In: 30th IEEE International Conference on Software Maintenance and Evolution, 2014, pp. 121–130 (2014)
16. Lima, L.G., Soares-Neto, F., Lieuthier, P., Castor, F., Melfe, G., Fernandes, J.P.: Haskell in green land: analyzing the energy behavior of a purely functional language. In: IEEE 23rd International Conference on Software Analysis, Evolution, and Reengineering, SANER 2016, 2016, vol. 1, pp. 517–528 (2016)
17. Liu, K., Pinto, G., Liu, Y.D.: Data-oriented characterization of application-level energy optimization. In: Fundamental Approaches to Software Engineering - 18th International Conference, FASE 2015, Held as Part of the European Joint Conferences on Theory and Practice of Software, ETAPS 2015 Proceedings, pp. 316–331 (2015)
18. Melfe, G., Fonseca, A., Fernandes, J.P.: Helping developers write energy efficient Haskell through a data-structure evaluation. In: Proceedings of the 6th International Workshop on Green and Sustainable Software, GREENS@ICSE 2018, pp. 9–15 (2018)
19. Pang, C., Hindle, A., Adams, B., Hassan, A.E.: What do programmers know about software energy consumption? IEEE Softw. **33**(3), 83–89 (2016)
20. Pereira, R., Couto, M., Ribeiro, F., Rua, R., Cunha, J., Fernandes, J.P., Saraiva, J.: Energy efficiency across programming languages: how do energy, time, and memory relate? In: Proceedings of the 10th ACM SIGPLAN International Conference on Software Language Engineering, SLE 2017, pp. 256–267 (2017)
21. Pereira, R., Couto, M., Saraiva, J., Cunha, J., Fernandes, J.P.: The influence of the Java collection framework on overall energy consumption. In: Proceedings of the 5th International Workshop on Green and Sustainable Software, GREENS@ICSE, pp. 15–21 (2016)
22. Pinto, G., Castor, F., Liu, Y.D.: Mining questions about software energy consumption. In: 11th Working Conference on Mining Software Repositories, MSR 2014, Proceedings, pp. 22–31 (2014)
23. Rashid, M., Ardito, L., Torchiano, M.: Energy consumption analysis of algorithms implementations. In: 2015 ACM/IEEE International Symposium on Empirical Software Engineering and Measurement, ESEM 2015, pp. 82–85 (2015)
24. Roy, S., Rudra, A., Verma, A.: An energy complexity model for algorithms. In: Innovations in Theoretical Computer Science, ITCS 2013, pp. 283–304 (2013)
25. Tibken, S.: Intel's skylake chips to power pcs as thin as tablets, with big battery boost (2015). https://www.cnet.com/news/intels-skylake-chips-will-power-pcs-as-thin-as-tablets-compute-sticks/
26. Tsifakis, D., Rendell, A.P., Strazdins, P.E.: Cache oblivious matrix transposition: simulation and experiment. In: Bubak, M., van Albada, G.D., Sloot, P.M.A., Dongarra, J. (eds.) ICCS 2004. LNCS, vol. 3037, pp. 17–25. Springer, Heidelberg (2004). https://doi.org/10.1007/978-3-540-24687-9_3

27. Vitter, J.S., Shriver, E.A.M.: Algorithms for parallel memory I: two-level memories. Algorithmica **12**(2/3), 110–147 (1994)
28. Will, D.: Head north for the data center gold rush (2017). https://blog.advaoptical.com/en/head-north-for-the-data-center-gold-rush
29. Yuki, T., Rajopadhye, S.V.: Folklore confirmed: compiling for speed = compiling for energy. In: Languages and Compilers for Parallel Computing - 26th International Workshop, LCPC 2013. Revised Selected Papers, pp. 169–184 (2013)

Author Index

Z. Porkoláb and V. Zsók (Eds.): CEFP 2019, LNCS 11950, p. 393, 2023.
https://doi.org/10.1007/978-3-031-42833-3

Printed in the United States
by Baker & Taylor Publisher Services